Letters to Virtue

Letters to Virtue

A Civil War Journey of
Courage, Faith, and Love

Edited by
Ann K. Gunnin

***BOOK*LOGIX**®
Alpharetta, GA

10 9 8 7 6 5 4 3 2   0 9 0 2 1 4

ISBN: 978-1-61005-520-8

Printed in the United States of America

Cover background image is the letter from December 8, 1862.
Cover photograph courtesy of Nancy Hinkle.
Chapter heading image from stationery used by C. W. Sherman.

♾ This paper meets the requirements of ANSI/NISO Z39.48-1992 (Permanence of Paper)

In loving memory of my mother, Natalie Sherman Kleinkauf.

This book is dedicated
to my great-great-grandfather,
Charles W. Sherman,
and to the brave men and women,
past and present, of the United States Armed Forces.

A soldier is not a hero in fighting alone; his patience under hardship, privation and sickness is equally heroic; sometimes I feel disposed to put him on a level with the martyrs.

—John William De Forest, *A Volunteer's Adventures*

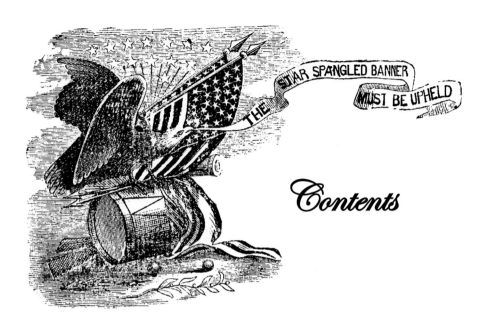

Contents

Preface

I do wish this Cruell War would come to an end, for this goin about to Kill one another has a unchristian look to me, when you come to look at it in that light, but it has to be don, I sopose.

The preceding words were taken from the last letter Cpl. Charles W. Sherman wrote to his wife, Virtue, and his family, four days before he was killed in the Battle of Cedar Creek, Virginia, on October 19, 1864. This collection of 160 Civil War letters chronicles his almost three-year journey as an infantryman in Company K, Twelfth Connecticut Volunteer Infantry Regiment. Charles enlisted as a private on January 31, 1862, and went into camp near Hartford just days after his fifth child was born. He was thirty-three years old.

Born in England in 1828, Charles immigrated to this country with his family in 1838. His father worked in a woolen mill in Connecticut and settled his wife and two sons near the mill town of Rockville. A decade later, Charles married Virtue James, also an English immigrant, and they had five children: Fanny, Angeline, Lewis, Arthur, and Charles Butler. Census records show that in 1850 Charles was employed as a harness maker in Connecticut, and, in 1860, as a carpenter in Webster, Massachusetts. Charles enlisted because of his strong belief in the principles of his adopted country as well as his firm opposition to slavery, and he served until his death in the Battle of Cedar Creek, Virginia, October 19, 1864.

The Twelfth Regiment left Connecticut in early March and travelled to Ship Island, Mississippi; on April 30, it arrived at New Orleans, the first Union regiment to occupy the Crescent City after its capture. The regiment spent the remainder of that year and all of 1863 in Louisiana and was involved in several engagements, including the Siege of Port Hudson. Charles reenlisted in February of 1864 and enjoyed a furlough at home. In July, the regiment, as part of the XIX Corps, was shipped from Louisiana to Virginia and, on August 7, joined the Shenandoah Valley Campaign under Major-General P. H. Sheridan. They distinguished themselves in the Third Battle of Winchester (Opequan), fought in the Battle of Fisher's Hill, and suffered heavy losses in the Battle of Cedar Creek.

During his near three years in military service, Sherman wrote at least 160 letters to his family. Discovered a century later in a closet in the house built by one of his sons and later occupied by a granddaughter, the sack of letters provides a fascinating view of the daily lives of Sherman and his fellow soldiers during their camp life and campaigns from Louisiana in 1862 to Virginia's Shenandoah Valley in 1864. These letters vividly describe the human side of war from an infantryman's perspective through his keen observations of life around him; the people in command, the countryside, the battles, the often-times-brutal circumstances of the soldiers or slaves, and the financial hardships suffered by his family back home were often topics of his letters. They also reveal Charles's sense of humor, his philosophy of life and war, his loyalty to his adopted country, and his endless faith in God, which carried him through many trying times. Charles's love for his wife and children along with his devotion to his parents is apparent through the constant concern for their well-being expressed in his letters. His colorful descriptions of people and places, along with his wry and sometimes angry or frustrated comments on national events, transport the reader back to the nineteenth century, immersing one in the emotions of the time and taking the reader on a Civil War journey not to be forgotten. The final letter in the collection is from Charles's tentmate, sadly informing the family of his death at Cedar Creek.

Most of Sherman's letters are in exceptionally good condition and quite legible. The handwriting, grammar, and format are typical of that era. To save paper, Sherman used no punctuation or new paragraphs, and his random capitalization seems to emphasize key words in a sentence. His phonetic, and sometimes original, spelling reveals his writing haste and English origin (e.g., "as" for "has," "thair" for "there" or "their," etc.). In the course of one letter, he often spelled a word or town's name in several different ways. Charles knew he wasn't a great speller, remarking one time that he didn't have "Webster's Unabridged" with him!

Upon their discovery in that cloth sack in the closet, the original letters were sent to my mother. I have scanned all of them for ease of transcription and digital preservation. I also have photocopies of several additional letters; their transcription is also included and noted where appropriate.

In May of 2011, I attended a meeting of a Civil War Round Table group in New Jersey. Dr. James I. Robertson, Jr. (then a distinguished history professor at Virginia Tech) was the guest speaker, and I had the pleasure of meeting him and discussing the letters with him. He encouraged their publication and suggested leaving the original spelling intact as much as possible so as to preserve the character and charm of the writing, so typical of that period. Dr. Robertson's advice has been followed, with the insertion of simple punctuation and paragraphs to help the reader. In some cases, words or letters have been inserted in brackets for the sentence or word to make sense. Era terminology regarding slaves, although not currently politically correct, has also been preserved to assure the integrity and the flavor of the writings; no disrespect is intended by the author as he was opposed to, and appalled by, the institution of slavery.

Terms, facts, people, and places mentioned in the letters have been researched with an attempt to present reliable information in the footnotes. Conflicting information abounds, both in books and in Internet sources. However, especially in cases of Internet information, more than one source has been sought to verify the information, although only one may have been cited. The information offered in footnotes is either to explain a term, identify a name, or to try to support facts stated in the letters. Because the human side of the war is the focus of this publication, the purpose is not to try to offer a definitive factual reference; however, every effort has been made to present correct information.

For the reader's reference, the Twelfth Connecticut's engagements during the war are listed in Appendix I, along with photos of Winchester National Cemetery where Charles is buried. Appendix II, titled "Family Information," contains biographical information on relatives mentioned in the letters, particularly his wife and children and what became of them in later years. Appendix III details the pay, bounties, and pension Charles and his wife received during and after the war.

Sherman's letters weave a story of courage, faith, and love. His sense of humor is wonderful; his selfless concern for his wife and family is touching; and his compassion for others, whether it was a fellow soldier, a slave, or a family chased out of their home, is endless. Knowing how it ends at Cedar Creek, there is not only a sense of sadness every time the letters from October 1864 are read, but also a feeling of pride. Charles W. Sherman was my great-great-grandfather. I found his journey through the Civil War fascinating and hope you will also.

Ann K. Gunnin,
Editor

Pvt. Charles W. Sherman
(This photo is mentioned in the letter dated November 29, 1863)

No 3

Camp Prophet New Orleans Jun 29 1862

Dear Wife & Mother & Father & Children

and we hope that we

shall have no ocasion to Distroy

this Part of the State it deserves

some punishment for the

usadge and insult thay

heaped on the Union

soldiers that came to Liberate them

from Worse then African

Slavery thay could not see that we

was their Salvation you ought to

see the Money thay had in curcelation

the araingment for Small Bills

is most Beautifull one of thair one

Collear Shin Plasters if you wanted

Fifty cents Chaing thay take a knife and

cut the Bill in toe and 5 & 10 s

thay do the same and I have seeing

a fifty cent Bill cut in too thair

is no Silver Chaing only what the

men Brought thair is nothing smaller

then 5 cents or a picune and those

1862

Background is the letter from June 29, 1862

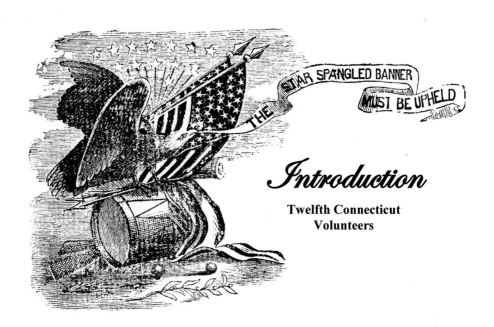

Introduction

Twelfth Connecticut Volunteers

The formation of the "Charter Oak Regiment," as the Twelfth Regiment C. V. Infantry was known, was authorized by the Secretary of War on September 16, 1861. Recruits began filing into Camp Lyon in West Hartford as early as November 11, 1861. Its Colonel was the Mayor of Hartford, Henry C. Deming, with Ledyard Colburn as Lieutenant Colonel. In January 1862, Frank H. Peck of New Haven became the regiment's Major.

Charles W. Sherman enlisted on January 31, 1862, as a private and was assigned to Company K. The regiment was equipped, drilled, and fully recruited (numbering 1,008 men) at Camp Lyon, until its departure on the twenty-fourth of February for New York, debarking from there on the steamship *Fulton* on February 27. Upon arrival at Ship Island, Mississippi, on March 8, the regiment was assigned to a brigade commanded by Brig. Gen. John W. Phelps, and remained on the island until April 16, 1862. On that date, the troops boarded the ship *E. Wilder Farley* and lay in the Mississippi River just below Forts Jackson and St. Phillip. However, once news was received that New Orleans had been captured, they were ordered to the Crescent City and, on April 30, was the first Union regiment to appear before that city. They landed the next day and went into camp in Lafayette Square.

In early May, the regiment, with its brigade, occupied the abandoned Rebel earthwork, Fort John Morgan, whose name was changed to Camp Parapet by Union forces. The regiment remained at this camp throughout the summer of 1862. On July 25, five companies (including Company K), along with a section of the Second Vermont Battery, participated in an expedition aboard the US gunboat *Grey Cloud* with the objective of destroying railroad bridges and routing bushwhackers. Bridges at Pass Manchac and North Pass were destroyed. They then proceeded through Lakes Pontchartrain and Borgne, up the Pearl River, and landed at Covington, Louisburg, Madisonville, and Pass Christian, among others. The expedition ended after ten days and returned to Camp Parapet.

The regiment was transferred on the twenty-ninth of September to the "Reserve Brigade" under Brig. Gen. Godfrey Weitzel and moved to Camp Kearney at Carrollton. The first engagement for the Twelfth occurred on October 27 at Georgia Landing, or Labadieville, in La Fourche Parish where the brigade dislodged the enemy. The Twelfth distinguished itself in the fray and was highly complimented by Gen. Weitzel. After this, the brigade went into camp near Thibodeaux with Maj. Peck in command of the regiment.[1]

---

[1] *Record of Service of Connecticut Men in the Army and Navy of the United States During the War of the Rebellion,* Compiled by Authority of the General Assembly under the direction of the Adjutants-General (Hartford, CT: The Case, Lockwood & Brainard Company, 1889), 471–2, PDF e-book; John William De Forest, *A Volunteer's Adventures, A Union Captain's Record of the Civil War,* ed. James H. Croushore (New Haven, CT: Yale University Press, 1946), 1–84.

Chapter One

Steamship *Fulton* and Arrival at Ship Island, Mississippi

Steamer Fulton, Gulf of Mexico, March 5, 1862

Dear wife & Chirldren,

I take this opertunity of writing a few Lines to you hoping thay may find you in good health has thease Leaves me at [present].[2] We are enjoying beautiful wether rather warm for some of the men but I enjoy it.

We are rather crow[d]ed at Present, nerley 2000 men abord and now thay have got over thair sea sickness enjoy themselves preaty well. We do not get anuff to Eat, rather slim rations are served out to us but it may be for the good of the men. A chaing of climeat might afect some of the men if thay was alowed to feed has thay whould if thay could get at the grul. It was rather Disagrible for a few days, so many men sick and Confind in service queartors. I did not have a very Flattering opion of Soldering from my experince of Monday the Day we left Hartford and Monday night. We was kept out in the rain all day Monday and the road was over our Shoes in Slush and water and we were soaked to Skin again. We got into the Cars for New Heven. We got into New Heven about Seven O'clock and had to stay in the Depot 3 hours till thay had stowed the right Wing in the Granite State. Our Company is in the Left Wing, and you can concive wether we was crow[d]ed or not to Put over one thousand

---

[2] Charles was born in England, and lived there until he was ten years old. He oftentimes says "has" for "as" and vice versa.

3

men in one steamer that was never intended to Carry more than 200 Pasengers, but all things have an end and that night did, much to my relefe if not others.

The men got Liqor or a grate many of them, and thay mad[e] things rather Lively for a spell. For myself I never got any I have mad[e] up my mind to Let it alone has long has I am away from hom, for it will not help me to do my Duty, and I tell the men that if thay wish to ever see thair homes thay had better give it up. If a man gets Wounded thair are nine Chances for him that dose not Drink then fore the one that dose. You need not have any fears for me on that account. We suffer for the want of Watter. Some Days I do not get any, only about a Pint of Coffe for brakfast and hardly that and about the same for super. I have not felt the want of it so much has I should if we had to work much. I am getting quite laze but when we get ashore I expect to have that taken out to me and the rest of us.

Tell William Ruby that I often think how he whould like to Plant Corn in this wether. It is about the same has good July wether now. Do you not wish you couled com out of that Snow and Ice? How the Chirldren whould sun themselves. I rather guess that Aurthur would fancy about bare footed.[3] Take care of them all. I shall be to home before 3 years unless I go under.

We have a splended Regment. We have six Hundred of the 13 Main[e] Regement with us and thay say that we take them down. The men do look healthe and tugh and in high Spirits and it will go hard if we can not wip any 3000 of the Rebls. We are armed with the Enfield rifel, good for nine hundred yards, and the 13 Main[e] have the same rifle and the fier of a thousand of theas well handled must be awful.[4] Last Sunday Morning we was lured up on deck has t[w]o Vessles, one on each side of the Steamer, was seeing and has soon has thay found that we was redy thay put out thair Lights. We had four rifeld Cannon, thay was cast Loose. We was in the Gulf Stream then and we did [not] know but thay might be seshe, but what ever thay was thay cleered out.[5]

---

[3] Arthur is the second son of Virtue and Charles, born in 1860. Given name is Henry Arthur.

[4] The Enfield rifle was a muzzle-loading rifle-musket, made by private contractors in the United Kingdom. Its caliber was .577 Ball. The British Pattern 1853 Enfield, along with the Springfield Model 1861 Rifled Musket, were the most widely used infantry weapons in the Civil War. Patricia L. Faust, ed., *Historical Times Illustrated Encyclopedia of the Civil War* (New York: Harper Perennial, 1991), 243–4.

[5] "secesh"—a slang term for a secessionist—Charles sometimes called them "seshe." There are a few other variations used as well.

We have been fore 3 Days on the Cost of Florida. We pas[s]ed Cape Florida yesterday. The shore Looked butifull. Coverd tall trees all in leafe. We expect to mak[e] Key West tonight and Ship Iland about Friday and the sooner the Better. I have had all the sailling I want fore this Time, rather to[o] many Passengers fore comfort.

Virtue you must keep up your Spirts and not be down Hearted. I shall come home when this Truble is over it can not last a year. The others that have been out before us have Preaty much Tamed that Southern Colt, and we are goin to Put the Bits in his Mouth and Lead him to the Stable whare he has Broken from and feed him with Reson and kindness so that he will be willing to Draw in the Old or New Fedral harness fore I Promsed him I whouled come if he did not come to Terms.

Virtue you must try to think that I am in the way of duty. Let others think has thay may. It whouled not be right fore me to stay to home and Let others Fight for me. Theas Southern Rebles have interfered with me and my rights and to alow them to Carry out their vewes of goverment whouled Reduce me and my Chirldren to mear Vassledge, to take a way every Sense of Independance and bring us on a levle with thair Slaves. Such Notions has that can not go down with me. That Letter with that Money I couled not find. It may Turn up. Do not Let that worry you, it was not much. I am sorry that I wrote for it. I will send you some more soon. Pleas Let me know if you got that Tresury Note and if Henry has sent you any. I give him a True account of how we stood. I know that he was owing me more then he thought and I should feell more Satisfied. I know that he will do what his right with you and the Chirldren. If I am not their I hope that he will see that you have some thing Planted or help Mother to get has much Planted has he can and Put somthing on that riey [rye] and get it cut and secuerd in good shape. I [may] not be able to do anything this sumer and I may. Some think we shall be to home by July. I do not count on that. Father must write me Every Chance he can. He nor Mother must not worry about me. I am in the Hands of One that rules on the Sea and Land and I feell that he watches over me and protects and that he will gard me from all dainger.

It is warm. We are near Ship Iland and Glad I be fore we have faird hard fore Food and Watter and thay give us nothing but Condensed water and that is warm. The pototisam [potassium] of the me[n] is geting Low, but the Fight in them is geting larger from Various Causes. Tell Lewis he must be a Good Boy and do all that his Mother wants him to do and try to Learn all that he can at Schoole and at home. You must get Father to write thease Letters over if you

5

want to keep them.[6] Tell faney to Learn to Write has fast has she can so that she can write to me. Let me know how you are geting Along and Angline must Learn to write.[7] Tell her I want a Letter from her.

March the 7
We had an aufful Gale of Wind. All right now.[8]

March the 8
Got to Ship Iland this morning.[9] Butifull Day rather Cold. Look has though it a bissness Place. Goin Ashore this afternoon. Low Sandy Iland not a Tree on it. I am well. Please Direct your Letter to Charles W Sherman Ship Iland 12 Redgement Compney K Captain Abbot.

Kiss my Chirldren for me tell Virtue to keep up good Pluck. I ain't scait yeat. I shall send again in few days. Please copy theas Letters so that you can read them. No Ink so that you will have to Put up with Pencl marks.

Your Affectnate Husband & Son,[10]

CW Sherman

Remember me to Mother and all enquiring Frends I shall write Mother a letter Good By

Direct to C W Sherman 12 Redgement C.V. Compney K Captain Abbot

---

[6] Some letters are written in pencil, and he mentioned in some to "pen" them over in ink. In those letters that survived, there is only one for which that was done.

[7] Lewis was born in 1854, so he would be about eight years old. He is the oldest son. Fanny is the oldest daughter and was born in 1850. Angeline was born in 1852.

[8] Charles wrote without punctuation or paragraph designations; therefore, all punctuation, including underlining and paragraph construction, is the product of this editor for the benefit of the reader. However, in the case of dates, there was no consistency (e.g., 7th vs. 7), sometimes using one form, sometimes another, and they are represented as he wrote them.

[9] Ship Island is off the coast of Mississippi in the Gulf of Mexico, situated between Biloxi and Gulfport. Adm. David Farragut's Union fleet sailed from Ship Island in 1862 to attack and capture the ports New Orleans and Mobile. "Ship Island History," Ship Island Excursions, accessed February 17, 2014. http://www.msshipisland.com /?q=ship_island_history.

[10] "Affectionate"—this word was spelled a few different ways in his letters.

Ship Iland, March 10, 1862

I take this oppertunity of writing a few lines to you hoping this may find you and the dear Children In Good health as bless the Lord it leaves me at present.

We got ashore Sunday Afternoon got up our tents after Smoothing the Ground over. The Main[e] Regements got ashore the Same day. 25 hundred men landed on Sunday, 2 battries landed today. There is 14 hundred cavalrey here from Main[e] and the 13 Connecut as got yet to come and Major General Butler and then these Rebels must Stand out the way for we Coming to this place is all the southern watering place they had. The Iland is about 2 miles wide and 7 long made with very white sand, white as milk. We get sweet soft water By diging about 3 feet And a Blessing it was to us after drinking condensed water for 12 days And not a half enough of that.

The Southern Chivalry [h]ad a very large Hold here but it got burnt with the fort. They Set fire to them when they see that they could not hold them. The men are in good heart But it will be hard drilling here. The men Sink over their shoes in the Sand. We have all Been cutting bushes to make Beds with and lay on the sand and I reckond I should [like] the team that was out Cutting Bushes to Cut Father's hay next summer.

We take steamers every day or so from the Rebels. No ship can run the Blockade now. We shall have some lively times soon and old Connecut will not be far in the rear. We have the 25 Machusetts with us and the 3 Main[e] Regements so that our Surthern Brethern can not say they have been unfairly delt with for all parts of the Union have turnd out to see that They have fair Play. I was Looking for Something to eat this morning and came across our Brigadear Genrl Phelphs and he took my eye as soon as I see him. I asked who he was—he Looked rather Rusty. He steped of[f] the Plank side walk and whent up to a Sergent that had an accoard [awkward] Squad under [h]is care and acquard they was But he talked kindly to the men and, if they can not learn and fight under Such a Generall they ought [to be] wiped. I could not help looking at him as the Papers had a good deal to Say about [h]is Proclamation that he sent over to the main land.[11]

Virtue, keep up your Courage. Kiss them Children for me I dare not wish I was home. I have a duty to do first And then I Can think of home. Give my love to Edwin, Father and all enquiring friends.

Your Affectate Husband,
CW Sherman

Ship Iland, March 10, 1862

Dear Brother,[12]

I take this opertunity of writing a few lines hoping thay may find you in good health as theas leaves me at Present.

We got out of the Steamer Sunday morning and pitched our tents. We had to smooth the ground first. Ship Iland lies low from ½ Mile to 2 Mile in wedth and about 7 Mile in Length. It is made of the fine white sea sand. Some Pines grow on the Northern End of it. It was a Summer Watering place fore this End, so to speak, of the Suthern Chivalery. Thay had a fine Hotel that Covered about one acre of Ground that was Burnt with the Fort when Phelps took it and the Fort. Thay have Built another Fort with Sand Bags and have some ninty Pound guns Mounted. It Looks has if it was bound to be Considerable of a Place. It Commands the Mouth of the Missippi and Lake Panchactrain.

The Day we got in, one of the gun Boats, the Newlondon, took one of thair steamers with over one Hundred thousand Dollars worth of plate and juewler[y]. The Plague thing had run the Blockade some half Dozon Times. It's speed is auffull, only 30 mile an hour. It is an Old Looking thing but Dose us

---

[11] J. W. Phelps, Brig. Gen. of Volunteers, Commanding, issued a Proclamation to the "loyal citizens of the Southwest" abolishing slavery on December 4, 1861, long before Abraham Lincoln's Emancipation Proclamation. He was headquartered at Ship Island at the time. The contents of his Proclamation are included in *Official Records of the Union and Confederate Navies in the War of the Rebellion*, Series I, Vol. 17, published under the direction of the Hon. William H. Moody, Secretary of the Navy, by Mr. Charles W. Stewart (Washington, DC: Government Printing Office, 1903), 18–20, PDF e-book.

[12] Charles's brother's name is Henry.

good service now. Thay took another steamer with her Loaded with Lumber that Comes [in] handy. Thay are building a Warfe and the Main[e] 14th come in on sadurday and them and we and six hundred of the Main[e] 13th that we Brought with us all of us got Ashore Sunday. We was rather crow[d]ed. You know how we was packed; nerely 2,000 of us on one Maile Steamer.

We have 3 Cavlery Compneys on the Iland. Thair is one Cavlery Redgement from Main[e] to Come and the 13th Connecticut. Buttler has not come. We have been expecting him. We are serounded by the Rebls on the Main Land. It is a Ticklish Place, but we Pay no Atention to them. We feel that when we move that it will be fore some purpose. We have got some good Tools to work with. The Main[e] Boys and us have the Enfield Rifle. The 26th Masachusets have the Springfield Rifle. This is Monday Noon and I, with the rest of our Company, have Just got one potatoe and one small pice of Pork. That is all that we have had since Sunday Morning and then we only had one potatoe and a small pice of Mule meat and that is about the still of our Treatment we have receved since we Left Hartford. Thair is some missmanedgement some whare. Thay gave us Condenced Watter on board the steamer that was half oily salt. By the way thay Manedge things thay do not Care wether men are well or not. I have bean well, not sea sick, nor I have not been sick as that of enlisted.

I think that this thing will be Put down and that shortley we are goin to Mobile first, has that Weakens New Orleans. I kind a hope that no stray Shot will take me down has I want to help my Suthren frends Build up thair Shanty fore it must get rather Leakey again [when] we get don[e] with them. You want to get a good Job and if thay give me a Chance I will see that thay shall want someone to set out a Frame or so.[13] All's fair in war. You do not know [how] good it feeles to get out of that everlasting Snow & Ice. I do not know but them Rebels may make it warmer then I shall fancy.

Let me know how your geting along and take Care of what Tools thair is in that Chest. I wrote to you when I was in Camp Lyon but never recved any answer. If you write Please Direct to CW Sherman Ship Iland 12 Redgement Compney K Captain Abbot C Vollenteers or C V or else whare; that is has plain has Mud. You can send me anything you want by Adams Express. I should Like some tobaco and a good Pipe. Thay only Aske 1 doller a pound fore tobaco. Some writing Paper, Ink Pens. Aunt Came Down and see me Friday before we

---

[13] Both Henry and Charles were carpenters.

Left and she Promised to send me some Paper & by Uncle has he was Coming down on Sunday, but he only Brought me a paper of Smoking Tobaco and I did not see him. I got a chance to run home Sadurday noon, to be back Sunday Noon, but the two Fellows that went with me on my Pass got Butifule Tight and has I was responsible for them I did not get Back till Dark. Uncl staied till 5 o'clock. He probably whouled send me, or help you, some Postadge stamps I shouled Like and a Hancerfer[14] to whipe my face for this dubile quick through this sand starts the greace. I want a Prayer Book. Derick sent me one with Aunt, two pair of stockings but the Soldier got Tight in Hartford and the Police Locked him up till morning and he Lost them.

Tell Elvira[15] she must write me a Letter. Give my respects to her and all inquiring frends, if I have any. See my wife and Cheer her up if you can and the Chirldren. God Bless them and make me Worthey of them. I shall see them again. I am not going to leave my bones hear. It looks rather tough to be bur[i]ed hear. Thair was two Poor Fellows Bur[i]ed Sunday afternoon just as we was Marching to take up our Ground. It Looked Solome. It made me think of thair distant homes that thay was not to see no more in this world. A Soldir's Funerl makes a man Feell that thair is some other Life beyond this. Thair is a over-ruling Providence that guides the Affairs of all men, and my nights when I have been on gard, I have Looked up to the Starrey Hevens and felt that the same Power that Called them into Beaing was watching over me and gives me Curedge to know and feell that thair was a Power above that Couled and whouled Protect me, and I shall Carry that same feeling with me to or whare ever I shall go. Under Fire it will give me Back Bone. I Laughf Some Tim[e]s to myself what Aunt said to me when she was goin home, to be sure that I did not get shot in the Back. I told her that the Shermans was allways afraid to turn thair Back. You must write to Virtue and keep up he[r] Curedge; now [that] I am away she will feell a littl Down some times and if you can help her to Plant some Land so that she can have some thing when Winter comes on.

I have just come in from cuting Rushes to lay on. The Sand is Wet, the watter Lies about 2 to 3 feet under so that we can get all the water without much truble. It is nice soft Water. I cannot account fore it has the sea washes completly over it some Times and in the Hollowes that the water has washed out thair is

---

[14] Handkerchief
[15] Henry's wife

Pooles of fresh water with fish in. The boys have got the most of them or will, thay that were Lucky enuff to Bring fish Lines.

Please Let Virtue see this letter when you get it. Copy it with ink. I have to write with a pencl and it may rub out. I have wrote a Rambling Letter. You must excuse all that is writen. Butter is worth Sixty Cents Per Pound, Molass 15 Cents a quart. I have Just heard of one soldier Paying 9 Dollers for 3 Pints of liqor. I do not Dout it. I know that abord the steamer the men Paid sixteen 16 Dollers Per Gallon or one Dollar for half Pint, 4 to six Cents for a stamp. Thay rob the men the worst way. I must Close.

Your Affectnate Brother,
C W Sherman

Direct to CW Sherman Company K in care of Captain E H Abbott, 12 Redgement, New England Divison CV

Ship Iland, March 12, 1862

if you think worth saving put it in ink and send it to my wife

Dear Uncle, Aunt and Cousins,[16]

I take this opertunity of writing a few Lines to you hoping thay may find you in good health has thay Leaves me at Present.

We had a good Pasadge considring we were Crow[d]ed some what. 3 men in a Bearth, nerley 2000 Men on Bord. We suffered for water, had to Drink Condensed watters and that did not smell or taste the sweetest. The 14th Main[e] Redgement got hear two Days after us. 3 batter[ie]s arived 2 Days after. We have 8000 Men hear now. 3 compneys of cavlery, the 9 Connecut has to come and 1400 cavlery from Main[e]. A Buley Crowed we shall all make. The men are full of Fier and it will go hard with the Rebles if we get a Chance at them. Thay must be geting sick of this Game by now. Not a single Sail can heave in sight, but they are over hauled. This is a Point that makes the Blockade effectule for the Missipie and New Orleans. They took a Cupl of steamer the other day. One Load[ed] with Lumber that was Just the thing and one had over

---

[16] Charles's aunt is his mother's sister, Elizabeth. His uncle is Elizabeth's husband, James Derrick. Cousins are Anne, George, and Sarah.

a Hundred thousand Dollars worth of Plate and Jewlry that was trying to run the Blockade.

Thair has been a stady stream of Mortar Boats Coming in to work on Mobile and New Orleans. This Iland was the summer Watering Place for the Planters of Leusana, I have not spelt that right. Thay had a splendid Hotel; thay Burnt that and the Fort when thay found thay Couled not hold it. The Iland is made of fine Sea Sand. It is about ten miles Long and 1½ Mile wide. The sand is very wet. We get good water by Diging 3 feet. It has been Cold since we have been hear and wet. If we can keep Dry we shall do preaty well. The water comes over the Iland in some se[a]sons. We stand a fine Chance of Drowning if not getting shot.

I like our Brigadier Generle Phelps. He is a rugh Looking Man; Black hair, Baird geting gray, and Looks rather rusty. Thay are Building a Warhfe, has everything has to be Lan[d]ed in boats from the Steamers and that makes it slow work. Thay lose a great maney Horses Coming hear and what they have hear have to stay out nights with no Covering and the Dew falls so hevey that thay will not Let the men stay out nights without thair over Coats and India Ruber Blankets. It will soke a man through. It comes down like fine Rain.

The Consti[t]ution has just come in with 3 Redgements. The Missipi we have Just heard has gon a shore with Buttler & Staff at or near Port Royle. The sutlers Rob the men the worst way.[17] Thay ask 10 Cents fore Cent Boxes of Matches, one Doller a pound for toba[c]co. Some of them have Bottled Cider which thay ask one Dollar Per Bottle of one Pint. I do know that some of the men have Paid 16 Dollars Per gallen for Liquor and other things in perportion. I suppose thease things will have to be.

I was sorry I did not see you, when you was kind enuff to come to see me. When Aunt came I did not know that I couled get a Chance to go home and had given up all hopes of seeing my wife and Chirldren but Luck favored me and I got 20 hours and I just got Back to Rockville Just 12 O'Clock Sunday intending to get into Camp by 3 o'clock and shouled if it had not been for Wickes.[18] He lived in Rockvill. It ended by my having to Leave them in Hartford and report myself to Captain Abbot, but you had gon[e]. I Left word with the Ordley to

---

[17] Sutlers were citizens officially appointed to a regiment to supply the soldiers with approved items such as food, newspapers, books, tobacco, razors, tin plates, cups, cutlery, etc. Faust, *Historical Times Illustrated*, 738.

[18] Wickes appears to be a family friend.

use you has well as he could if you come. He told me he did, but I was vext about it has I should have seeing you if those other two men had kept themselves right. I found your Present all safe. You do not know how I wanted a Prayer Book and that one that you sent to me that Fish Fellow Lost. I have wrote to Henry to send me a little Tobaco and if you couled write to him that I should like a few Boxes of Mattches, and fix it with him to send me nother Prayer Book and Put it in one small Parcl and send it by Adams Express, Direct [it] to CW Sherman Compny K Captain Abbot 12 Redgement Cn Vo New England Division or Elswhare.

We are filling up Fast hear. Six redgements since we came, four batterys of Atilerys and more Coming. You ought to be heare to see. You whouled think you was in new york to Look toward the shipping. 27 sails Left us Last night to go some whare we know not. You get all the News.

The 14, thay wanted vollenteers to go some 12 miles to Raft Wood. Some 20 of us vollenteered. We was gon[e] two Days and a Tough Time we had. Thair came up such a storme of thunder & Lightning, rain that it astonished me and the rest; it was Auffull and the sea Liked to have washed over the Iland. Has it was, it knocked the Tents over, the wind I mean, and blowed a Leuatenant and 7 men; thay was given up for Lost but thay was saved and came into Camp Sunday noon with a Contraband.[19] Thay was goin to Bring some of thair men that was up geting wood. The storme took them and Landed them on the Mouth of the Missipie but thay fell among Union frends that used them well and thay said that [they] Long for the day when we shall Cross over and straighten things out fore them.

We have about 12,000 men hear now and the Constitution has gone to Fortress Monro for 6000 more. She brought 5000 this time. We expect to move soon. The Mortar Fleet Left on the 5th to clear away the road for us.

I have wrote a Rambling letter. You must make it out the Best way you can. I will send you again if you can make this out. Please send to my wife that I am well at Present. Tell her that I want to know if she has recived that Paper that Col Demin[g] gave me so that she couled Draw her pay from the town of Willington and if not to Let me know.[20] Tell her to kiss the Chirldren for me. I

---

[19] Contraband: A term describing the new status of an escaped slave or one brought behind Union lines. Faust, *Historical Times Illustrated*, 161–2.

[20] See Appendix III "A Connecticut Soldier's Pay" for an explanation of the quarterly bounty Virtue received from the town.

send my love to Father and Mother. Give my love to Ann and her Husband and Sarah, Aunt and G[e]orge and accept the same yourself. The Boys have Just Brought in to Camp a Aligator about 9 feet Long.

Yours Truley,
CW Sherman

Ship Iland, March 18, 1862

Dear Mother, Wife and Chirldren,

I take this opportunity to write a few lines to you hoping thay will find you Enjoying Good health as theas Leaves me at Present. I kind of Pity you Poor Frozen Cri[t]ters down in Willington. We are Enjoying the Tallest kind of Wether, butifull Sea Breazes Blow off the Sea. It is very warm in the middle of the day. Thay do not think of drill, only 4 hours per day and that gives us fits. Some Days has been quite cool but now it begines to Grow Warmer.

We have to turn out at 5 o'clock in the Morning at Roll Call. Brakfast is at six, Gard Mounting at 8, Drilling at half past 8 till half past 9, one hour off and then another hour Drilling. The Sand is soft and it makes it hard fore the men. This Iland is about 11 Miles long and about 2 Miles wide. I speak of my own knowledge. We wanted some Wood and 20 of us Vollenteerd to go and get some. We took 2 days rations and started and in 3 hours got into the Woods. You whouled have Laught to have seeing us, we had to wade through the Water up to our waist, some took off thair Pants, but thay soon Put them on again. The bite of those miscatoes [mosquitoes] is butifull to them that Likes it. I fore one do not Admier them over much. Thay are as big has a common house flie.

On the 10 of March we had to sleep in our wet Clothes and such a storme of Rain, thunder and lighting. It was butifull. We bilt our raft of the Tallest kind of Fat Pine Logs. The Lumber that [was our] boards whouled make Henry's Mouth Watter. We had a Tugh Time getting them to Camp. We had to go out to sea so far to avoid the Sand Bars, the Rollers did go over us, faith, such getting a wood pile I never did see.[21] Wading 14 or 16 miles is a Little to much. The Boys Brought an aligator about 9 feet long into camp. We did not see any when

---

[21] The word "faith" seems to be a euphemism for a swear word.

we were out, but thair is some we took, or the gun Boats Bring in Prizes every day or so.

27 Sail Left us to Clear out the road for us the other day. Troops are Pouring in every Day and batterys are Landing from the Ships. We have redgements from half the states hear, faith, I never see a City grow up so fast. Col Demin[g] has the gout. He has not been out with us since we Landed but our Leutanant Col is anuff for us. He gives the Boys all thay want in the shape of Drill. He intends to make us the Crack Redgement.

We had another hard Blow Last night, another lighting and thunder storm. The surfe roars awfulley in the night. It looks very funey to look towards the Beach to see the Men that have to go there, rain or shine, for cirtain purpose, Loom up Like Black spirits of Darkness when the Lighting lights up the Hevens. It is butifull. The Morning is fogge when thair is the Least Cloud to shut out the sun, till the Sun gathers strengh.

Thair is another Large Steamer just come in firing Big Guns. We think it is General Buttler Coming in it. A beautiful morning. I want to be a moving so that we can be doing something. This Drilling all the time I do not fancy. I know that it is necessary to fit the men so that thay may be able to rally to and know where thair places his. Thay are building a railroad hear and building store house and which do not look has though thay were a goin to give up this Point right away. We are filling up quite fast. 2 Redgements landed yesterday, of them a New Ham[p]shire Redgement firing artilery and batterys and Buttler has come with the 12th. Have just got served with 22 Rounds of ball carteridges and the quicker we get to work the Better. We have a nice day after our storm not a cloud. We have heard that Manassas and Charleston have been taken by the Federal Forces, but do not know for cirtain.[22] Give my love to Mother and Father and Virtue. Kiss my baby.[23]

Yours Afectnatle, CW Sherman

---

[22] This was a rumor as neither city had been taken as of this date.
[23] Charles Butler Sherman was born on the sixth of January, 1862. C. W. Sherman enlisted on the thirty-first of January.

Ann Gunnin

Ship Iland, State of Missipi, March 22, 1862

Dear Wife,

I want to hear from you and the Children and if you have had any Truble to get what is alowed from the Town and if you got that recpt that Captain Abbot[t] give me to enable you to get it. I sent it to Father. I am well and hope this will find you and the Chirldren in good health.

You must not expect to see me right away, not till we have Put this rebellion down, and down it shall go for I am hear myself, faith. I am goin to see if thay are goin to kick the House down and raise the Old Boy genraley, and I stand by and not Pitch into them, not has long has my name is Sherman, as if I go down you must train up my Chirldren to fall into the ranks has fast has thay get Big anuff, if the war should Last so Long. Keep up your English Curadge. Your Father and Mother and Brother will give you a Lift.

I want to hear from them. I have wrote to Uncl and shall expect to hear from him. Tell me how Lewis behaves himself. I want him to Learn all he can and do all that he can to help you. Tell Fany to Learn to write. I want a Letter from her. Let me know how the Cows come out and if you have recived any Money from Henry, and if Father is goin to have William Redy plow for him and how things are genraley, and how this spring is coming, early or late. I have Lost sight of the Sesans. Some days I think it must be July and then it puts me in mind of May. It has not got settled seas yeat, but it may be all the best for the men.

Right opsite the Compney's Street Lies a English ship that was Wrecked some 8 years ago and all hands Lost. She is most gon. She lays Beded in the sand. At that time this Iland was washed over by the Sea and everything washed off the Light house every Living thing drowned. When the Wind is blowing a Gale in the night, I think of the sea washing all of us into the Sea.

Sunday Generl Buttler came Ashore and took command. His wife and Daughter are with him. Thay are Building a two story House for him and staff. We are Brigaded off. The 12th are in Genral Phelps Brigade and that we are Bound for Texas if thay give up New Orleans without Fighting. We are anxious to get off to get whare we can see something besides Sand. Thay tell of Moving next week.

I am cook fore the Compny today. We chaing cooks every day. All have to take Turns, only think of my Cooking fore nerley one hundred men. I cut up four smoked hams for brakfast. Beans and pork for Diner. Faith, I think I shall take a Hotel when I get home for I am learning how cheap I can keep borders.

16

I should Like to dip into your swill tub and get some of your potatoes that you feed your Pig on. That is tru. I couled make a good Meal out of some Pig Trough that I have seen. I think I shall not make much fuss about food if I can get into Old Connecut once more.

March 23

If we was on the March I kind of recon thair whould be some Droping out of the ranks, but I can stand it if any of them can. I have not Lost a single drill or shirked Duty once. Thair is a grate deal of that and some men is sick and have been that. If you couled have seeing them in Camp Lyon in Hartford, you whouled have thought that thay couled have stood anything. We are making quite a graveyard. Some Poor Fellow Bur[i]ed every day away from is home and Frends. Our redgement is pretty healthy, only nine in the Hospital. None died has yet.

Mother and you must do the best you can fore the Children. I wish I couled see them. I shall, I am confident and I think I shall never want to rome any more. I shouled not now if my Confounded southern Brother had Behaved him self like a Christian. He is in fore a thrashing now that he will remember has long has he lives, if he dies in any resonable time.

We have just heard heavy firing toward Cat Iland. We shall be in fore it before Long. We have to Carry forty rounds of aminition in our Belts to Drill and every whare we move and for one I shouled Like to Lighten mine in such a maner that thair whouled be no ocasion to carry any.

Remember me to Edwin and Harriet. Give my love to Henry and Elvira and if you shouled see them, tell him that I will remember him to his southern frends if I find them. I expect to see Ben McElhaney, the Texas Ranger, for we are Ordered to Texas. Good by Virtue and all of you. Kiss my Chirldren.

April 6, 1862

I have been walking round our camp and I can not realize that this is onley the 6th of April. To see the Potatoes in Blow and the Oranges on the Trees,

Onions full grown, Corn has high as the first of August with us, every thing so high, Different then with us.[24]

I have seing some of the Canester and shell that the Rebles threw into the River. Some of the Boyes have been in swimming and fished them things up and a large Reble Flag that they put in.

I do not know how this thing will End. I know that we can wipe them, but this Negro question Comes up. The Planters will want the help of the Negro and how is he to get along if the Negro shouled refuse to Labor for him. Thay are enteligent, thay know all that is Pasing around them. I heard one of them telling some of the men that it is the Creole Master that is the most hard on them. The American Master that uses them Best that is down here in Louisisana; they have a Notion that slaves are used Better in Virgian [Virginia] then down here.

I wish I couled get some Soupe. We have Been kept on salt Hor[s]e and Pilot Bread and we are geting weak and Poor and unless Buttler gets us some Fresh Food we must go off this summer. That is if they keep us hear. My health has been good so fare and I try to keep it. It depends a grate deal on a mans mind how well he will be. My hope is very Large and it is Luckey fore me. I write nothing about how you get along. My mind is all taken up with what is Pasing a round me hear.

---

[24] This letter is missing the first and last pages.

April 25, 1862, ship E. Wilder Farley

. . . Boat.[25] She tried to go between us, but maneged to carry the bowsprit of the Mortar Boat and Tear her own anchor off. The Snaping of the Bow Sprit and Riping of the Anchors off the Gun Boat in the night made us get to our Feet in Duble quick. We thought the Steamer had Cut the Mortar Boat in two. As she car[ri]ed the mortar boat astern of us we thought she had gon down, but after a Due quantity of yelling, things got Straightened out and in the morning we found the Gun Boat ashore and the Mortar Boat with her Nose broke.

This morning the River was full of Fire Rafts that the Rebles tried to send down fore our Benifit, but burnt out before reaching. Lots of cotton have Been floating down has though it was of no account. The Captain sent out a boat and saved some. Genral Phelps has Just pased, giving the Oficers orders to have the men down below if we see anything coming down the River.

---

[25] The first pages of this letter are missing.

April 26

This noon has I was eating my dinner an Aligator came out of the River about 4 Rod from us and Climed up on a log and went to sleep but some of the Oficers got thair shooting Irons to work on him, but he Paid no Atention to them till one of them took one of our rifels and slipped a Mine Ball under [h]is forleg; that made him turn over onto his back. Another was droped into [h]is bowels, if he has such a thing; that made him take to the Water in duble quick.

That night about midnight, all of [us] sound asleep, [we] heard someone in a boat singing out "Starboard your helm," and then down went the Ship on her starboard side. The Anchor Chains rattled, smash, something struck us in the bow that shook the ship as if she was going down. The Captain run up in his drawers but it was too late to avoid whatever it was. The men Trubled out thair bearths in duble quick. If thay whouled handle themselves has lively all the time, our Lieutenant Col whouled be in a perfect state of Bliss. But thay did Pour on Deck singing out. The Ram[26] was [star]board of us[27] and I for one did not know what it was, but soon something give and the ship righted and thump, thump. Some came by the side of the ship Looking has much Like what thay said the Ram was. It was partly under the Water with a Black Smoke Pipe. It was soon astern and we all Breathed Freer again. In the morning we found out what it was. Our Lieutenant Col was out all the Day before with a boat and up among the Rebl Boats round the Fort. It was a Reble Gun Boat that our fleet had sunk and it was Drifting about, but he had no thought that it whouled Truble us. It was an Iron Clad Boat with her guns and everything abord and it was no wonder that it give us fits Coming with the stream at the rate of 7 mile an hour. It was our Anchor Chain that saved us or we shouled have stood a fine Chance of goin down. It stove our Pipe that the Cable Chain runs through.

April 27

We started to go up to Fort Jackson, pased by the Boats that the Rebls had Buoyed thair Chain, and Anchored Alongside the Fort about 11 o'clock at night. As we came to anchor, our Captain hailed the North America to know what

---

[26] A ram is a projection on a ship whose bow is hardened and reinforced. The ram is used as a weapon to penetrate the hull of an enemy ship. *The Free Dictionary* by Farlex, s.v. "ram," accessed April 20, 2012, http://encyclopedia2.thefreedictionary.com/Ram.

[27] Meaning the Rebel Ram *Manassas*. De Forest, *A Volunteer's Adventures*, 15.

News. We learnd that thay was negotiating for the serender of New Orleans. In the Morning we had a view of the two Forts. It was a nice, buatifull morning and the Place Looked well, we having [not] seen anything for a long time. The Stars and Strips Looked well in thair Old Place. The Fort was not Injuerd so much has we had thought. It was not taken without more or less of loss. How much we do not know. It is very wet inside and stinks. Thay have a dich on the outside and Being Built in [the] Swamp must be very unhealth[y]. Our oficers went ashore and saw the Place. Thay had landed the 30th Masachucets, 5 companies in Fort Jackson and 5 in Fort Philips. Fort Philips is the same kind of work as Fort Griswold at New London. All Earthworks that were not injured much. Thay mutinied and whouled work the guns; the Oficers Run away and left them. It was a long string of them. Poor Fellows, two hundred of them we have alongside in the Gunboat that is Towing us up the River. We expected to leave two companys, the right Left, and thay had all fell in and thay was geting up rations for them when Buttler Came Down and said up the river, and, if we were not tickled worse than any Chirldren, and up we went.

When we was about Six mile up a Sail Boat came down with 5 men from the Missippi. Thay were goin at a rush on the Tide, Portside, to Come on Bord. We flung them a Rope but thay was goin so that thair Mast struck one of our boats, ti[p]ped them out, but we had a Boat out in no time, stopped, drifted down to them, took them [on] borde all safe.

And the morning that we got to Fort Jackson I was on gard on the quarter Deck to keep the men from intruding on to the Oficers. Looking toward the North America thay was taking Troops from her to put in Fort Philips. One of the men fell into the Stream, knapsack, Belts and all. Thay droped a boat in duble quick. It was not a mineut before thay was rowing after him and we couled see them Grasp the knapsack that was floating and lift that into the Boat but no man. Thay had 3 boats down then and thay looked for him some little time, but found him not and that Poor Soldier will never be found. The Stream runs 7 mile an hour and it is very Deep and when he struck the water is knapsack flipped over is head and the undercurent kept him down and carried him downstream. There were 5 drowned at Ship Iland the same way. Thay were in swimming and the undertow carried them out till thay were drowned and then Flung them Back dead.

We pased the Steamer Frigat Missippi and our Col had us give her 3 rousing Cheers fore runing that Infernal Ram down and has She went down, she exploded and Blowed the Railroad Iron that she was covered with more than a half a mile.[28] The Captain [of the ram] had Both Legs Blowed off and one Arm. Some of our boys saw him in a tent over to Fort Philips. He and one niger was all that was saved. The Missippi gave us some tall musik. She has a very nice Marine Band and thay know how to Play and Cheer and Raise the Old Boy with all Reble Craft that gets in her way.

It was dark when we got by and we turned in till morning. We cannot make very fast time, geting so that we make but about fort[y] mile all night. We was up be time in the morning. It was a butifull morning and the Little Darkeys whouled rub thair eyes and look and those up who could go astern did and the women whouled wave thair hanchefers. It looks very preaty, the Banks of the River and the Small Houses of the Coulerd People that apears about all that is left. The White Part Looks has if thay did not know what to make of it. I have seeing today what I have heard and read of; a gang of Slaves at work in the Feild with thair Driver. Little Chirldren and grown up men and Wemon Hoeing Sugar Cane. The Plantations on the Streame is all Sugar. It looks like Corn Coming up. Some of the plantations are very Large. I Counted Sixty or more in one Field. These plantations are Laid out with much Taste and looks has if thay was coltivated up to the handle. The Negros quarters are small, only two rooms down below, built in Streets. All that see us and one Womon, a Slave, sung out, I know, when she see the Stars and Strips and, by the way we had our Redgemental and State Flags out on the quearter Deck, that She knew Dat Old Flag and Acturley roled on the Ground! She was so ticuled to see it. We was very near the shore and heard and see it. It made us Laughf some. One plantation that we pased, the Slaves and thair Mistress and a Portley Looking Coulerd Gentleman with a White Vest and drest very neat manefested the most pattrotism. The lady waved her kembric and the Col had us give her 3 rousing cheers.[29]

---

[28] The paddlewheel frigate *Mississippi* disabled the Confederate ram, *Manassas*, during the capture of New Orleans in 1862. Stanley Sandler, *Battleships: An Illustrated History of Their Impact* (Santa Barbara, CA: ABC-CLIO, Inc., 2004), 57, http://books.google.com/books?id=i9-0ZuKsMvIC&printsec=frontcover&dq=stanley +sandler+battleships&hl=en&sa=X&ei=upECU7SROMidyQGylYCoDA&ved=0CC kQ6AEwAA#v=onepage&q=manassas&f=false.

[29] Cambric (Charles's spelling is kembric) was a fine lightweight linen fabric, cotton or batiste, possibly referring here to a handkerchief or a piece of clothing, possibly an apron. *Encyclopedia Britannica*, s.v. "cambric," accessed April 20, 2012, http://www.britannica.com/EBchecked/topic/90639/cambric.

We have been all up before Col Demin[g] by companies and he gave us some good Advice and to have us Answer to our names on the Mustering Roll. He told us our first stop whouled be the Old Battle ground 3 miles below New Orleans and we must give the People, he did not call them Rebls, a Chance to see that New England Troops was Gentlemen and knew how to behave themselves for it all depended on the next 20 days. One man in the morning has we were goin' along sung out to a man on the shore "you damd Reble, come hear!" The Col did talk to him some for it and we are not to insult any man, not by look, much more by word. Some plantations that we passed had Flocks of Sheep there and the little Pickaneneys, just of a size, thair parents were out in the Field, looked too Primitive and Inocent for me. One plantation was a Sample of all Big White house for Massa and one or more Streets of Small Shantys for thair Slaves; the same Uniform Look to all. No variations. That Comprises all that is on both Banks of the Missippi from the Belize[30] to New Orleans.

I am writing this 3 mile below New Orleans on the 1st of May. We are waiting for [the] rest of the expidition. The 12th is first in the Pet Lambs, is the name we go by, and the Pet Lambs is a going to win.[31] We are Anchored just below the city that thay call Algiers. It is the Oldest Port. It does look as if we were in some diferant Cuntry to see the Orange and LemonTrees and Live Oak. When I was Coming up the River I thought how I should like Virtue and [the] Chirldren to see it.[32]

Missippi Ship E. Wilder Farley April 27, 1862

Dear Wife and Chirldren,

I take this opertunity of writing a few lines to you hoping thay may find you Enjoying the Blessing of health has theas Leaves me at Present.

We are geting near Fort Jackson. We have been Anchored some 10 mile from the Fort most [of] the Time thay have been Shelling of it. It serenderd at

---

[30] A pilot station situated at the mouth of the Mississippi.

[31] Coincidentally, there was a group of soldiers also called Wilson's Pet Lambs referred to later in these letters. There was no more mention of the Twelfth being called that nickname.

[32] No more pages to this letter were found.

8 o'clock this morning and the Stars and Strips flotes over it now. We are orderd up to take care of it fore Uncle Sam till Such Time has he thinks that he can take it off our hands.

We left Ship Iland the 16 of April fore the South West Pass in companey with the 9th Connecut in the Matanzas gunboat. She towed us. The 9th has a nice Brass band and thay gave Dixie Land with all the variations. The Missippi steamer took 2 Redgements; the Great Republica carried 3 Redgements. When I first saw the Mouth of the Missippi I thought it was the fag End of all Creation. The watter where it joins the Gulf is of a Clay colour, Dirty, full of Sedement. The Current runs 6 mile a hour and that keeps it riled up, to say nothing of taking the wash of 6 or 8 States. We Passed the Blockading Squadron. Thay Looked Grim and savadge with thair guns run out. The Colarado Looked Like a Tower of Strength, but when I come to think that Wooden Walls was all Played out, it took her Affectiveness from her has nothing but Steel Plated Ships will have any Chance in this Age of the World. Thay have brought the licence of War to Perfection or nerley so it will have a Tendency of Shortening the Evils of war.[33]

When we began to Ascend the river, it Looked some Better. Pilottown had quite a home Look. It Looked quite Preaty but must be very wet and Damp being low and nerley Levle with the River. No bisness, there, only to Supli Pilots for the ship. We pased quite a number of Houses. Some put me in mind of home with thair Farm Look. Some had quite a number of Cows and Cavles feeding in what Looked Like wild Rice. We pased a Splendid War Steamer Belonging to John Bull. I thought he Looked Surley about his Cotton. Higher up the River we pased a French Corvette. She dipped her coulors which Compliment we returnd. The Band Played some Patriotic Airs. Thay gave us 3 cheers and we returned them with a Will. We pased quite a number of Gun Boats and as we Pased them thay manned the Rigin and a give us Cheers and I am thinking the 9th and 12th did not Spare thair throats. The Band gave them some of thair Best Musik. It was more Like a Picnick than a Broken Family. One Part goin to Pull the House down and the other to Punish them if thay did not stop in thair Fratricidl Course and Build the House up Stronger than it was. We soon Came in sight of the Fleet. Thay had begun to work on the Fort that

---

[33] The ships and gunboats mentioned in this paragraph are: *Matanzas*, gunboat; USS *Mississippi,* a paddle frigate; the *Great Republic*, a wooden sailing ship used for troop transport during the war; and the USS *Colorado*, a steam frigate.

morning. We couled see the smok roll up Like a Furnice. Thay droped us about 6 mile from the Fort. We have since Learned that if the Fleet had kept up the Fire that night thay whouled have had to serender, has it was thay Stoped and it has Cost 11 Days and nights stedy Fire and the Rebles must have Sufered Fretfull. Them Mortars kept a Purfect Streame of 250 Pound Shells Pouring into them. It seemed has if the Infurnal Regions was Pouring Distruction upon Frends and foes. The Rebles made a Large fire round the Fort the first night and it Looked has if the Fort was on fire and that was the reson the Fleet stoped firing. It was a blind and it answered thair Perpose till thay Couled Repair Damadges. It was splendid fire. It Lighted up the whole hevens fore hours. The Fleet stoped Firing and Commenced again this morning and has kept it up. All the Fleet couled not get to work at the same Time has thay couled not get above the fort on account of the Chaines the Rebles have drawn across the River. Genral Phelps is with us. Buttler is on the Missippi. The boyes have Great Confidence in General Phelps and non in Buttler. Phelps is Cool. Buttler, his Head thay say, is too hot rash.

17th[34]

There was some excitement this day. Boat Sunk alongside – got her up after some Swearing. A Boat Came alongside with two men with oysters that our Col bought of them. We have faired hard since we left Ship Iland. [We have only had] hard bread [and] salt horse. The men I see have Lost flesh very much this Last 15 days that we have been abord ship.

The Saxon Gun Boat has just gon down [the river] with Major General Buttler. The boyes ventlated them Selves and he Pased along. Last night we Cut the Anchor Chain fore fear of Fire Rafts; [we are] redy for Droping Down the Stream if thay shoulel get by the Gun Boats. Phelps ordered us to Drop down to the South Pass. Thay are goin to Cut the Chain tonight that keeps our boats from goin up the river. That was a Ruse of the Rebles to get our Gun Boats near to them by making belive that thay had set thair Fort on fire and I think it was a Tall Joke. It did Look has if thair cake was all Dough, but we shall get to work

---

[34] Charles took notes of their activities and would occasionally write a letter that encompassed an accounting of his experiences over the past several days, or even weeks. This letter is dated April 27, but he goes back several days to explain what they have been doing. Here he goes back to April 17 and then to the 20th.

soon. Buttler was Down Last night and ordere the Matanzas to Cast Loose from us and go Down to the South Pass and Bring up the Great Republica. She has 3 Redgiments on Bord, Western Redgiments.

20 of April, Sunday was a Cold Day, Wet. The Gun Boats kept up the Fire all day [and] night and Monday it was hevey and has Continued ever since. It is a hevey lot but must come. We had a Deserter Come to us from the Fort. He was impressed into the Fort. Thay have impressed all that thay can into thair Service. Thay have 3 chains drawn across the River and, in fact, thay are goin to make it warm for us. Today a Gun Boat Came down the worse fore whare. One mast knocked out and more room in her side than is generally good fore health, in fact, Solid Shot do not improve the bueaty of a ship. The Gun Boat Wallice that we took a few Days since over to Blixoo [Biloxi] from the Rebles sunk Coming hear. We had a hard Storme and she was hurt some taking her. She whouled have been of use to us.

I write this in a hury from a few Notes that I have kept.

New Orleans, Louisiana May 1, 1862

Dear Wife and Chirldren, Father and Mother,

We have got to the Cresent City all safe so far. The Troops are Landing. We Shall not have any Truble. The People do not Fancy us, not a Single Cheer. I shouled like to see you and the Chirldren. This war is Drawing to a Close, You will see by the Papers Long before I shall get thair. Do the Best you can. Tell Mother and Father that I think of them and our Father in heven will bless them in thair old age and to keep up, I shall be a Plaguing the life out of them again. When I see the wemon with Babys in thair Arms, I thought of that one that I left and them two Little wemon that Plagues you so much. I shouled like to see [them]. Tell them thay must Love one another and that Boss Farmer that Chops the wood and thinks that he knowes it all, tell him to learn all that he can fore he will need it if he shouled live to grow up. I hope he loves to go to School and be a good Boy.

This City is Built on the Right Banke of the Mississipi and some on the other. It [is] Built very well considering.

May 2nd

Thay are down on us hear but thay will have to take this Medicin. The wemon hope the Yellow Jack[35] will take us off. We shall get quartered today. We had to Lay on the wharf Last night when thay heard that Jackson and Philips was taken.[36] Thay Burnt up over a Million Dollars worth of cotton and More in all thair Sugar, Mollasas, Hogsheads and about 15,000 Troops took to thair heels.[37]

It is a butifull morning and we feell in first rate Spirits. Has we landed by Companeys from the Ship we was Drawn up on and the Folks gathered around us. We were ordered to Load so that thay couled see that thair must be no Foul play.

Kiss that baby fore me and good bye Wife and Chirldren, Father & Mother. Give my regards to all enquiring frends and may God Prosper the Right.

Camp Parepet, May 4th, 1862

Dear Chirldren,

I have Just got through Morning Drill and have taken a walk up the Mississppi on the Levee. The water is very high at this time. It is very mirky water, so many Rivers runing into the Mississippi Brings down a great amount of Wash from the Differnt States that thies Rivers Drain. It looks very butifull on the Bank. You whouled Like to Live hear. Lewis whouled Like to be hear so that he couled Sail Boats and fish. It is a Noble River and in good Tim[e]s the River is Coverd with Steam Boats and Ships and Fortun[e]s are made hear in a Singl Summer.

About 4 mile from our Camp,[38] up the River, grows any quanity of Blackbear[i]es. Lots of the Poor People Pass our Pickets every Morning to Pick them. I have never been up thair but thay tell me that thair is any quanty of Snaks among the Briers; Black and yellow and Spoted, all coulors and Large. I

---

[35] Yellow Fever

[36] Fort Jackson and Fort St. Phillips

[37] A hogshead was a unit of measurement for sugar in Louisiana. *The 1911 Classic Encyclopedia,* s.v. "hogshead," accessed April 20, 2012, http://www.1911encyclopedia .org/Hogshead (site discontinued).

[38] Camp Parepet

shouled not want you round them Berries. It is a very Low, wet, and Swampe in this Part of the South. The River has a Belt of Timber on Both sides of the River. The Wood has been Cut off and Plowed and Brought into a high State of Cultivation and Planted with Sugar Can and Sweet Potatoes, Ric[e] and Corn. Sugar Can is what thay make the Sugar from. Thay have Large Gangs of Slaves to do all the work. Thay have to work from Sun Rise to Dark with a Driver Standing over them with a whip to make them do thair Task.

I had to go up the River one afternoon to help stop the Wicked men that is hear that was Cuting the Levee so has to Let the Water out so has to Drownd us out and Distroy the Growing Crops thay Left. Has we Came in sight, the Planters Turnd out thair Slaves to repair the Crevass that the water was making. If you couled have Seeing the Little Black Chirldren ho[e]ing with thair Mothers and Fathers in the Cane Fields you whouled be thankfull that you was not Born with a Black Skin and that you Enjoy the Blessings of Liberty and the Privlidge of goin to School. Dear Chirldren, you must make the most of your Time when you are at Schooll and when you are asked to do anything by your Mother you must Jump and do it and then it will not be so irksom and you will not Consider it so much of a Task.

Lewis whouled Like to see such tall Corn has growes hear. He couled not reach the Ears thay grows so high. Corn now is Tasseled out and is some 12 feet high. Thay Plant the Hills 6 feet apart, the Rowes are Longer then from your house to the Schooll. In one field I see 16 Pair of Mules Plowing Sugar Can all in one Estate. It belongs to a Northern Man Born in Massachusets by the Name of Mason. I went up to his overseers quarters and Swaped some hard bread fore a Corn Cake. Not so good has your GranMother makes and your Father used to Turn up his Nose at them. I think you do not know how I shouled like some Milk and Can not get any. I think you must do all the Milking for I Can not be Trusted to Milk a Cow. If I shouled Live to Come home I shouled Drink all the Milk.

It is very warm Wether and dry and the nights are very cleer, no Clouds. The Stars Look down on me with Brighter Eys than thay seamd to do in Old Connucut. We are not Plagued with that hevey Fog that we was wrapt up in in Ship Iland nights and mornings. Some Times I think I shouled Like to Live hear, but the Cuntry will be a long Time in geting quieated and Calm again.

Kiss that Little Roger, Arthur, and that Baby.[39] Kiss your Mother for me and tell that I shall Come home again I Trust. Kiss your Granmother and Gran Father and be good Children.

Your Affectnate Father,
CW Sherman

New Orleans, May 6th 1862

Dear Wife, Father and Mother,

The 12th is all right. We have not been eaten up by the Rebls and have not seeing any of them, only has Prisners and some that did not Fancy the Rebl Servis. We got into New Orleans after Some Time. Thay did not think that it was posable to get by Fort Jackson and when the Newes got up to the City, the Rebles took to thair heels. Thay had about 15,000 men in the City. Thay kept the Engine Fired up for more then a week, night and day, redy fore a move if our Gunboats shouled get by. Buttler Put us right in the Center of the City. We Lay on our Arms down by the wharfe the first night when we first Landed. We marched out into the Street and Let the Crowd see that thair was not to [be] any Fooling with them. Each man was Directed to Let them see that it was Ball Catridge that he was Loaded with has it was intemated that thay was goin to Mob us. The People greeted us with you Damn Yankes and that the Yellow Jack whouled have us. It was the wemon that were the most Bitter on us.

The next Day we was taken to Lafefeate [Lafayette] Square, a most Butifull place, Shaded with Trees. The City Gards was EnCamped in it, but thay made themselvs safe by runing and Left a very Preaty Camp Ground all Fenced in with Iron railing. We did not see many of the Better Class of Citizens the first Day or so, Stors all Closed. Thay Told us that when the News Came up to the

---

[39] "Little Roger" appears to be a nickname for Lewis, though this is the only letter in which he uses the term. Casual family records list a "Roger William Sherman" that turned out to be Lewis. Pension records also cite a "mistake" in his name, calling him "Roger"; however, the sworn testimony from Virtue and other family members state the correct name is "Lewis William" and that there was no child named "Roger." The National Archives, *Case Files of Approved Pension Applications of Widows and Other Dependents of Civil War Veterans*, ca. 1861–ca. 1910, Catalog ID 300020, Record Group 15, www.fold3.com.

City that our Gunboats were By The Rigolets.[40] The Point whare the Forts are Built, thay Set Fire to all the Cotton. Thay say some 15 hundred thousand Bales and all the Ships and to see the Places whare thay had it Stored, I think it must have been more then thay say. Thay Roled all the Sugar and Molass barrles into the Street and knocked the heads in and thair is Streets that the Flies have taken Poss[ess]ions of through it. After Buttler Put out is Proclimation the Citizens apeard to have mor Confidance. Thay whare not goin to Print it fore him, but he Just Marched a Gard into the Delta Ofice and took Printers anuff to do what he wanted frome his men and Put his Proclamation through. The Owners of the Saint Charles Hotel whare not goin to Let him into that, but make it his headquarters he whould and did. He placed a strong guard in and around it with a strong . . . [unreadable] . . . this paper that I write this letter on I took out of the telegraph ofice that is under the Hotel. I shouled not want Buttler to know it but I wanted a Sheet or so and took it. We made a good impresion I think on the People. We behaved has men, Answered not back, used no insulting Language and Bought no Liquor or Shine has thay had Put Poison in it, so the Union men told us. I have not had a Tast since I was in Tolland.[41] The 9th Connecticut is all Ir[i]sh and thay Landed a Day after us and thay was soon Drunk. Thay Lost one man; he went into some Place and got his Abdomen Cut so he died. Thay have 2 to be Shot fore leaving his Beat and Geting liquor when he was on gard.

Thay have moved them and us about 7 Mile up above the City into an Intrenchment that the Rebles have built. Thay have Spent a great Deal of Labor and time in a work that thay got up fore Halle[c]k. Thay Counted that we couled not get by [Forts] Saint Philips and Jackson and have been labering, throwing up Brestworks. This one that we Occupi, the work runs back in a line some 3 mile or more Mounted with some very hevey Guns and Mortars. Thay Burnt the carridges and spiked the Guns and the Folks say thay have thrown a great quanity of Arms into the River that we shall get when the water goes down. Thay say that thair is a Large Forc Living back in the woods. Thay have thought that Halleck whouled have to Face these Brestworks and thay had cut a great Dich and to Cut the Leve and Flood the Ground that the Union Army whouled

---

[40] The Rigolets is a straight that connects Lake Pontchartrain and Lake St. Catherine to Lake Borgne and, eventually, the Gulf of Mexico.

[41] Tolland, Connecticut, is listed as his home town in the *Record of Service of Connecticut Men*, 496.

have had to Stand on and a hard fight it must have been, but it is in our hands now and we must hold it. Beauregard is in between us and Halleck.[42] Thay say that Beauregard has Lost Army but we can not find out how. The Battle goes away from us. You can get all the News before us. We have to wait for the Papers. We are in Phelps Brigade and our Col. Deming has got the Ofice of Provost Judge fore the City of New Orleans, but we are not Left without oficers. We have a Leutenant Col. that is a Brick.

I hope you will not take any Truble on my account. I hope to come hom again, how soon we can not tell. You know how the war goes, Better that we do out hear. Mother, this is a Butifull Cuntry along the Banks of the Missippi, but to see the Gangs of Slaves working fore theas planters, thay have to work rain or shine. We had one come on Bord Last night has we was laying in the streem. He stole a small skiff and come abord. He was ticuled, laughfed and told how the Rebles run when thay found we were coming and how the slaves talked and laughed. It looked rather hard to see the Polic Driving them to the jail. Thair has been a great many run down to the City lately when thay found that we was thair.

If anyone shouled ask you anything About me, tell them that I am all right. Give my regards to all those enquiring friends. Tell Virtue that she must kiss that baby fore me and tell the Chirldren that thay must be good and kiss them fore me. You do not know how the Poor of New Orleans have sufferd fore food. When we were Coming away, I took our mess Pan and gave all the Meat that the men couled not put in thair haversacks to some Poor Chirldren. Flour not dollars will [be good as] 75 cent found. Thair will be a famine south this summer.

Yours truly,
CW Sherman
Please send me a few letter stamps.

---

[42] P. G. T. Beauregard was Louisiana-born and a prominent general for the Confederate States Army during the Civil War. He trained as a civil engineer at the United States Military Academy. Maj. Gen. Henry Wager Halleck commanded the Department of the Mississippi before Lincoln appointed him General-in-Chief of all Union forces in July of 1862. "P. G. T. Beauregard, General, May 28, 1818–February 20, 1893," Civil War Trust, accessed February 15, 2014, http://www.civilwar.org/education /history/biographies/p-g-t-beauregard.html; Bruce Catton, *The Civil War*, American Heritage Press, (edition unknown), 306.

Camp Paraphet, Jefferson Parish, New Orleins, May 14, 1862

Dear Father and Mother,[43]

I am well but Reduced in Flesh. My health has been good but our Comissery has been manadged in a way that People have no Idea it Couled be Posable. The Feeding of the French and Austran Soldiers has been Reduced to a Sicanse [scant] cup. If thay Can beat our feeding Troops it dose not Come so hard on thair or our Goverment. But we shall live through it.

I hope the Rebles do not Let Day Light through us. Thay kept it a respectful Distance from us so fare, not becaus thay are less Brave but becaus we are ahead of thair time and thay are having a Bad Cause and thay begin to see it. This war has been Cause by Ignorance of the People South. This State is filled up with French and Creole and Germans and thay are Down on all Yankees has thay Call us.

Every poor Man must have one or more slaves and that helps keeps them Poor. Thay Labor under the impresion that it Adds to thair importance. Thay do not think for themselves but let thair Political Leader Lead them by the Nose whare ever thay please. Thay never stoping to re[a]son with themselves if this thing right or that thing wrong. Thair Leaders have Drilled it into them that the Contraband was given to them and thay whare made Expressly fore thair use and that Slavery is the Normal Condition of the African Race, and that it is derogatory to the White man to Labor and serve. And Black hearted Northen men with Southern views of the Beauties of Slavery have helped to back the Southern Politican; pull the Wool over the Mass of the Southern People. And that every movement of the North to Save his Southern Brother from bean [being] Swallowed up in the Black Eliment that he was, and is serounding himself with, in the Shape of this Slavery of another Race to Minster to his Plesuers and Lusts, that every movement that was made North of Masons & Dixons Line was made to destroy thair Political Power and Bring them to Play Second Fiddle to the North, and by every way in thair Power thay have Inflamed the Peoples mind with the Idea that we was thair Enmy and wanted to Bring them Down to our Low Level; that is thay have been Brought up in such a way that everything Conected with us at the North is Low and mean, and that

---

[43] This letter is transcribed from photocopies.

every thing Southern is high, and that thay have all the Virtues and that, as Southern Planters, a Embodyment of all that is manley and good in our Comon Natuere. Thay are down now and the Back bone of the Reblion is Brock; the Stars and Strips Flote over this Part of Rebledom and it will take a big Fight to take them down. We fished up the Confedrate rag out of the River and it Looked Just like thair Cause, torn and dirty.

Thay have a Splendid Climate and a half the Labor that is nesary to home to get Prepared fore Winter will get a good living hear. The Orang and Magnola Trees Look very Preaty and when thay are in Bloom thay Cent the Place whare thay are and thay give the Cuntry a Tropical Look.

The Principle Inhabitants have Left, but thair Slaves Carry on the Plantations. Thay Come into Camp Every Morning. Thay travel in the night to save Bean [being] Picked up. Thay Come in and Claime Genral Phelps Protection and thay get it. He is down on the Perculer Institution and he is in the right Place and he has had a great maney Calls from Owners of Stray Cattle, and I have a Notion thay go away with a Flea in thair Ear. He talks kind of Fatherly to them and Exhort them to Flee from the wrath to Come. I was on Gard by is Tent the other Day when two Overseers Come to see him and he Put some straight Forward questions to them and thay was a little taken Back. I wish some Northern Democrats Couled have heard the Old Man. He Advises them to Put thair House in order and begin to Pray. Says the Genral, "You have a thin Boiler and you have been Putting on Steam and Crowding the Safty Valve down. You Put on a Forty Pound Shot and other weights and now you have Piled on Canon and the first thing you will know, you will be Blown up." "We of the North," says the Genral, "when anything goes wrong Pray to Congrass, but you walk in and tell Congrass that unless your Demand are not complied with you will Dam the Cuntry. We Pray and you Curse and that is Just as things have been."

Last Sunday our Chaplain held a Meeting by the Gard Tent. Our Camp was about full of Sable Visitors, Wemon and men and Chirldren. Lewis whouled have Laught to see them Little Black Boys with thair Curley heads. Poor things, thay have not the same Priveledges that he has to Atend Sunday School. I have not seeing a Single Church all this way from New York till I got to New Orleans, although we Pased numbers of Villidges on the Florida Co[a]st and the Banks of the Missippi. The town of Carlton (Carrollton), 3 Mile below us, has not a single Church.

We went down to Carlton the other day to Bring up some Canon and I see some Chirldren Swinging in one of those swings that I had seeing used at Fairs in England when I was round in them Parts. It Put me in mind of the Tims of old Langsyne, in Fact the Band Played that Tune has we Marched into Town. Yesterday I went with a Foragin Party to get some Corn Shucks to Put in the Hospital, and the way the Planters whouled like to get rid of letting us have any was a caution. We had Orders to let them keep them if thay whouled not let us have them Reasable, but thay are spoted if we shall want any, and we have not time to look around has it was. We went from one Plantation to another till we found one Planter that Let us have t[w]o Loads, he finding Teems and Drivers. He sent his Overseer with [us] to Camp to get his Pay. We Pay for every thing that we want and it whouled go bad with a Soldier that shouled Dare Lay his hand on anything that was not his. Thay must not pick up so much has a Orang without leave.

When we are out to see how thay [Rebles] look and when thay see us Coming, how thay whouled like to Bite, but thair Teeth is Pulled and thay Can mearley Growle. The Poor class rejoices that we have Come and Buttler is putting the screws Down on thair Cause, and them, and the way he dose Come in over them is a Caution to Evil doers. Our Coming is a God Send to the Slaves. Thay Come into Camp and desire our protection and so think that those that have helped to Carrey this Reblion on will in the End, regreat that thay ever Put thair hand to this War, for thay will Come out the Little End of the Horn. Thay had made great Preparations to give us a warm welcome but that God that Looks over the afairs of Nations overruled thair desines and turned thair Works to non affect.

Your Affactnate Husband and Son,
CW Sherman

Camp Parepet, New Orleans, May 23, 1862

Dear Wife,[44]

I take the Pleasure of writing a few Lines to you and the Chirldren hoping thay may find you all in good health has theas leaves me at Present.

---

[44] This letter is transcribed from photocopies.

I send you a Order fore 10 Dollers fore my State Bounty. It will be payable to Virtue in the Town of Willington at the Town Treasury. I was Payed 10 a few hours before I left Hartford and this is the Second Payment. I hope you will receive it safe. Pleas Let me know If you do and if not you must take the Truble to get a Afidavit from the Town Treasurer that he has not Paid you no bounty on this Second Payment and I can get another order for you. We have not been Payed any United States Pay since we left Hartford. I shall have 3 Months Pay Due me the first of June. Most of the Redgiment have 5 Months Due them. As soon has I recve my Pay you shall have it. It may be soon and we may have to Waite another month.

I hope you keep up your Curedge and makes the Best of your Lot. You can not Concive how much the Poor Wemon of the South have had to enduer Since this Reblion has Desolated this Fair Land. Thair Husband and Sons have been forced into the Reble Ranks or be Shot, and thay have been left with thair little ones to get a Living how thay Couled.

Thair has been great Suffering in all the Citys South. When we Came into New Orleans thay did not have 3 Days Provisions in the City and great fears was entertained of a Famin, and whouled have been if Genral Buttler had not taken mesures to get Provisions fore them. He, by good luck, found a large quanity hid that the Rebles had taken from the People and he Distributed about one thousand Barles [barrels] of meat, Coffe & Sugar to the Poor till he couled find means to have Provisions Come into the City. Thay come into our Camp and exchaing a few Onions for some of our hard Bread, swap milk for some of soft meat. Thay ask 10 Cents a quart fore Milk.

You have begun to Plant about this time. I hope you will have good Crops. You are about 3 months behind in the seasons. Corn hear, what little I have seen, is Tasseled out, Sweet Potatoes is about a foot high. Irish potatoes are in the Market, and green Peas, thay are for those who can get them. We Poor Soldiers have to Put up with Salt Meat and hard Bread and what thay Call Coffee. But what thay call coffee and this thing was never within speaking distance.

Our redgiment has been Trubled with the Disentery but thay are getting over it some. I have been very Lucky so fare. Thay Call me the Toughest one in the Camp. I tell them it is a Cleer Conscience and Patrotism that keeps a Soldier well. If the Boyes couled only get to Hartford it whouled . . .[45]

Camp Parepet, New Orleans May 24, 1862

Dear Wife and Chirldren,[46]

I recved your & Mother kind letter of April 10th and was Glad to hear from you and that you was all well. I am very well at this time. I have not been Sick a Single Day, for wich Blessing I can not be to Thankful to my Hevenley Father fore his kind care of me. I was disappointed in not recving more Letters from home. We have been waiting so long fore a Maile. Six week and some of the men got 3 & 4 Letters. I have wrote home has maney has 20 Letters. I sent 2 Letters by a man by the Name of Leaver, a Member of our Compney that got his Discharge in Ship Iland. If you get any Letters Mailed in New York or Westerley Road Iland, you will know that he Mailed those Letters. I shall send Virtue 10 Dollers, the Second Payment of my State Bounty. Please Let me know if you get it all safe.

May 26th

Yesterday I was on the Brigade Police, that is the day after we Stand Gard we have to do Duty round Camp. Go round and Colect [all] things wood and we was Detailed to go Down the River to Jefferson City to help the Citizins stop the crevas[se] in the Levee. It had given away and most of the City was Flooded. It did make a Cleer Sweep to Lake Pontchrain. Boats had to be used to get round in the Streets. The Mississippee has not been so high for a great many years. The Watter his maney feet higher than the Serounding Cuntry. The Water is Confined in the River by Embankments of Earth Called Levees. You Can Concive what Distruction of Property and Life thair whouled be if we Shouled have a very hard Storm, when the watter is so high, if the levee shouled give away and have a fair Chance. It whouled Put New Orleans a great many

---

[45] The rest of the pages are missing.
[46] This letter is transcribed from photocopies.

Feet under water. It has Caused a great Deal of Distress and Suffering all the way on the River, but the high Watter has helped our Cause by Enabling our Gun Boats to get round.

We had a very large Mail Come Sadurday night and did get but that one Letter from home of April the 10 and I had been expecting some half Dozen, and no Paper. Tell Fany that I got her First Letter and was Pleased to think that she Couled do so well. I had wrote a Little Letter to her and Angline and Lewis, and shall write another to her. You must take Pains to Form your Letters and take time and She will soon be able to write.

Dear Mother do not be unesey About me. I have had very good health and have Enjoyed my self well, Considering, and thanks to my Parents fore a good Constitution and the Free Mountain Air of Old Connectcut, all given to me by a kind Father in Heven who will Protect and Preserve me.

I shouled like to see you all but I thought my Duty to Follow the Stars and Strip[e]s out hear and I have seeing them raised in Places whare thay had been Puled down and the Old Flag looked all the better fore having been Absent a Short Time, and whare ever that Glorious Old Flag is needed to regenrate and revive Old Memorys of the Good Old Tim[e]s when we Lived in Peace and hapeness, why, I am bound to help Cary it. Why, it is like a river running through a Thirsty Land giving health and peace & hapeness. It is fore the healing of the Nations, and when its Mission is fullfilled and this Deluded People have been Brought Back to the Faith and Love of its youth, then Charley will be redy to Follow it to is Old New England Home and will be ever redy to Invite is Southeron Brother to a good Old Fashiond Thanksgiving Dinner. The boys think that it will not be long before thay will see thair Homes again. We have as many Rumors in Camp has the Papers to home have of Telegraphic Dispaches, and thay are about as relible. We Trust in Providence and our Rifles to Put an End to this Fraticidle Strife.

The Chirldren tell me that the Snow was two feet Deep. I can not realize that it is only 3 Months Since we left home and we have been under July Wether all the Time, and when we left, we was most Froze and 2 Days after the "Fulton" left with us we was in our Shirt Sleeves and some of the men are Tanned so that it will not do fore the Rebles to get holt of them or thay will be goin into the New Orleans Market.

Yesterday we whare hurred up some 6 mile at a Duble quick. The Rebles had Come down and Cut the Levee and was Tearing up the Raile road Track.

Thay Left when we Came in Sight and we had the Priviledge to get Back to Camp the Best way we couled.

The Wether is hot fore some of the Boys; I like it. Corn is tasseled out, New Potatoes is gon, Sweet Potatoes are about half grown.

You must have got my letters by this time. I hope Mother and Virtue will not worry about me. I expect to come home all right. You will have planted all you will by this time.

Ask Edwin to write me and tell me all the news and buy yourself a bow if you have money enough. I shouled have some soon and I hope that thay have paid you the state pay. I sent you an order for 10 Dolars and I do not want you to deny yourself anything you want, nor the children. When I get my monthly pay you shall have that. We expect to get it every day now and the sooner the better.

Also ask John Fisk to write me and tell me how things are in Stafford.

You must keep up your spirits. I am all right as present and it may not be long before the 12th may be home again, sooner than we think.

Your Affactnate Husband and Son,
CW Sherman

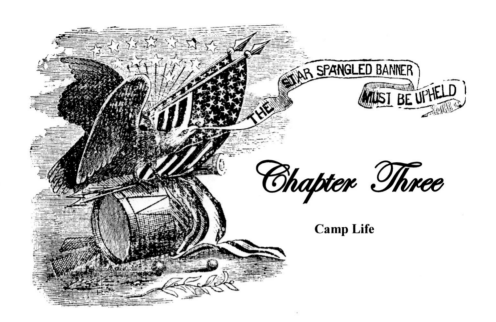

Chapter Three

Camp Life

Camp Parepet, Jefferson Parish, June 9, 1862

Dear Wife and Chirldren,

I have been waiting to get a Letter from you. I expected one Every Week, but have only recved 3 Letters up to the ninth of June. The First one was Dated the 10th of April and I have wrote as much has 2 Letters a week and have sent them all to Rockvill as Father and Edwin are thair and are goin home Every week or so. I did send one to Stafford. You Can send every week as we have a reglur Mail run from New Orleans to the States and we Shall Stay here this Sumer. I think we may go highier up the River and in fact a soldiers Life is very uncirtain.

My health has been very good but it takes all that I know with the help of my Father in heven and He has been very good and kind to me. All of the men have been Sick but my health has been so very good that that thay Call me the Toughest man in the Crowed. Virtue, I hope you keep up your Spirits and do Dance round the house and Shake up that Arthur for me.[47] I sopose he takes geting up Earley and Padles round with them Little Feet of his and that Old Lady called Faney Sherman has her hands Full in Puting things Straight and

---

[47] Henry Arthur would be about sixteen months old, Fanny almost twelve years old, and Angeline just ten years old.

Spanking the Baby. Angline dose all the Chors and sees to things genrally. Lewis cuts all the Wood and Draws all the Water and runs away every Chance he gets. Mother Dreaming about her Wicked Boy and Father Puts on the Armor of Faith that makes Strong the Weake, mighty keep up all of you, fore Charleys Worth ten Ded men as yeat, and he feels thankfull that he has been Preserved so fare.

We have any quanity of Camp rumors of goin home but if we do go any whare that way it will be on the line of the Potomac and Let the Western Redgiments take this Line. Our Col has gon to Washington and we are waiting for him to Show us his Jolly and Portley Presence. Our Boys are doing Better now. Thay have been Trubled with the Disentery but are geting Acclimated and if the yellow Jack keeps off we shall do very well. Our Leauteant Col Flies round and imparts some of the Snap that he Calls it. He is getting the Redgiment up to a high state of Disaplin. The other Redgiments have Orders to take thair Calls and other Arai[n]gments from the 12th and in fact we can Drill with the Best Redgiments that Old Connecut has Sent.

June 10

We have Just Come from escorting the corps[e] of one of our Oficers, a leauteant of Co. I. The Body is on his way home. The whole of the Redgement Turned out with Genral Phelps at the Head with the Redgimentl Oficers. Sunday the 8th the Chaplain Preached to us.[48] He dose every Sunday Afternoon but the men do not Turn out as thay ought. We have a Great Number of Slaves Come into Camp Sunday and thay apear to pay Great atention to the Services. Thay read Some of the Church of England Service and Combine with the Modist [Methodist] and a Little of Both. We expect to get two Months Pay Soon, 26 Dollers. You can Look out fore it has I shall send it home. I hope you will get that Town Money, Virtue, and that 10 Dollers of the State Bounty I have sent you and 26 Dollers of my United States pay fore the 2 months of March and April.

---

[48] The Chaplain of the Twelfth Connecticut was James H. Bradford from New Haven as listed in *Record of Service of Connecticut Men*. His name was often listed in the return address on the envelopes since he handled the mail as one of his duties. *Record of Service of Connecticut Men*, 474.

The wether is very warm. The River is goin down and the water is drying up in the Swamps, but thair is no way of Draining the water that has got over the Cuntry but by the Action of the Sun, and it is to be hoped that no Evil afects will arise from it.

The other day a Slave Came into Camp that had Come 60 Mile down the river. He had a Large Hay knife to Protect himself. He had one of thos Iron Collers round [h]is neck with 3 Long Pieces riveted on runing Straight up by his head so that he couled not Turn his head.[49] It was one of thos Araingments that Shows off the Beauty of Slavery.[50] This makes the Second one that our Blacksmiths have taken off. The first one was taken off a womon. Onley think, Virtue, of having our Chirldren with such Ornements on. And thay Claim the right to do what ever the Devil Puts them up to and it is time thay was Brought up Standing with a round Turn.

Thay ask the soldiers one Cent a piece for one Small Potato. Cotton Cloth is worth 150 Cents Per yard, Shoes, 4 Dollers Per Pair, Boots, 15 to 20 Dollers Per Pair, Flour, 20 Dollers Per Barrle and Salt meat, 50 Cents Per Pound and that was not to be had till the Yanky Came, and Buttler has been trying to bring things down but the Cuntry was Draind so that it was take some time to fill up. It is a nice Place Virtue to Bring up Chirldren. You Can Let them run Bare footed and one Shirt on. Save lots of Washing and Ironing. In most of the front yards thay have one or more of those Plants that never Flowers only once in a Hundred years and when thay do it is worth Living a hundred years to see the Flower.

Mother, you must make Father write me more Letters. I have not receved but 3 Letters Since I Left home and this is the 12th of June. We have had quite a number of Mailes and it Comes Tugh to see the Boys have Letters and narey one fore me. I want to know if Henry has Paid Virtue any Money and how you have got along and thair was one Spell that we all thought we shouled get home by the 4 of July, but things have Chainge so that we may have to Stay till fall. Virtue you must keep up and Show them that you are one of the Spartan Wemon

---

[49] Please see the following website for a photo of this horrible device: "Photo of slave wearing collar device from Ken Burns documentary," August 20, 2011: http://civilwartalk.com/threads/photo-of-slave-wearing-collar-device-from-ken-burns-documentary.26352/.

[50] Tongue-in-cheek—he often used the opposite word of what he meant to stress a point.

of Old. This thing has to be Put through if it takes a Leg. Father you will do the Best you Can this year and I hope you will Prosper and that you may have good Crops this year. We have had no rain but one Little Shower since we have been hear. Thay tell me the heat is so great that you can not Sleep nights but we stand it. I lay my India ruber Blanket on the ground and Put my Over Coat on that then take off all my Clothes and throw my woolen Blanket over me and sleep like a Log. I think we can get along if we did Come frome a Cold hard Cuntry. Another Mail came into Camp last night and nothing fore me. I shall not write anymore. It is no use fore me to write and never get anything. If any one thinks the Truble is to much or if thay will take the [time] to write Direct thair Letter to New Orleans, Company K, Captain Abbott, 12th Redgiment CV, New E Dision,

CW Sherman

New Orleans, June 14, 1862

Dear Wife and Chirldren,

I write to [you] again to Let you know that I am well and hop this will find you and the Chirldren and Mother and all of you Enjoying the Blessing of good health. I have been favored more then I deserve by my Father in Heven. I fore one fore get to[o] often that God that Preserves me and keeps me in health.

I am put in mind of the Shortness of Life by seeing the Firing Parteys of the 8 Vermont as thay Pass by with the Corps[e] of Some of thair Members. Thay have Buerd quit[e] a number of thair Comrades Since thay have been with us. Thay have gon up the River now and we want to go but must wait fore our Fatherley Col. We are waiting with all the Pactance [patience] that we can muster. I Sometimes think I shouled like to Drop in and see how you are and take a Little Beer. I hop you keep Some on hand. I may Come like a theif in the night and I may have to Stay a Spell Longer. I have to go a little dry sometims has I do not want to Drink so much of that Delectable Compound Called Mississppi Watter. We Lost one of our men by Drownding Last night. He was a good swimer. The Missippi is a Dangrous Stream. It is full of Eadeys and the under Curent is so Strong that it is Daingrous to Drop your self under has you Can in most Streams. The Body has not been found and Probley will never be.

<u>Sunday the 15 June</u>

We have Redgimentle Inspection every Sunday Morning and we have to be Paticular how we go out. Our Knapsacks have to be Packed neater than any Lady keeps her Band Box. Our Rifles and Belts are kept so that you can see your Face in Plates and the Mortar Fleet of Comador Porter have been Passing up by our Camp this Last Week in tow of Comador Fareguts Gun Boats.[51] Thay have got one Gun Boat and Mortar Boat aground right opersite to us. The Contra Bands Come into Camp More Sadurday nights then any other night. Our Pickets have the Road full Every morning but it dose no good. Thay are Sent Back or up the River and thair Masters gos up and Gets them and Gives them a Auffull W[h]iping after thay Gets them Back on the Plantations. I know not how this qustion will be Settled, but Some thing more then talking will have to be don. The Suthron People are Just has Bitter now has thay ever have been and thay tell us that we may hold thair Citys and towns but we never Can Subdue them. Thay hate us Yankees as thay Call us more than any thing you can imadgin. The English whouled be welcomed or fore that matter the Devil and all his Angles [angels] whouled be taken by the hand and Welcomed but we must have faith that Every thing will Turn fore the Best.

I hope the riey [rye] will do well and what you have Planted yeld a hundred Fold and that our Father in Heven will Bless you all and keep my Little ones safe and in health. Keep up your curedge Wife I shall return home safe. Never fear you are not agoin to get Rid of me so Easey. I have to stay by the Old Flag aspell Longer. Thair is a few more Places whare we have to Unfurle it and give it to the Breezes. Kiss my Babys and tell them to be good.

Your Affectnate Husband and Undutiful Son,

CW Sherman

---

[51] Adm. Farragut

Camp Parepet, New Orleans, June 22, 1862

Dear Wife and Chirldren,

I take this opertunity of writing a few Lines to you, hoping thay may find you and my Chirldren and Mother and Father and all of you well has Bless my Father that is in Heven fore his many Merceys to me, it Leaves me at Present.

The Wether is Splened, 95 Degrees in the Shade and how much Warmer it will be I can not say. Our Canvass Houses keeps the Sun off us in the Day and Cool nights. Tell Faney I Lost her Hancherf [handkerchief] and I wish I had a nother but thats out of the question has Cotton Cloth in the New Orleans Market is Worth 150 Cents Per yard and other small things in Proportion. The Merchent that gets hear first with his yenkee Notions will make his Pile. Ships are Coming with Ice; that is a Leuxery that we shouled Like to enjoy but shall have to get along with out.

You will have Planted all that you will fore this year and I hope you will have good Luck this year. We are Suffering from a Long Drouth that has dryed up all the Gardens so that we will have to go with out garden Sauce. I get a few Tomatoes, but thay do not Taste so good has thay do to home. Thay ask a Pickeune[52] or five Cents for 4 or 5 of them but thay help get down our hard Bread. With me Salt Horse and Sea Biscut dose not go quite so good has Soft Bread and June Buter. Buter his a thing that I have not seeing since we Left home. We get Pork and Beans twice a week and that his the best meal I get through the week. The men swap thair hard Bread for one thing and another. The negros come into Camp and trade Principley molases that the Planters Alow them to has. Thay are hard up fore Corn Meal. Thay [are] not raising any Last year but this year thay have a large extent of ground Planted but the dry wether has kept that Back. Thay Plant it in Drills about 4 Inches apart and it runs up not quite out of Sight. [Thay] use no manuer has the Land requirs non. It Bakes up hard the Same has the Bottom of a Mill Pond when the Water has been drawen off and the Land that we are encamped on dose not need a strong Team to Plow it up. Then I do not know what mud is well Trod down and Baked well.

Father Say I do not write often a nuff. I have wrot anuff Letters to averadge 2 a week, 2 I think you never got. I sent them by a man by the Name of Richerd

---

[52] Picayune—A small Spanish coin worth about five cents. *Merriam-Webster*, s.v. "picayune," accessed April 20, 2012, http://www.merriam-webster.com/dictionary /picayune.

Lever living in the Town of Westerley, Raod Iland. He was discharged in Ship Iland and sailed a few Days after we Left fore New Orleans. I hope you will get them. Virtue we have been Paid fore 2 months and I send you 27 Dollers by Adams Express. I sent you a Order for Ten Dollers a few weeks a go and Pleas Let me know if you get it safe. 25 Dollers is in United States Notes and 2 Dollers in Gold. I hope we shall get through with our Trubles by Fall so that we can get home. I do not wish to Leave till this War is over for my self, all though thair is not a Soldier hear that whouled Like to get home Better than me but I Put my Hands to the Plow with my Eyes Open and Counted the Cost and have never regreated that I Enlisted. I know that there was others to home that Couled have Left Easyer then me, but thay thought that thay Couled not Leave, but the Old Flag needed a few more hands to help up hold it and hear I be and shall stay under its Folds till it Flotes over Every Foot of Soil that it Claimes Aligance from. May heven Bless you all. Keep up you Curedge. We shall Com out all right.

Your Affectate Husband,
CW Sherman

Camp Parepet, New Orlean, June 25, 1862

Dear Mother,

I take this opertunity of writing a few lines to you hoping thay may find you in good health has theas Leaves me at Present.

I am Siting under a nice Shadey Fig Tree but it is not mine. It belongs to a Bi[t]ter Sesash Col that is now away frome home Fighting against the men that is Garding his Property. I am on Picket Duty. It is very warm. The men are all Laid out a sleep in the Lot or Field. In Front of us has been Planted with Assparrow [asparagus] and it Looks very Preaty in the Middle of the Furrows. Thay have Planted Corn only one stalk Left Standing and on Each one thair is from 2 to 3 Ears of Corn big anuff to knock a man down and it takes a Tall man to Top it in fact.

Mother this is a Splended country if you onley had Money anuff. Faith, I am geting lazey. You do not Feel Like Work and if we had any Marching to do, I do not know who whouled do it. It is so warm in the Middle of the Day that for one I do not care wether School keeps or not. We can not Drill but two hours and a half a Day. One hour in the morning and one half or from 7 to 8 in the morning and from 5 to half Past 6 and then Dress Parade so that we do not Eat sup[p]er till after 7 o'clock.

We have 3 Redgiments Encamped hear. The 12 Connecticut this is the Crack Redgiment.[53] You ought to see the Colord Individuals that come to see our Dress Parade. We do look kind a Slick and the way thay roll up the White of thair Eyes when our Col Calls out Charge Bayonets. We are expected to Look Savedge or Wolfish, but when I see the Face some of them Put on I kind a Laugh inwardley.

The Chaplain gave them the use of our Canvass Meeting house Last Sunday and thay had a good Time. The Colord Preacher Preached what you whouled Call a Old Fashind Methodist Sermon. I liked [it] much and a Prayer that one of the Slaves made I shouled like fore some of those men that Look down on the Colord Race with Contempt to have heard. I Claim with Greeley that every shot Fired from eather Side in this War is a Link Broke in the Chain that Binds the Slave.[54] Thay look on our Coming with delight and thair is nothing that thay are not Willing to do for us. Thair is quite a number in the three Camps and we Couled not get along with out thair help. Thay Bring Water fore the Different Compneys and help round the Cook Tents. Our Genral whouled give them all thair liberty but he is Tied by the Short Sighted Policy of the Cabnet at Washington.

We have been Paid off and I have sent my too Months Pay home. I sent it By Adams Express. The Chaplain took it to New Orleans fore me. I Directed it to the New Rock Mill, Rockvill, to Father. I expect that it will be Put into his hands. Thair that is how Samul Wicks Directed his to his Wife. I hope Virtue will get it all safe. I Insured it. It Cost me seventy Cents to Insure 27 Dollers. That his the Amount I have sent. I was Paid up to the first of May so that I shall have 2 Months Pay Due the first of July and I hope thay will Pay up then so that I can send 2 Months more Pay home. I sent Virtue my second State Bounty

---

[53] Under Lt. Col. Colburn, the Twelfth attracted notice for its high state of discipline. He insisted upon company-drills every morning and brigade-drill every afternoon. W. A. Croffut and John M. Morris, *The Military and Civil History of Connecticut During The War of 1861–65* (New York: Ledayrd Bill, 1869), 160, PDF e-book.

[54] Horace Greeley (1811–1872) was an American journalist and politician who was a radical anti-slavery leader. Catton, *The Civil War*, 306.

of Ten Dollers and I shall feell Anxious till I hear that she has recved it. Tell her to keep up her Curedge and Trust in Providanc for He doeth all things well. Tell her to kiss that Baby for me and that Arthur give him a good Shake every Morning. Kiss the Chirldren all around. May Heven Bless you, Mother, Father, Wife and Chirldren.

Your Affectnate Son,
CW Sherman

Camp Parepet, New Orleans, June 26, 1862

Dear Wife and Chirldren,

I am well at this time and hope this will find you and the Chirldren all well. I am waiting anxiousley to hear from you. I write but do not get any in return. I hope you will write oftener. I have recved but four Letters since I left hom and one of them was from Henry. I recved that Paper that Father sent me, but it was so Old that the Boyes Laughed when I told them the Date. We are hungre for Newes and the way it is Devouerd is a Caution to those that Neglects or For gets thair Frends.

This Climate is not a good Place to keep Butter or Fresh Meate. Very Fat People do not Admire the heat. 95 Degrees in the Shade Day after Day and not one Drop of Rain. The ground is Baked hard so that it begins to Crack. It is a kind of Clay Mud and when it dose rain it makes it very Disagreable fore Ladys to get round. It must be very Plesent Travling after it has Raind for 2 months has it dose. It sets in to Rain in June, but this year it has been dry and we must get the Wet Se[a]son in July. We thought once that we shouled be to home by the Fourth of July. It dose not look has if Col Demin[g] Can fulfill his Promis to us in that Matter. It is two Months since he Left us to go hom and we have not Seeing him Since, but have heard that he sailed in the Road Iland from Boston on the 10 of June and to Day is the 29.[55] We want to have him with us. The Boys think that the Leauteanant Col works us to much and that Col Demin[g] will use more Judgment in what work thair is to be don.

---

[55] Ship USS *Rhode Island*

We are Puting up a Covering in our Compney Street with Poles and Brush to keep off some of the heat. It begins to make some of the men wish for the Green hills and Cooling Breezes of thair Old Northen homs. I fore one whouled like to be to day Layed out under that Maple Tree below the Barn with some Beer and a Pipe. If [I] was, you may take my hat if you whouled get me whare I am now. Thay have issued out some Miscatoes [mosquitoes] Bars to the men and thay will Sleep with more Comfort then thay have. You whouled not beleve that Miscatoes are as Blood thirsty has thay are. The men are more Afraid of them than Beauregard and his men.

I hop that some of my Letters will get home. Virtue, you must Cheer up and do not be afraid of any thing you shouled hear in regard to the 12th. Thair has been things said at differant Times Calcalated to Alarm the Frends of those that are in this Redgiment. We shall do our Duty if Called on and we shall not all be drove into the Missipipi. If Baueregard shouled come this way, we have a 22 Gun Sloop of War Covering our Camp that whouled make it nearley Secure if we couled not help our selves, which is not the Case. Thair are 3 Redgiments in this Bigade now, 2 having Left us. We have 4 Batterys of Rifeld Guns that, with the Sloop of War and what Guns we have on the Parephet, whouled make it unconvenatly warm fore any one that Shouled Dare to Molest us and Genral Buttler has given them Notice that before he will be Driven away he will Burn the City and make it so that it never will be the Place for man to Live in a gain. By Cuting the Levee he can Turn the Missipipi all over this Part of the State and thay will think twice befor thay will Act once or Compell the Federl Commanders to resort to such a Measuer and it is most imposable for any Desaster to befall us to Compell us to give this Place up again into the hands of Traitors . . .[56]

---

[56] This letter continues on June 29, 1862, but starts with a new date and salutation. There were apparently three letters in an envelope June 25, 26, and 29, numbered 1–3.

Camp Parephet, New Orleans June 29, 1862

Dear Wife and Chirldren and Mother and Father,

. . . and we hope that we Shall have no ocasion to Distry this Part of the State. It deserves some Punishment for the usadge and insult thay heaped on the Union Soldiers that Came to Liberate them from Worse then African Slavery. Thay Couled not see that we was thair salvation. You ought to see the Money thay had in Curculation. The Araingment for Small Bills is most Beautifull. One of thair one Dollers Shin Plasters,[57] if you want Fifty Cents Chaing, thay take a knife and Cut the Bill in two and 5 & 10 thay do the same and I have seeing a fifty Cent Bill Cut in two. Thair is no Silver Chaing, only what the men Brought. Thair is nothing smaller then 5 cents or a Picune [picayune] and those are made of Paste board. The Suthron Curancy is or was Easely made but Genral Buttler has straighened some of it out and heald others to their Promises to Pay.

June 30, 1862

Dear Father,

We are expecting a Mail and I hope it will Bring me Some thing in the Shape of a Letter. I keep on writing and Shall till I get Some Letters. I have wrote to Henry and Derick since I recved that Last Letter from you that went to Ship Iland and then to New Orleans.[58] I am well at Present and we have had two Small Showers of Rain, the 28th and 29th of Jun. It has been very Dry and the Corn Crops that the Planters have Put in this year will and have Suferd from the Drouth. I am on Picket Duty out side of the Camp in the Road. [We] have to Stop all Teams and Foot Travlers and some of them do not Fancy Such Fun. Thay that have Passes go along rejoycing. The Spot that we are Placed is alongsid the Missippi and all Boats goin up and down we Bring to with Mine Ball Picked a head of the Boats and thay must Submit to be Serched. We have a house that has been Deserted by the Owners and the Genral has it about full of Contraband. A Sessash Col Living on the other Side of the River had a Smart

---

[57] A common name at the time for paper money of low denomination—privately issued paper currency, especially devalued and poorly secured. *Merriam-Webster*, s.v. "shin plaster," accessed April 20, 2012, http://www.merriam-webster.com/dictionary /shin+plaster?show=0&t=1335120056.

[58] His brother Henry and his uncle James Derrick

Coulerd Boy that Came over to our Camp and told the Genral that his Master had a seshe Flag and arms hid, so a Leauteanat went over with the Slave and made him give up his Straing Gods wich did not improve his Temper and he sent over all of his Nigers and a great maney more have Come Down the River and thay make this Place thair Head quearters, and how thay will ever Settle this question I know not.

Before this Letter reaches you, you will have begun your Hayien [haying] and how you will get it, I know not. I hope Henery will Bring a Cuple of good men and get it in good Shape. I think he ought to aford to do a Little that way fore me has I am out hear Trying to help keep this Distructed Cuntry togather so that he can have Bissness. He has gon into the Wagon Trade and a man will not want to by a wagon if he has no Cuntry to ride in and I want him to bear that in mind. Your or my Frend Frink, ought to give me a days work for old acquaintance sake. I hope you will get along with your Sum[m]ers work. Edwin will be able to give you a Lift and Lewis.[59] I expect that you will have to stand out the way when he brings that Rake round. Be carfull and see that he dose not hurt him self if you Put him on the Cart to Tread the Hay down. Tell Mother and Virtue to Put on a Stif uper lip and Trust in Providance. I hop to Turn up all right. I did expect to get home By the Fourth of July from what Demin[g] Told us, but I must spend the 4 in Camp Parephet. I have sent Virtue 27 Dollers. Tell her not to Truble on my account as my Father that is in Heven will take care of me. He has, and I feell that I shall Come home all safe. Kiss the Chirldren for me,

Your Affectnate Son,
CW Sherman

Camp Parephet, New Orleans, July 2, 1862

Dear Wife and Chirldren,

I take great pleasier in Writing theas few Lines to you, hoping thay may find you in good health and the Chirldren, Mother and Father. I recved your Welcom Letter of June the First and was Glad to hear from you and that you

---

[59] Edwin is his cousin, and Lewis is Charles's eldest son, not quite eight years old here.

was all well. I am well at Present, thank the Lord for is Great Care of me and mine.

I see that you and Mother have Turned Farmers. I hope that you will have good Luck in raising Potatoes. When I come hom I shall want some one to help me by thair Parctuel [particular] Knowledge of Agruculturl. I expect to see your and Mothers Names of those that have had Prizes Awarded to them fore the crop of Turnips and Cabadges. I think more of a good Crop of Hay, but it is all Nessary for a Suckcesfull Farmer.

I am Sorey to hear that you did not get your Town Pay till the Middle of May. You did right in geting what ever you need for your self and the Chirldren. I couled not send you any Money befor I recved my Pay, but has soon has I got it I put it into the Chaplains hands to take down to Adams Express in New Orleans. I recved 26 Dollers, two Months pay.[60] I sent you 27 Dollers, a Doller more than I recved and hope you will get it by the 10 of July. I sent it to Father to the New Rock Mill Rockvill.[61] I expect it to be Put into his hand thair. It was insuerd and I have the recept of the Compney so that if any thing Shouled hapen to it I can get the Amount again and I had Sent you my Second 10 Dollers Bounty from the State of Connecut. I sent that in a Letter and you must have got it by this time and if not Let me know and I am expecting my 10 Dollers from the town of Stonington which you Shall have has soon has I get it. Please do not whorrey your self on my account has I hope to get home some time.

The Road Iland got in Last night Bringin me two letters, one from you and one from Henry and Alvira.[62] The Raine Seson, we are expecting to set in soon; that we Dred the most. It is so mudey when it dose rain and the Sun Comes out so hot that it makes it very unhealthey. I recved those Postadg Stamps and thay will Come [in] handy. Thay Pass our Letters home by Franking them but you

---

[60] Charles generally spelled "two" as "too," and "too" as "to," but I felt it was confusing to leave that spelling intact.

[61] It is evident that Charles's father, Thomas, and possibly Edwin, worked at the mill in Rockville, Connecticut. Various family members worked at woolen mills near Putnam after the war, according to the 1870 Census, most particularly Fanny and Angeline. Rockville is approximately eleven miles from Willington where the family lived during the war. His father went home every week or so.

[62] Charles sometimes spells Henry's wife's name "Alvira" and sometimes "Elvira." Family and census information indicates the latter spelling.

will have to Pay fore them thair I supose.[63] Money is Cicurlating around hear some now. The men are making up for Lost time and Put thair Oficers to some Truble. We had Ten men in the Gard House out of our Compney and other Companeys in Proportion. Men will drink if thay can get it. Col Demin[g] has got has far has New Orleans.[64] We shall see him soon.

Write has often has you can. Tell Mother I often think how we used to talk about this war and now I am in it and have a fine Chance of seeing how things are don in this heathenish Cuntry. How long it will last I know not but the sooner it is ended the Better for me. Keep up your Curadge, I am right and the Old Flag still Waves and the Clouds of war will Blow over and Leave this Cuntry still entier and our Southeron Brother will be Taught a Lesson that he will not soon forget. Tell the Chirldren thay must try and do all thay can to help thair mother. This month will Put me in mind of home, not that thair is any grass hear, but I shall be Put in mind of what you are doing and this Sun that we have whouled make hay has fast has it couled be cut. Tell Lewis to Learn all that he can if he Learns a little every day he will be astonished how much he can Learn in a year. Give my Love to Fany and Angline and tell them to see how much thay can do in the house to help thair Mother and Grandmother. Kiss them all for me.

Your Affectnat Husband and Son,
CW Sherman

Samul Wicks is well.

Camp Parephet, New Orleans, July 7, 1862

Dear Wife and Chirldren,

It is with pleasuer that I write these few Lines to you hoping thay may find you in health has thay Leaves me at Present.

---

[63] "Franking" meant that the soldiers could send letters home without paying postage, but the recipient would be charged the postage. Many of the envelopes that we have show a postmark as well as a stamp "Due 3" or just "3." A few have stamps. The return address would start with "Soldier's Letter." Janet Klug, "The advent of postage stamps did not end stampless covers," Linns Stamp News, accessed April 20, 2012, http://www.linns.com/howto/refresher/20110530/refreshercourse.aspx.

[64] "As far as"; "has" and "as" are often used for "as" and "has."

We was all in Bed when Leauteant Roch[e] came along and told us that he had some Letters for us. You can guess that I did not get my Candle Stick ready. That is my Baoyenet. It makes a good Candle Stick by driving one in the Ground. One of the men Jumps up in his undress Uniform, that means his shirt, and soon Brought those letters and the way we all went to tearing Envelops open was a Caution to those that take the Truble of Puting Letters into them. I read Part of mine when a Poor Fellow Came over to me and wanted me to Read his for him. That his a service I have to do fore 4 in our Tent and I have to Answer them for them. Thay think thair is no one in this Part of the Worled Equeal with your humble Servant in Writing a Letter or holding forth to the Tent in Tall Talk. I used to have some 8 or 9 against me but the fact of it is has the Orderley tells them thay might has well Dry up has I have Talked them out of Sight, so thay take me for Law and Gospel now but it whouled make you Laugh to hear our Discusions and I have to give any quanity of Advice. We get Along first rate.

I get the Corprals Berth every Time it comes my Turn to Stand Gard. That gives me a Squad of 12 men and saves me Standing Gard. All I have to do his to releve them and Put some more men in thair Places. I have not got my Warent [warrant] yet. It will give me a Chance of Sargent's Bearth when thair is a Chance and our Corprals and Sargents are Played out in our Compney. Some will be Coming home soon or we shall have to give them a Soldier's Grave. It is quite Plesent now. We have been having Some Showers and the Fourth of July was one of the most miserable days that I ever Sufferd in. It Raind nearley all day and when I was goin round with my relefe it Comencd to rain so that I was soaked before I Put the Last man on and had to stay in my wet Clothes till the next morning. The Sun came out and Dryed the Ground and the Rest of us. Thay was goin to have a Time in New Orleans but the Rain damped thair Patrotism. It Deluted mine some.

I was Down to New Orleans the day before the Fourth. I hapen to be one of the few that has. Lord Gough Said of Hav[e]locks men allways redy and never Drunk. I am Praising my self but I feell Preaty well and you must not read my letter to the Publick. My Oficers Let me go Down to New Orleans Last week, gave me a pass to my self, a favor that Every one do not get, and a great maney whouled Like. I did not Enjoy my self very well. I was all alone and the City Looked so Dull. All though we have been in Posi[t]ion nearley 3 Months the People are Suffering from the want of Food. Buttler has don all that he Couled to help the Poor of the City. 18 Hundred Famleys are Fed Dayle from the Free Market and he has 2000 men imployed in Censing [censuring] the streets and he Payes them one Doller Per Day and those that have Famleys he Alowes them a Soldiers Rations Per day to take home to thair Famleys. Flour was 40 Dollers Per Barrle the Day I was thair and Couled not be Bought for that. The people say that it is our Fault that we will not let things Com into the City, that Buttler keeps the Flour out and makes them feell the Hand that keeps them in Check.

I vewed my Old quarters in Laffeyeat Squear and was thankfull that I was not thair now. The 14th Main[e] was thair and thay have Sufferd much from Desentery. Thay have recruted Largely from the City to keep thair ranks full. 200 of them have been Discharged and are waiting for Transportation home. I whouled rather Stay a Little Longer and Com home well then be Discharged on account of Sickness. Thay look forlorn and has though thay had not a frend in the World. New Orleans dose not strike me as Looking like what thay Call her the Quean City of the South. Her glory has departed to my Vew of her. The City is Built on Both Sides of the River and must be one of theas days when Yenkee Energy and Captal get to Work on her, a Second New York. It is the onley outlet fore the Bordar States and the Produce of the great West can all ways find an outlet when the Northern Lakes are Closed up in Winter.

The People have the same kind feelings in regard to us has thay had when we first Enterd the City.[65] One of the men asked me if we did not feell afraid that first night we Enterd the City. I told him New England Troops did [not] know what fear was and we did not Leave our New England Homes to be Frightend from anything that thay Couled get togather to stop our Landing. It was a Bold thing in Buttler in Landing with such a small Forc[e] and Entering a Large City with onley two Redgiments, but to speak the truth for one, I felt Just has safe has though we was goin into Hartford. I did keep one Eye peeled for a shot from some of the Windows. Thay have not got over that night yeat by thair asking me two months afterward if we did not feell afraid. Thay will get a Better Answer then I can give them if thay will give us a Chance.

We have any quanity of rumors. We find that thay can Tell Just has good a Lie hear has any that can be got up North. In fact thay can tell a Biger lie then can be told North. We are under Marching Orders and our Cooks have Orders to keep two Days Cooked Rations fore us and that means that we are on Ship

---

[65] Tongue-in-cheek

Board. If it is up the River it will Suite me, if Down it wont. The Steamer Fulton is downd to the City and she may Carry some of us the way she Brought us. If thay whouled not Cram us so Close togather has thay did Bringing us, I whouled not mind. Uncl Abrahams Paying my fare Back.

In goin down to the City we Passed the English Man of War Rinldo,[66] that took Mason and Slidal[67] from Boston. She was Anchord Just above a French Brig of War, a nother English Brig of War of 12 Guns came up that Morning and Anchord in the stream. Thair was a row of Uncl Abrahams Gun Boats Down below them. One, the Pensacola, was having some of her Wounds Dressed that she got at Fort Jackson.

Dear Wife Pleas do not Fret about me but think that I am Just gon out to what thay might Call a Big row and has I like Fair Play I am mearley Looking on to see that Boath Sides gets it. Rember me to all Enquiring frends and may hevens Choices & Blessings rest on you and the Chirldren. Tell them I do not know when I shall be to hom. Kiss them fore me. You will be through your haying before this reaches you. Give my love to Mother and Father. Keep up your Sp[i]rits, all will End for the Best. Trust in Providance, he doeth all things well.

Your Affectnate Husband,
CW Sherman

Camp Parepet, New Orleans, July 16, 1862

Dear Wife,

I take great pleasuer in writing theas few Lines to you hoping thay may find you and the Chirldren in health has theas Leaves me at Present.

---

[66] *Rinaldo*

[67] Senator James Murray Mason and John Slidell, CSA Commissioner to France, were Confederate diplomats that tried to convince Great Britain and France to support the Confederacy's case. The incident was also known as the Trent Affair (Nov. 1861–Jan. 1862) because they were removed, along with their secretaries, by force from the British mail steamer, *Trent*, and were taken to a Boston officers' prison at Fort Warren. This incident brought great stress to the US and Great Britain relations. The British demanded Mason and Slidell's release, with their secretaries, and the four were released and boarded the British ship *Rinaldo* bound for Southampton. Catton, *The Civil War*, 103–5.

The wether is very Lowery and we are having a Mudy time of it. I recved that Last Letter that Father wrote of the 19th of June and was glad to hear from you. I often think how you will get your Hay Crop. I hope it will turn out Better then you Expect. The Riye, I have been afraid, whouled be Light but we must hope fore the best. It may Turn out Better then it Promises. I though[t] it was Put in in good Seson and recond that it whouled take good root that fall and Winter. Your Corn and Potatoes I shouled think will do well by all the accounts that I have seeing.

We have had 3 Mailes this week and I have recved but one Letter. I expect one or more every Mail. I have waited for one from Uncl Derick and do not Consider his excuse good for not writing to me has thair is 3 men in my Tent that Live at the Point and he couled easley have got all the Directions that was needed. I have wrote Letters for some of those same men and have written 3 Letters to him and if he dose not Consider me worth writing to, well and good. I am good for myself and shall try to Prove good fore one or more Rebles.

I feell Just has Independant out hear has to home and shall keep a Preaty Stif uper Lip for all Triles that I may be Called on to go through. I intend to Show theas Southron People that a Northen man his has good [68] if not better than anything thay can raise South of Masons & Dixions Line. I think Old Connecticut will Prove to theas sesahs that She is not to be Sneezed Down and when she goes down thair will be a big Pile go down with her.

The River is open all the way now. Vicksburge his Preaty well Batterd thay say and Porters Fleet has been Droping Now by our Camp to Pay thair respects to Mobile and we hear that the Stars & Strips ar flo[a]ting thair. The river has fallen some 7 feet and the Banks do not improve. Leaves them very mudy and the water gets wors; more mud in it now then when we first Came and it dose not improve our Coffee. If thay whouled use Coffee it whouled be all the Better. The compound that is served out to us is made of more things than one.

You can tell the Chirldren that I often think of them and hope I may see them soon. Thay must be good Chirldren and not Put thair Mother to no more truble then thay can help. I hope thay will go to Sunday School and Learn all thay can. I have sent them a Pictuer, a Pice of the City of New Orleans or Differant vewes of the City. You may not think much of them but you must save them and I may send you some thing more valuable. I shall send a Letter every

---

[68] Keep in mind his English roots; with these extra "h's," this would be "is as good."

56

week as long has I stay hear and all Letters sent to me if Directed has I have Directed will find me if Living.

Pleas Virtue, do not take any Truble on my account, has the same Father that waches over and as Protected me so fare will, in his own good time, return me safe, and if he shouled, in His good Providanc take me, I hope to Meet you in a Better Worled. I am no Better then others that have given up thair Lives in this war. It is not what we can see of this war at this time, it is the afect that it is goin to have on Generations still unborn. The Father of us all works his own good Pleasuer in his own way and Time, and Punishes the Nations fore thair Sins as a Nation. This Nation has sin[n]ed and gon astray from the Primitive Faith of the Fathers of this Republic. I hope that he will not Punish has we Deserve and that he will Bring this Wasting Civle war to a Close and open the Eyes of the blind that thay may see the Rock on wich thay have Split the Worled never Looked on such a Strife and Carred on on such a Mighty Scale.

It is one thing in our favor to have Frinke out of the way. He has Lived a usless Life, no good to him self and onley a Curse to the Comunity in wiched he has Lived. I hope those that will Carrey on the Place will do what is right with you. If you have to Come in Contact with them taxes will be high for some years to Come and we must have more Incom Coming in to meet them.

I want to Come home Safe and hope I shall, but I have to see 2 and 3 Firing Partyes go by every day to Carry some Poor Soldier to his Last resting Place. The Main[e] Redgiment has Sufferd most. We have Lost 16 men Since we have Left home. A great maney have and will get thair discharges and go hom. I shall have to stay unless Sickness shouled bring me down or some Accident. The Horspital araingments are very Poor, nothing to give men but quinine, Murcury and Blue Pill.[69] When the men have Lived through thair Doctrin of him and he want a little of something to Strenghen him he can not get any thing but a Little Mudy Mississpip Water and some Saw Dust Sprinkled in it yelped Grule. Coffee his made of Tan Bark. Thay get a Compound of what thay Call Tea by

---

[69] Blue pill, or "blue mass," was a medication for a variety of ailments which was made by grinding mercury with other ingredients, such as licorice root and rose water, into pills. Later researchers found, when recreating the formula, that the pills exceeded daily doses of modern safety standards for mercury by 120 times. Lincoln took the pill for a time, but noticed in 1861 that it made him "cross" and he discontinued its use. Various sources; Hillary Mayell, "Did Mercury in 'Little Blue Pills' Make Abraham Lincoln Erratic?" *National Geographic News*, July 17, 2001, http://news.nationalgeographic .com/news/2001/07/0717_lincoln.html.

Boiling down Dryed Skunk Cabbaege and Sole Lether. We have not been over fed. Hard Bread the men can put up with when thay know it can not be helped but we are Living near a Large City and Boats runing every morning and night and it whouled be Cheaper for the Goverment. A Lofe of Soft Bread and nothing but Water I can make a hearty Meal and whouled ask for nothing more. Thay might have thair Salt Mule meat. It is not me. [I] whouled Weep for the Flesh Pots of Egipt if thair was nothing Else in them.[70] Potatoes his out of the question. Thay ask and are selling them for only six Dollers per Bushl. We want some Vegeatables and must have them or the men will have the Scurvy, but Little thay Care for us. We have had potatoes sent to us and thay have kept them so Long that thay have rotted and we have had to stand Gard over them when the Smell was a nuff to knock us Down. After keeping them Long a nuff to Scent the Camp thay have Carted them off. The men whouled Look on those Potatoes and the Tears whouled Come in thair eyes when thay thought what a waste of the very thing thay wanted.

I fill up my Letter and do not Put in half what I want. Virtue you must keep up your curadge. Do not be afraid of any thing in this Little Worled. I can not come home as yeat. You must rember that Non Comisioned Oficers must be up and Dresed. I have all that I can do. I have to atend Oficers Drill 2 hours every Day besides our reguler Battalion and Brigade Drill. It keeps me Preaty Busy. You must kiss Mother and the Chirldren for me. Bless you all

From your Affectnate Husband,
CW Sherman

Camp Parepet, New Orleans, July 23, 1862
Dear Wife and Chirldren,
I take this opertunity of writing theas few Lines to you hoping thay may find you all in Good health has I am at Present.

---

[70] "Hard bread" was also known as "hardtack." "Flesh Pots of Egypt" is an expression that means an abundance of appetizing food. It is also used to mean a "hankering for good things no longer at your command." E. Cobham Brewer, *Dictionary of Phrase and Fable 1898* (Philadelphia, PA: J. B. Lippincott Company, 1905), 470, PDF e-book.

The Wether is very Warm and I often wish I couled Just Lay my self out under one of those Mapple Trees up in the Pastuer and take a good Sleep. I think I shall be good fore nothing when I do get home. I shall want some Lazey Job whare I shall not have to Work much. This Climat is to[o] much of a good thing and thair is no Soci[e]ty hear, only the Poor Class of Whites. The Planters Owne all the Land and thay form a Distinct Class of themselves and Look down on everything Els[e] that is not of thair Set. Thay take the upermost Seats in the Snegouges [synagogues].

It is all Slaves hear. You find all the Slaves have been Raised in the Carolinas and Virgina and Maryland and Sold down hear. Thay are geting quite Num[er]ous. Thay took off a Boat Lo[a]d Down to Fort Jackson to work. The Goverment are a Isuing rations to them. We had 13 Hundred in Camp one Spell and the men Complain that thay ought to be set to work so has to save them. I think thay ought to be made to save the soldiers and do what thay can.

We had quite a exciting time the other night. News came down the River that the Rebles had another Ram that had sunk a number of our Vessels and Gun Boates and was Coming down and Shell us out of our Camp. Thay turned us out about midnight on a false alarme. We have nothing to fear from it now as Faregut[71] has knocked it into the middle of next week but it did us a Lot of Damaege and Cost us many Lives but Vicksburge will fall all the Sooner has it has Waked up the Fleet.

I shall send you my third Payment of State Bounty. I have made it Payable to Father has that will save him and you Truble if he can get it Cashed in Rockvill. I want to hear if you have recved that 27 Dollers I sent you. I hope I shall hear from it the next Mail. 10 Dollers will help some. You shall have some more as soon has I can get it.

Keep up your Curadge Virtue. Do not be afraid. My Father in Heven Cares for me. He will Provide for you if He shouled see fit to take me. I shouled Like the Minetuers[72] of the Chirldren and you. Thay take them on Cards. See if you can get them taken and send them to me if you think Proper. I do not know what you can get it don for. Mother, I shouled Like to see you. Do not work so much has you have. Take it Easey. I shall be to home again soon and forget all my

---

[71] Rear Adm. David G. Farragut
[72] Miniatures—a popular photographic format at that time

Trubles, but I am hear and you whouled have me do my Duty and I shall never fear. If I am not on hand when wanted no one will be . . .[73]

July 26

We had a Reagular Tropicle thunder and Lighting Storm Last night. It put me in mind that storm we had in Ship Iland. It was so hot that the men Sweat like Rain. It came on about midnight. You have Storms to home at this Time, but those are mearly sun Showers to what we get hear.

You will have got Preaty much through your Haying be fore this gets to you. Let me know all the News and write oftener. I wrote the Chirldren 2 Letters and never heard from them. I think you do not get all of them. Virtue you must Put them up to write oftener. Give my Respect [to] Harreat.[74] She must write to me. Give my Love to all the Folks to home. I send you my Love. Kiss the Chirldren. Tell the Chirldren to write to me. If the Gulf of Mexico was not so deep I whouled try to Wade home and see you all but must Put it off for this.

From your Affectnate Husband and Son,

CW Sherman

---

[73] He must have gotten interrupted here as this sentence is incomplete, then he starts with three days later.

[74] Harriet is his cousin Edwin's wife. Edwin's father is John, Charles's uncle and brother to his father, Thomas.

Chapter Four

Expedition on
the *Grey Cloud*

Lake Ponchatrain, July 28, 1862

Dear Wife, Chirldren, Father and Mother,

I take this opertunity of Writing theas few Lines to you hoping thay may find you all in good health has theas Leaves me at Present.

4 Compnyes of our Redgiment are Scouting round Looking up Bush Wackers.[75] Compny K is on hand has thay allwayes intend to be. We have been Waiting to move some time. As you couled see by my Letters we Left Camp Parepet July 25th. Friday the 25th Marched to Carrolton.[76] Took the Cars thair fore Lake Pontchtrain, got thair at night. One Section of the Second Vermont Battery, one Sa[w]yer 6 Pound Gun, one 20 Pound Parrot Gun got on Bord the Steamer *Grey Cloud* Comaned By 1st Leautenant Buchanan of the New London. I have told you the doings of the gunboat New London round Ship Iland and theas Watters. She has been a thorn in the Side of all Evil doers. Her Captain has made his Pile in Prize Money. She is our Escort. We have 2, 62 Pounders on this Boat.

---

[75] Bushwhacking as a form of guerilla warfare was prevalent in rural areas during the Civil War.

[76] Carrollton, Louisiana

Our orders were to Burn 2 Bridges on the Line of the New Orleans and Jackson Rail Road. Drive out all Bush Wackers, and Visit our Southron Co[u]sins in a Frendley way. Sadurday Morning we Started up the South Pass of Manchac and a Secret Place it was.[77] It is about has Wide has the Quinebauge at Southbridge.[78] Our Boat took up Both Sides of the River. The Aligators thought thay was taken the way the Boat Brushed them Ashore. Any quanity of those Varmints were in the Pass. Some Large ones. The Oficers ki[l]led quite a number of the Ugley Looking Criters.

The Sides of the Stream was Lined with very hevey Live Oak and was Just the Place to have a Masked Battery open on us but we got through to the Bridge all right. Just has we got thair a Reble Put to Shore and made Tall time Down the Rail Road. Our first Leautenant Called for Six men to go ashore with him but was too Late. The Fellow had too much the Start of him. After Chasing him 4 mile or more he took to a Small Creek and got away and our men Came Back Some what Jaded out. Thay over hauled 2 Old Shantyes and got a Larg Carpet Bag filled with Powder and Bulets, found a Dubled Barled Gun, a Single Barled gun, Pistols and Brought them Abord and Fierd the Bridge in some 20 Places. Made Shure work of that and Burnt the Buildings and went Down the Stream Rejoycing and up a nother Pass to the other Bridge. Burnt that without any Acident. The New London Couled not go with us, She Drawing too much Watter. We found her Waiting for us and we Started for Masonvill,[79] got thair about Dark, Anchored off that Place till Morning and Started for Madison. It was a Beautifull Morning. We soon got to Whare the Cuntry Put us in Mind of Old Connetucut. In Pasing Madison a Shot was fired at the Boat, Pasing over the Heads of Some of our Oficers on the uper Deck. The Boat returned it with a Shell and Pased on. Our Destination was a Town Called Coventry[80] whare we had heard was a Body of Rebles, or Bush Wackers but we was Brought to a Suden halt. The Rebles had Sunk 2 Gun Boats right across the Channel. That Put an End to our further Progress by Watter. Our Major soon had us all Ashore.

---

[77] A pass to Lake Pontchartrain from Lake Maurepas
[78] Quinebaug Valley in Southbridge, Connecticut
[79] Madisonville is on the Tchefuncte River leading to Lake Pontchartrain. It's likely that "Madison" should be Madisonville as well as there is not a Madison close to there. De Forest, *A Volunteer's Adventures,* 32–35.
[80] In his letters, Charles spells the town as "Coventry," however records show they went to Covington, and he mentions it correctly a few sentences later.

Landed our Battery and Manned the Drag Ropes and was Soon on our way to Covington. I felt first rate. The Cuntry Suitead me to a Charm and by a Little Streatch of the imadgination I couled Fancy my Self to home. We was then in the State of Mississppi. The Day was very warm and Some of the men Sufferd from the heat. It Cost the Lives of two Corproals, Partley by thair Drinking too much Watter.

We reached the Town a little before noon and Drew up in the Main Street. Thair was not more than a Dozen men round but any quanity of Wemon and Chirldren. When we Stoped and faced the Buildings the Wemon Set up Such a Screame that and took on so that I had to Sing out to them that thay was Perfectley safe that no one whouled Injur them. Thay Said that thay was unprotected. We Enquird for the men. Thay Answerd that thay had all Left.

After Satisfieing our selves that thair was no Soldirs in the Woods round by Sending out Scouts, we Faced about and took up our line of March Back. Just as we got ready to Start the Captain of the Boat Sent us two men that had Come Post from Madison with the News that thair was two thousand Rebles with a Battery of nine Canon [that] had Come in to Dispute our Return Back. That was [not] what I considered Plesant News under the Circumstances. Hear we was with a Comon River Steamer with Some 300 men and four Peices of Canon in a narow River whare thay Couled make every Shot tell on our Small Band, but we soon made up our minds to Fight our way through, Sink or Swim. Our Compny had, or has, the Luck to have a Fighting Leutenant. He is our Acting Captain and will soon be full Captain has Captain Abbott[81] has resigned. Our Second Leutenant is a nice Fellow with not quite so much of the Military in him has our first Leutenant but with Pluck anuff in him. We got Back to the Boat after a time. Quite a number of the men was about used up, two have Died from the Afects of the heat.

We were soon Abord and the Boat Headed Down Stream. I Put up my Equipments and Walked forward to whare our 32 pounder was. We had two of them. Thay are manned frome the New London. The Captain sung out to the Crew to know how thay was loded. The Captain of the Gun told him that it was with Solid Shot. He told them to Put in a Case of Canister. The men did has thay was told and I was talking and Laughing with one of them how that Charg

---

[81] Infantry Company K, Capt. Edward K. Abbot[t] from Norwich, Connecticut. *Record of Service of Connecticut Men*, 495.

whouled astonish them Down to Madison when Crack Crack went some fort Rifles from the Bushes. The Bulets Came Preaty near us. Thay was Intended fore the Crew of that Gun and me. We all Droped and I made Tall time for my Rifle that was at the other End of the Boat, but had to Dodge behind the Boiler. I recon thair was quite a number of the men kiled the way thay Droped Down but has Luck whouled have it we all got off without a Scratch. One of the Sailors had 2 or 3 Buck Shot through the Flesh Part of [h]is Arm. We were soon to Work and the way Shell and Grape were Picked into those Woods whouled have done you good. We soon Put an End to Such Murdering Firing as that was.

We Lost not a Singl man and Put our way down Stream, Stoped at a Small Place, Landed a Compney, threw them into the Woods, and Overhauled a Cane Factory. Found nothing but a small Canon. Brought that Abord and started for Madison Shelling the Woods as we went. Just has we got in Sight of Madison we Came upon a Beautifull English Flag held by a Little Boy. His Parents stood around him. Two Ladyes Dressed very nice and the Whole Party Looking Better than anything in the Shape of men or Wemon that I have seeing since Leaving home. The Ladyes waved thair Cambric and your humbl Servant took off his hat for one. Thay made quite [a] Pictuer has thay Stood on the Rivers bank all Woods around them no house in Sight.

The Afternoon had Cloueded up and it had begun to Rain. We Continued down the Stream, Stoped a few Mineutes, threw Some Shell into Madison by the way of Feelers but got no response but kept our Eyes Peeled fore the Bushes. When we reached Madison thair was some runing About some. A Large Boat was filled with Wemon and Chirldren with what Bed Clothes thay Couled Carrey. We give them a Taste of our Feelings by Shelling Differnt Parts of the Town and one house in Partictular whare the Shot Came from in the morning. The men had hid themselves or gon. We found no Battery and was not Fired on anymore, but we had to stand ready for what might come. The Batterys kept throwing shell, Shelling all Supious [suspicious] Looking Places. We all Breathead Freer when we got into the Lake[82] again and found the New London Waiting for us. Thay had heard the Firing but couled not come to see what was up, onley with Small Boats.

We had a quick run across the Lake to Pontchtrain; Staid thair all the next day. Sent the bodys of the two Corproals to Camp for Beurial and got a nother

---

[82] Lake Pontchartrain

Gun and Put abord and Started for Pearl River. Stoped a few hours at the mouth of a Small Creek to Alow a United States Captain to run up and see his mother that he had not seeing her for 3 years. It was but a Short Stay for those that had been Seprated for so long a time. We stoped whare the Lighthouse had stood but the Bush Wackers had burnt it down and we made Coffee from the Charred Timbers. We cannot have anything Cooked unless we can run on Shore and make a fire. After Supper we Put out into the Lake and Anchord for the night.

The next morning we entered Perle River and went has fare has we couled. The Bush Wackers had Cut the trees on Both Sides of the River in a narrow Part that has soon has we shoueld get through, a few Cuts of the Ax whoueld throw them into the River so that we couled not get Back. We did not give them a Chance to Blockade us in. We Landed and Examind the Cuntry but couled not find no Trace of any Troops. The People Said that thair had been no one thair for Some time, but you must take a Wife's Word for the Whareabouts of her Husband.

We couled find nothing and took our way Back. Cut the Telegraph Poles down and took the Wire up whare it crossed on the Bottom of the River and at night stoped at a small lighthouse that was Deserted and our Cooks went Ashore and made us some more Coffee and the rest, or what wanted, went in for a good Swim. Thair was any quanity of Oysters on the Bottom near Shore. Some got thair haversacks full. We Anchord hear for the night and in the morning Started for Pass Christian Land. All the men and one Six Pound Sawyer Gun took our Coulors and started for Christian through the Woods, most of us without Eating anything. We found nothing hear, no men. All the men have been Forced into the Army. Thair had been a Force of 500 Caverley in the town a few days befor but had all Left so we had to leave that Place. The Boat Came round and took us on Board and whare next we are goin I know not.

The Cuntry Apears to be Draind of men. Every thing Looks Dead and dull, nothing doing Except a few Saw Mills. Thair is no life in any of the Towns or Villidges. Every one Apears Sick of the War and the Poor Fellows that has been Forced into the War must be Sick anuff of it.

We have Brought up at Shieldsburogh.[83] Compny K and Compny B went Ashore to Look after two Peices of Canon that was known to be in the town. It apeard to be quite a Preaty Place. The Wemon and Chirldren stood and Looked

---

[83] Shieldsboro Harbor, now known as Bay St. Louis, Mississippi

on a few mineuts and then run away. Our Captain told them thay need not fear, we did not make war on Wemon and Chirldren but thay Put themselves out of the way. We Put most of the Compny out has Pickets and the rest Called on the Principle Houses for information but thay all Claimed thair had been no Canon thair and it began to get Dark. Thay Called in the Picket Gard and went on Board and Steamed away at Missippi City. We called thair but found nothing at this Place.

Some few Weekes before the Gun Boat New London Buried one of its Crew and Called about ten days after to take the Body up and bring it away but when thay came to take up the Body, thay found that someone had been thair and Pulled the Teeth out as Relics. The Captain Landed [h]is crew and went and serche every house and found 2 of the Teeth in a front Window. Thay Assembled the Mayor and the Comon Council and Tryed to find the Frends that had Desacrated the Grave, but couled find nothing to Satisfie them and to Burn the Place whouled have made the Inocent suffer with the Guilty. This is fact.

Buttler has 2 men on Ship Iland for exhiting [exhibiting] the bones of Fedral Soldirs. Since we have been hear thay are not Human Beins, theas Southron men. The Wemon Scowle on us when thay Dare to and thay will have to be Converted by beaing made to Pass through the hot Furnace of Affliction.

We steamed all night and About noon the next Day we Called on our Madison Frends again. Thay was taken by Surprise. We was soon Ashore, but Couled find nothing. A great many of the Wemon and Chirldren had gon away. One Poor Womon with one Chiled in her Arms and two hangin on her Clothes Pas[s]ed us. She said that she whould have gon but she Couled not has she had too many Chirldren. One of the Little ones asked her to go home but she said that she had no home now to go to now. A nother Womon with a Baby in her Arms that we Called on said that she was Glad we had Come and hoped we whouled stay. She said that thay had nothing to Eat but Corn Bread.

We got into the Post Ofice by Braking open the Door but found nothing Except an Old Flag that was made when thair was but 15 States in the Union that we hung up on a tree in Front of the Post Ofice and gave it 3 Cheers and Left the Place for home or Camp Parepet. Got thair about sundown.

August 3

Was Complemented by the Major for good Conduck and other qualities and were Promised another Cruse soon. It was a very Daingrous Mission we was on but I shouled like a nother has I am Tired of Camp Gard Duteys.

Give my Love to the Chirldren and Mother and Father and Virtue you must keep up your Sprits and Cureadge. I hope to see you all again. This War can not Last for Ever. I expected a Letter from you when I got Back to Camp but the Blackstone that was Bringin the Mail was Detain. You know the Cause better then me. The Creole is expected up every hour and I hope will Bring me some Letters. August has set in Wet but I hope to Live through it. You must all Pray for me. I hope you got that money I sent you all safe and my third State Bounty of ten Dollers. You must have got it all by now. Mother, kiss my Chirldren for me and Wife you must Shake that Arthur and kiss him for me. I am in for this war. I see that it will not end this year but I must Do my Duty and shall, Let it Last 3 years or Six. I send my Love to you all. You can tell my Frends that I still Wave in the Land of the Orange.

Your Affectnate Husband & Son,
CW Sherman

Father, I hope you got through your haying all right. I am bound if I get through this all safe to farm for a living. I feel as though all the rest in the world is taken and enjoyed by the farmer.

Chapter Five

Camp Parapet

Camp Parepet, New Orleans, August 6, 1862

Dear Wife & Father & Mother & Chirldren,

I take great Pleasuer in Writing theas few Lines to you hoping thay may find you all in good health has theas Leaves me at Present.[84] I recved your kind Letter of July the 15th and was glad to hear from you and that you was well and the Chirldren. I hope to see them all again but that is in the Futuer and non of us knows what is in Store for him. I have been Preserved so far for Which I am thankfull to my Father in Heven for his many Mercys to me and mine.

Thair has been a great many Deaths in this Brigade but our Redgiment has been quite healthe Considering the unhealthe Natuer of the Ground and Climate. Our Northen Soldiers have not been taken away by the Yellow Jack as our Southron Brothers have prayed that it might be the Case.[85]

---

[84] As I have typed many of his letters beginning with this sentence, I became curious about it. It apparently was a common way to begin a letter, perhaps from English or Scottish origin. He spells the word "these" as "theas," but it could also mean "this," making the phrase "as this leaves me at present" which is also common. Here it is "as these [lines] leave me at present."

[85] Camp Parapet was "terribly muddy" and typhoid fever raged in late summer. Many lives were lost from the fever and other causes before the regiments faced their first battle. Croffut and Morris, *The Military and Civil History of Connecticut*, 306.

thay have not writen me any Letter to me Latley and I have been expecting one from them. I hope you will get your Hay in good Shape. The Goverment Payes one Hundred Dollers Per Ton for Hay. It is worth something this way. I do not Drink any spirits. You need not take any truble on that Acount. If I had Money I shouled Drink a Littl Beer.

I received a Letter from Henry and 3 Papers and shall write him. I have Sent E[d]win a Letter. De[r]rick has never Sent me no Letter and he need not Truble himself to now.

We are getting along Preaty well. We have Put Floors down in our Tents and that makes it more Comforable for us then it was before.

Tell Virtue to keep up, all will yeat be well. We must Trust in Providance for health and Life and all Blessings that we recve. I try to Trust in my Father in Heven for is blessing to rest on me and my Wife and Chirldren and my Father & Mother and that he will Permit me to See you all again. Give my Love to Virtue and kiss my Chirldren. Tell Mother that I often think of the Truble I used to make her. Give my respects to all enquiring Frends. Tell them that I am trying to do my Duty.

Yours Affectnately,
CW Sherman

Camp Parepet, New Orleans, August 10, 1862
Dear Mother and Wife, Chirldren,

I am well at this time and hope this will find you all in good health. Thair is Some Poor Soldier Carried to is Last resting Place every Day from one Redgiment or the other. We have three Redgiments at this Camp Parepet and two full batterys. Thair was a Leautenant of one of the Batterys Drowned Wensday of this Week. His Body was not found till toDay, Sadurday. He got into one of the Eadeys[89] or Worlpools that the Mississppi is toubled with. Thair is no hope of anyone if thay Fall into the Curent or is Sucked down in the Pooll formed by the Curent meeting one another on the Sides of the Stream. The Watter runs up and then Down.

---

[89] Eddies

Thair is quite a number of Bodys Floting in the River at this time has one of our Gun Boats run into a Steamer that had over a Hundred of our Wounded on Board that was Wounded in the Late Battle up to Baton Rouge. The Reble Genral Van Dorn under took to Drive a Part of this Division out of that Place. Genral Williams who Comanded thair led the 21st Ind[i]ana in a Charge on four Redgiments of the Rebles and Drove them, but Lost is own Life. [H]is body was on Board of this Steamer that was run into and was found the next morning Floting in the Stream. The Pilot and Captain was Brought in Irons to New Orleans and the Furnal[90] of Genral Williams took Place in New Orleans yesterday.

Our Forces Drove Van Dorn 10 Mile and took 3 Canon from him. [H]is force was three to one of ours. That dose not Look like Wiping 5 to one has thay have allways Claimed thay couled. We are Redye for Van Dorn. He has Sworn to Drive us out of New Orleans and Every other Place Whare we be but thay had Better Let that Job out. We Came near Falling into his hands when we was out Scouting a Short time since. He was Notified of our Trip and as we Pased Masonville[91] he Came in Sight with 2000 men and 21 Peices of Canon. Some of the Canon he had we was Looking for and had Landed in Differant towns to find. You need not be Alarmed about me has I am in the hands of one Mighty to Save and Who will Protect me.

The Slave Population is Coming into Camp and we have a nuff now to make one full Redgiment and Genral Phelps Gets Cursin a nuff from Some of the men about [h]is nigers as thay Call them. He has Formed a Camp which thay Call Camp Greeley and he is Drilling Some of them in thair Facings. Thay have no arms has yeat. He is waiting I think for the Goverment to give the Word when you will see Black Redgiments Sping up anuff to give the Finishing Blow to the Reblion.[92] The Goverment have Co[a]xed and Flatterd the Slave Holders and it has threatend and thay have Paid no Atention to what was to thair Interst but have Fought us Like Feinds and thair Brutal Acts to our Dead and Wounded Soldiers will Stamp them with Eternal Infamey.

The Boys in my Tent call me a Black Abolintionst [abolitionist]. We have Considerabl Talk about this state of things and I try to make my Side of the

---

[90] Funeral
[91] Madisonville
[92] Rebellion, spelled "Reblion" throughout the letters

Argument Good. I give some of them fits and the Truth of what I tell them Crawls through thair hair and thay are glad to Let me be.

Phelps says that he can make Just has good Redgiments out of theas Blacks has any on the Ground and if theas Slaves can not help Fight for thair Freedom what is the use of our Wasting our selves in fighting a usless War. Slavery is the beginin and End of our Present Trubles. We have fought so far at Disadvantadge. The Reble Leaders have used the Slave to Dig in the Trenches and Perform other Camp Dut[i]es and Saved thair men to Fight us. At the Same time we have used our Soldiers to Dig in the Trenches under a Broiling Sun and in a Climat that thay was not used to and Do a large Share of Camp Work and an Auffull Lot of Gard Duty with insuficant [insufficient] food and rest and it is this thing that Reduces our Armey Down, so I say use the Slave to do our Camp Work and save us. I speak from Experance for I have gon through the Mill has the saying is but thair is any quanity of Crackers to home and in the Army that Cry out "you must not use them nigers. Thay are a nother mans Property and you must not Meddle with that instution that is Sacred. We are Fighting fore the Constitution and the Laws. We did not Come hear to Free nigers or Slaves." But such talk is about Played out.

We have protected Reble Property about Long a nuff and it is time that Rebles were made to feel the Waight of this war Coming onto thair own Shoulders. The way we have been Careing on this War so far will use up the Resorces of the North and Leave us whare we began.

For some time after we reached this Place the Chaplain held Meetings every Sunday after noon and after a Spell the Chaplain Tent was Put up but we have never used it. The Atendance began to Drop off and the Tent has been used for a Gard tent. The Slaves hold Meetings on our Ground and thay Enjoy them Selves Preaty well. It Looks kind a funey to see how thay will Dress. If thay can thay Come with the Cast off Finery of thair Mistresses and Masters. That is some few of them. The Wemon whare gay Coulord Hanchfers [handkerchiefs] tied round thair Heads. Thay go in for Bright Coulers. Some apear to Enjoy Relegion and Pray well. Thair singin is kind of Old Fashiond, the Leader giving out two lines at a time. Thay think that we have Come to Liberate them and thay have Flocked into us in such Numbers that it gives the Lie to all that say that thay are satisfied with thair Condition.

I hope you will have good Luck with your Crops. It does not Look as if we Shouled get home soon but we know not what may Turn up to favor us. I shouled like to get the Minetuers of all the Chirldren. The men recve some most every Mail. When we are Paid off again I think of having mine taken if alive and well.

Tell Father that he need not be Scart about the Number of Letters that I write. He says that I write to many and I write a great many for other Poor Fellows and it is all the amusement I have is writing to you all. My wife and Chirldren want to know how I am geting on. Tell Virtue that she must still keep up her Curage, set her Face as flint against all Desponding Feelings. It will be all right soon. Our Trubles will soon be over and the Old Flag will come out all right. Kiss those Chirldren for me and Cheer up.

Your Affectnate Husband and Son,
CW Sherman

Camp Parepet, New Orleans, LA, August 19, 1862

Dear Wife and Chirldren,

I recved your Favors of July 24th and August 3rd and was glad to hear from you and that you was all well. I have good health all the time and have had. The Wether is a very Little Warm in this quarter. I make it go. The Meat has Left me or what Littl I had. Hard Bread and Salt Horse is not Just the Feed to Put men in Working order but fits men for Runing. That is if the Bones are Tied togather.

We are Waiting hear in Camp Parepet for What ever may Turn up. The Talk now is that we shall be kept near togather. We have been Strung some 300 mile up the Coast, had to Hold a great many Points to Prevent the Rebles geting Aid Comfort from thair Frends in the City and with all the Wachfullness of Buttler thay have manedged to Suply the Conffedrate Cause with many things and that Dash of Genrals Van Dorn and Brckenridge on Baton Rouge whare Genral Williams was Stationd has opend the Eyes of our Leaders that thay are not Subdued in that Battle. Our men in Buring the Dead and Picking up the Wounded found a great many of the Citizens of Baton Rouge on the Feild and in the Ranks of the Rebles. We had been Protecting thair Property and the first opertunity thay had Joind the Rebles and help the Confederat Cause. It will be some time before thay will have Such another opertunity of Playing that Dodge on us.

Buttler has orderd all Arms to be Brought to him in the Custom House New Orleans and given up under heavey Penlitys if any one Dare to keep Back thair Privat Arms of What ever Discription. Any one wishing to Send thair Arms North Can have that Privleadge. Thay must Bring them themselves and see them Sealed up and Deliverd up to the Provost Marshal of New Orleans and the way Arms are Pouring into the City is a Caution. Thay Dare not Trifle with Genral Buttler. Thay know to a certainty that what he tells them will rigedley be Performed.

Thay are waiting fore a favorable opertunity to Fall on us and if thay do not get the Concert taken out of them it will [be] because we are not Abl to do it which you know we can do it to Perfection. It will be sooner or Later thay can take thair own time and thair own way. It makes no differance with us. All that we have got to say is to come on MacDuff.[93]

We are Pleased to hear that the North has got Waked up. It is most time. Eather get a Sound Licking or give one that will not soon beforgot. We have men anuff if thay will turn out to Bring this War to a Close and I think thay are offering good Bounty if that is what thay are after and thay are no Better men than those that is all ready hear. Thay need not Flatter themselves that thay are the Cream of the Nation. That is not the Case as any good Farmers Wife can tell them that the Cream rises to the Surfice first and is taken off first but if thay will onley Bring Willin Hearts and Hands with them we will Condecend to Admit them into full Membership. Thay will have no Easy time of it. It will be expected that thay Work hear if thay never did fore. I for one say Com on.

I hop you do not Fret yourselves About me.[94] I shall take all needfull Care of myself that can be taken with out Shirking my Dutys that you may beleve. I shall Alow no man to do my Duty if Able to do them my self. Thair is a great Deal of that don hear as well as Elsware. That is not my Style and so far I have been favord with good health and when wanted thay have allways found me in my Place. How men can Shirk and have any quanity of Ailins when thay go to

---

[93] An expression having roots in Shakespeare: "Before my body I throw my warlike shield. Lay on, Macduff, And damn'd be him that first cries, 'Hold, enough!'" William Shakespeare, *Macbeth*, Act 5, Scene 8, Shakespeare online, accessed February 17, 2014, http://www.shakespeare-online.com/plays/macbeth_5_8.html.

[94] A second letter with the same date and salutation starts here. The two have been combined since the second seems to be a continuation of the first, in spite of the second salutation, because the date is the same and there is no closing signature at the end of the first.

the Doctors. I for one cannot see. Thay have got to be excused by the Doctor. Thay carred this thing on so when thay Alowed thair Compny Oficers to excuse thair men, that this order was given and some manedge by one way and another to be sick most of the Time, but when the Pay Rolls have to be Inspected it Surprises me whare thay get all the men from, as each man has to Answer to is name if Able to Stand up. I never see them on Drill or Gard Duty but at that Pactuler time thay are round. I sopose it is all right but why not send such men home if thay are not fit for Duty and our Sergons ought to know if a man is sick.

I have not recved any Line from Derrick Since Leaving home and do not expect any or anything from him. I was in hopes that Henry whouled be Able to help you get some of the Hay but if he couled not he has good and Valid Resons why and I hope that he will if Posable fix the House up a little. I shouled like to have been thair when that was don, but if Henry Comes I think that he couled and will do it as Good as your humbl Servant who has good and Sufficant resons why he couled not be thair but Lives in hopes that he may see you all again in that Old House. No other house whouled Suite him. Van Dorn may have a Spare Shanty for him yeat or Louisana may find a home fore him by Mississppi's yellow Watters.

Tell Arthur that he is Perfectley right in sayin that his Father whouled like that if it was of the eadabl kind. Potatoes whouled not go Bad or some Beets and Greens. If ever men wanted anything we Poor Fellows want Potatoes. We are Poisend up by Eating so much Salt and Dry food and if I had any rich Frends I cirtainly shouled Aply to them for some thing to Clense my Blood. Some of the men suffer from the Prickley heat and the Doctors have nothing to give them but quinine without the Wiskey. Some have been Trubled with Ring Worms. Non of your small kind but such that you couled Jump through taking up the whole neck and Body. I have taken no Medcin since Leving home. I recond that some of the men took anuff for me and themselves. It must have Cost the Goverment as much for quinnie and Murcury as for Powder and Lead.

We hope that you to home will turn out the men in such numbers that thair shall be no Chance of a Faileur. We hear are waiting for a Chance and it may Come sooner then expected but we shall try to do our Duty. Let it turn whatever way it will. Give my Love to Father and Mother and Let them Pray for me. I have faith in a Prayin Father and Mother. Keep up your Curedge, Virtue let nothing Daunt you in the Present or Futuer. Kiss them Chirldren for me and may Heven Bless you all and keep you.

From your Affectnate Son and Husband

C W Sherman, La

Camp Parepet, New Orleans, La, August 20, 1862

Dear Wife & Chirldren, Parents,

I am well at Present. The Wether is very Warm and dry. We want some Rain very much. The Corn Crop is Burnt up. The Sumer has been very Dry. Thay Planted more this Seson then usal by Order of the Conffedrate Goverment and Less Sugar Cane, but thair is a very Large Extent of Ground in Sugar Cane Planted more then Suites some that has got up this Worl Wind of Destruction and Suffering. The Oranges are Just begining to Turn a very Little. Thay are not very Temting to Look at on the trees, but some of the men Pick them and Eat them. Some men are Worse than Chirldren in Some things. The Fig Crop is all gon. Thair is some very Large and fine figes raised hear. Thay are very rich Eating. I did not induldge myself with Eating of them. The Planters make Pies with them and I shouled think thay whouled make very nice Pies but that is a Luxery that we Poor Fellowes are expected not to know anything about.

You Speake in the Letter that you have sent me a Small Box with a few things in but I am afraid that you have sent me things that I do not Want. I shouled have Wrote you what to send if I had known that you whouled send me a Box. The Freight Comes about half when Sent to Soldiers. I shouled think you Couled find out at Rockvill or Stafford what the Freight whouled be in all Cases. The Freight Shouled be Paid has thay will not move any thing till it is Paid. The men in my Compney that has had Boxes sent to them have allways recved them allthough sometimes Delayed. I have not recved that Box as yeat. I will Let you know when recved and Can speake more at Length about the Contents when I have Vewed them.

Tobaco, both hard and soft is allways welcom to us Poor Miserabl Sinners. A few Pair of Cheap Suspenders is very handy; I am rather hard up for a Pair. Pipes is Just the thing, a few Needles & thread is not to be overlooked, Writing Paper & Pens and Ink. Be very carefull not to send any Butter unles Put in some thing that whouled hold, has this Climat is very Apt to Put such things in a

Melting Mood. One of the men in my Tent Whose Wife thought a Little Butter whouled be a welcom Present Put some in a Tin Pint Cup and Put it a top of all the Rest and Tied some Paper over it but it got Spread over every thing and all togather it was a Buttered Box.

Some Hanchfers is Just the thing hear, Cheap White ones. I have at Present [one] in the Top of my hat and have Worn it Ever since I have been hear, a Red Concirn that Father give me when I Left him. I never thought a Hanchfers Couled do so much good, but that Red Bandana has Saved my Bacon, I have not the Least Dought, has I do not Consider my self Equiped till I have Been to the Mississppi and Washed it and Stowed it in the Top of my Hat. When that is don I am ready fore the day. It is geting the Worse fore whare at Present and the Tears very nerley Came into my Eyes this morning has I vewed the Rement [remnant] of what was onece a thing of Beautiy but it has a straing way of Floting in Differant Directions when it gets into the Water.

Those Minetuers that you are goin to send might Come by Mail or in that Box that you have sent. I hope thay will Come safe. If you shouled Put a very Little Stimulent[95] it whouled not be very Wrong as men have a Straing way of Expecting such things. I do not induledg in any hear for it wont do, but in certain Cases it is very Proper and right. Just a nuff to go round the tent. I am Chief of 16 men, thats the number in my Shanty, and am responsable for them and some of them have given me a smile when thay had any sent to them. Tell Lewis to Learn all that he can and those young Ladyes that Cut such a Swell do all thay Can to help thair Mother and are respectfull to thair Gran Parent. Plese Let me know if thay Like thair pictuers.

From thair Affectnate Father
CW Sherman

Please Let me know what those Minetuers Cost.

---

[95] Alcohol

Camp Parepet, New Orleans, August 28, 1862

Dear Wife & Chirldren,

I recved that Little Box Last night all right. It was Packed tight. Everything was Just what I wanted. Those hanchfers is the very thing; I had often thought Little what I whould give if I onley had a few White hanchefers. Thay Cost fablous Prices hear. If thair had been one Shilling Pair of Suspenders I shouled have been Set up all my wants Suplied but I must get me a Pair. Thay ask so much for any small thing that you want that it takes a Months wadges to Pay for a few things. Those Pens whare Just the thing. Thay are the Best Pens that I have seeing. That Pen Holder Suited me to a Charme but that Hot Drops[96] was the very thing of all that was sent. You must not forget to send me more of that if Posable. Every thing Showed good Judgment. The Boys Laughed when thay see the Box but when thay come to see what was in it thay owned that it was a Small Box well filled. I couled not find out how much you Paid for fraight.

We have been having quite Lively Times hear. Buttler has taken all the Troops from Baton Rouge; 7 Redgiments with two full Batterys and Brought them Down to our Lines to make a Stand hear. Coll. Cahill who took Charge after Williams fell Put every thing on board about 25 Large Steamers and Droped down to our Camp. When I looked out on the River that morning I couled not make out what had Brock Loose, the river full of Steam Boats and the Boats full of Armed men. The Soldiers Gutted Baton Rouge be fore leaving, undermined the Captal Building and Left it a warning to all futuer Evil Doiers. Thay Brought away some 3000 Contrabands and all the Mulles and Horse thay Couled Lay thair Hands on.

Van Dorn and Brackenridge lay some seven mile out [of] the City. We have 3 Gun Boats to hold the City and thay have Orders to Burn the City if the Rebles undertake to Fortifie it or enter the City. Thay tryed to anoy the Troops when goin on board but the Steam Frigate Mississippi open her allfull hevey Batterys and thay soon Skaddaled [skedaddled]. Her fire is Dreatfull so thay say. It was she that Coverd the Fleet when Pasing Fort Jackson Last April.

We had a Revew yesterday by Buttler and he has Promised us that if thay do not Atack us soon we shall go and Look up our Enmy. He told us that the 12 whould have to stand the Brunt of the fight and Every one of us must Drop in

---

[96] Hot drops were cough suppressants. "Stabler-Leadbeater Apothecary Museum," Confederate Book Review (blog), Saturday, December 3, 2011, http://confederatebook review.blogspot.com/2011/12/stabler-leadbeater-apothecary-museum.html.

our Tracks before we allowed the Rebles to mount the Parapet. We are in the same situation hear in Camp Parepet has the Rebles are in at Richmond. We shall try to keep them out and save the City but if forced to Leave wont thear be a smoke.

Keep up your hearts it can never Come to that. I hope you will get good News before this reaches you and that Destruction has fallen on Richmond. Give my Love to the Chirldren and tell them that I am glad to hear that thay try to do all that thay can and that Lewis Learns fast.

Thay are firing Mineut Guns to Day in honer of Martin Van Buren. Give my Love to Father and Mother and remember that baby for me. Kiss Aruther and tell him that he must not make so much noise.

From your Affectnate Husband & Son
CW Sherman

Camp Parepet, New Orleans, August 30, 1862

Wife & Chirldren,

I take this opertunity of writing a few Lines to you hoping thay may find you in good Heart health & Strengh. I am better then I have been for 2 Weeks. I have had a Smart tuch of the Agu[e] in the Face with a Little Fever. I am all right now. My Gums are Swelled some and I find that my Teeth wont take hold of the Hard Bread as usale.

We was paid two month's pay yesterday. Thay kept two Months Back. I put 25 Dollers into the Chaplains hands to Send by Adams Express to you. I sent it the same has the last to the Rock Mill Rockvill. It Cost me Seventy-five Cents Freight & Insurance. I hope it will go safe. Virtue must be in want of some of Uncl Abraham's Shin Plasters. That Town Money is Due Virtue by this time. Please Let me know if she gets her Pay all right and in a Proper time. This making my Wife waite a Month after her Pay is Due dose not Suit me and thay may hear of a Large Flea in thair Ear yeat. The Whole Town is not worth the Death of one Single Soldier. It has not one Spark of Patrotism or manhood no Generosity no nothing. I do not know how thay used me in many ways do I, O no, I forget.

We are having a Wet time at Present. We got one of our men Shot yesterday.[97] He was in the Gard Tent. He has made a great Deal of Truble ever Since we have been hear. He has Served one Month in the Parish Prison in New Orleans. When I have had Charge of the Gard I have placed men with Loaded Rifles over that Same man with Orders to Shoot any one that shouled undertake to make any Desterbance. I hop it will be a warning to the Rest. I whouled rather the Rebles whouled Shoot our men than Shoot them ourselves.

We were all Turned out Last night. The 12th took to the Parepet but it did not amount to much, a false Alarm. Genral Cahill Comands our Brigade now. Genral Phelps is goin to have Buttler's Bearth. Buttlers goin to Charlston to take Charge of that City. I do not Like to lose Buttler but the Cuntry Needs is Services Elswhare and whare ever he goes he will win.

Thair has been a Sleight Differance of opinon betwen Phelps and Buttler in regard to Drilling & Arming the Contrabands. Thair is a Large Peice of Woods on the right of our Camp that ought to have been Cut down Long before so that the Gun Boats can cover our Camp from Lake Ponchtrain some two Mile Distant. Buttler wanted Genral Phelps to set his Contraband to Choping the Woods down and Phelps Wanted to Arm and Equip them has United States

---

[97] This same incident is portrayed in De Forest's book, *A Volunteer's Adventures*, 41–42:

> One toper has lately got a stinging lesson. Charley Counsel, a huge, rawboned Irishman is one of the regimental nuisances and spends half his time in the guardhouse. He has been in three different companies, captain after captain getting wearied of his rampaging and transferring him to whomsoever will take him. Yesterday morning, being in the guardhouse as usual, he swore he would break out of it, whereupon the officer of the day ordered the sentry to shoot him if he tried it. Counsel rushed at the sentry with a yell and wrested the bayonet off his rifle.
> "Try that again, and I'll drop you," said the man.
> Counsel made another plunge, and fell with a hole through his thigh an inch or so in diameter. Braley, who is Counsel's present captain, came up and gave the sentry five dollars. The lieutenant colonel followed shortly and asked, "Did you shoot that man? All right; I'll make a sergeant of you."
> Counsel was borne off to the hospital, where he got up an outrageous rumpus, throwing a spittoon at his nurse with such force as to smash it against the wall, and yelling loud enough to be heard across the Mississippi.

Soldiers but Buttler whouled not Isue the nessary Arms & Clothing to them till he recved Orders so to do from Washington and in the mean While Let the Nigers do what work thair was to be don.

I want you to home to hury up that recruting and Crowed the men forward to the Front and fill up the Old Redgiments. No time to get up new Redgiments and when got up thay are of no use. Fill up the Old Redgiments I say and then you will do some thing. This fiddlin with the men is about Played out. We are in great Heart at Present and Waiting for Van Dorn and if he dose not Come soon we must go after him.

Give my Love to Edwin & his Wife. I shall never get over Dericks not writing to me. Give the Chirldren that kiss for me. Give my Love to Mother. Tel her that I thought of home when I had that fevor and Agu[e] in my Face. Give my Love to Father and Virtue keep up your Curadge. I am all right and shall Come home all right. Kiss that baby.

CW Sherman

Camp Parepet, New Orleans, La, Sept 5, 1862

Dear Wife and Chirldren,[98]

I take great Pleasuer in Writing theas few Lines to you hoping thay may find you all in good health has theas Leaves me at Present.

I have been some Down in the mouth. I had a Tuch of this Confounded Swamp Feavor. I Doctord my Self. If I couled have my way, I [would] Shoot a few M.D.'s that I know of. I had a Sweet tuch of the Ague in my Face and it whouled not of been healthy for Van Dorn to have troubled our Lines at that time. I felt very much Like goin into Somebody or some thing at that Particuler time. I am all right at Present but want Some thing to do.

We are kept in a Sweat Waiting fore the Rebles to Drive us out and Buttler Promised us the other night that we Shouled go and find the Enmy if thay did not Come Soon. I wish thay whouled End this War if thay are goin to. I want to Come home. Pope is the onley man that wants to Bring this thing to a Close. He is Willing to fight and is bound to make Somebody do something. I do think that the Rebles have had the Better of us. Hurry up them Reinforcements.

---

[98] This letter is transcribed from photocopies.

Genral Phelps has resined and Col Cahill of the Connecticut Ninth is Acting Brigadier Genral of our Brigade. Buttler has taken the Colors of the 7 Vermont from them for Bracking and refusing to Support the 21 Indana at Baton Rouge. It is very Straing that a Vermont Regiment Shouled Disgrace itself in Presence of the Enmy. The Col Lost is Life trying to Bring them up to the help of the Indana Boyes that was covered with Rebles but beat them off. It is unf[or]tunate that it Shouled have hapened but Genral Buttler has Promised them that thay Shall have the first opertunity to Redeem thair manhood and thair Coulers.

We are kept more Stricked then we was. Thay will not Let [us] out [of] Camp now. Thay used to Alow us a Mile outside of the Lines. The Days are a little Cooler and the nights, but it is Warm anuff for Comfort.

Still, we are very Anxious to hear that Richmond is taken but shall have to Waite Sometime before that will be don. We whouled much rather be in front of Richmond then hear Waiting to be Atacked. We are Turnd [out] every other night and that dose not improve Temper of the men.

I recved a Letter from Uncl Derick. It was a very good letter. He told me of Mother's Staying a week with him and how he was going to Rockville to see Father. I shouled like to go myself but shall have to Put of[f] my Visit for a Cuple of years, I expect, the way things are goin on now. By that time the Chirldren will be grown up and thay will have for got all about me, has I expect to come home with a Wooden leg or my Sleeve Emty, and then I may be all right, but those things truble me but very Little.

Let me know how the Folks are at home and how you have made out farming. Henry Wrote me a Letter from Troy, N. Y. and how he got into Work has soon has he got thair, but manedged to Bruise is foot, that was Natural. I hope he will get along well. He tryes to and I think he will Suckceed.

Please kiss that Baby and I want to know how soon I am goin to have all of your Minetuers. I expected to get them in that Box. You will get no more money till I do get them. I want the Whole or none! Virtue, I have sent you 25 Dollers, or the Whole of my two Months Pay, and hope you will get it safe. I shouled like to have sent you more but thay keep two Months Back. Give my Love to Father & Mother and accept a Large Share your self. Shake up that Art[h]ur fore me.

From Your Affactnate Husband,
CW Sherman

Camp Parepet, New Orleans, LA, Sept 8, 1862

Dear Wife and Chirldren,[99]

Last night was a Beusy one in our Camp. The Gurelles have come Down to within 10 Mile of our Camp on the other Side of the River and have fired upon our Small Boats. So Buttler Sent up two Stemers with 4 Companeys of troops Sunday morning, but thay had to Come Back and reported Troops on both Sides of the River and thay had not force anuff to do anything. So Buttler Ordered out the 7 Vermont, 14th Maine, 21 Indana, 9th Connectcut, 21st Masachusetts along with 4 Batterys. The Frigate Missipip went a Head to Cover the Landing of the Troops and Shell the Rebles. She can throw Shell 5 Mile and is the Hevast [heaviest] Armed of anything in the Navey. In getting the Ninth Abord, one of the men got in [a] muss with one of [his] Comrades and Struck him over the Head with the Butt of is Rifle and Knocked is Brains out. So that takes two of that Redgiment before thay Started. Thay got away about Midnight.

We had Just turned in when one of my mess, who has been Sick ever Since he Enlisted, under took to get up to go out and fell over and Died before we couled get a Light. Has I am Cheef of the tent, it fell on me to hunt up the Brigade quarter Master, get a Ambulance, get the Corps[e] to the Hospital, Wake up the Coll to get a Order from him fore a Coffin. Thair is Plenty of Red tape Routine. I had to get a order from the Redgimental Sergon to get the Ambulance. When I got through I felt like Cursing Genrals, Cols, Sergons & Captains and the Service in Particuler that Shouled, or was, tied up with so much Tape. Our Sergons are not fit to atend a Sick Cow. This man, Pratt, I have taken to the Sergon and he Claimed that he was fit for Deuty, only a Slight Cough.

Our Wether is all that Couled be Desired and I feell first tip top. Keep up good Heart to home, Wife Chirlden, Father & Mother. Let me know if you get that Money.

Your Affactnate Husband & Son,

CW Sherman

---

[99] This letter is transcribed from photocopies.

Camp Parepet, New Orleans, LA, Sept 9, 1862

Dear Wife and Chirldren,[100]

It is raining and I set Down to write you a few Lines. The 15th Maine Left us Last night about Midnight for Washington. That Expidition that Left us the other night has got back all right. Thay Captuerd the Whole Party. Thay Proved to be Texans. Thay are all Safe now. One of the Boats went above thair Camp. Thay See the Boats but thought thay was not goin to land. One of the Redgiments went by Land with the first Main[e] Battery. The Texans Drew up in Line and waited fore our men that went by Land thinking thay Couled retreat, if Wi[p]ped, up the River, being Mounted on thair small Mustang Pon[i]es. But the "Mississppi" soon Brock thair Dream. She gave them a Aufful Shelling and when thay retreated thay road into the Ninth. Thay then took to the Swamps, but our Boyes Chased them into the mud and Serounded them so that thay had to Serender. Thay Brought 25 of them into our Gard House and a Dirty Looking Set of men Thay whare, regular Bush Wackers. The Boats Came in about noon with some 400 of them with thair Horses. The Wounded Gurrelles whare Laying on the up[p]er Decks.

Our Boyes Seamed to think that a Little poultry whouled go well and do them as much good as the Sesh Rebles that owned them. All of them had Turkeys & Geese, Hens and some of them had what Beer whouled do them good. Thay found about 400 Barrles of good Brandy that thay had Colected to take to thair frends. Thay was taken too nicely. Thay said thay knew of the Expidition, but trusted to geting away by thair Pon[i]es, but was Cut off and now thay will have a Chance to see Old Hair Triger. Thay whare all taken Down to the City, but what thay will do with them I know not.

Sept 11th 1862

We are goin to lose our Genral. He resigned. The Officers and men of the Brigade Payed him a Parting Visit with the Band of the Ninth which Played Some Pattrotic Airs and our Glee Club sang some good Songs when the Col of the 8th New Hampshier Stepped forward and Expressed the regret of the Officers and men of having to Part from So Able a Commander, and our Major Peck next stept forward and in a few Choice words, expressed the regret of the

---

[100] This letter is transcribed from photocopies.

12th. Genral Phelps Came forward but is feelings seemed to get the Better of him. He expressed the Pleaseur he felt for the high Compliment that was Paid him. He said it was the highest Compliment that a Soldier couled recve. He said that the Course that he had taken he couled not Avoid. He couled not do violence to is feelings. He beleved that we ought to make use of all the means that Providence had Placed in our hand, and he beleved that he represented the free Sentement of the Whole Devision. He expressed my Sentements to a Charm but I couled not tell him so. The Officers all went and took Leave of him, but I couled not. We Poor Privats must keep at a respectable Distance from Brigadier Genrals, but he has my good wishes for his futuer wellfair. He will be to the North now in a few Days, and I expect a Major Genrales Comission for him. I have all ways felt safe to go into Battle with him for a Leader and that is the feellings of all the men. Thay feell that if it had been thair Luck to have been Called to meet the Perjured Rebles in fair Fight, thay Couled have Bourn the Stars and Stripes over all opersition. It will be some time be fore I for one will feell all right, for I Claim thair is not another Officer in this whole Division that has the Ripe Judgement and Experiance which Long Service alone can give.

We are having any quanity of Bad Rumors in regard to our Armeys in Virginia. We are anxiousley waiting for Newes from home. Thair has been three Mailes in, but no Letter for me. Most all the other Boyes got Letters. I wrote Edwin a Letter but never got no Answer.

Virtue, you and Mother will be gathering you[r] Crops before this reaches you. I hope you will have a full Crop of the Golden Ear[e]d Corn and that your Bins may run over with the Root that thay call potatoes and the Frute that hangs on the Tree that makes the Cider Press run over may be Plentifull.

Cheer up, I shall be thair some time I hope, and, for one, I shall never want to see Dixie again, but we all have our Dutys to Perform and you and me must do them with a Will. Forget all other Considerations but the Dutys befor us and a half of the Ills of Life is Conquered, and the rest of the Dutys before us is nothing.

It is geting cooler Wether and I hope it will stop Some of the Deaths. We have Buierd two of our Companey this week, but Both the men whare not well when Enlisted, and this Climate will soon Pull such Down. I had Charge of the Burile of them and it made me feell that this war was Costing us very Dear when I Looked round at the New Made Graves and thought of the homes that was made Desolate. I hate to Leave our Poor Fellowes in this Land but it is the Fortune of War.

Mother, you must keep up your Anglo Saxon Curadge and Father Cheer up Virtue and all will be well yeat. Kiss those Chirldren, that Baby and those Old Ladyes that board with you, Let me know how thay Prosper.[101] That Old Gentleman, a Cirtain Mr. Lewis Sherman, dose he Travle from the Schooll House as he used to? Give him my respects. I should Like to Drop in a few Moments to see you all, but Couled not stay Long. Uncl Abraham whouled be after me with a Sharp Stick and that whouled Spoile the Visit. The Old Gentleman Called Uncl Sam we hope will give us a Long Furlough soon, we Trust. I Send Fany & Angline a Song that thay can Sing. We are about as usale except for the Loss of our Genral. I see by the Evaning Paper that Jeff Davis has Put him and Genral Hunter of North Carolina out of the Pule of Prisnors of war. Thay are to be Treated the same as the Greatest of Crimnales if ever taken, but the Second Brigade whouled very much like to be thair at that Particurlar Time.

I must Bid you all good By fore the Present. Acept my Love, Wife, Chirldren, Parents and all that have a Intrest in my welfare. I have Sent Virtue another 25 Dollers by Adam's Express. Please Let me know when Recved.

From Your Affactnate Husband and Son,

CW Sherman

Camp Parepet, New Orleans, September 17, 1862

Dear Wife & Children,

I recved your kind Letter of August 30th and was glad to hear from you and that you was all well. I am well and feell first rate. It is very Mudy and Wet when it dose rain, it dose, and thats a fact.

We are not Drove out of our Camp. Thair was a rumor Last night that a Flag of Truce Came into the City with a Ultamatum to Vakate New Orleans within 4 days but as we have taken the Truble to Come and Pay them a Visit and our Old man[102] is never in a hurry and has a way and a Will of is own and

---

[101] His daughters, Fanny and Angeline
[102] Gen. Butler

it is my opinion that when he gets Tierd of staying and thinks of goin he will Let them know. He is a curious Old Codger and thay had better not get his back up has he as a habit of Doing Just What he says he will. Funey man, Buttler, and he has a Buley Crowed to back him. It is that that makes him so Saucy.

A Cleer feild and no favors is all that we ask. We shouled Liked to have had Phelps with us if it shouled be our Luck to have to repell the Enmyes of our Cuntry. The men had unbounded Confidenc in is Judgment and Skill, but we shall meet them with Stout Hearts and Strong Arms and as Free men knowing thair rights and knowing them Dare to maintain them. Cheer up you to hom. It will never do to give it up.

So we have for Ten Days been kept on hot Brick with rumors of Defeat and Disaster to our Armey on the Potomac. Thay Came through Reble Sources, but thay createad Great Excitement in New Orleans. Buttler Alowed them all to be Printed all though he knew them to be false. Theas Rumors have been hashed up every Day since and when the Stemer Came in with the Papers thay was Devouerd by hungry men and thair has been a Differance of opinons in regard to how fare we was whiped or wether we have been whiped or not. I take the Ground that we have not and as a [con]sequence I have to fight every man in our Tent. Thay can not see but what we got the Worst of it. Thay can not imadgin how a Army can Fall back but still get the Advantadge. If thay Alow one of Stonewall Jacksons men to get away or Lee's I shall feell like Swaring. Has to having any fears has to the Safety of Washington is Just simpl nonsense.

If the New England men can not turn out now to make good that Liberty that thay have been Enjoying and that was Transmited to them by a former Genaration has thair Birth right to Defend and Transmit unimpaird to thair Chirldren now is the time to Com forward and vindecate thair honer and stand up for thair right Like men and as men that has been insulted and sneerd at and Looked Down upon by theas Southron Chivlery as the Dirt and Scum of all Creation. Now is your time to Show them the Differance between Blowing and Blows. Now is the time to Strike the Fetters from off the Nation that the Rebles have been Forgin for 30 years to Bind us hand and foot so that thay Couled Crack the Whip over our Backs and force us to help Draw the Freest Goverment that the Sun ever Shone upon into Perdition and Distroy us with themselves. But, thank God the Scales have fallen from our Eyes so that the Nation sees and our Ears are unstoped so that we can hear the Warning of the Past and the Experance of ages that is Past. We hear that Stonewall Jackson is in Maryland and holds Fredrick City. You must turn out and seround them. Never Let them get away. What are our Genrales doin to Alow them to get into that Hot Bed of Secssion? It is unacountable that we shouled be Drove to the Wall in this shape. Brigadier T. W. Sherman has Come to take Genral Phelps Place so thay Say.[103]

We are about as usal. Shall have to stay this Winter hear I supose but that is not Cirtain. The Wether is very Plesent when it dose not rain, real September Wether but a Trifle Warmer then to hom. The skies are Cleerar than North with you.

Father tells me you will have Preaty good Crops this Fall and how he has Bought a yoke for those Steers and is goin to get a Small Cart for them so that Lewis and the Girles Can get your Crops in this Fall. I hope the Chirldren will not get hurt handlin those Steers. If thay can manedge them it will be a good thing and Save Lots of hard Work for you. Do the Best you can this year be Carefull to get your Winter Wood up befor the Snow Falls. You know that when Winter sets in it is no time then to get Wood.

I am Sorry that Henry has not Come Down to help Fix the House up as Long has you had got Clap Bords all ready. I recved a Letter from him with the one you sent. He was in Palmer then. He had Left Troy having hurt his Foot.[104] He said that he was goin to work in Springfieald. He may have Paid you a Visit befor this time. Please Let me know if he dose.

Edwin sent me a Letter and I send him one with this. Derick sent me a Letter a few weeks since, which I Answered. Write me has often has you can. I hate to have a Maile Com in and not get no Letter from hom. I get all that you send. I hope the Factorys will not Stop this Winter. Thay must keep those runing if thay Expect to Save the Cuntry and keep hard Tim[e]s from the Door.

Tell Lewis to be carefull and not get hurt and Faney and Angline to keep out of the way. Do all you Can to help your Mother and do not make her any

---

[103] Brig. Gen. T. W. Sherman who later lost a leg at the siege of Port Hudson. Edward Cunningham, *The Port Hudson Campaign, 1862–1863* (Baton Rouge: Louisiana State University Press, 1963), 59–60.

[104] Troy, New York. Henry had gone there to find carpentry work and was employed as a foreman for Brown and Johnson on State Street. His wife, Elvira, stayed in Connecticut. This information is from a letter from Henry to his parents dated August 10, 1862. The next one is from September 16, and he states in that letter that he had hurt his foot and was working in Springfield, Connecticut, with Elvira staying in Palmer, Massachusetts, with her father. There are a few letters from Henry during the Civil War period, and several from his stay in California during the Gold Rush in the 1850s.

more truble than you can help. Give my Love to my Mother and Father. I hope I may be to hom soon but can not tell how soon. Virtue you keep up good Heart and do not take any Truble. All will be well. Trust in Providence. He doeth all things well.

Kiss that Baby for me and Aruthur, you have Buried Nep, I am Sorry to hear and Father tells me he Brought home a nother to the Chirldren. I thank him for that has I like to see a Dog whar Chirldren are. Those Minetuers have not got a Long to me. I send my Love to you all and may Heven Preserve us all.

Your Affectnate Husband & Son,

CW Sherman

Camp Parepet, LA

Camp Parepet, New Orleans, Sept 26, 1862

Dear Wife,

I want a Letter from home and that is the reson that I write now. The Maile Steamers have been Coming in for 3 Weeks and I want a Letter with every Mail that Comes in. I have recved all that you have Sent. Those Pictuers I have not recved and unless thay come soon I shall be Wading the Gulf of Mexico and Coming home to get them.

We are still hear but expect to go and Brake up a Gurilla Camp. General Sherman[105] has Come and is goin to revew us tomorrow in hevey Marching Order. The men are a Little afraid of him that he will work them too hard. Thay Claim he killed is men in Port Royle working them in the hot Sun and thay are afraid that he will Spair the Negro. Buttler wants the Niger to do the work of Digin and Choping and the White man to do the Fighting. Now that is all right as fare as it goes but Benj. F. Buttler has raised a Free Coulerd Redgement in the City to have the same Pay and Rations for thair Famleys and Bountys as the rest of Uncl Abrahams Vollenteers and Now all the Differance between Buttlers and Phelps Police was that Phelps wanted to recrut from the Slaves that Came into is Lines with out regard to the State that thay had been in has he did not recognize the right of any man to hold a Fellow man in Bondadge and the same

---

[105] Brig. Gen. T. W. Sherman

Freedom that he Claimed for himself he wanted to Extend to all men no matter what thair Coulor or Complexion and Uncle Ben had been one of the first or the first one that Decided that Slaves was Contra Band of war. That was the Differance that was between the two Genrales. One wanted to take all the Material that a State of war put into is hands, the other must humor the Slave holding Comunity that was using all the means in thair Power to Distroy the Goverment that he was Sent hear to Preserve and Sustain. Phelps believed that him and his men was sent hear not onley to Fight the Comon Enemy but represent Free men and Free Inst[i]tutions and to Show the Rebles the Differance between a Slave holding Comunity and men Brought up as thair Maker intended free as the Air thay Breathed.

We miss Genral Phelps. The men hold Differant vewes in regard to is Politics, but all agree that he was the Soldiers Frend and felt Perfect Confidance when under is Command both in is Judgment and Skill knowing that he never made any Blunders and whare he Led, Victory was Shure. Buttler has made one great Mistak. He may be right but it dose not Look so to me at Present.

Dear Wife if you couled see the mud that we have to Waddle through at Present you whouled wonder how we can Stand it and it is not half as bad as it will be. We have to Shovle our Tent out every morning the same as thay Cleen out a Pig Pen. It makes Plenty of work for the men to Wash thair Clothes as the mud is slipery and you do not know whair your feet is. You may think your feet is in the mud but you find your mistake as you take your meseur in the mud. I have got my Warrent and I feell Just as Proud of it, more so than any Col dose of his Comision from the Govner. I will try to Deserve it by doing my Duty Faithfully.

Mother you must kiss my Babys for me and Virtue do not Let your Curadge go Down a moment but keep up a Stout Heart. Trust in our Father that is in Heven all will be well. We must have a Little more time to Crush this Reblion but we shall shurley do it. Thay or we must go Down. Give my Love to the Chirldren and Accept the same your self. Father keep up a stif uper lip.

From your Husband and Son,
CW Sherman

Camp Parepet, New Orleans, Sept 26, 1862

Dear Chirldren,[106]

I take this opertunity of writing to you hoping theas few Lines may find you in good health, as thay Leaves me at Present. The Rainey Seson is upon us now and we, that is the Soldiers, have to take it rough. The mud is Auffull to get round in. Our Tents are Like a Pig Pen. The mud you Can not shake off your Shoes, nor Scrape it off your Shoes.

I often think of you, Dear Chirldren, and hope and pray to my and your Father that is in heven that we may be Spared to see one another again after this Wicked Rebllion is Put Down and Peace is restored to this happy Land. I hope you may be Spaired to grow up and be good men and Wemon and that you try to so Live that the World may be the Better for your having lived in it. You will find as you grow up that thair is many Dutys Neglected by the many that ought to be Performed. I want you to get into, or acquier, a habit of Promtness, of doing what you have to do with a Will. You will find that it will help you to get through the World, Easier and with more Respect to yourselves. Men and Wemon Love to see Energy in thair Fellows if thay do not Possess those qualities themselves. You have many things to Learn and I Shouled like to have you begin to see now while you are young what may be fore the Best in the years that is to Come. I Hope and Pray that your Father which is in Heven may open up a Bright Futuer to you, Dear Chirldren, Brighter then what has been my Lot, but I have not much to Complain of, but much to be Gratfull for. I want you Chirldren to learn Perfect Obedance to your Mother first, and your GranMother & GranFfather next, and to Pay Proper respect to your Eldiers at all times, and in all places, and to Learn to be Polite and forbaring toward one another and to be Polite and Perffectley Easey in the Preseance and Company of Straingers. Dear Chirldren, you must allways Bare in mind that God sees you at all times, and in all Places, and you must try to not offend him that has been so good to you and me and whose Merceys are around us at all times. You and me must try to relye wholey on is goodness and Loving kindness to us. He is willing to Protect and Able to Save all that will Call upon and Put thair Trust in him.

You whouled Like to be hear at this time. The Trees hang full of Oranges, but thay are green. The men Pick them and Suck the Juce from them. It will not

---

[106] This letter is transcribed from photocopies.

do to Eat the Meat, that is tough and it has made some of the men very Sick. To squeeze them into Water makes a very Preaty Drink. Thay are not Sweet, but full of Acid that when you Bite one, it sets your Teeth all most on Edge, but the Tast[e] is very Agreable. You never Saw Aples so thick as Oranges grow. The Sugar Cane is nearly Ripe anuff to Crush; it is very Sweet. The men make it a Bissness to Stop Every Negro that has got any or that is Comin into the Lines with any.

We hear Conflicting Rumors in regard to our Armeys on the Potomac.

I send my Love to you, Dear Chirldren, hoping that heven may Bless you and that we may all meet again.

Your Father,
CW Sherman

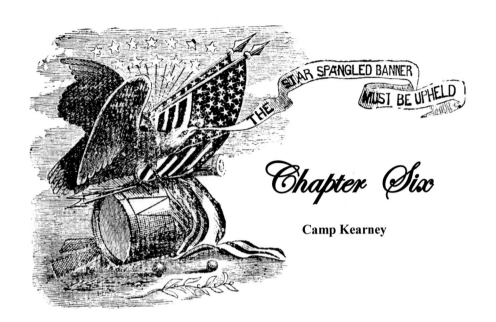

Chapter Six

Camp Kearney

Camp Reserve, New Orleans, October 2, 1862

Dear Wife & Chirldren,

I take great Pleaseure in writing theas Few Lines to you hoping thay may find you in good health as theas Leaves me at Present.

The 12th has got Shifted and the Brigade got Mixed and Scatterd round and Brigaded with other Redgements. We are in a Reserved Brigade. Major Geneal Buttler gave is Chife of Staff is Pick of the Best Redgements in is Division to form a Reserve so Brigadier Genral Go. Weitzel,[107] a United States

---

[107] Brig. Gen. Godfrey Weitzel commanded "The Reserve Brigade," which was stationed at Camp Kearney. The Brigade consisted of the Twelfth Connecticut Volunteer, Colonel Colburn; Thirteenth Connecticut Volunteer, Colonel Birge; the Seventy-Fifth New York Volunteer, Lieutenant Colonel Merritt; Thompson's First Maine Battery; Eighth New Hampshire, Colonel Fearing; First Battery Massachusetts Light Artillery ("A"); Troop C Massachusetts Calvary; Lieutenant Carruth's Sixth Battery Massachusetts Volunteer; First Louisiana, Colonel Holcomb; Williamson's, Barret's, and Godfrey's companies of the Louisiana Cavalry; Perkins's company of Massachusetts Cavalry. De Forest, *A Volunteer's Adventures*, 53; Frederick H. Dyer, *A Compendium of the War of the Rebellion* (Des Moines, IA: The Dyer Publishing Company 1908), 551, PDF e-book; and Homer B. Sprague, *History of the 13th Infantry Regiment of Connecticut Volunteers During the Great Rebellion*, (Hartford, CT: Case, Lockwood & Co., 1867), 74, PDF e-book.

Oficer, Picked the 12th Con Voll, the 13th Con Voll, the first Louisiana Voll, the 7th Vermont Voll, 75 New York Voll, the first Louisiana Cavllery and Nims Battery and Mannin[g]'s Battery[108] and if you know anything of the names I have given you, you will know that when we move, if thair is any thing in the way God help them for thair Father the Devil will not.

We have been having good news from home. I hope the Boys will be Able to Lay that Stone Wall Jackson so Low that the Frost will not Afect him. Keep that Ball in Motion the good time is Coming. This State of War can not Last much Longer. The men are geting Tierd of it and whouled much rather go out and make one or more Big Fights of it and go hom. This Chaingin Camps is not to my Liking has you can not Chaing for the Better.

We are goin up the River but Whare this Child knows not. Coll Deming is with us now and after Inspection Last Sunday Morning Complemented the Redgement on its good Discpline, Cleanleyness and Curadge in Facing the hard Dutys of Garrison Life and having to See thair Comrads carred to the Grave every Day and to tell the Truth it dose requier a higher and more Elavated Class of Curadge in men then Facing the Enemy in the Open Fieald.

It has been a trying Summer with us. Deming told us that he had been Promised a Conspicuous Posision in the Fieald for the 12th. We are Waiting for the Brigade to be formed and have a few Days Brigade Drill togather and then Forward will be the Word and for one it is what I have been Waiting for. The 12th has Drilled has a hevey Artlery Redgement as well has a Infantry Redgement. It is that that Brings its Valeu up has we are Able to Fall behind Stone Walls or Parepets or take our Stand in the Field and out Drill any Redgement in this Division. This is not Blowing or Gas but the Naked truth. It has Cost us maney a Wet Shirt. Our Leautenant Coll is not a Sunday go to Meeting Coll but one of those that takes his Coat off and Rolles up is Sleeves and says Com in Boys we Came hear fore Work not to Play. He has got many

---

[108] Maj. Ormand. F. Nims, Second Massachusetts Light Artillery and Capt. Charles H. Manning Forth Battery Massachusetts Light Artillery both in the Department of the Gulf. Dyer, *A Compendium of the War,* 157. Both were at the battle of Baton Rouge. Manning resigned on October 20, and Trull of Nims' Battery took over. A section under Lt. Briggs accompanied Weitzel's brigade to Labadieville; Nims proceeded to New Orleans. *The Union Army,* Vol.1 (Madison, WI: Federal Publishing Co., 1908), 220–222, PDF e-book.

a Curse from Lazey men that whouled never get off thair Backs if thay Couled have thair way and when the Enemy was upon us whouled be found wanting.

The Wether is geting Cooler but the Sun Shines quite Warm anuff for me. I know that I got one Wet Shirt Marching to this Camp. The Raile Road runs by us and you can immaegin yourself in Old Connectcut if you keep your Eyes off the Moss that hangs from all the Trees in this State.

Please Direct your Letters to Captain Roche instead of Abbot has he has gon home for good. Give Love to Mother Father and all Enquring frends. Kiss my Babys and tell Faney and Angline that I am waiting for that Letter. I send my love to you and remain,

Your Affectnate Husband,
CW Sherman

Camp Reserve, New Orleans, October 2, 1862[109]

Dear Wife and Chirldren, Mother,

I am a live and well at Present but we have 4 Poor Fellowes Laying Dead tonight. Thay Died in the Hospital. We Shall be represented Preaty Largle[y] by our Dead in the State of Louisiana befor we get out of it. I for one do not want to Leave my Bones in this Cuntry but I know not what may be in Store for me. I shall try to do my Duty and Leve the rest with my Father in heven. Do not worry about me. I know that you Pray for me. I often think of you all to home and may Heven Speed the day when this Reblion Shall be Put Down and the Olive Branch of Peace once more be over and around this Land.

We have been taken from our Old Camp and the Chaing was not for the Better. We are for a Reserve under the Comand of Genral Weitzel. We have had Some Little Truble about who should have the right of the Brigade. The 13th Claimed it but the 12th Put its foot Down and told them thay Couled not Com[mand] it. The 13th is quite a Dandy Redgement. Thay have all ways [been] in Barracks and thay have not Dirtyed their Clothes. Thay whare white Gloves and Brass Epaulets on their Shouldiers. Our Coll told thair Coll that thay whouled have to take those White Gloves off before thay got ahead of the

---

[109] This is a separate letter also written on October 2.

12th. Thay have been Put with us to Learn and if we do not Put them through a Course of Sprouts,[110] Coll Deming told them that thay whouled have to Drill for the Right Flank befor thay got it and toDay we gave them a Chance and Left them so far in the Shade that thair will be no more truble. Genral Weitzel was on the Ground and expressed him self highly Pleased with our Performance. We have Earnd our right by maney a hard days work in this Blistering Sun and Shall Alow no Redgement to step in ahead, no sirree.

You to home are getting your harvesting don. I hope your Crops will Turn out Better than usaley and that the Frost may keep off. I shouled like to be to home but that can not be but that time will shurely come. Lewis I hope will do all that he can and when Schooll opens he must Learn all he can. I want a Letter. I do not get any. It apears to me onley in a age. You must write oftener. The Fall hear dose not Look much Like Fall. Everything as green now as in June. Mother you send me a Letter and give me all the newes. Virtue and her baby I hope is well. Little Arthur you must give him a kiss for me and all the Chirldren. May Heven Bless you all. Give my Love to Father and Mother and the Chirldren and Accept a Large share your self.

From your Affectnate Husband,
C W Sherman, La

Camp Kerney, Carrollton, October 5, 1862

Dear Wife & Chirdlren,[111]

I take this opertunity of writing theas few Lines to you as I may not be Able to write again for Some time. The 12th is goin to take a Little run into the Cuntry to see the Folks and get some Peaches but whare we shall Bring up we know not. Thair is various rumors some say Gavelston Texas and others Mobile but whare ever it may be I hope you may hear good Newes of us.

Yesterday our new Brigadier Genral Godfrey Weitzel inspected us and did not find us wanting. He put us through our Paces to our Hearts Content. Faith, the moon was up before he got through with us. Today Sunday thay have taken

---

[110] A term used for company or squad drills
[111] Camp Kearney, where "The Reserve Brigade" commanded by Gen. Weitzel encamped, is the same camp Charles called "Camp Reserve."

all our Sick and those that have been off Duty and had them examind as to thair Ability to Stand the Tug of War and all that is unable to keep in the Ranks [were] Sent to the Genral Hospital to recover in the City of New Orleans.

I find myself in good health at this time by the goodness of my Father who is in Heven who has kindly Wached over and Presearved me till this time. Thair as been quite a number of Deaths in this Redgement Since we have been hear, more then it runs to the Lot of any Redgement in a hard Fought Battle. This Place as Cost us men by Dease [disease] if not by the Fortunes of War. I hope I may return from this Expidition Safe. Do not Worry I shall Com out all safe I trust.

You will have got through your Harvesting befor this reaches you and Cold Frosty Wether will be upon you. Hear things are about the same, the Same Hot Sun shines upon you now as Last July. The Trees and all Natuer Dressed in her Green Robes, the Same as if She had Just Put them on. The nights are Beautifull and Just Cool enough to sleep good. I dred to have it rain. Every step is Like steping into Glue with a very Little Grease to have you Slide down. I wish I was to home at this time to see our Woods Put on that Beautifull Dress that old King Frost Paints for us in our Northen Homes. I look in vain for signs of Winter or Fall, but see non. Thair was something so healthey and invigerating in the Cool Bracing Air to home at this time [of year] that it makes me feel the Hot Breath of the Southern Clime with more Force. To Talke to me of the Balmey Breath of the South, I fail to see the Point.

I have filled this Sheet and must ask to be excused for not Puting any more in it. Kiss that Baby for me. Give my Love to the Chirldren & Father Mother and Virtue take a Large Share yourself.

From your Affectnate Husband,
CW Sherman

Camp Kerney, October 5, 1862

Dear Wife & Chirldren,[112]

Our Camp is so hot that I have got into the Chaplain Tent. It [is] pi[t]ched in a Grove and feells Cool and Plesent. We have a Long Table and thair is some 8 of us Writing home to the Girls we Lef behind us. The Band Playes that Tune some times and it must and dose Turn our thought to our homes and make us forget, in the thoughts of the Past, the Hard Work that is befor us.

Coll Deming has Left us again. He has been apointed to fill the Mayors Chair for the City of New Orleans and if [he] cannot fill it to Perffection the 12th whouled like to know who can. It is no Bed of Roses or Downy Seat but he will Bring Light out of Darkness and Show his Southron frends how a City shouled be Govnerd. The People say thay never knew Mart[i]al Law was such a Blessing till Genral Buttler undertook to Adminster it to them.

We have one Captain coming home in Disgrace for taking money from the Rebles who wished to Cross our Lines with Medcins for the Enemy. How he can Escap Death I can not see. Thay Some Thing about free Masonry[113] but that ought not to Shield the man that couled so far forget himself has to give Aid and Comfort to the Enmy. He is a German and thair is a great maney hear and he was a man that Drank and Played and the Devil soon Bought him.

You have Plenty of Apples to hom this year so I Learn and we have Plenty of Oranges and I shouled like to make a exchainge with you. It is wicked how we have had to Cut Whole Plantations of Ornges trees to give our Guns fair Play but thay whouled make us do it and if thay whouled have a Dance thay must Pay for the Musick. I have had no Letter [for] so long that I do not know but I can get along without any.

General Sherman has Charge of the Brigade & Camp that we formed a Part of our Camp Parepet.[114] We have a West Point Officer the same one that Built Forts Jackson and Fort St. Philip.

When you write direct to Captain Roche, Company K, 12th Redgement Conn Vol & New England Division or Els Whare.

---

[112] This is a second letter written on this date.

[113] Masons formed military lodges within their regiments during the war. Their sense of brotherhood sometimes transcended political lines and the battlefields. "Masonic Civil War," Beardan Sharpshooters, Civil War Reenactors, accessed April 21, 2012, http://www.berdansharpshooters.org/masonic.html.

[114] Brig. Gen. Thomas W. Sherman

Tell the Chirldren to be good and do all thay can to help thair Mother and Virtue keep up good Heart. Our Old Flage must be Carred to Places whare it has been Banished and I am Bound to see it don. Pray for me that I may be spaird. I am in the hands of one that can make all things Possable. Give my Love to the Dear Chirldren. I shall write again as soon as I can. We may not move as soon as thay tell of. Do not be Afraid we may meet with no opersition but if we do it will soon be moved.

Your Affectnate Husband,
CW Sherman, La

Camp Kerney, New Orleans, October 9, 1862

Dear Wife & Chirldren,

I tak this opportunity of writing a few Lines to you hoping thay may find you all in good health as theas Leaves me at Present.

I recved your kind Letter of Sept 21st and was glad to hear from you. I have not had a Letter [in] so Long that I had given up all hope of geting one. We have Steamer Coming in every week so that Letters whouled reach me every Week & the 12th has not gon as yeat.

We may go into quarters in the City of New Orleans has our Coll is Mayor and the 9th Connecut is quartered thair now but thay Raise the Devil thair so thay Can do nothing with them. It is a Irish Redgement and thay will Drink. You want to know how we Spend our Sundays. We have no Preaching and have had non Since Last July. The Redgement Came away from Hartford with a Chaplain Tent that Cost over 200 Dollers. It never was used hear for Preaching. The Chaplain Put it up but thay Put our Prisnors in it and used it for a Gard tent from that time till this. It is rotted and will fall to Peices. This Climate Mill Dewes our Tents. Thay have isued New Tents to us and all the Redgements. We was half Drowend when it Raind be for. Now we can keep Dry but can not keep the Mud out of our Shantys.

We have a good Chaplain, is name is Bradford. He whouled willingle Preach to the men if thay whouled hear him. At Dress Parade every night he Prayes for the Redgement. He is our Post Master Genral and helps the men in various ways and is Liked by the officers and men and we couled not get along without him.

We are getting Redy to move on [to] Mobile. That is our Destination so thay tell us. Thair is no more Bounty Money for us till this year is up. Thay ought to Pay us some Extra has we have taken the heat and Burden of the day. It is wrong to Pay such Large Bountys to men who are no Better then those that have gon before Draft. If the men will not turn out, Force them. The men do not Grumble if thair Naibors do get a Larger Bonus then themselves. We all have a Duty to Perform and we must see to it that we do our whole Duty.

The President Proclemation Suites me to a Charm. Genal Phelps was right. He all ways heald that it was the true Policy to get at the Heart of the Reblion. In this State alone thair is over 200,000 in this State and we must Arm them.[115] We can not move with out the Pro[tec]tion of the Gun Boats. It will be a Death Blow to the Reble Leaders. Thay will have something Els[e] to do besides invading the Loyle states. It will give us something more to do. We will have to use Judgement in handlin this new Element of our Armeys. Thair will be some Bigotry but it will whare away in time.

Give my Love to the Chirldren and Virtue Mother and Acept the Same yourself. I am well at Present and hope to be Preserved. I have to take my Chances with the rest. I shall Trust in that Providance that has all ways Preserved me.

CW Sherman

Camp Kerney, New Orleans, La, October 9, 1862
Dear Wife, Mother & Chirldren,[116]

I am glad to hear that your Crops Turn out so well. I hope you will think of me when you are Eating those nice Mealey Potatoes. How I shouled Like to have a Chance at some, Less then a Bushel to say nothing of the Aples & Cider that would Disapear & I do not know but a Pound of Butter whouled not Last long. I am glad that the money was recved safe. I know not how soon we shall get anymore. I want some to Buy myself a Pint of Milk & if I ever get home you must Look out for the Milk Pans. I am goin to have one Cow for my own Easpacil use and behalf. I never Cared much about Milk till [now] since I have been away Drinking Mudy Water and what is, by Courtesy, Called Coffee.

---

[115] "Them" meaning the slaves.
[116] This is a second letter written on October 9, 1862.

The Camp whare we are at Present is Laid out so that we can see all that is goin on and at Drill times it is Preaty Livley with Musick and Marching. Thay are Puting the 12th through the Scershmersh [skirmish] Drill and a Livley time we have Laying Down and Duble quicking of it and Chasing round. Faith, if anyone thinks we have a Easey time Let them Com and try it. I never worked much harder at any thing then I have in the School of the Soldier.

October 10th

I have Just taken a Squad [of] men to the River & we got a Boat, went over to the west Side. The 8th Vermon[t] has a Pickit over thair. We went to a Planters and a nice Place. He has every thing on is Estate to make Life go Pleasant. He had a Mule grinding Corn in a Primative Mill, Slaves Wemon doing all kinds of Work. His House Serounded with Orange & Magnola Trees. We asked him for Some Oranges. He told one of is Coulered womon to Bring us some. She Brough[t] about a Bushal and the Boys went in. I though[t] that Virtue whouled have Liked any Share as She is fond of them. I Eate some few for her and some Less then a Peck for myself. Oranges the men go in fore. Thay are geting ripe now.

It is a Great Pity that things are in the State thay are for a more Luxorious Life then a Southeron Planters is hard to find and I am thinking that Uncl Abraham has set some of them to thinking how thay are to get out with thair Property all safe.

We are waiting with Patience for News from home. I am sorry that Henry has not been Able to help you get the House fixed some what. I hope he will spend a few Days to home. Give my Love to the Chirldren and kiss that Baby for me and Arthur keep up good Heart. Virtue and Mother and all of you write me so that I can get a Letter oftener. I am well and hope this will find you all well. Give my respects to all enquiring Frends.

Yours truley,
CW Sherman, La

Camp Kerney, New Orleans, October 13, 1862

Dear Wife & Chirldren,

It with Great Pleasuer that I now write theas few Lines to you hoping thay may find you in good health as theas Leaves me at present.

We have had quite a Cold Snap. It Froze me some. I whouled not have beleved it Posable that a Little North East Storm whouled have had such affect upon us. It will not do for me to Come home this Winter has I shouled Stand a mighty good Chance of geting Frost Bitten, but as things go now I need not be afraid of Seeing old Connectcut right away.

We have not gon away as yeat but as soon has thay can get ready. We are geting Put through the Skirmsh Drill and our Compney have an Ordley Sergeant from the 4th Winsconsin Redgement to Learn us the Bayonet Drill. That is a Drill with work in it but well Learnt. It will make a Redgement worth two and Save maney a Poor Fellows Life.

We Leave in Six Days so thay Say but whare I cannot Say. You to home must keep up your Spirits. When this Brigade mov[e]s the war will soon be don with as the Twelft wants to get a Chance to hurt some one or get hurt. We are goin to have New Brech Loding rifles, Greens Patent.[117] Thay will Put a Ball 2 Mile and a half so that the Rebl Regiments had Better get out the way of the 12th when thay Draw a Bead. It is a Fact theas Rifles will Throw a ball 2 Mile & half. Our Enfield Rifles are not Slow but those other Rifles Leaves the Enfields so far in the Shade that thay will not be mentiond in the Same Day.

We are waiting for a Mail from home and are not more then half Satisfied that our Genrals on the Potomac Let that Reble Army get away from Maryland but we must Let things take thair Course. It was all for the Best or it whouled not have happend. This War will be the Means of Freeing the Slave. I do not know what we shouled have Don with out is help this Sumer doing all the Hard work and Saving the men. We have one to Look after our Tent, wash our Tin Ware, Black our Shoes and do our washing.

---

[117] A breech-loading weapon is a firearm in which the bullet or shell is inserted or loaded at the rear of the barrel, or breech—the opposite of muzzle-loading. The Greene rifle used rotating bolt-action and was fed from the breech. Breech-loading rifles held a significant advantage over muzzle-loaders in loading time. It appears as though they did not receive these rifles; Charles mentions "our Enfields" in the letter dated November 17, 1862. Arcadi Gluckman, *United States Muskets, Rifles and Carbines* (Harrisburg, PA: The Stackpole Company, 1959), 3–4, PDF e-book.

In Serving out theas New Tents we get 3 Tents to a Compney more then the Old Tents. Thay was made to hold 20 men, the New ones 15. The Non Comisiond Officers have a Tent or thay ocupie one Tent and that makes it more Plesent. Samul Wicks is a Little Sick at Present. He Drinks a good Deal and Last Sadurday night Slept out Doors and took cold. You need not tell is wife has she whouled tell from whome she got her information and it whouled do no good. He has don him self no good. His Compney officers are all down on him through is own Fault.

We have a new Captain and one that the men Like. One that says Come not go. Things remain hear about the same.

Kiss that Baby for me. Tell my Mother to Pray for me. Virtue you must kiss that Arthur and give him a shake. Those young Ladys and that young Gentleman give my Love to them and Father Mother and Accep a Large Share your self. Keep up a Stout Heart, all will be well.

From your Affectnate Husband and Son,

CW Sherman

Camp Kerney, October 20, 1862

Dear Wife & Chirldren,

I take great plesuer in Answering your kind Letter of October 7th and was glad to hear from you and that you was all well as this Leaves me at Present.

The Wether is Delightfull at Present. The nights are quite Cool so that the Gards have to whare thair over Coats night which is quite a Chaing from the great heat that we have had to enduer fore Six months. The men have Stood it like Salemanders. It astonished the Southron men who own up that our Northen men Can Stand more hardship then Southron men to the manor Born.

Sadurday the 18th this Brigade was Marched to the City of New Orleans to be revewed by Major Genal Buttler and he Put us through our Paces to our Satisfaction and a Splended Aperance thay made. 5 Regiments 6 Compneys of Callvary 2 Batterys. The Citizens turned out and thay Treated us with a little more respect than when we Last or first Paid our Complements to them Last May.

General Buttler looks some Older then he did in Ship Island. He as had a heavy Burden to Carry on is Shouleders but he Puts things through with a Stif uper Lip and the City of New Orleans never was Governd so well as Since Buttler took it in hand.

I see by the papers that he Feeds 3,500 Famileys, over 1200 are the Famileys of Confedrate Soldiers. He as tryed by all the means in is Power to win over those that have been Deluded into this Reblion and Bring them to a Sense of thair ingratude to the Best and kindest of Goverments that the Sun ever Shone upon. We are Slowly but Shurely doing the good work. We have to overcome a very Large amount of Prejudaic that is in the Southron mind regarding the People of the North but it will Shurely be removed.

This war will be a Blessing to all Coming time. It will open up the Southron States to those of Northen Origin. Thair will be fore years a Bitter Feeling against us by those that will and have Sufferd by the Chances of War.

This Brigade is goin up the River fore a few Days. We Start on wensday the 22nd and I hope to get Back Safe but must take my Chances. I tell you this not that you Shouled Worry yourselves about me. I am no better then Thousands that now Sleep Peacfulley in thair Graves but we must Trust our Father in Hevan. If He sees that it whouled be for my good in this World that I shouled return Safe, I shall. I shouled like to see you all and that Baby. You must kiss him fore me. All the Chirldren must kiss for me. I hope this war will Com to a Close soon so that we can return but not as Long as the Rebles hold out, I do not wish to return. I have Enlisted for the War. One of us must go down. I wanted to have a hand in this Pie and if Providance preserves my health I mean to stick to the old Flag and help Pull that seven Bar[r]ed Rag that thay have insulted heven and Earth by raising. Never Fear we shall Com out all right. It may take some Time to finish up this Bissness, but finished it will be and, faith, it will finish some of us.

I am Sorry that Virtue Couled not have those Minetuers taken at a resonabl Price, but it may be all for the Best. I thought if Virtue couled get them Taken in a Cheap Form I shouled have liked it but I can Waite. I may be Coming home some fine morning and if thay shouled keep me a spell longer it will not matter much. Father tells me that he will Put some Cider in the Celler. I shouled Like to Drink some of it. I hope I shall help Father next time he gets is Hay. Hay is Worth 125 Dollers Per Ton in the City of New Orleans. What the Goverment Pays I know not but a nuff no Dout. All that Come from the North Brings a high Figuer. The men Pay our Sutler 50 Cents Per Pound for Butter and Po[ta]toes 15 Cents Per Pound, and Chees 40 Cents Per Pound and every thing Els inproportion. Some of your Store keepers whouled Like to Sell to the Boys.

I was Sorry to hear of Mr. Brooks Son Geting Wounded. It is Lucky for the young man that he had a kind Father that was Able to go to is Asistance for the Armey Hospitals are not the most Plesent Places for a Sick man to be in. Those that we have are the Last Place for Sick man to be in. I do not know but the Goverment intends that the men Shall have good Atendance and Care but thay have not got it. I have known men that has been told that nothing was the Matter with them and before midnight thay was Dead men. That is the Class of Doctors we have with us and if Justice was meated out to one that is with us he whouled be hanging on the first Tree the Boys couled get him to.

I hope the Factorys will not stop this Winter.[118] Thay must keep runing evan at short Time. It whouled Cause a great Deal of Suffering. You tell me that Virtue has got a Loom for Fany so that she can help her Mother. Angline has written me a Letter for which I send her my Complements hoping she will Contineu to send me the News about home. Bless her Little Heart. I shouled Like to see her and Fany. She say she has got Tierd of Choping. I do not intend she shall if I can get at that old Wood Pile once more but I must waiet a little Longer. Keep up your Curadge Chirldren. I hope to see you all again. Write me again I will answer it. Chirldren Please Pray for me that I may be Preserved.

I was Sory to hear of Poor Old Neps Death. I shall miss him if I ever get home but you have another Dog so your Granfather wrote to me he had Brought you one. You and Lewis must take Care and not get hurt with those Steers. Keep out of thair way. You must Learn all you can this winter and try to help your Mother all you can.

We Leave this Camp to morrow morning for a few Days. Thay have told of it so many times of goin that we get to Dout the rumors that we hear but go we do to morrow.

Let me know if you saved any Hazle Nuts and get all the Wallnuts and Chessnuts you can. We get no nuts here but Oranges thay sell 4 for 5 Cents. Thay Look very Preaty on the trees now. Thay are turning yellow. Fig Trees Bare all the Time no soon[er] one Crop gets Ripe and are Picked then thay begin to Form again.

Mother you must kiss my Babys for me and Cheer up. Virtue do all you can to make Life as Plesent as you can. We have Evils anuff Come on us from

---

[118] His biggest concern here may be the woolen mill in Rockville where his father works.

with out. Trust in a kind Providence. He will do all things well. I send my Love to all the Chirldren Virtue Mother & Father and all Enquiring Frends. I will write again if all goes well with us.

From your Affectnate Husban,

CW Sherman

Wicks is sick. He is goin to the hospital tomorrow Morning. He made himself sick and must take the Consiquances. The Last time we went away he was sick from the same Cause. Do not tell is wife, he will be better soon. I am goin to write to his wife by is own request. He will get over it.

Camp Kerney, October 24, 1862

Dear Wife and Chirldren,

We did not go that day that was Set. We went Aboard the Boats that was got ready for us and had Just got settled when Genral Buttler sent one of is Aids up to have the men go Back to Camp and Waite 24 hours has the Fleet couled not be got ready in time. He [was] having to get a heveiry Force to go with us then was intended at first.

The Maile that the Trade Wind brought out was Delayed. She [was] having to Put into Ship Island having got Disabled and she Just got up to the City. I was glad to get your Letter of September 30th. I got one from Henry at that time and two Papers. He was well but he had not got his Pay of[f] Marcy. I am Sorry that he can not Pay Virtue. He is owing me and if he never gets any thing from Marcy I shall have to Lose what was my Due.

We are Ready to move once more on Board the Boats. The time is fixt at Noon to Day. The other Day when we went on Board thay Arested 3 of the Piolets [pilots]. Buttler has Detectives all around him and thay found that theas three men whare goin' to run thair Boats under the Batterys and get us knocked into a Cocked Hat. Thay must get up very Earley in the morning if not befor when thay get ahead of old Hair Triger. We have been Reinforced by 4,000 men. Billey Wilsons Lambs from Penscola is one of the Regiments[119] and the

---

[119] 6th New York Volunteer Infantry, commanded by Col. William Wilson, known as the Pet Lambs. It was a regiment of New York City firemen, and the term "zoave" was used to describe the regiment, generally referring to the "rough" nature of the men.

21st Massachusetts, the others I do not know. Pleas do not Worry about me. I hope to return safe.

Virtue must not be afraid. It will do no good. She must keep up her Spirits for the Sake of the Chirldren. I must do my Duty. Let whatever be the Consiquance. It was for that I enlisted. Cheer up thair is hope. I recon I am Worth 10 Dead men as yeat. We shall Put this Reblion Down and what is Left of us return to our homes. We can not all Com Back, that whouled be out of the Natuer of things and it is onley a question [of] a few years more or Less to Sleep in our Graves. If it shouled be my Luck to go Down you can allway think that I went Down Like a man and in the Pathe of Duty.

I shouled like to write to the Chirldren at this time but can not. I will on the Boat. We Expect to be abord 3 Days. Whare we shall Bring up I know not but hope to give a good Account of ourselves. Thair ought to be some thing don by the 12th. Every man Carrys one Hundred rounds of Ball Cartridges.

Winter is Coming Fast upon you to home. I hope you will have your Wood Pile Cut up and keep your selves Warm. I shall take things as I find them. To morrow is my Birth Day. I expect to be Steaming up the Mississippi in Compney with 8 or 9 thousand more Poor Fellows and Uncl Abrahams Bleu Jackets with thair Thunder. I intend to Enjoy the Ride and make the most of it. Be of good Cheer. Providance will Favor us and Bring us all safe and sound out of our Trubles.

Give my Love to the Chirldren and kiss the Babys. Tell Lewis to be good and take Care that he dose not get hurt with the Cattle. Give my Love to Mother & Father and Virtue be not Down Hearted. You must have the Pluck of the Spartan wemon of Old. Keep up a stif uper lip. Let what will happen and may heven have you in is keeping is the Prayer of your Affectnate Husband

CWS

The New York Times, Tuesday, December 23, 1862; New York State Military Museum, *6th Regiment of Infantry New York Civil War Newspaper Clippings*, New York State Division of Military and Naval Affairs: Military History, last modified March 27, 2006, http://dmna.ny.gov/historic/reghist/civil/infantry/6thInf/6thInfCWN.htm.

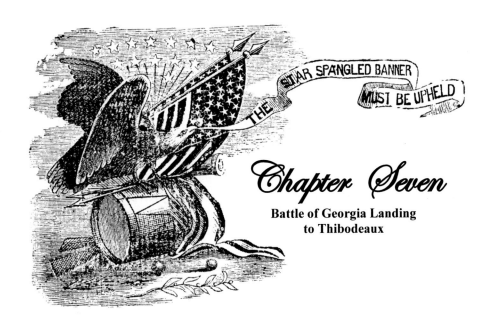

Chapter Seven

Battle of Georgia Landing
to Thibodeaux

Camp Tiveadore, Bayou Fuche, La, November 2, 1862[120]

Dear Wife and Chirldren,

It is with great Pleasuer that I write thease few Lines to you to let you know that I am well at this time and safe. So fare Providance has Brought me out of the Fire without a scratch. I wrote you that this Brigade was Ordered up the River to Clear the Cuntry of Gurilles and whatever stood in the way.

We landed at Donsonvill[121] 75 miles from New Orleans. Staid thair that night in the Catholick Church and the next morning Started again after the Rebles.[122] Thay [were] keeping ahead of us. We got to with[in] two mile of them that night and Camped. The next morning started again, the 12th Acting as rear gard. The 8th Newhamshier having the right in front on account of the Cols Comisions having been made out about a month or so be fore Deming's.

---

[120] Camp Thibodeaux (as it was spelled from 1838 to 1918), Bayou Lafourche, La, was really called Camp Stevens. See letter November 6, 1862.

[121] Donaldsonville

[122] They were in pursuit of Confederate Gen. Alfred Mouton, a West Pointer, and his forces which consisted of the Crescent regiment, the Eighteenth and Thirty-Third Louisiana, the Terre Bonne militia, the Second Louisiana cavalry and Semmes' and Ralston's batteries. Captain De Forest of the Twelfth Connecticut estimated the force to muster about 2500. De Forest, *A Volunteer's Adventures*, 54.

Deming is Mayor of New Orleans and Laeutenant Col Colburn is in Command of the Regiment. The 13th Connectcut [is] to the right of the Newhamshier Boys. The 75th New York was on the other side of the Bayou. The Rebles had Burnt the Bridge but Genral Weitzel had Caused a Flat Boat anchored and by the help of Planks made a Bridge.

About Noon Col Colburn rode Down to us [and] told us the Enemy was in Front. [He] Caused every mans Canteen to be filled with water, took off our Knapsacks. [He] Detailed two Left Companys to take care of the Baggdge Wagons with the Old gard that had stood the night be fore and who was under the Charge of our First Leautenant Francis, to stay By and help. In a few mineutes a Aid from Genral Weitzel Came with an Order for the 12th to move up Dubble quick and we did move. We soon Came to the Bridge and the way thay Pi[t]ched the Shells into us was a Caution. The 12th paid no Atintion to them but it did Look a little Squalley. Our Compney was thrown out has Skirmshers to feell the Enemy. We soon found whare thay was hid. Thay was in a Rifle Pit with a Fence befor them. We couled not see them but thair Bulets kicked up some Dust. I can not tell you all about the fight now.

Genral Weitzel Came on with us, the other regiments having gotten Broken up. The Rebles Paid Particuler Atention to us, gave the whole weight of thair fire on us. The Order was give to Charge and away we went. The Rebles Brok and we had the Day. The Col of the 13th Came up and Proposed three Cheers for the 12th. Genral Weitzel propposed 3 more, [and] Gave us the Credit of Win[n]ing the day.[123] Compney K took 27 Prisnors. Our Captain Shot the Col of the 18th Louisiana [of] that Redgiment we Brok up. That Redgiment took some 250 Prisnors and did things up Brown. Our Compney Lost one man Kil[l]ed, one Wounded. The Redgiment Lost six Kil[l]ed, 15 Wounded.[124]

---

[123] De Forest's account of the General's praise is as follows: "Twelfth Connecticut, you have done well. That is the way to do it. Never stop, and the enemy won't stay." Ibid., 67.

[124] Depending upon whose accounting one is reading, the numbers vary. De Forest's book states the regiment lost three killed, sixteen wounded, and one officer captured or missing. Sprague gives three killed, fifteen wounded, and Lt. Francis taken prisoner. *Record of Service of Connecticut Men* and Croffut and Morris both state nineteen killed, wounded, or missing. Regardless of the source, all state that the Battle of Georgia Landing (sometimes referred to as Labadieville) on October 27, was a decisive victory for the Union forces. Ibid. 70; Sprague, The *History of the 13th Infantry*

I write this in a hurry. Give my Love to the Chirldren and give me your Prayers for I feell that I may have to Die but I Trust in Providence. Kiss that Baby Mother. I send my Love to you all. Virtue keep up your Spirits, all will yeat be well.

Your Affectnate Husband,
CW Sherman

Camp Thibdaux, November 4, 1862

Dear Wife & Chirldren & Father Mother,

This Brigade is in the Field and has Don so far all that it was expected of it. We have Cleard this Part of Louisiana of all Gurillas and those that had Banded themselves to gather in opersition to the Laws and to the Preduice [prejudice] of good Order.

We Left Camp Kerney October the 24th on Board 10 River Steamers Flanked by 6 Gun Boats, and all to gather we made quite [a] Show. If nothing Els [we] must have Astonished the Darkeys as thay apear to make the Poppalation of this State.

We Drew into Shore in the Morning. Theas Flatt Bottomand Boats are Just the thing to Land Troops from but not to stand Fire, as thay are only Ginger Bread. A Grape Shot Passing through one [is] Like sticking your finger through wet Paper. The one we was aboard of, having been bored through by the Gurillias at the Place whare we Landed but a short time before. We soon got Ashore, the Cavlery taking the Back Road for Don[ald]sonville. The 75th New York took to the Cane Fields as Skimshers Taring the Fences Down as thay Spread out. To tell you the Truth Fences Suffer some if thay are in the way but at night all the Fence for a long way round the Camps are Torn up to make Fir[e]s to Cook our Food.

We got to Don[ald]sonville about noon and Stacke Arms and went to gnawing hard Bread. Every man was expected to Carry three Days Rations and one Hundred rounds of Catteradges [cartridges], 40 in is Belt & 60 in is Knapsack and it makes a hevy Load to Carry. The men Growle some. The

---

Regiment, 91–2; *Record of Service of Connecticut Men*, 471; Croffut and Morris, *The Military and Civil History of Connecticut*, 316.

Afternoon Turned out Cold, a North Eastern storme. It did not Rain as we expected but the men Huddled togather Like you have seeing Sheep. It took me all Back. Thair was a Catholic Church that the Prist Promised our Col he shouled have if he whouled have the men respect the Place and not Deface it. The Col Promised and after a few words to the men we took Poss[ess]ion. I Guess that Old Church never was so well Filled as it was that night. It was a Curious Looking Congregation. We stayed thair that night. It was my Birth Day the 25th and I never spent a more miserable night then in that Church.[125]

The next morning was Sunday. We started at Six Oclock the 26th. The Wind Blew the Dust into our Eyes and a more Dusty Lot of men you never will see. The Roads a[re] good, not a Stone in the Whole State, as I know. Large Fields of Sugar Cane Line the Roads, Ripe but no Laborers to Cut it all. The White People gon into the Army. All the Negros that we Pased Joind us and it Looked as if our Bissness was to Pick up all the Colerd men and thay to Pick up all the Horse and Mules that thay couled find. The men whouled call a niger up to them and Strap thair Knapsack on thair Back telling them to keep up with them.

We went about 15 mile that Day and Halted for the night. The nigers and men Picked up all the Gees[e] and Turkeys, Chickings and some made good Sup[p]ers. Our Buchers Kil[l]ed Beef anuff for the Whole B[r]igade, takes about 10 to go round. These Cattle are Picked up by our Commissarys as thay Carry nothing but Coffee & Hard Bread for us.

The 27th saw us again on the Road, the 12th Acting as rear gard. About noon [we] Came in sight of the Enmy. The Col halted us, Caused Every mans Canteen to be fil[l]ed and all that had Knapsacks to unsling them, Leaving the two Left Compneys as gard with Fifty men that was on gard the night before. Thay was in [the] Charge of our First Leautenant Francis.

Soon the Ball was opend. The Rebles were on the Right Bank of the Bayou. Thay had Burnt the Bridge and Genral Weitzel had Caused a Flat Boat to be Brought up and had extemprized a Bridge for us to Pass across on. Soon Weitzels Aid Came Down after the 12th. We was orderd up Dubble quick. The Distance was some 2 mile. When we got in sight the Road was full of Cavlery and men retreating out of range of the Shell. We Couled see no Troops but gards and on the other side some 200 nigers Diging Down the Bank so our Artliery

---

[125] Charles turned thirty-four in 1862.

couled get across. The Reble Guns was Droping shell all around us. Thay struck into the Water Close to us as we was Crossing the Bridge that was up to our knees in water but we kept right on. The Screming of the Shell was Muisick that was not to my Liking. Thair Batterys was Paying thair Atention to us having Drove Back our Battery because thay over reached us. Being hevier thay had Forced Back the 8th Newhamshier, 13th Connectcut and 75 New York. The 12th took to the Lots to the Right. Our Compney was orderd forward as Skimshers. We spread ourselves in the Lot and soon found whare the Enmy was hid. Thay had a Large Dich with a Fence in Front. We fell Back on the Redgiment.

Col Coburn gave the word Forward[126] and forward we went over Diches, Fences & Bryers thorn Bushes. The 8th Newhamshier came up at that time. Thay was ordered to take the Battery but thay Brock [broke] and spread themselves over the Ground. We kept on Firing as we went, stoped for nothing. The Rebles was 17 hundred Strong and thay Pi[t]ched thair Le[a]d all over and around us. The Battery gave us six shells a mineut and the only reson that we did not suffer more. We Came up Faster than thay couled get the range. Colburn gave the Word Charge and away we went. Them Guns was Limberd up about suden as thay can do those things. The three Regiments of Rebles took to the Woods right Back of them and the Day was ours. That Fence that thay Lay behind Came Down suden and into the Woods we went or Just before the 13th Came up and Dressed on our Left. Col Burge Came Forward and Proposed three Cheers for the 12th.[127] Thay was given. Then Genral Weitzel Proposed three more and gave us a high Complement. I did not realize that we had don any thing till afterwards. It turned out that we had don all the Fighting.

The Prisnors, Poor Fellows, began to Come in. Compney K was orderd into the Wood and in we went. We soon Brought out a Reble Leutenant and 27 men as Prisnors. We took in all about 200. Picked up some 400 Muskets & Rifles and Lots of Blankets & Canteens that thay had thrown away, took one Brass Canon. Thay [thought thay] had made shure of Capturing the Newhamshier Redgiment [so] thay had sent away thair Cavlery to Cut off our Baggage Train By a nother road. Thay knew nothing of the 12th till we Came upon them. Thay said that if it had not been for the Bleu Hat Regulers, that what

---

[126] Lt. Col. Colburn
[127] Col. Henry W. Birge, Thirteenth Connecticut. Sprague, *History of the 13th Infantry Regiment,* 61.

thay took us for, thay shouled have won the day. After thay Brock our Artilery with a squadron of Cavlery [we] took after them [their cavalry] but thay had a Farry Lower down on the Bayou on which thay Crossed and Burnt the Boats so that thay manedged to get away safe. We Kil[l]ed thair Col. He was Acting Brigadier Genral. He was a fine Looking man. Our Captain Roche Claims the Honer of shooting him. He was shot through the uper Lip the Ball Coming out at the Base of the Brain.

We Camped on the Field with out Over Coats or Blankets. Thay not beain able to Bring the Waggons across till next morning. We have not been given any thing to Drink only Water since we Lef Home. Other Redgiments have had Rations of Wiskey Delt out to them. Our Col and Major is dead set against giving the 12th any Liquor but I have seeing the time when a Little whouled have don the men good. We had a hard night of it.

The next morning, the 28th, the Genral gave us the right of the Brigade. We are marching Left in Front that being the Post of Honer. We having Fairly won it. It was a Beautifull morning. The Brigade Beaing Devided into divisions; the 75th New York and 13th Connectcut taking the Left of the Bayou with one Battery, the 12th and 8th Newhamshier with Perkings Cavlery, the right.[128] Genral Weitzel was Bound not to Let them get away. We felt our way till noon when we found them in our front Drawn up ready for us. Our Line was soon formed in a open Feild. The town of Tibdaux [Thibodeaux] between us and the Rebles. Thay sent us word that thay whouled stand Fight. We sent our Cavlery Down to Road to Draw thair Fire but thay Brock and run. Thay Formed twice for us but whouled not wait but made the Best of thair way toward Berwicks Bay Burning the Bridge Across the Bayou and Setting fire to the Rail Road Bridge 4 mile below us and Burning the Depot whare was stored 15 hundred Hogsheads of Sugar. This is a Sugar Cuntry. We have Come into Poss[ess]ion of any quanity of Sugar and Corn that thay had Stoard but had no time to Distroy. Every Barn is full of Sugar and Corn.

We was sent to open the Opolusia [Opelousas] and Algiers Rail Road so that we couled open up and get Pos[ses]sion of that road. Thair was a nother Brigade that was to Come by the way of the Rail road and meet us at this Place. This Brigade was under the Comand of Genral Dudley. He has two Regiments of Negros that Buttler as Organnized to help and the Rebles undertook to stop

---

[128] Perkins's Massachusetts Cavalry. Ibid., 74.

them but got the worst of it. Thay had to stop and build the Bridge that the Rebles had Burnt about 20 mile from hear. Weitzel sent the 13th Connectcut Down to help them through if nasaray [necessary]. Found them all right and Building the Bridge up and so returned to Camp such as it is.

We started with our Tents and we find the night very Cold. The day after the 13th returned news came that the Gurrilias had Shot six of our Sick men that had to be left in the Hospital with the Wounded. The next morning, November 1st our redgiment with Thomsons Battery[129] and Perkings Cavlery was orderd to return and Punish them if found and Bring our Wounded up to Camp. We caught 30 Gurrillias goin up but when we got to the Hospital we found that thay had not been Molested or injuerd in the Least and that the Inhabitants, or the Wemon Portion of them had been to the Hospital and Brought Beds for our Wounded and thairs Cleen Shirts for the men and every thing that thay couled do for them was don. Thair Wounded was Left on our hands. Thay had about 80 Wounded and thay Promised to do all in thair Power to help our Poor Fellows and we left them and returned to Camp having Marched 26 mile. We got to Camp Preaty well used up and have not been away since.

The Genral and Staff took up is quarters in the House of the Reble Genral that Comanded in theas Parts and [h]is time has been taken up Adminstering the Oath to all those that wish to return to thair Aligance and to thair first Faith. It is a Creole Poppalation that Settles this Part of Louisiana. Thay are as Differant to the rest of the Southron people as two Races can be. Thay are very Rich, own all the Land and can do Just as thay Please, make thair own Laws and read them to Seute themselves. Thay are very Proud but some of that Pride has been taken out of them. The yeenkee thay have never seen till now. Thay Left thair Houses and Put Back into the Cane Brakes. When we first Came we couled not see no one. Some of the me[n] got into the House and helped themselves to what ever thay couled cary away conveanley [conveniently]. Some got money, some Jewlery, someone thing and another. You whouled have thought that thay saved all thair Terkeys & Gees[e] & Chickings for us the way the men and Nigers Brought them into Camp the first two or three Days . But that is played out. The People have taken the Oathe or those that are hear and have Printed Protections so that those that are given to taking things that thay

---

[129] Thompson's First Maine Battery

find in thair way find a Stop Put to thair Pickings and for one I am glad of it for the Inocent Suffer with the Guilty.

What thay will do with all the Nigers that is with us I can not say. Thair is a Big Pile of them. I have one to help me. Nigers and Horse have been very Cheep Latley. The Poor things think this is thair Day of Divliverance. In Pasing by some of the Large Plantations, the Owners having Left them to take care of the Plantations, the Wemon whouled come out and say God Bless you Massa. We do not know you but God in Heven knows you and will Bless you and much more that I cannot rem[em]ber. The men whouled Fall in the rear and it Looked as though we went about Picking up the Slaves.

I must Conclude. I will write you more soon. Virtue you must keep up your Spirits and Cheer up. Providance will do what is Best. Let what will Hapen. Never give up. Keep right on. Kiss that Baby for me and Mother Pray that I may be Preserved from Daingers seeing and unseeing.

From Your Affectnate Husband,
CW Sherman, La

Chapter Eight

Camp Stevens

Camp Thibdaux, La, November 6, 1862[130]

Dear Wife & Chirldren, Mother & all to hom,

I recved your kind letter of October 20th and was glad to hear that you was all well as this Leaves me at Present.

We are Camped at this Place without our tents and have had a North Estearn Blowing for the Last 24 hours and we feel most Froze. You can not Concive how it takes hold of us. Overcoats amounts to but Little to keep out the Wind and the Cuntry is so Level that thair is nothing to Brake off the Force of the Wind. The Sun Shines Bright but thair is no Warmth in it. You to hom I Pictuer to myself setting round a good warm Stove taking what Comfort you can and if you do not it is your own fault.

We shall not stay much longer hear with out our Tents. If thay was hear I whouled like to remain as it is highier & Dryer than to Camp Kerney but we Poor Fellows must go or stay as our wise men that is over us thinks Best for us, but Just now thay get more Curses than Prayers. But it will not all ways last. This war must

---

[130] After the Battle of Georgia Landing on October 27, Weitzel's brigade made a camp, which was called "Camp Stevens," one mile south of Thibodeaux. Food supplies were insufficient, and the troops were sometimes quite hungry. Foraging was a frequent activity. Croffut and Morris, *The Military and Civil History of Connecticut*, 316.

have an end and the Blessings of Peace once more be over this Land. I am glad that you have the Old House repaird. It will be so much Warmer this Winter and save Wood and that is money to say nothing about Comfort.

I recved two Papers from Henry and a Letter. [H]is Writing he can mend. I shouled think I recved two Papers from G[e]orge Der[r]ick but no letter from him or is Father, save one some time ago which I Answerd at that time.

We are goin, so I understand, away from this Place in a Day or so and if you shouled not get any Letters from me for a little time you will understand the Cause. Your Letters will Reach me, go whare ever the good Cause may Call us in the Work of Bringing this Wicked Reblion to a Close. What the End may Be, we can not tell. Please do not Worry about me. I am afraid that Virtue Trubbles more than thair is any need of. I wish she whouled Trust in that Providence that as wa[t]ched over us to this time and relize upon his Providances and goodness to us all.

Fany Sent me a Little Letter which I was Pleased to get. Contineu to Write to me and you will soon learn to Compose. She told me about her and Angline goin to William Hortons Funeral.[131] It was nothing more then right that the People shouled turn out. Thay will realize more of the Horro[r]s of War and the Distress that is in the Land.

What I want to ask you, Wife & Chirldren Mother & Father is this - that if it shouled be my Fortune to Fall in this War, is to Bare it with Spartan Fortitude. The same God that over rules the Destinies of Nations over rules the Destiniey of each Human Beain or Mortal that he as Createad and we must Obey Each Mandate that he sees fit to Issue. I shouled like to return but must do my Duty what ever the Consiquances may be. I do not write in this way to have you truble your minds, but to meet Truble Manfulley and you will be shure to Conquor. You must steel your Hearts in a way so to speak but I have said anuff on that.

We are making Progress. The Planters Come in all the Time to take the Oath and every Little helps to Put a stop to this Truble in this quarter. Genral Buttler as come up from New Orleans this Afternoon and when he moves it means something.

This is a Beautifull Cuntry, raise anything and the Climat suites all Classes of men but still I Fancey Old Connectcut and my Old New England home but

---

[131] William Horton, from Stafford, Connecticut, was a First Lieutenant who fought with Company I, Sixteenth Infantry Regiment Connecticut, and was killed on September 17, 1962, at Antietam, Maryland. *Record of Service of Connecticut Men*, 685.

Money can be made Faster hear then in the Older States but thair is maney things that you whouled Miss hear.

Chirldren Winter is upon you. The Winter School Fire Welcomes you to warm your Little Hands and your Hearts by Learning. Do not Let a single opertunity Escap you to improve your minds. Be Cheerfull but not Boisterous and Loud in your Plays. Love one another and Cause you[r] Mother and Kind Granfather & Mother no more Truble than you can Posable help. I often think of you how you are geting on and how I shouled Like to see you. Dear Wife those pictuers that you have taken the Truble to get I won't have sent. I couled Carey it well anuff in my Knapsack, but I might Lose it Marching round; so a great maney of the men has Lost thairs and all that thay containd. Latley we have to Leave them sudenley sometimes and Trust to Chance to see them again. I am sorry but must forgo the Pleasuer of having them for the Present. I am glad that you got them. Kiss all my Babys and may Heven Bless them and you all is the Prayer of your Affectnate Husband,

CW Sherman, La

Camp Thibodaux, November 8, 1862

Thair was a Tirable Acident on this Rail Road that we have opend from New Orleans to this Place. A Car Load of Aminition exploded Killing 11 men and Wounding 10 more. The Aminition was for this Brigade. We are expecting to go to Berwicks Bay on the Gulf of Mexico. The Corps[e] of one of our men has Just gon Past to is Last Resting Place. He was Shot through trying to get across the Bayou to get out to Forradge. He and a nother was some what in Liquor and was Orderd to stop but Payd no Atention to the Order. The Ball Pased one Inch below is Heart. He lived 3 Days afterward. He Leaves a Wife and two Chirldren and the Maner of is Death will [put] is Poor Wife off from geting any Pension. So you See that when the news of her Husbands Death, there will be another Hearth Stone made Desolate, another Heart whose Sun has gon Down in Darkness, two more Orphans thrown on the Cold Charity of a Cold World. Good By for the Present.

Your Affectnat Husband & Son
CW Sherman, La

Camp Stevens, Bayou Lafauche, Near Tibodauxvill, November 12, 1862
Dear Wife, Chirldren, Father & Mother,

I take this opertunity of writing theas few Lines to you hoping thay may find you Enjoying the Blessings of good health and Contentment for unless you are Contented you can Enjoy no Blessing that our Father gives us.

We are still Encamped on this Bayou and Shall remain hear Some time. Our quarter Master has gon to New Orleans to get our Tents. We have been without Covering now for three Weeks and the nights have been very Cold heavy Frosts such as you do not get, not in Connectcut in November. I have been Laboring under the impression that we was Down South but it must have been a mistake if the nights are anything to Judge by. The Days are Comfortable anuff and we make the Best of our Situation. We are out of Tobaco and that Dose not improve our Tempers. I hope Bragg and Van Dorn will not Molest us at this time as we shall not Leave anuff of him to Swear by. The men feel Crabed and out of Sorts having no Wiskey & no Tobaco. You can Judge how we are but things will Chaing. We are waiting to get our Pay. Thay ow[e] us 4 Months Pay, but we shall not get but two Months.

This Section of Cuntry is a Sugar Cuntry. We are goin to Colect all the Sugar and Molasses at Tiger Vill 12 mile from us. The 8th Newhamshier found 5000 Barels of Sugar Stoard and the Rebles had fixed them so that when our Troops shouled force them to Ske[da]ddle thay Couled Start some Wedges and Let it all go into the Bayou but thay Left in Such a hurry thay forgot to do it and so Left it for us. We Captuerd 1000 head of Cattle and a Lot of Waggons & Mules. Thay Retreated to Berwicks Bay and have thair made a Stand but our Gun Boats have made that Place uncomfortable for them.

November 14th

I recvd your kind Letter of October 20th and was Pleased to hear from you and home. You waite to hear from one and write only one Letter. I write every week if Posable and when not, write 2 or 3 so that I keep ahead. I have never recvd any from Edwin in Answer to my Last and when Henry writes, [h]is Letters have the Look as though he was hard up for time and couled not Dwell or form [h]is Letters. He sends me Papers and that must Cover is other short Comins.

It dose me good to hear that Virtue and the Chirldren & you and Mother are well. It whouled take what little Plasuer I might find in this Life if anything should hapen to any of you and me away. I know that you all think about me and Pray for me and we must Leave the Rest with that Providence that Dose all things well. If you couled get those pictuers taken in a Small or some taken from them I shouled not Care about having them unless thay couled be taken good and Nattural.

Our Tents reached us the night that I got you[r] letter. Thay was Just 4 hours too Late. We have been having the most Splended Wether for two months Past but the Rain fell Just 4 hours before the Tents Came. That made it Bad for us as the Ground was Wet, our Clothes & Blankets all Wet and that is one of the Evils that we have to Enduer.

You say you Shouled Like to have my Minetur but you whouled be Disapointed. I am Preaty Poor in Flesh. I am not as good by one half as when I enlisted. This Life that we have to Lead is trying to the Constitution and we have to make Graves whare ever we stay two Days. Men get Broke Down and soon go under. I can not Stand much Fatague with out Feeling of it sooner than I Fancy but I hope to Pick up this Winter if we do not have any Fataguing Marching to do.

We shall stay hear till we have Colected all the Sugars and sent them to New Orleans to be Sold and in the mean time we [are] goin to have a Millitary and Civile Comission Set hear in Thibodauxvill to hear all Cases. The Planters that is hear have got to Prove that thay have not helped by word or Deed to Carrey on this Reblion. If thay [the Commission] Prove thair Case thay [the planter] Can not recve no money for what ever the Goverment may Se[i]ze of thair Property till after the War Comes to an End and all Plantations that thair Owners have run away and Left, the Comission have Power to work and save what thay can of the Crops of Cane. Thay have the Power to take the Slaves and work them in geting in the Cane. The Goverment [is] finding Rations for them and Paying them Wages. The goverment [is] taking a Lien on the Property for all Expenses Incured of geting the Crops in and geting them to Market. If anything remain the owners get thair Just Share if all as been right with them. Those that are Fighting us at this time if thay Come in and give themselves up take the Oath thair Case will be Sent to Uncl Abraham and recomend them for Mercy.

We are goin and have Se[i]zed all the Property Both Public and Private and all to gather Buttler is doin the thing up Brown this way. If all our Genrales will use a little of Buttlers Firmness and Sound Judgement and do what thay Promis to do if our Public Enemys do not Return from the Evil of thair way. We are at Present Living on the Enemy taking is Sugars & Molasses and Horses and Beef. Our Caverley Bring in some of the most Splended Horses and Mules that Eye whouled wish to see. We have Mules that in good times 6 & 800 Dollers whouled not be to high a Figuer for them and Horses that Cost thair owners over one Thousand Dollers.

We have two Redgiments of Colerd men Holding the Raile Road from Algiers to this Point. Thay are doing us good Serv[i]ce. Thay have Orders not to take any Prisnors so I have been informed. A few Days after thay were Placed on the Line of the Road the Gurrillias took 2 of them and Cut thair Ears off. A few Days afterward thay took 15 Gurrillias, Shot 14 of them, took the other, tied him up over night and the next morning made him Dig is Grave and then Shot him and Coverd him up. Thay have no mercy to Expect from thair Southron Foes and thay must use Serverity to Protect themselves and Compell thair respect. Thay have Enlisted quite a Large number from this Section. Thay make quite good Looking Soldiers. Thay are strong made men, stronger than we are. Thay have nice Frames but we are a Little Tougher then them. A great maney of them take Cold easely.

I am glad to hear that you have the Old House fixed up. It must Look more then a nuff Better to Pay fore the out Lay. I hope to come home and see you all again but thair is much for me to go through before that can be unless this Reblion Shouled come to a Suden End. We are all wishing this thing Brought to a Suden Halt. We see many things that you and those that think thay are Posted in regard to maney things thay can not see or know.

November the 15th

I am well, but a Little Weak. This Fresh meat that we have to Eat makes us some what Loose. Boiled Sweet Potatoes Phisic us.[132] Thay do me. We are geting things in Shape again. The Brigade as got thair Tents and we are Cleering up a nother Drill Ground. We are 70 mile from New Orleans on the Bayou Lafoach[133] and we are sending Ten Thousand Dollars worth of Sugar to New Orleans. We shall Pick up a Large quanity and I hope the other Leaders that have Charge of other Sections of the Cuntry will go and do Like wise.

---

[132] Physic—a remedy for disease, a cathartic, an internal application for the cure of relief of sickness. Used here, the boiled sweet potatoes "cure" the looseness caused by the meat. "Definition of Physic," Brainy Quote, accessed April 23, 2012, http://www.brainyquote.com/words/ph/physic202600.html.

[133] Bayou Lafourche

Virtue keep up your Spirits and Laugh Dull Care a way. I shall come along some fine Morning and take Brakfast. Kiss that Baby for me and Mother Shake up that Arthur for me and Kiss them all round. I shouled Like to see them but must Stay hear or Some whare Els a Spell Longer till Uncl Abraham Calles us home and that time cannot be far Distant.

Give my Love to the Children. Tell them to be good to thair Mother and Granmother and not make them any more Truble than thay can help. Give my Love to Father. Tell him that I will try to do all that he recomends me to do but we have many things to do that is trying to one. Pleas Rember me in your Prayers. I have Faith that my Father in Heven can and will Protect me.

Your Affectnate Husband & Son,

CW Sherman

Please direct your letters as usual. I wish you couled send me some Tobaco but how I can not see. It is worth 2 Dollers a pound here and will be more

Camp Stevens, Louisiana November 16, 1862

Dear Children,[134]

It is with much Plesuer that I answer your Letters. I have been or have had my time so taken up that I couled not atend to you before and that must be my excuse.

I am in a part of our Cuntry that has tried to throw off Alegance to the rest of her Sister States. I never see any Chirldren hear such as you see around you when you go out or go to School. There is no School Houses hear. I have never seeing any. Thair is any quanity or number of Coloured Chirldren, but they are not reconized as Human Beaings but as Chattles by the Local Laws of these Southron States. Thay has been held as property or Slaves with no Will of thair own. Thay has been used as Horses and Mules. It is all Colerd People hear. The White having gon away to fight us. Thair Poor Slaves whouled com out into the road from some Large Plantation House where thair Masters had gone away and Left them. Thair Poor Slaves whouled Bless us as we marched by saying

---

[134] This letter was transcribed by the editor's late father, many years ago. Unfortunately, the original letter has been lost.

that they did not know us but thair Father in Heven knew us and would bless us as they all have an Id[e]a that this is thair Deiliverance and that we have com to Free them. Thay all desert the Plantations all round us, this Section of Cuntry whare we are and Com into Camp. The Goverment has to feed them.

The other morning [while] I was on Gard at the Quarter Master quarters a Mule Team came and brought some Beef. A Cupl of Darkies came and Cut it all up into small Peices and put it into one pile. Soon there came all of the Negro wemon in Camp in two Ranks the same as we Soldiers are some times and has fast has thay came up thay were asked how many Chirldren they had. Some said four, some six and they recved Peices of Meat acording to the number of Little Mouths they had to feed. Thair was not near anuff to go around. You never see such a looking lot of Wemon, bare footed, bare headed and nearly naked. The Goverment can not Clothe and Feed so many people without help from the people to home.

I have written you a very Poor Letter, have not said what I wanted. Tell Lewis to be carefull and not get hurt when he goes into the barn. I send my love to you, Angline, Arthur. Kiss your Mother & Baby & Granmother for me.

Your Father,
CW Sherman, La.

Camp Stevens, Near Tibodaux, November 17, 1862
Dear Wife & Chirldren & Parents,

It is Storming this Morning and I thought that I whouled write you that I am Still alive and well at this time and under Cover and feel much Better Mornings when I get up. The night Dews is what we have to gard against. Thay are Poisenus and very unhealthy. We had Floors in our tents in Camp Parepet and Camp Kerney. Hear some of the men have got Boards about thair Length to Lay on. I have made me a Bunk raised from the Ground and in two Parts so that I can Shut it up. One half makes me a good Seat to set on Deuring the Day. We try to make our selves as Comfortable as we can. We have New Tents, the ones we Brought with us from Old Connectcut got Rotan. This Climate Mildawes everything that has to be exposed to the Wether. It is so Damp in this State. The Land Lays so Low that it is one Cause of Sickness among the Troops and the men are not Carefull anuff to Put on thair over Coats when it Coms night unless thay are on Gard and then thay are Compeld to ware them.

Camp Stevens is Laid out much Better than Camp Kerney. We have more Room. The Land is very Levle hear. We Cleard up the Brush and have Swept the ground Clean and Di[t]ched round our Tents. That is nessary to Carry of[f] the Water when it rains and it dose rain. We are expecting a spell of Rainey Wether but may be Disapointed.

We have the Raile Road open from New Orleans to Berwicks Bay and are Bringin the Sugars in to New Orleans. We have all of Last years Crop and this years we Shall make ourselves so that the Rebles will not get it to sell and use the Money to Buy Arms and to Fight us with.

Genral Weitzel is Disarming the Cuntry and making Every man Bring in is Arms of what ever Discription and if he Proves himself a Loyle Citzen is allowed to keep them. The Arms that we get most of is Duble Barrled Shot Guns and Old Horse Pistols and not very daingrous Arms Alongside of our Enfields. I Fancy them. It is all Day with a Fellow if one of our Mine Balls hits him and he must stand at a Long Distance to get out of the way of them. Thair is some Talk now of the 12th goin Down to the City this Winter and thair may be some Truth in it as our Col is Mayor of New Orleans and our Conduck Latley meets with Buttlers Aprobation.

November 22nd

We are having a nother Cold Spell. It dose nip us some but we must Stick it through at night. I am Put in mind of that Fire that we used to have in that North Room. We have been Burnt this Summer that we feell the Cold more than we otherwise shouled if it had not [been] so hot.

You will have had your Thanksgivin Diner befor this reaches you. I hope you will enjoy your Selves. I shouled Like to be with you but must Put it off this Some more Peacefull tim[e]s. I am in hopes to Live through it, but I find it tryes me some.

We have lost the two Doctors that we Brought out with us and have younger men. Doctor, or Sergeon Le[a]venworth was a very Old man [and] had had great Experance having Spent the Greater Portion of is Life South and knew how to Treat the Peculear Deases that Northen men was Subject to in geting Acclimated. The Boys Called him Old quinine. He having to give them that Drug to them most. He Brought this Redgiment through this Sumer that is Past with out Losing near the men that other Redgiments did. The Vermont & Newhamshier & Maine Redgiments Lost 3 to our one. The 7th Vermont has had to go to Fort Pickings[135] to recrut and Billey Wilsons Lambs have taken thair place.

November 23rd

Dear Wife & Chirldren & Parents,[136]

I recved your Letter of November the 9th and was glad to hear from home and that our Father in Heven as so kindley Wa[t]ched over and Protected my Little ones, Preserved them in health till the Present time. I am well at Present and to Day is Splended. It really makes one feell well if he is not . . .[137] The Wether Puts one in mind of the Best Part of the Indan Summer that [we] have [in the] North Some tim[e]s.

You must not Let the Simple Fact that I am trying to do my Duty Truble you. If it Shouled be my Fortune to Fall it whouled Still be your Duty to your Self to Put on a Stiff uper lip and meet the Frowns of this World as you all ways have and again you whouled still have the Satisfaction of knowing that I Lost my Life in a good Cause and that no one have given more for the Cuntry of thair Adoption then you had. You couled Still hold up your Head that you had Paid as havey a tax for the Presarvation of the Union as the Proudest in the Land. Do not be Disheartene God will in is own good time Bring order out of Disorder and the Olive Branch of Peace will once more Shed its Blessings over this Land. The time can not be fare Distant when the Old Flag of the Union will Flote in undisturbed Poss[ess]ion of the Whole of theas Confederat States. The People of the now Disturbed States rejoice when ever the Old Flag Come near them in the Tide of War. When ever we can Asuer them of our Protection from thair more Rabid Naibors, thay Flock round Headquarters to take the Oath[138]

---

[135] Fort Pickens
[136] Part of the same letter, but new date and salutation
[137] He didn't finish this thought.
[138] Butler issued General Order No. 41, which stated that all foreign-born who had lived in the US for five years and had not sought the protection of their government in that time were deemed to be citizens and must take an Oath of Allegiance to the United States. John D. Winters, *The Civil War in Louisiana* (Louisiana State University Press: 1991), 130, accessed April 23, 2012, http://books.google.com/books?id=PjicJWUQhPYC&printsec=frontcover&dq=th

and those that still hold out are Brought by the Force of Circumstances and by kind Word and a Knowledge that any Duble Dealing Leads to shure Distruction, keeps them true till the Trubled Waters settle. We are working slowley but Shurely in Bringin this Part of the South Back into the Union.

I am Sorry to hear that Virtues Sister is so Daingerously Sick. I do not know how Virtue couled do otherwise then to go to see her Sister and do what she couled for her but am afraid that she will Work her self Down Sick. She ought to be carefull for who whouled Come to help her? As to taking her Sisters Baby I do not see how She couled as She has work anuff to Look after her own Babys and I insist that thay Shall not be neglected. It is hard to Put the Little ones out to the Cold Charitys of this World but such is the Fate of many in this World. What is right I am willing Virtue Shall or may do but to Burden her self at this time whouled be doing her self Wrong. [I am] hoping that Mother and you Father will co[u]nsul or Advise her for the Best which [I]know you will.

That Snow Storme that you had must have taken you all by Surprise. I hope you have a good Wood Pile to meet the Rigor[ou]s Cold Wether that must be upon you by this time. Those Pictuers I know not what to say to you. I shouled like them. If we get down to the City this Winter I shall Cirtainley have them [take] my Pictuer. You can not have [it] at Present as I am 60 mile from New Orleans and have no money. When thay will Pay I do not know. Virtue must be in want of some Money. She shall have it as soon as [I] can get Payed.

Tell Virtue & Mother that thay must keep up thair Curadge and be of good Curadge for all will work round for the Best. Kiss my Babys and may Heven Preserve and Bless them and you all. Give my Love to Virtue. Mother and Dear Father take a Large Portion to your self and what Ever betide. Never give up is the Motto of your Husband & Son,

CW Sherman

Camp Stevens, Near Tibodaux, November 29, 1862
Dear Wife & Chirldren & Parents,

I am well at this time and Enjoying Some of the Tallest kind of Wether at this time. Our thanksgiving Passed over with some Little Fun for the Boys. The Officers Put up 50 Dollers in prizes. The first thing was a Race for 3 Greac[e]d Pigs, Shaved and Greac[e]d so that those that Loved that kind of Sport had thair fill. The next was Climing a Greac[e]d Pole with a Orange on top. The one that took it Down to have Ten Dollers. No one was Able to Clime it but one of the men he Put two Rop[e]s round the Pole and took a Bag of Ashes and Sprinkled the Pole so that he couled hang long anuff to move up is Rop[e]s. He got the Ten Dollers after every one that was a mind to had Greaced them selves up to thair Hearts Content.

The next thing was a Runing Match which was won by one of Compny K but what Pleased me was we got two Months Pay on thanksgiving Day which you will get as soon as I can Send it. Thair is some talk of thair Paying two Months more and if thay do it will be Just what will Suite me and you will be Able to Buy the Baby a Frock and Mother do not for get to Lay in a suply of Snuff. I can not be thair to do it my Self. Please to think that I shouled Like to See you all and know that you was Comfortable and making the Best of what Fortune may have in Store for us all.

I am geting to be uneasey at the Delay that our Generales have Weasted Valueable time on the Potomac. No one that knowes that two and two makes four can Deny thay have had Drilled Redgiments anuff to Steady the Raw Recruits or the New Redgiments that have has[t]end to Soport the Stars that had begun to Wane, men anuff to have Turnd the Tide of Suckcess in our favor with such a Rush that it whouled have Swept the Reblion out of the Land but thay Let the Day go by and can not be Brough[t] Back only through the Loss of 30,000 men for us. I may be mistaken but I am Afraid that it will be to[o] True.

The Newes of the Removel of McCellen[139] has Just Com to us and for one it is what I have Prayed for and have allways told those that I have talked with when

---

[139] George Blinton McClellen. Various sources show that he had many differences with Lincoln and other military leaders, which ended his career as a Union Army leader. He often had to be ordered to take military actions, defied his superiors, and had an overly cautious attitude. He avoided battle and, apparently, threw away many opportunities for victory, which would have meant an earlier end to the war. He was removed from

Speaking of our Leaders that Burnsides[140] whouled Com upermost and Lead us through the Darkness that was Gathering over the Land. This making a Suckcessfull Retreat is not the thing that News Paper writers Represent and how the People can Suck such Nonsens Down is Pasing Straing to one that has had a Smal Look behind the Curtain. But some men are not Satisfied unless thay are Fooled with and Rob[b]ed of what Little Sense and Money thay Posess and then it is a hard matter to make them beleave that thay have been used as the Monkey used the Cat to Pull the Chestnutts out of the Fire. But we must still Press on through all Difficultys and Blunders. We shall all see Day Light again. It is all ways Darkest Just befor Day. Uncl Abraham and Burnsides will Clear up the Clouds that now hide the Sun of Freedom from us all. It will be all right.

Cheer up we are sending the Sugars of Louisiana to you to sweeten things North. Kiss them Babys for me and shake that Arthur up for me.

Your Affectnate Husband & Son,
CW Sherman

---

command on November 5, 1862. He opposed Lincoln in the 1864 election. Charles Bracelen Flood, *1864 Lincoln at the Gates of History* (New York: Simon and Schuster Paperbacks, 2009), 37–8; Catton, *The Civil War*, 60, 62, 310; Kennedy Hickman, *American Civil War: Major General George McClellan*, accessed April 23, 2012, http://militaryhistory.about.com/od/americancivilwar/a/McClellan.htm.

[140] Maj. Gen. Ambrose Burnside, Rhode Island. He took over for McClellen on November 7, 1862. He tried to get around Gen. Lee's forces at Fredericksburg, but waited too long for transport across the river, giving Lee enough time to fortify the heights west of town. Burnside suffered heavy losses in the Battle of Fredericksburg on December 13 and offered to resign. The next month, he attempted a second offensive, which was unsuccessful due to heavy rains and was dubbed the "Mud March." Lincoln replaced him with Maj. Gen. Joseph Hooker on January 26, 1863. However, Burnside later had a successful command in Tennessee. Flood, *1864 Lincoln at the Gates*, 127; Catton, *The Civil War*, 115–119, 127; Kennedy Hickman, *American Civil War: Major General Ambrose Burnside,* accessed April 23, 2012, http://militaryhistory.about .com/od/americancivilwar/p/burnside.htm.

Camp Stevens, Bayou Lafourche, Reserve Brigade, LA, November 30, 1862
Dear Wife and Chirldren, Parents,

I take this opertunity of Writing a few Lines to you hoping thay may find you Enjoying the Blessing of Health and Contentment as the Good Book says a Contented mind is a Continual Feast.

I am well at Present and Waiting for Newes of the Taking of that Last Reble Strong Hold, Richmond. If Burnsides will only Brake up that Army and Send Part of the Troops this way we shall be Delighted to Recve them. We are on the only Road that thay can Come and it will be thair Fault if we do not Meet. Onley Drive them this way, thair Travling Expenses will Be Paid to New Orleans with the Greates Pleasuer and Board thrown in By Genral B. F. Buttler. We were up throughout the other night by the Long Roll being Beaten and a Continus Fire kept up by the Pickets. It did Look a Little Squalley. We was all ready. Genral Weitzel Rode along our Line and then our Major Sung out to by the Right of Companeys, "to the Rear Parade is Dismissed," and the men Turnd in again. Genral Weitzel Complimented the Brigade in a Genral Order on thair Promptness in Turning out. It Showed that when thair is any Work to be Don this Brigade can Walk in and do it up in a Work man like maner. When we go in we shall Win.

I told you that when we Started from Camp Kerney that if thair was anything in the way we shouled move it and we did. The Rebles had us at a Disadvantadge but we soon Put them to thair Mettle and found that thay whouled not stand Cold Steel. Thay waited till we got about two Rods of them with a Fence between us then thay Brock and Skaddled [broke and skedaddled]. Thay gave us Fits. Thay Brought 6 Canon to Bear on this Redgiment and 17 Hundred Rifles. The only thing that Saved us, we came up Faster then thay Lowerd thair Guns, or Range — thay had it maney times but we stepted out of Range and Left them to get it again. Thay had a fair Chance fore a Mile and a half in a Open Lot. Thay was in a Dich and thay ought to have Cleand us out with the Advantadge thay had of us. Thay formed in Line 3 times to Dispute our Pasadge to this Place. We formed to meet them, but thay thought thay might as well get out of the Way and retier wich thay did, Burning the Bridges to Prevent our Foll[ow]ing them, one of them was New cost 25000 thousand Dollars, and Burnt 27 hundred Barrles of Sugar. Thay Left in Such a Hury thay had not the time to Spair. Genral Brags home is in this Town and the Reble

Govnor Moor[141] and Reble Legeslatuer was hear but thay kept out of the way and got to Berwicks Bay but thay have beaing Drove out of thair, but whare thay are now I know not and do not Care. We are good for them.

December 1st, 1862

Dear Mother, this morning is the first of December but as unlike what the first Month of Winter is with you as two things can be Differant. This Morning is as Miald as May in England not the Mays we have in New England, but the first thing we Shall have will be a North Wind that will Cut through us, the Sun Shining all the time and not a Cloud to be Seeing. Our Redgiment is getting all the Detached Service. Our Col Deming is Mayor of the City of New Orleans. Our Leautenant Col Colburn has taken Charge of the New Orleans and Opolousise [Opelousas] Rail Road that we have opend and others has got apointments of Different Dutys. If G[e]orge De[r]rick had Enlisted in this Redgiment he whouled have Got a Bearth hear as thay want good Penmanship and a Knowledge of Bissness. I know of Some [who] are qualified that if thay will onley mind Number one, can make a Pile and not Rob the Goverment. Theas apointments are Permement as the Goverment will keep a Strong Grip on this State. I wish that I was Able to get on Detached Service, Let it be ever so Sleight as it whouled give me 40 Cents a Day besides my Pay from the Goverment as an Enlisted man.

I hope that Providence will Spair my Life and Prosper me so that I can give my Chirldren a good Bisness Education so that thay Can take Advantage of what Providence may Put in thair way and that thair Path May be Easier and Brighter then yours or Mine. Dear Mother, your and Fathers Expearance of Life has had some Bright Spots with many Dark ones. I Shall try to make your and my own Days, if I am Spaird to Return home again, Safe, Easyer then it has been. If I can not Live without Racing all over the Cuntry I do not wish to Live but I think I can. I Shall try to if I ever get home again.

I wish you whouled get a few Sheep and Let me know how Virtue gets along with her Cow and how those Steers get Along. I expect you to get me a teem by the time I get home So that I can do some thing for my Self if things turn out right. Let me know how things go round Home and what is the Prospect

---

[141] Confederate Gen. Braxton Bragg; Confederate Governor Thomas Overton Moore of Louisiana

& Henry ought to have helped you fix up the Old House and Saved you a few Dollers. Henry Sends me Papers for which I am thankfull to him for his Letters is Breife anuff, but is time is taken up in Bisness so that he has no time to write very full. I must be thankfull fore Small Favors. Uncle Derrick has no Paper I sopose and G[e]orges time is taken up so that he has but verry Little for himself. Theas People may think it a Small thing and of no account but any one out here among Straingers Like to hear from America for this Place is not in the United States, nor never was and only Federal Bayonets will keep it whare it is.

Father you whouled Like to be in our Tent Some times. We have a Sargent of the Good Old English Stock who gives us Some of the Tallest Fiddleing. He has a Fidle that he Confiscated when he came hear that whouled make is Fortune if it was to Home. Amos Bray is Ready to give us, 'is Frends, Sweet Straines from is Fiddle, or give his Enemies Mine Balls from his Good Enfield Rifle. His Fidle knocks of[f] the Rugh Corners of our other wise Tough Times.

Virtue, I have a Prospect of Sending you 40 Dollers at this time. You must have thought that I had forgot you and them Babys but that is not so. We have to Waite for the Pay Master and he Genral[ly] takes is time before he Showes is Face to Poor Fellowes like us. I hope you have not been in want of anything Since I sent you the Last Pay. I may get my first State Bounty for this year that will soon be up on us. If so I shall Send it all to gather. Things is very High with you at this time So I understand. Do the Best you Can and keep up a Cheerfull Disposition and a Stout Heart. Let nothing Daunt you but think of the other Poor Wemon that have Lost thair Husbands. Providence as Mercifulley Spaird me to the Present time and we must Trust in Providence and hope allways. Never give up. That is the way Difficultys are overcom. It may be Dark now but Light will Come and the Clouds will Pass away and Times will Brighten.

I Hope you will have a good Schooll this Winter and that the Chirldren may be Able to go Steadley and then thay will Learn. Give my Love to them and have them kiss thair Mother and Gran Mother for me and may Heven Bless them Preserve them in health. I want them to be good Chirldren and Help thair Mother all thay can, give her as Little Truble as Posable. She as Care anuff and maney things to Truble her that thay can not understand.

Please do not Truble about me, my Father in Heven will do with me what Seameth him good. I send my Love to you all. Do your Duty to yourselves and Leave the Rest with God.

Your Affectnate Husband & Son,
CW Sherman, LA

Please put me a good pen in your letters to me. Thay ask 5 Cents for a pen. This way you can send a extra Sheet of paper in your letters and a few Postage Stamps. I shouled Like in writing to you it whouled be better to have one and it 5 Cents for what you can get for one to home and a Pen or more can be Sent as well as not. Thair is nothing Lower then 5 Cents hear, no Pennes.[142]

Camp Stephens, La, December 3, 1862

Dear Wife & Chirldren,

I take this opertunity of Writing theas few Lines to you hoping thay may find you in good health as theas Leaves me at Present. I have Just Sent you 40 Dollers by Adams Express Freight & Insurance was one Doller. I hope you will recve it Safe. Please Write me as Soon as Recved. My First State Bounty I expected to get to Day but must Put it off as the Captain has to make out two New Pay Rolls and did not have the Time to Spair. It is not Due but if I can Send it you may Proberley get the Money on it of[f] the Bank. We Shall have to waite along time before we Shall get any more Pay. I hope we Shall not get Payed but once more but we can not tell. It may be Some time yeat befor this Truble may be over and it may be over befor Spring. The Sooner the Better.

Keep up good Heart, make your Self as Comfortable as you can. I shall be along Some Day and if we do not have a Time it wont be my Fault. Clear the Kitchen Mother and Cheer up. I kind awant to See those Snow Drifts that you will be having Soon. This Continual Sameness Dose not Suite me. I want Chainge. It Comenced to Rain Last night as we had Just Turnd in and as our Tents did not Leak I Fanc[i]ed that it Felt good. We have had no Rain [for] so Long we wanted Some but it makes Preaty Mudy Walking and our Tents Dose not Look as though thay was as Clean as thay might be but we Put up with theas Inconveance and Laugh and Talk. You would think that we was Settling this or our Trubles by making our Tent as Noisey as Posible. It Cirtainley Dose not Sett a very good Exampl for the men to go by, for the Non Commissiond Tent

---

[142] This was added at the bottom of each page, written upside down. Some of the writing was cut off during the copying process. This letter was transcribed from copies.

to raise Ned,[143] but the Fact is men can not forget that thay Whare Boys once and a little Fun hurts no one.

December 4th

One of our Corproals and a Sargent got a Little High. The Corproal took the Sargents Money, Went out and Gambled it and is own away. 70 Dollers or so but no one will Suffer but themselves. A Grate many Lose thair Money Every Pay Day but still men will not Learn by Expearance. Still Punish themselves and Bring thair Frends into Truble. Do not take any Truble on my Acount. I shall Let thair Louisiana Rum alone as it has Bueard [buried] numbers of our men and will. You Can not keep Liquor from men if thay have Money to get it.

This morning is very Dull, Wet and it makes things Look Dull in Camp, but the Sun is Shining and will warm us up again. I Should Like to See how the Old House Looks now it is fixt up. You will be all the Warmer this Winter. Dress the Chirldren Warm and make them as Comfortable as you can. I should like to See them and Shall Soon. I know this War can not Last much Longe[r]. The Cuntry can not Stand the Strain. Whare is the Money to Com from? This question must be Settled. It can not be Carr[i]ed on a nother year. If thay intend to take up the Paper all ready Issued thay must Come to an understanding, Conquor or give the thing up. So Hury up the Cakes, do what is to be Don right away.

Give my love to the Chirldren and tell them I want them to go to Schooll and Learn all thay can. Kiss that Arthur and give him a Shake for me. I Send my Love to you all and all Enquiring Frends.

From your Affactnate Husband & Son,

Charles W. Sherman

Ne[a]r Tibodaux, Bayou Lafoursh, La

---

[143] This was a common expression in New England during that time, meaning to create a disturbance, similar to "raise Cain." James Maitland, *The American Slang Dictionary* (Chicago: R. J. Kittredge & Co., 1891), 217, PDF e-book.

Camp Stevens, Bayou Lafaurch, La, December 8, 1862

Dear Wife & Chirldren,

I take Grate Plasuer in Writing theas few Lines to you hoping thay may find you Enjoying the Blessings of Health and having a Hearty Relish of Life so that you can Enjoy all that the Giver of Life Intened. We all Shouled without Murmering or finding fault with our Lot in Life.

To Day is Sunday. We have Just Come in from Inspection. We have to be up and Dressed Sunday Mornings. Clothing all Cleand and nicly Packed in our Knapsacks, Plates all shined, Rifles in Such a State that the White Gloves of our Officers Can not be Staind nor a Speck of Dust on them. Everything as Neat as though we was goin to Church. The unluckey Fellow that forgets to Shine is Shoes gets Extra Duty. If the men Cary out the Habits of Neatness that thay have to Learn hear, thay will go home Better men then when thay Left Old Connectcut.

The Wether is quite Cool, the nights Frosty. Our Tent as manedged to Get hold of a Small Stove and Pipe and as we turn in for the night get out the Coffins, as some of them Call our Bunks, [and] mak[e] up a fier. It dose Put one in mind of the Comforts of home. We Expect to Winter hear as far as we can See at Present. Some thing may turn up and give us Some thing Els[e] to do besides Gard Duty and Drilling. Things Remain about the Same. The Leafs of the Trees are falling Except the Live Oak and Cypruss and Natuer is Puting on or making Praperations for her Winters Sleep South. You are Wharaped up with a Mantle of Snow and Ice by this time in your Northen Homes and as the Long Winter Months Come and Pass away we Shall be remined of the Seleigh Rid[e]s that we have had and the Cold Cuting Wind & Snow that we have Faced and wish our Selves Back again.

And we live in Hopes of Seeing our homes once again but till that Day that the Order Shall be given to Pack knapsack and Fall in for our March Homeward, the Union all Safe and the Reblion Put Down and our Old Flag Floting in Security over a once Devided but now United and Contented and Happy Nation, till that time arives, we must Put our Best Foot Forward and with a Steady Front to the Enemy Crowed him into the Gulf of Mexico or Some other Hot or Wattery Place.

The 12th is Doing as well as men can. The Redgiment is Preaty healthy. We can muster about 600 men Which is Doing well for a Redgiment in this Climat and that as been in Servic one year. We started from Hartford with 950 men. You can see how it is that our Armeys Melt away when thay get to work.

The ninth Connecut has been filled up twice and to Day thay Can not turn out men anuff for Gard Duty. Thay have been in New Orleans for the Last 4 Months. Rum and Wemon as used them up as well as Service. The Vermont and Newhamshier and Main[e] Redgiments have Sufferd in the Loss of men more then the Massachusetts and Ind[i]ana and Michagan Redgiments. The Loss of men in Battle is Small Compair with the Loss of men by D[is]ease and Pining away. Men get Home Sick and get Down and then it is all up with them. If thay get in the Hospital it is Shur Death. You need not have any gloome fears about me. Give my Love to the Chirldren and accept a Large Share your Self.

Your Affectnate Husband and Son,

CW Sherman

Camp Stevns, Bayou Lafaurch, La, December 8, 1862

Dear Wife & Chirldren & Parents,[144]

I recved your kind Letter of the 22 Second. I was glad to hear that you had recved that Letter as I knew you whouled be Anxious to hear from me from what I wrote when we Started from Camp Kerney. I am as Tickled as you that I was Spaird to Come out Safe. It was a warm Road that we had to Travle for two Hours. The acount that I see in the Papers is a one Sided acount. Genral Weitzel ought to have given the 12th more Credit, but that he couled not do I sopose with out making hard Feelings between the other Redgiments, but the Fact is the 12th Saved the 8th Newhamshier from Being Cut off and did all the Fighting. The 13th never Came up till after the 12th had forced the Rebles to Skeddall. The 13th fierd one Volley over our Heads as thay was Coming up which did no good and was as likely to kill Some of us as the Enemy.

I want our Frends to home to understand the Real facts as the 13th as one Officer that as had Some Conection with News Papers that Puffs them to thair Hearts Content and the Fact that we marched Left in front the next Day, that is the 12th had the Post of Honer, till we reached this Place. It may be a Small matter to Some, but those Engadge[d] feell and know that we have not had our

---

[144] He wrote two letters on the eighth.

meed of Praise and Soldiers love to be taken Notis of and Praised as much as Smaller Fry.

We do not expect anyone to truble us whare we are at Present. Thay are making Araingments above us to Cleen the River out and make a Cleen thing of it. The Enemy has Drawen immense Suplies by the way of Texas and the Federal Army has not being in a Condition to move Afectiveley till the Present time.

I shouled like to be to home to Help you get that Pork in the Celler, but you must excuse me for the Present. I Hope Henry will make you a Visit. I have writen 3 or 4 Letters to Henry but have not recved any Answer. I sent two or more to Southbridge and two to Springfield but Wether he as got them or not, I know not. I shouled like to know.

Virtue and the Chirldren, I hope, will Enjoy them Selves and make themselves as Comfortable as thay can. Mother and you must take Life as Easey as you can and I shall Write as often as I can and I hope this Winter will Witness the Down Fall of Reblion and the return of all the Armeys of the Union to thair homes and Frends. Thair has been Blood anuff Spilt in this Fratcidal War. Maney a Home will be Desolate for ever, the Light of whose Hearth Stones having gon out in Darkness.

I do not know but I shall go Down to New Orleans this Week and if I can get my Minetuer taken with out Costing to much I Shall and Send it Home. You can send me those of the Chirldren if you have got them Taken Smaller. I shouled think you couled get them taken good and Sent to me. Whare are all the Degarian Seloons[145] that was in Evary Villige? Mother, you must see that Virtue dose not work herself Down Atending on her Sister. As to her taking that Baby, I do not see how She can do it. Give my Love to the Children and kiss that Baby. I send my love to you all.

Your Affactnate Husband & Son,
CW Sherman, La

---

[145] Daguerreotype saloons. A daguerreotype is an early type of photograph developed by Frenchman Louis Jacques Daguerre. Kenneth E. Nelson, "A Thumbnail History of the Daguerreotype," The Daguerreian Society, accessed April 23, 2012, http://daguerre.org/resource/history/history.html.

Camp Stevens, December 14, 1862

Dear Wife & Chirldren,

I take this opertunity of writing a few Lines to you to Let you know that I am well at this time. I have being waiting fore a Letter and expected one by the Last two Mails, but was Disapointed.

We have being having a Spell of Lowery[146] wether and have being having a therough inspection by Acting Brigadier Genral Dudly of the 31st Massachusetts and he found things not what thay Shouled be. He found the men in our Redgiment wanted Shoes, Shirts, Caps & gave the Major Fits. Told him that any man that whouled Leave is Redgiment to go Railroading or at anything Els[e] in the state thay was in, whouled Steal. He hit our Coll in that. I am glad thay or Genral Buttler will have a Chance to know how we have been used and Enspected our Quarters. [He] came upon our hard Bread, Looked at, Smelt of it. "Is this what you feed soldiers on?" says Dudley, "It is not fit to Feed Hogs on." And that was the Truth. When we Started from Camp Kerny thay Put 10 Days Rations aboard the Teams for us and that Hard Bread was full of Worms and Bugs. I for one Couled not Eat them till Hunger Compeld me to. I do not know but that is the way to Treat men. If this Goverment can not give its Soldiers Decent Bread it is time to Stop runing the Machaine. The Regulations Say that the Rations shall be So and so, weigh so and so, but in one years Expearance I have not found the first thing Come any whare near what the Regulations Says thay Shall. Our Redgiment has gon Hungery when thair was no Acasion for it and no excuse to use men so.

I do not write this because I am Dissatisfied with my Condition or to find Fault but to tell the thing Just as it is. When our inspector Genral finds Fault with the Manedgement of things it is no harm to State what he found Fault with. Genral Dudley stated to us that Genral Buttler Loved is Soldiers and wanted to know how thay was geting on and had Sent him to See into the Condition of his men as he Couled not Come himself. He [h]as a Chanc[e] of informing Genral Buttler that he found some of his men Bare Footed, Shirtless and Bare Headed nerley and now he can have a Chance of doing Some thing for is men.

---

[146] Lowery, Adjective, 1. Cloudy; gloomy; lowering; as a lowery sky; lowery weather. *Merriam-Webster*, s.v. "lowery," accessed February 17, 2014, http://www.merriam-webster.com/dictionary/lowery.

I have been trying to Get to New Orleans for two Weeks. The Major Gave me a Promis that I shouled go and I shall this Week and if I do I shall Send my Profile if you will take it.

Samuel Wicks I have not seeing Since Leaving Camp Kerny, but I expect to if I get down to the City. We Left him Sick in Camp Kerny when we came away. He has had the Chills Caused by his own carlessness.

December the 16th

The most of our Boys that was Left behind Came up Last night from Camp, but Wicks. He and a few more was Left. I must tell you a little news. Major Genral N. P. Banks with [h]is Fleet Lays Down to New Orleans. The River is full of Transports with Troops on Board. It is a great thing for Banks to get away with out Letting everyone know whare he is goin. It Looks like Work some whare. The Missippi will Stand a Chance of Being Cleerd out and Vicksburge will get Warmer.

The Wether is Just right for work and the Rebles this way will be kept moving. Pleas keep up your Curadge and take Care of your Selves thair to Home. My Little ones are Treading the Snow Down on thair way to Schooll by this time. Snow has a Peculer Charm for me and I Shouled Like very much at this time to be to home. Give my Love to the Chirldren and Accept a Large Share your Self,

CW Sherman

Camp Stevens, Bayou Lafourche, La, December 21, 1862
Dear Wife, Chirldren & Father & Mother,

I take this opertunity of Writing theas Lines to you as I may not have a nother Opertunity for Some time as we are under Marching Orders onece again, but whare to, we can not tell, but Rumor Says we Shall Bring up at Baton Rouge the Capital of Louisiana, and whare our Forces have being but was with Drawin after the Battle Last Sumer. But now Genral Banks has taken the Comand of the Department of the Gulf. Banks has Relieved Buttler. Banks takes in Texas. He has Brought 30,000 men with him, So thay Say, and are goin to Reform the

Brigades. We are goin to be Brigaded with the Connecticut Redgiments, one Ola [Oklahoma] Redgiment with 4 New Redgiments.

I have not being Able to get Down to the City and Shall have to Put it off till a more Favorable opertunity. Genral Weitzel is Acting Major Genral and Some thing has got to be Don if I have to do it my Self. The first of Janury is Preaty near and I for one feell Anxious to know how the Leaders of the Southeron People will Act in regard to Uncl Abraham's Proclimation.

We are Crowding them hard this way, Bringin them into Short Corners. Thay have no Flour, Salt, Shoes, Clothing, nor anything, no Tea, Coffee and thay must have Sufferd more than thay are willing to own up to. Thay hang out with a will and are Bound to give us all the Truble thay Can but we Shall have to give them a few more Lessons be fore thay will own up. Beat to all Apperances at Present, thay are goin to give us Some Truble to get into Vicksburge but it must be taken, Cost what ever it may. It makes me feel Sav[a]dge to think how we have to be moved about and knocked round through them but thair time will Come and then the Day of Reconing will Come. If our Leaders use the means that thay have in thair hands with a will this Winter, this Reblion will be Crushed and Peace Rain onece more a round us and over us.

The Whether hear is Cool and Plesant Days but the nights are Frosty. I have had to get me a nother Blanket. The one I Drew in Camp Lyon was very Poor nothing to it. I took as much Care of my Blanket and more then Maney did, but my Blanket got thinner every Day.

Thair has being a great Deal of Cheating among those that had the Fiting out of the Redgiments.[147] The first Clothing & Blankets that was Served out was much Better then those that was Drawing Later. I have, with others, got to Pay as much as thay that had Better things Served to them. I Shouled Like to Send my Ind[i]a Rubber and Woollen Blankets home to Let you and others see how theas Contractors Punish the Vollenteer in Selling him Poor Clothing & Blankets at a Price that ought to buy him good Servisable things. Thair are hundreds of theas Blood Suckers that are Sucking the Life Blood of the Nation in a thousand ways. We are Allowed 42 Dollers Per year for Clothing but most of the men will be in De[b]t to the Goverment for the first year. All those things that is furnished by Uncl Sam for the first fiting out is Charged to him, but if

---

[147] He's referring to the sutlers, contractors in charge of "fitting out" the Regiments with various supplies.

the things are good, the Second year the Soldier will not want to take up the 42 Dollers Allowed to him unless by Carlessness he loses them. In our next Payment the Money will be Deducted from it what is taken up Above what is Allowed by Goverment.

My State Bounty I can not Draw till next Month. The State having sent a Ci[r]culer to the Officers not to give them out till we have been in the Service a year from the Date of Enlistment and if a Poor Fellow Shouled Die be fore the 4 Months was up, he not have it Drawn or whouled not be Entitled to it. I am writing of things Just as thay are, not to have you feell Down or Dispirited. It is allways Best to know how we stand and what is to be Expected. 30 Dollers Per year is all the Bounty that I am Entitled to from the State of Connectcut. The Nine Months men get more but I have no right to Complain.

We Shall have to have two more Sergants apointed for our Compney. I stand a Little Chanc of geting one of the Bearths but can not tell. Thair is our Old Ordley in the way. He is in the Ranks now having had is Stripes taken off Last Sumer. He may be Chosen has he is one of the Best Drilled men in the Redgiment. I shouled like to get in has it whouled give me five Dollers Per month more. If I can hang on till next Sumer, thair will be Chances anuff.

You to home are keeping your Selves warm. I take it that the Winter as set in by this time. Lewis and the Girles are Sliding Down Hill I sopose. I hope thay will Enjoy themselves and have all the Sliding down hill thay want. I used to Like to Coast it Down Hill and Stay out in the Moonlight Evanings and Enjoy my Self, nothing Like Good Frosty Wether. I wish I couled be thair but must Stay a Spell Longer.

I wish we was Back to New Orleans as the Oranges are Ripe and you can get them Ten for a Dime. Thay Bring them up to Camp from thair and Sell them 5 cents a Peice and thay go like hot Cak[e]s. Thay have Cut Down any quanity of Orang Trees round our Old Camp, Camp Parepet, to have a Chance to use thair Big Guns if Van Dorn Shouled give them a Chance.

Give my Love to the Chirldren and may Heven Bless them and you all. I Send my love to you. Keep up your Curadge all will be well.

From Your Affactnate Husband & Son,
CW Sherman

I hope you had a good Thanksgiving.[148] We did not have much of a Time. Some of the men Enjoyed themselves Some but that kind of Fun did not Suite me. I am glad to hear that you had a good Pig this year. That is some Encuradgement. I Shouled like to have being to Home but we will waite till a nother thanksgiving Come round.

I hope you had a good Crope of Oats. The Straw is worth Something and I think that thay may be raised in Willington to Pay with Buckweat. I want to finish what we begun and I think with that Little Farmer that will be Climing whare he ought not that Some thing can be Don Evan in that Poor Town. I was Sorrey to hear that Lewis has got hurt again. Tell him that he must be more Careful or he will not be Able to Hold that Plow and Cut that Swath of Grass that I expect him to. Tell him that he must be more Careful and not Climbe whare thair is no use for him and to Rember that I want him to help me when I come home and he will not be Able to if he Contineues to Brake and Sprain is Limbs. He must keep off the Ice and not get on to that Pond this Winter.

You tell me that Virtue as taken that Baby of Sissions.[149] I was in hopes that She whouled not take it as she will not get any more then what She as taken, that old Cow will not near Pay her for what She has don allrady for her Sister. Virtue [h]as, or did have, work anuff before She took that Baby. Must She take every young one that Comes along? If we did not have so many Chirldren to take Care of, it whouled not be so far out [of] the way. That Sissions will not Pay any more then he [h]as. I do not Fancy the Breed. I know it is hard for her Sister but She Brough[t] it upon herself. She Broke the Law of her Being and Natur has Pun[i]shed as She will when her Lawes are Broke. I do not think it was right to take that Baby, but as She [h]as taken it, She can keep it. If Virtue can take as good Care of her Chirldren as befor well and good, but I am afraid She can not. She must be her own Judge as to Matters and things in Genral. It is well to do all the good we can, but we are not bound to Injuer ourselves by so doing. I hope it may be all for [the] Best. I may be mistaken, but we will Trust in Providance.

Chrismas as Come with us but it was rather a Sorry Chrismas. Soldiers do not get much Chance to Enjoy themselves. Thay keep us Pend up with Gards,

---

[148] This letter is incomplete and has no date, location, or salutation. By the contents, I have placed it at the end of December 1862. The location at that time would have been Camp Stevens, Louisiana.

[149] Sissons, Virtue's sister

can not get out side of our Camp, Gards between Each Redgiment as though we was Enemyes. I have not been Able to get down to New Orleans and I do not know that I can. I do not Fancy the Araingments but must Put up with it. Nothing but Shouleder Straps[150] can have any Chance. Thay can go and Come, do about as please. The Poor Privats are of no account, onley as food for Powder. If we go to Baton Rouge, I shall try to go down to the City unless thay Rush us into Fight and I get knocked over, but we will hope for the Best, take all that is in Stoar for us and make the Best of every thing. The Old Flag must be upheld, Cost what Ever.

Yours,[151]
CW Sherman

Camp Stephens near Thibodaux, Bayou La Fourche, December 27, 1862
Dear Wife and Chirldren,[152]

It is with much Pleasuer that I write theas few Lines to you hoping thay may find you all in good health as theas Leaves me at Present.

We are having a Wet time at Present, mud being the Principle thing with us. At Present this Redgiment is still in Camped on this Bayou. We have being under Marching Orders for two Weeks Past. Thay are Pouring Troops up to Baton Rouge, but have not made any Atack on Port Hudson as yeat, and as to this time have not Fierd a Shot into Vicksburge, but will get to Work soon. The Wether is very Miald at this time unlike what you have to home as two things can be.

We have Just got the News of the Crossing of Burnsides into Fredricsburge and we shouled like to know how he as Suckceeded, but can not till a nother Steamer Comes in. The movements of the Armey of the Potomac we watch as anxiously as the Frends of those Composing the Rank & File of the Armey with us hear. When we do move, some thing has got to give away, and we want to

---

[150] "Shoulder Straps"—officers. "Civil War Jargon," ACWS Newsletter, June 1998, quoted on American Civil War Society, http://www.acws.co.uk/archives /index.php?page=jargon&dir=misc.

[151] This closing leads this editor to think the letter was written perhaps to his brother or his aunt and uncle.

[152] This letter is transcribed from photocopies.

see the Rebles give away before our Boyes that are at the other Sides of the Union, but we must waite a little Longer.

I recved your kind Letter of the Seventh of December and was glad to hear from you. I expect a Letter by every Maile that Comes in, but that whouled be keeping you writing all the time, but do what you can. My Brother dose not write as often as he might. He sends me Papers, the New York Tribune. I wish he whouled Send me a Plug of tobacco in is Papers. Those Small Plugs can be Wraped up in a News Paper and sent Safe. Some of our men recve Tobaco that way; it is a Novel means of Cheating the Post Office.

I am as well now as when I left home. Better then I have being for 6 Months. I have not being under no Doctors Care being to Work every Day; Lost no time. Do not Worry your Self About me. We can not get what we want hear, have to Put up with what we can get and Consiquencly we get out of Fix, Like any Machinery that is run the Whrong way, but with Care can be Brought to run Right and well again. All I need when I get down is a little Rest and that Puts me all right again. I, for one, have to thank my Father in Heven for a Healthey Organization and using the Means which he as Placed in the Reach of all is Creatures.

I was Sorry to hear that Mother has had one of those Bad Turns that She as being Afflicted with so maney years. I wish that when She wants to go any whare to get a Teame and Let Virtue Pay for it, if She has the Money. Mother can not Walk 3 or 4 Miles at her time of Life with out Aff[ec]ting her, and Mother must not do it. I want to Come home some time and a Great Part of my Plesuer whouled be Distroyed if Death Shouled take Either of my Parents away and me a way. Mother, you must be more Carefull of your Health. I hope you and Father may live Maney years after our Present Trubles have Ceased and the Present War is forgotten.

Yours,
CW Sherman

Camp, Stevens, January 18th, 1863
Bayou, Lafourche, La

Dear Wife & Children

I have got back again to
our Old Camp Safe again
thanks to the Protecting care
of my Father in Heven
who has Brought me through
the Fire with out harm
this Brigade was orderd last Sunday
to Berwicks bay to Support the Gun
Boats in the Command of Comodoar
Buchanan to Distroy the Robl Gun
Boat Cotton that was up the Bayou
Teish and was Blockedad in in Such
a maner Supported and coverd by
Roble Sharp Shooters that our Gun
Boats could not get to work on
her with out losing every man
that showed himself as to work
the Guns the men had to be un
coverd and the Guns whould
need a new crew every time

Background is the letter from January 18, 1863

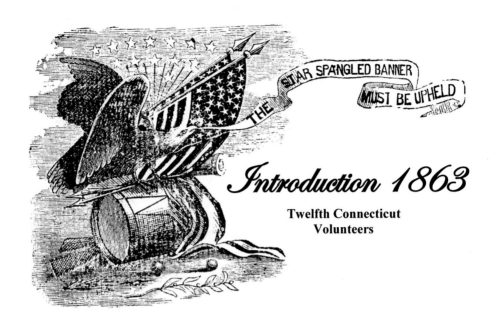

Introduction 1863

Twelfth Connecticut Volunteers

January of 1863 found the "Reserve Brigade" with an increased force proceeding up the Teche River with the intent of destroying the Rebel gunboat, *Cotton*. The brigade attacked on January 14; the *Cotton* was destroyed, the enemy dispersed, and the brigade returned to camp at Thibodaux.

In February, the Twelfth moved to Brashear City and remained in Camp Reno and Bayou Boeuf for the next few weeks.

The gunboat *Diana*, along with Company A of the Twelfth Regiment under Lt. William S. Buckley, and other troops were captured on March 27 near Pattersonville. Lt. Francis, who had just returned to his regiment from being taken prisoner at Georgia Landing, was shot through the body, but not killed. The *Diana* was now in enemy possession.

In anticipation of a long march, Maj. Gen. Nathaniel P. Banks restricted what the men could take; the remaining property was stored in trunks in a sugar-mill warehouse, however, the warehouse was burned in June by enemy troops.

Maj. Gen. Banks commanded a large force which embarked on April 9, crossed Berwick Bay, went up the Atchafalaya and the Teche, and, on the twelfth and thirteenth, was engaged with Confederate Maj. Gen. Richard Taylor's troops, the latter leaving Fort Bisland in the night of the thirteenth. Banks pursued the retreating Confederates on the fourteenth and, after several skirmishes, reached Opelousas, Louisiana, on the twentieth, where the regiment stood picket duty for the next several days.

Continuing its forced march, the Twelfth joined the troop advance on May 4 to Alexandria on the Red River, ninety-six miles away, reaching that city on the seventh; on the ninth, they marched another thirty-six miles to Piney Woods and back to Alexandria on the twelfth, where it remained until the seventeenth. The troops then marched to Simmesport, proceeded on a transport to St. Francisville and Bayou Sara above Port Hudson, and reached that area on the twenty-fifth of May. On the twenty-seventh, it joined in Gen. Banks's general attack on that Rebel stronghold. It eventually took position about 150 yards from the Rebel earthworks where it remained, under continuous fire, until the surrender of Port Hudson on July 9, 1863. During this period, the regiment participated in two attacks on the enemy: June 10 and 14. While suffering losses of 108 killed and wounded during the forty-two days under fire at Port Hudson, Gen. Weitzel and others frequently complimented the Twelfth on its "staying and fighting qualities." The victory at Port Hudson was strategically important in obtaining Union control of the Mississippi River, as was the surrender of Vicksburg only a few days earlier; however, the victory was not without high cost in the loss of lives, nearly as many died from disease as those killed in battle. Charles himself came down with yellow fever in mid-June.

Transports returned the regiment to Donaldsonville, then to New Orleans, and finally to Brashear City on Berwick Bay, arriving on July 25. They were accompanied by gunboats and occupied that post with the Thirteenth Connecticut, with Lt. Col. Peck in command.

Throughout this time, the men were not paid, many were sick, and morale was low. Sickness and malaria incapacitated so many it was difficult to find enough officers or men to perform their daily duty. Charles's spirits reached a low point during this period as well, as he suffered from yellow fever starting around June 16, but he eventually recovered, got paid, and his optimism returned.

The troops were moved to Algiers, opposite New Orleans, on the second of September with preparation to join an expedition to Texas, but circumstances developed that led orders to be changed. In October, the regiment reached

Opelousas[153] where it remained until late fall, when it returned to New Iberia and went into winter quarters. During the period from mid-October to the end of the year and possibly into January, Charles was retained by the surgeon in charge of the hospital in New Iberia and later Franklin. Apparently, the hospital was shorthanded and the surgeon obtained approval for Charles's temporary assignment as the regiment was not in demand at the time.[154]

---

[153] Opelousas is west of Baton Rouge, in the center of the state and north of New Iberia. Brashear City is now known as Morgan City and is approximately ninety miles southeast of Opelousas.

[154] *Record of Service of Connecticut*, 472; Croffut and Morris, *The Military and Civil History of Connecticut*, 320, 403, 409–16, 514–16; De Forest, *A Volunteer's Adventures*, 85–158.

Chapter Nine

Camp Life, Gunboat *Cotton*,
Standing By for Orders

Camp Stevens, Bayou Lafourch, Janury 1, 1863

Dear Mother,

This is the begining of a nother Year. Maney Chainges you have seing in this World, but a great maney things are Coming to Pass that Looked uterley imposabl when the Years was younger with you and me. But thair are maney things for you and me to be thankfull for in the years that have gon. I am thankful for the meseur of good health that I have Enjoyed Since Leaving my home and fore the Preservation of my Life through maney Daingers till the Present time. I know that I am not Greatfull a nuff for the maney Blessings that I have being Serounded with. My Wife and Chirldren have being kept in health. I hop[e] thay may live many Years and be Usfull men and wemon and that you and my Honerd Father may be Preserved to me to help me Bring them up and guide them by your Counsl and Riper Judgement. It is a great trust that I Confideth with and unless we have help from one that is mighty to Save us, all our Labor is vain. I hope you do not truble about me. I am in the Hands of a kind Father that will help and Preserve me if I call upon him in Trusting Faith. Without Faith we are nothing, can do nothing, within or of ourselves. Faith in a overrulling Providence that guides and govnors the Nations. If it was not for Simple Faith I shouled not have being able to stand the Whare and Tear of this Life that I have being Leading fore the Past year. It is this Faith that keeps me well and makes as Strong as ten men for the right, a Knowledge of the Justness of our Cause, and that God whouled so order things that the right whouled Prevaile.

We may be under the Cloude at times but the Sun whouled and did Shine again, and we forgot the Darkness that had Coverd us and Serounded us as with a Mantle. Never get Down Hearted but allways, when you feell that things do not go Just as you think thay ought to, we must stop and think, I may be wrong. We expect more then in the Natuer of things can be accomplished, and tharefore we find fault but we must use the means that a good God has Placed within our reach and Trust Providance for the result. In the time to come if my Life Shouled be Spaird, that I may repay in Some meseure the De[b]t that I owe to the Best of Parents for thair kindness and Forbarance towards me when I have, by Rudeness of Speach and Conduck, Caused them unessary Pain. I never willfulley meant to Pain them but I know that you have allways meant my good and may our Father in Hevan Reward and Bless you and that your Road through the remainder of Lif[e']s Jurney may be more Plesent and Easey, less thornes and more Flowers in your Path. Life at the Best is but a Pilgrimadge. Nothing Shure hear, nothing to be depended on. Life is Short and Death Cirtain for all of us at the End of the Jurney. Keep up your Curadge Mother, we will hope fore the Best. Kiss Virtue and the Chirldren for me and may our Father in Hevan walk over and have you all in his holey keeping is the Prayer of your son,

Charles W Sherman, La

. . . Let me know if Henry Comes Down to see you and if he Payes Virtue any Money as he, according to my Rec[kon]ing, owes me.[155] I know not if he can do anything at this time. I hope that Marcy will do what is right with him, but if Marcy has not Payed him, it Looks as though he did not intend to Pay.

I am glad that the Manufactering is good. I have being afraid that it might Suffer some. Every thing here is Dead and had being Since this war began. What Little thay had, thay have Sufferd more then you have aney Id[e]a of. I never thought that Cotton Goods whouled rise so high. It will make it hard to

---

[155] This next letter is incomplete, missing its first page with the date, but content places it most likely in January 1863, in Louisiana.

Live this Winter. I hope that Virtue and the Chirldren will not want for anything. She must get what ever she wants, do the Best She can for herself and Trust in Providance. I hope to get home but have to go and do as I am bid, but things will Turn round all right if we will only have Patience.

You do not fancy Paying that tax but it can not be helped. I ought to have some from the Town, but can not get one Cent. You ask if I ever got that 10 Dollers from the Town of Stonington. I have and Spent it and couled have Spent 10 more if I couled have got it. It came very handy I can tell you. If you think men hear can live on goverment Rations, you are mistaken. We have to get a few things, Butter I never tasted till a Month ago Since I left home. In the Scorching heat of Last Summer, I did get me a glass of Beer, no Liquor that whouled not do, those that did Put themselves under the Sod. It takes all the Judgement and a Knowledge of himself a man can Bring to [h]is Aid to live.

Samuel Weicks has come up to Camp. He has not Don any Duty for a long time. Rum Put him whare he is. I did all I couled to keep him Straight, but Drink he whouled. You must not Let [h]is Wife know what I write, he will com round all right.

You want to know what a Corproals Ofice is, or Bearth.[156] It gives me no Pay a Month more then I was geting befor, it mearley Saves one from Being Put in the Gard House if you shouled by any Accident do anything Preducil [prejudicial] to good Order and Military Disciplin. Thair is 8 Corproals in a Compney and 5 Sergants. The Sergants are taken from the Corproals. We have to Stand gard in our turns. The gard is taken from the Differant Compneys, 10 or 12 men from each Compney. Every Day the gard is Deivided into 3 Releefs, Each Releef is in [the] Charge of a Corproal. Each Releef Stands 2 Hours and 4 off. The whole Camp is in the Hands of the gard. No one can get off or on with out a Pass. The Corproal [h]as to Read all Passes. He can let any one on or off if he thinks Proper without a Pass. The Whole Gard is in [the] Charge of a Leautenant and one Sergant. Thay take the Sergants from the Corproals and Comissary Sargents. The Corproals are Acting Sargents. Thay are expect to keep the men Straight and See that thay keep Cleen and thair tent. Corproals are expected to be Modles of Soldiers, the Morale of an Armey & good

---

156 I believe this refers to the Corporal's Warrant that was given to him by Colonel Deming, which serves the purpose of giving him safety in case of disciplinary action.

Disciplin and the Non Commissiond Oficers are Expect[ed] to be all that is good.

Give my Love to Mother and Virtue and the Chirldren. Kiss the Baby for me a keep up a Stout Heart. Trust in Providence.

From your Affactnate Husband & Son,

CW Sherman, La

Camp Stevens, Bayou Lafaurche, La, Janury 18, 1863

Dear Wife & Chirldren,

I have got Back again to our Old Camp Safe again thanks to the Protecting care of my Father in Hevan who has Brought me through the Fire with out harm.

This Brigade was orderd Last Sunday to Berwicks Bay to S[u]port the Gun Boats under the Comand of Comodoar Buchanan to Distroy the Rebl Gun Boat Cotton that was up the Bayou Teish[157] and was Blockedad in Such a maner, Supported and Coverd by Reble Sharp Shooters, that our Gun Boats couled not get to work on her with out Losing every man that Showed himself. As to work the Guns, the men had to be uncoverd and the Guns whouled need a new Crew every time it was Fierd. Thay had thrown up Intrenchments and any quanity of Rifl Pits. The Rebls had some 32 Pi[e]ces. We took 17 Rifled Pi[e]ces and the 12th Con Voll, the 75th and 160th New York, 8th Vermont, 21st Ind[i]ana, 114th New York.

We started Earley Monday morning and was the Last to Leave the Camp. We Re[a]ched Brashaw City[158] Just at night and we Passed through the Wildest Looking Cuntry that I have Seeing. The Raileroad runing from New Orleans to Brashaw City gives us the Comand of this Part of the State to Berwick Bay and the Gulf. The Rebles Burnt the Bridges and all the Cars and Rolling Stock. We Pased one String of one Hundred Cars Burnt. We have Just got the Road in working Order and Buchanan had got every thing ready for us. We Camped the first night in Brasheur City and the cold wet ground recved our weary Limbs. We was soon a Sleep and, for one, I slept quite Comfortabl. Got a Cup of Coffee

---

[157] Bayou Teche
[158] Brashear City

and a hard Bread for Brakfast. We Left our Knapsacks in a Building under a Gard and took our over Coats and Rolled them in our Inda rubber Blankets, threw them over our Shouldiers and Marched on Board the Diana Gun Boat. The Batterys had beaing Put over During the night with the 21st Indana and 6th Michagan Redgiments, and one Companey of Cavlery.

We Started up the Bayou on Board of 4 Gun Boats. Berwick Town is on the other Side of the Bay; not a Solitary Famley in the Place as I couled see. We went up about nine miles and Landed under Cover of a Large Shugar House. We formed and marched up about 2 mile and turned in a Barway and Formed in Line in a Large Canefield, the Batterys on the right, one in the Center, the 75th New York had the right of the Line, 160th New York the Center, the 12th Connectcut the Left. The 8th Vermont was Landed on the Left Side of the Bayou to Cleer the Banks and Brushs of Sharpshooters so that the gun Boats couled work without losing thair men. The 21st Indana and 6th Michagan were held in reserve. We waited a long time to give them a Chance to Come on or thair Caverley a Chanc[e] to Charge. Thair was a Chance for them and thay though[t] of improveing it, but a few Shell from one of our Batterys soon set them a Skeddadling and the whole Line was orderd to move and into the Cane we went and if that was not work to get through that Cane, then I do not know what work was; into the woods and through the Cane, but no Enemey was found. We couled hear the gun Boats throwing Shell into the Rifle Pits on the other side of the Bayou whare the 8th Vermont was working up with the Boats. The Enemys Cavlery Showed themselvs, but what few we had Put after them, but after fiering a few rounds thay Brok and Turned Tail and our Boys after them. Thay got two; one died Bringin him into the Line.

It was Dark by this time and we was orderd to Sleep whare we were was, wet through and Tierd, no fire and no Watter and Just begining to rain. It was my luck to go on Picket. I had Just got my Back against a Post when the Ordley came and told me to take 7 men and go. It was not very Plesent after Such a Days Labor to go and Stand on Picket all night, but it must be don and away we went, 8 of us.

We took the front of the 12th. We was Posted on the Eadge of a Cane Field. I was Left with 6 men with orders to Fall back on the reservs if we was Driven in by the Enemy. A little Past midnight I stood looking towards the Bayou whare the Gun Boat Cotton was Anchord. I heard one of the Sentniles Challenging, who goes thair, then a Shot, then carack went the Rifls. The Bulets came right over and a round whare I was standing. The men with me fierd and ran, Left me alone. I couled not Leave my Post, as the Orders was to Stand unless forced to fall Back. In about half a hour, the Officer of the day and gard came round to see what was the matter & he wanted to know whare my men was. I told him thay had run in. He said that he whouled see that thay came Back. It was not a Plesent thing to be Left so but in the course a hour, the Leautenant cam[e] with the men, gave them a few words of Advice that thay will rember the Longest day thay live, told me to be shure of one of them if thay undertook to run again; I promised him that thair whouled be one short in the 12th.

The Rebles tried thair Old game but found by the fire of our Pickets that we was redy for them and thay did not truble us again that night. About 4 in the morning we was taken off. The Line formed and forward we went, wet through for it had raind nearley all night. No Brakfast and a Fight a head for us. It was decid[e]dly Pleasent.[159] The Travling was hard. The cane so thick that it was with the greatest Difficulty that we made our way through and cut up with the Di[t]ches that kept us Jumping and Falling in.

During this time the Gun Boats was throwing Shell and the Cotton Answering Back. The Cotton was Anchord under a high Bluff so that it was next to imposable to do her any Damadge unless you couled Bring a Force to the Left of her. She was Coverd with two thicknesses of Railroad Iron Forward and Coverd with about two Thousand Sharpshooters and thay had 15 Hundred Caverley to Truble any Infantry that shouled be Brought to Bare on her. On her uper Deck she had mounted two Pi[e]ces of Canon that gave us Shell filled with Rifle Balls that Sung nicley round our Ears. The Best Shots was Placed on uper Deck to Pick us off. Our Skirmshers forced thair Line Back. The 75th New York had the right of the Line. Thay had Picked 60 men to Cleer the Deck. Thay Drove the Guners from the Guns and couled have Borded it but thay whouled have Being Blowing up. Her Captain was a Northern Renagnade Named Fuller. He was a Bold man. He walked the Deck as Cool and whouled Point to the Spots on [h]is Person whare our Bullets did Strick him. He had a Coat or Vest of Mail, but he got kil[l]ed. One of our Balls went through it after a Spell. She couled not stand the Presseur that was Brought to Bare on her.

One of our Batterys Came up behind or in the rear of the 12th and we was Orderd to Ley Down while the Battery Played over us and between the Shell from our Battery and round Shot & Shell from the Rebl Batterys keeping us

---

[159] Tongue-in-cheek

between two fiers, but as Luck whouled have it non of us got hurt. The Reble Shell Bursting in front of our Line and the Pi[e]ces flying over us, thair we had to Lay till the uper works of the Cotton got knocked into a Cocked hat; when she thought it was time to be moving, and as she had to work Backward up Streame as She Fought head on, and was not Iron Clad — onley forward and round her Boilers. You can Guess the Dainger our Gun Boats was in from the fact that the first fier the Gun Boat Calhoun recved from the Shore kil[l]ed 30 of her Crew and Comodore Buchanan[160] and thay whouled have Captuerd the Boat if the 8th Vermont had not come up at the time and made a Charge on the Rifle Pits that was on the other Side of the Bayou, Driving the Sharpshooters out of them and Capturing 200 or more of them.

At the time the Cotton Backed up Stream, our Gun Boats couled not Follow as the Rebles had sunk two Flat Boat[s] Loded with Stone and a Powerfull Torpedo at the Entrance of the Blockade. We took the Torpedo up in pi[e]ces. It was a Slow and Daingrous Job but our Brave Tars are Able for any thing. Thay took out Seventy Gallons of Powder a nuff to have Disstroyed the four Gun Boats. The Shelling Contineud all day and we had to keep Shady tward the night.

The Fiering Stoped after Dark. Our Line was in the Cane field and thair we Slept that night. The rain came Down as though thay was bound to Drown us. It was a Long night. About 4 in the morning the Cotton got a Ground and the Rebles set her on fier and we wa[t]ched her Burn and knew that the Rebles had Skeddalad. Thay knew that we shouled stick to them and that we shouled get the Cotton and raise the Blockade and thay had had anuff and in fact, I had, for one. About 10, the Major came along the Line and gave us the welcom newes that the object of the expedition was acomplished. The Cotton had com[m]it[t]ed Suicide and that thair was no use to follow the Rebles as thay whouled not stand and it was us[e]less to go after them.

---

[160] Under Gen. Weitzel's orders, Union cavalry and artillery crossed Berwick Bay during the early morning hours of January 13, while infantry landed at Pattersonville. On the 14 of January, Weitzel and his troops ascended the Teche, accompanied by the gunboats *Calhoun, Estrella, Kinsman,* and *Diana,* under Lt. Cdr. Buchanan. Their successful assault forced the Confederates to destroy their gunboat *Cotton.* The Union forces took fifty prisoners with a loss of six killed and twenty-seven wounded. Among the dead were Lt. Cdr. Thomas McKean Buchanan and Lt. James E. Whiteside of the 75th New York. Richard B. Irwin, *History of the Nineteenth Army Corps* (New York: G. P. Putnam's Sons, 1892), 72–74, PDF e-book.

We formed our Line once more and Lef in front for a spell then; we then by the Left Flank into Column. Every house was set on fier by the Gun Boats and the Town Burnt down. Thay will have a Chance to rember that the Days of Grace is over and that the Days of Venjance is upon them.

We reach Berwicks at Dark and crossed over to Brashaur City got our Knapsacks and Lay Down for the night. In the morning we got ready to Leave for our Camp, got thair after Dark, found that our Cookhouse and Tent Floors Burnt by order of Genral Weitzel so if any Rebl force came round while we was away, thay shouled not get any comfort from anything we had Left. Such a Looking Camp for tierd men to fix up again I do not wish to see, but Sadurday night found the most of us with a floor to thair tents and things Looking like home again.

The wether was afull Cold and it took us by surprise. The Watter froze in our Canteens and Such a frost I whouled not have beleved that things whouled live through such wether, but we see some of the Best Gardens while we was gone that we have seing. Green Peas and Cabadges and all kinds of garden Sauce, but we were not Alowed to tuch anything.

We got our mail in Brashuer City the morning that we came away and that Plesed the men. Thay forgot that thay was about used up. I was for one, allthough my fingers Ached with the Cold. I recved your favor of the 21st of December and was glad to hear from you and that my Wife & Chirldren and you & Mother was well. I am sorry that Mother has been sick but hope she is better now. It might have being the Chaing in the Wether that causes those spells of Sickness that mother is subject to. I am glad that you have recved that Money as Virtue must have being in [need of it].

I hope Lewis will be more Carfull and not Climbe round so much as hurting that Arm so much will make it weak when he growes up and thair is nothing like having a Strong Hand in this World. I am glad that the Chirldren can all go to School and I hope thay will be atentive to thair Studeys and Learn all thay can, for if anything Shouled happen to me, thay whouled not stand the Same Chance of being able to go to Schooll. I hope I may be spaird to help them through till thay can help themselves. I trust in Providence that I may.

You say the Wether is Cold. I have a notion that it is Cold hear. Sometimes it takes hold of us some. Henry sent me a Letter in this Mail. I hope he will come round and see you and write me if he dose. He says that he is doing quite well in Springfield. He is one of [those] men that any one will take to and is able to take hold and work with Tools thanks to my Training. Have you got that

Box [of] Tools of mine yet? And if not try to get them. I wish I couled Drop in and see you and Henry & all of the Folks. If thair wouled not be a time in that Old House, it wouled not be my Fault for I can make as much noise as any other Chiled, if not more.

You hope that the Rebles will not kill all of us off Down hear. When thay do that thay will be smarter then Com[m]on. We have travled after them anuff but couled not get them to waite for us long anuff to do them all the good that we Entended to.

Your are wide of the mark in regard to Banks. He [h]as come to see us through our Trubles hear and some thing will be done that will wake up the Rebles some fine morning.

Mother and Angline Shall have a Dress if I can get one and shall not want for anything. Time will be Better soon and things will take thair Natural Channel. This war cannot Last another year that is cirtain.

Samul Wicks is well at Present and with is Compney and doing Duty. Virtue has Turned Farmer, gon into the Cattle Bissness. I hope she may suckceed [in] raise all the stock She can. Thay will bring her Money. I wish she had 25 good Sheep. Try and get some if you can. Thay must be high but be carfull to see that thay are not all withers. I must Close. I have not wrot all that I wanted to and must Put it in another. Tell Mother I recved her Letter Sunday night and will Answer it. Give my Love to Virtue and the Chirldren and you & Mother and all enquiring frends,

CW Sherman

Camp Stevens, Bayou Lafourche, La, Janury 25, 1863
Dear Mother & Wife & Chirldren,

I recved your kind Letter of December the 13th and was glad to hear from you and Virtue & Chirldren. I was sorry to hear that your Old Enmy had made another Atack upon you. I was in hopes that you whouled have Peace in your Old Age, but you are not Old. It was but a Short time ago that I was a youngster runing round your knee and making all the Mischife that I couled and Probley got a Spanking for my Pains. I have no Dout I Deserved one. I wish that you couled get me a Letter every Week. I shouled Like to hear and know how you are geting along.

We are hear in the Swamps of Louisana; can not see any one but the same Faces every day and if any New Face turns up it is a Black one. We Naturley want Chaing and the Problity is that we shall start for Baton Rouge the first of this Week and have a hand in taking Port Hudson and any other Worke that is to be Don. The 25th Con Vollnteers is up to Baton Rouge and I shall have a Chance to see Ira Sissions[161] and Gorge Frink[162] and any others that I know that is in the 25th.

I am Glad to know that you keep up your Curadge and have Faith that I shall come out of this War with my Life and that my Father in Heven will Preserve me. It Dose try any ones Faith when Shell and Grape & round Shot is Flying round us as thay was the other Day, but we came out with only two Wounded men. But the next time we may not get off so Easley, but I beleve with the Girl that a Dead Hero was better then a Live Coward.

The 12th will give a good Acount of themselves. Cheer up that Disponding one to home and never say Die till all the Aminition is shot away and when every hope of suckcess is gon. We must make one more Charge on the Enemy, one more Ralley, and then we have no Bissness to serender that Old Flag or our hopes. I shouled like to see that young Buttler that you have to home.[163] I was sorry to Part with the one that we had down hear,[164] but the Cuntry wanted the Services of the one, and the other one is Better with is Mother for the Present. I envey the Position of eather one but it was not all roses that B F Butler Picked when he was with us and thair will be many Thorns in the Futuer for him and the Little one. The Chirldren I hope will Enjoy and improve all thair opertunitys and take as much Pleseur in thair young Life as is Consistan with health and thair Studyes.

---

[161] The only name close to that in the 25th Connecticut is Ira P. Sisson. There are conflicting records as to his wife at the time, so it is unknown if this is Virtue's brother-in-law. The 25th Connecticut Volunteers served from November 1862 to August 1863, as a nine month regiment. *Record of Service of Connecticut Men*, 790.

[162] Various members of the Frinke family are mentioned a few times in letters. Census spellings have it as "Frink," whereas the military record of George spells it ending with an "e." As far as this editor can tell, they are acquaintances of the Sherman family.

[163] Charles Butler Sherman, the youngest child of Charles and Virtue, born in January 1862.

[164] Referring to Gen. Butler

You must have all that you can do at Present with Six Chirldren round you. You say that you need no Piano, and fact I shouled think thair must be musick anuff for one Famley. I hope Virtue will not take upon herself more then she can do but if she thinks that it will help her as well as save her Sisters Chiled from the hard lot of Being Brought up by Straingers hands, I am willing. It is a Posistion that I, for one, shouled not Covet to take any ones Chiled to Bring up for fear that I shouled not do what was right by it, and we having all that one Womon Shouled have at one time to take care of and Bring up. A Cow or a Barrel of Flour whouled not tempt me to take two Chirldren and if that is the way to fill a House, I can suply a Small City for thair is Plenty that whouled like to get off so Cheapley by giving a Cow, but she will meet with her reward. She tries to do her Duty towardes her Sister and the Comunity that she lives in and I hope Virtue will have good luck with her Cow and Yearlin. I will try to get them something to Eat and she must see to the Milking as that is something that I never Fanc[i]ed when thair was anything Els[e] to do. Virtue may think that I Censur her som what, but it is not what I Intend by what str[i]ctuers I have writen. It was the Best that she couled do under the Circumstances. If Virtue had not taken the Chiled the Naibors whouled have taken the Liberty to Talk and whouled not of lifted thair Finger to help. I hope Luck will Foller her and the Chiled will live and Prosper and do well and may heven Preserve you all and keep you in Safty.

I am sorry that things are so high with you as a Doller dose not go Far with you at Present. I never thought that Cotton Cloth whouled rise so and Calicoes, but I hope it will not be so Long but we must take things as we find them. You have sent those Minetuers to me but I have not recved the Box as yet but thair as been no time lost. If you have sent it I shall get it. I shall send it back to you again if I can not take it Easley.

I am sorry if I have Judged my Uncl harshley.[165] I am sorry but I knew nothing of the Truble that he has being having. I hope nothing serious will grow out of it. It was very unfortunate the young man did wrong in Trubling his mind about the Drafting, for it was Clearley his Duty to Enlist with out being Drafted if is Cuntry needed is service, and that ought to be anuff to Satisfie any man in

---

[165] James Derrick

regard to is Duty to is home and Cuntry, for without Cuntry, where is your home?[166]

I am glad to hear that the Lord has Dealt Bountifully with you the Past year and that your Barn is over flowing and your Celler is full of the Good things that go to make Life Plesent and Contented & Happy and may you, Dear Mother & Father, live maney years to Enjoy the Blessings of this Life and that Contentment that will all ways Follow those that try to do thair Duty to themselves and thair God & Cuntry. I am glad to hear that your Steers have got to be so us[e]ful and handy to you. You must have two Pair Coming on by this time. You have a nice Lot of Pork. I shouled Fancy some of that with some Cabbadge and Potatoes. That is what we can not get and we often think of the Din[n]ers that our Mothers & Wifes did get for us at this time and we long to get to Old Connectcut to get something to Eat. Most of the men spend thair Pay to the Suttlers for things to Eat besides what Uncl Abraham finds for us. We have being Preaty Short at times, but that is soldiers Luck and we must not Complain at everything that goes wrong.

Help must be scarse to have to Pay one Doller Per Cord but I shall turn up thair some fine morning and we will go in for a Woodpile and variouse other things. I take from what you say that Henry has not Being to see you but I hope he will come. I recved 3 Papers from him in the Last Maile and a Letter from Father Janury 5th and was glad to hear that you was all well and that you had sent me a Box. It will come safe no Dout. One Hundred Boxes was recved by this Redgiment Last Thursday and that one will come.

Give my Love to Virtue and the Chirldren and Harret & Edwin.[167] Tell Harret that I am Ablidged to her for writing for you. I will send you if we move. Trust in Providence. I must do my Duty, Let what ever hapen. Keep up a good heart and we will Trust in a Mercifull God.

Your Affactnate Son,
CW Sherman

---

[166] He may be referring to George, James and Elizabeth's son, Charles's cousin. There is a draft registration record for George, but no record of his having served.

[167] Edwin is Charles's cousin—his father's brother John's son. Harriet is Edwin's wife.

Camp Stevens, Bayou Lafourch, Febuary 4, 1863

Dear Wife & Chirldren,

I take great Pleasuer in writing theas few Lines to you hoping thay may find you in good health as theas few Lines leaves me at Present.

The Wether is very Plesent at times and Puts one in mind of Spring onley it is warmer, but when it is Cold it takes right hold of you more then I ever thought Posable, and if we couled get home at this time thair wouled be a Shivering Crowd.

Vicksburge is not taken up to this time, or Port Hudson. Banks as not moved from Baton Rouge and what thay are waiting for, I know not. It can not be for the want of Water as the Mississippi and all the Bayous are full and our Gun Boats can go whare ever thay Please.

Your box has not got to me up to this time, but it will come sometime. I want it to come before we go away again. The Talk among the men is that we shall go back to whare we Burnt the Reble Gun Boat Cotton and from thair to Franklin and open the Rail road to Jackson and from thair to Texas, if we can get Forc anuff to move with as the Reble Genral Magruder will block our way if he can. He has the State of Texas and Mississippi asinged to him and he is one of theas men that will give us Truble if thair is half a Show.

We are anxiousley Looking for Newes from home. The Proclamation of the President is working. We are Picking up the Slaves and Drilling them. We have but very few in Camp at Present. If a fellow can get a recomend from the Redgimental Oficers and has a little Money, he can get a Comission in theas Negro Redgiments as the Redgimental Oficers must be White. I whouled take a Position if I couled get one and Let Jeferson Davis hang me if he couled. 100 Dollers Per month is a Little Better then 13, I think, but I shouled have to stay after the War is over, but what if I did so I couled get the Green Backs.

I do wish thay whouled fight or let us go home, for I have got Tierd of Uncl Abrahams Rations. If we move it will give us a Chance at the Gees[e] and Chickins. Thay do Suffer some. Thair is not a single one round us hear at Present, thay have gon the way of all Poultrey. Not a Poor Old Cow to be got at, everything Cleand up. Our Foragin Teams have to go long Distances now to get Hay & Corn and thay have Brought us Down to Salt Pork and short at that.

Febuery 5th

The Wether is very Cold to day and that is Just how it is, Cold or Hot. The Creole is Come in and we expect our Maile to night and my Box but may get disapointed and I was, for the Mail did not come till the next day. My Box came Safe and the Pictuers. Thay Pleased me very much. It is a good Pictuer. The Chirldren are Looking well, those two Little Genrals are Looking as though this World was made for them and it was our Duty to Admier them and do them Homadge. Little Buttler Puts me in mind of is NameSake.[168] I hope that he will not begin to Show that Sparit that is name Sake is renownd fore not at Present, as it might interfear with is Education and he must Learn to govern himself. The Pictuer is as a Whole got up in good Shape. Virtue Dose not Look to me as Nattural as the Chirldren. I am afraid that She worries herself, now that is Wrong, she must not do it. I shall do well. I have a Kind Father in Hevan that will not Suffer me to Fall unless it is for some good End and I Shall have Faith that I shall come out of this War Safe, I trust. Do not Fear, have Faith in Providanc and keep up a Stout Heart, never give up. You do not know how Easey it is to do ones Duty by Meeting things with a Stiff uper Lip.

Fany & Angline, Lewis & Arthur Looks as Natrul as Life. I can see them Just as thay are and thay are Looking quite well. The Opinion of the Boys in the Tent was, after seeing them, that thay was the Hansomest Chirldren thay Ever see and to tell the Honest Truth, thay can not be Beat. I hope thay will Prove as good as thay Look as thay grow up. May Hevan Bless them and keep them Safe from all harm.

I recved your kind Letter of Janury 17th. You have it December. I was glad to hear from you and that you was all well. I am well at Present. We are Expecting to move again Soon, but whare it is useless to Say as an Armey is Governd by Circumstances, but you Shall hear. I hope to write you the Particulers. I try to write to you so that you can have a Letter Every week, but the Steamers do not all ways go at the time Advertised and if a Letter dose not Leave Camp in time for the Mail it will have to Lay over till the next one Sailes.

Those Aples rot[t]ed, thair were but two Sound ones among them. I saved anuff to give the tent a taste of them and the Cake was a little Moldey but it was

---

[168] Gen. Butler was in command earlier. He really isn't named after the General as he was born before Charles enlisted, but he calls him the "little general" after the big general.

anuff to give Each of the Boys a Slice. I Passed my Butter round and Let them have a nuff for thair Supper of Northan Butter. My Pudding, I shall Pass round the Same. When thay have Boxes from home, which thay do, and thay have all ways given me a Share. The Ink was Spil[l]ed and what Ever was in the other Bottle was spil[l]ed. If it was those Drops that Jackson makes,[169] it was what I wanted as I am Trubled with the Wind in my Stumach that makes the Sweat Pour off me Like rain. I am not Trubled much but when I do, or have had it, I all ways make me think of those Drops. As a Rule I am all ways well, never Better then at Present. I avoid this Louisisana Beef. It is so Tough that it strains any ones Stumach to Digest it and we can not get it Cooked as it ought to be. To Day the Boys have Bought some Irsh Potatoes and are goin to Draw our Rations of Pork and have a Pork Stew and with your Pudding we expect to get up quite a Tall Dinner. I will Let you know what thay think of your Pudding after Dinner.

We have Just Signed the Pay Roll and shall get some Money. We shall all of us come short this time as thay will take out what we have taken up over and above what the Goverment Alowes. Thay Alowes us 3 Dollers 50 Cents Per month for Clothing and all [those] that has not being Enlisted one year or 12 months have 3.50 Per month deducted from thair Pay till thay have, or up to the first of Janury. The Goverment must have everything Settled and have a New account opend for the Coming year. Some owe more then thay have coming for Extra Clothing & the first year we have to [unreadable—original is torn] . . . we do not have to get the Second year. Blankets or over Coats is two things that is expected to Last 3 years & the Clothing that is furnished to us is not what it shouled be or what the Goverment Pays for. If any one did not Look out thay couled Easley take up thair Pay besides the 42 Dollers Alowed them for Clothing. A great many of the men send home for Shirts & I shouled have Liked two good thick Woollen Shirts. I have had to buy one. What the quarter Master 'as Drawn for us the Last year I whouled not take one of them that I drew in Camp Lyon, make what I have got do. I have had 5.80 taken out of theas Last two Months and thay owe me one Months Pay; the first of March, two months, but we may not get it then. I shall send my Bounty Check this time and you can

---

[169] Probably stomach bitters. There was actually a Stonewall Jackson Stomach Bitters sold. Ferdinand Meyer V, "Stonewall Jackson Stomach Bitters & Ja[c]kson's Stonewall Bitters," Peachridge Glass, December 8, 2011, http://www.peachridgeglass .com/2011/2012/stonewall-jackson-stomach-bitters/.

get the Money off the Bank, I hope, instead of your having to send to Paymaster Fitch for it.

Febuery 9th 1863

I have Lost one Mail waiting to see if I couled go Down to New Orleans to have those Minetuers taken, but we are under Marching Orders and the Major will not give any Passes except to Shouldier Straps and thay are the Meanest and Lowest and most Degread Class that is in the Armey and I must wait a Spell Longer. I shall give this Pictuer Case into the Hands of the Chaplain to take Care of it till we get Settled again as I do not want to risk it in my Knapsack & the Tobaco that you sent was Just what I wanted. It is 2 Dollers Per Pound with us. Dryed Aple is what you want to Put in a box to send hear. Fill up the sides and in between whatever is in it. To anyone Dryed Aples will keep and we can Boile it in our Cups and make Aplesauce and it Taste quite good to us hear & that Black Pepper was one of the things that we want. Red Pepper is Best. We ought to have it so that we couled Put it in our Watter & a great maney men hurt themselves Drinking this Water, when Heated and a Little Red Pepper whould make it safe. The Suspender was Just the thing I wanted and those Hot Drops, it you shouled ever want to send me anything, put in what will keep. That Pudding kept good. The Pie that was a top of it, I couled not make out what it was. I had to throw it away. The Paper and Pens I wanted and I am in hopes of writing maney Letters with them. I shouled have fanc[i]ed the Ink but that got spilt and all togather it was a very good asortment. The Penhandle came very handy and the Paper and Envelops, Stamps. I thank you all for all the things & a Bottle of good Gin whouled have being very Aceptable. It is a thing that we can not get. I have not tasted any Liquor 6 times since Leaving home. I shouled sometimes, if I couled get any that was good, and had the Dust.

We are expecting to move every Day. Two of the Redgiments forming this Brigade have struck thair Tents and gon and the 12th will Bring up the Rear Gard. I am sorry that you will have to waite some time before you will get any Letters. I will try to do better but I have waited for a mail and then to get a Pass to go to the City and must wait still, but I shall get away some time. Vickburg is not taken up to this time, but we hear that thay are to work on it so if you read that it is, you can tell them Better.

Give my Love to the Chirldren and kiss them for me. Keep up your Curadge, all will yet be well and I shall be Free to go whare ever [I] want to and not have to wait after no one.

I send you my Check and Ten Dollers is theas two Letters, that is all I can do at Present. I expect if things turn out right to get 5 Dollers per month more but it all Depends on what Luck some other get in Raising Compneys of Negroes & thay are Picking all up thay can and for one it is Just What I have wanted the Goverment to do. Thay must Arm and Drill the Slaves if we ever get out of this War and Put the Reblion Down, but a great many of the men say thay did not Enlist to Free Nigers but old John Browns Knapsack is Strap[p]ed upon thair Back. Thats what I cajole them with. The good time is coming and we must work and waite in Faith. I send my Love to you all. Write if you do not get any Letter from me.

Your Affectnate Husband & Son,
CW Sherman

I have wrote Fany and the Chirldren and thay must write me again.

Camp Stevens, Bayou Lafourch, La, Febury 7, 1863

Dear Chirldren,

It is with Pleasuer that I answer your kind Letter. I am glad to hear from you and that a kind Providanc has wached over and Protected you and me from Daingers Seing and unseing. You and me can not be Greatfull anuff to that God that made you and me and that keeps us in Being and that as made this Beautifull Worled and all Created things that as Life.

I am at Present in a Part of the United States whare the People never See Snow, but Ice is made in the Small Pools of Water, but never Stays Long for the Sun to Look at. It is a Beautiful Cuntry but the Scurdge of War is Desolating it. Millions of Dollers worth of Sugar Cane has being Left on the Plantations by the owners who run away when we come to See them, and the Frost came and Spoilt it befor the Goverment could get Hands to Cut and Boile it down. So you See you will not be Able to Sweeten those Small Teeth of yours. I sopose you will make up for the Shortness of the Sugar Crop by Drawing on the Maple. In all the Sugar Houses hear thair is any quanity of Mollasses and what thay Call

Mollasses Sugar. The Goverment might Save more of it if it whouled [let] the men go and fill thair Canteens and most of them have a Sweet Tooth Like Chirldren of a Smaller Growth. You will think that this Land is one that Over Flowes with Sugar and Mollasses and it is a Literal fact that I have seing the Sugar & Mollasses runing in Large Streames whare theas Deluded People had Burnt the Warehouses and Depot Buildings to keep it out of the Hands of the Yankees, as they Called us, but I have written anuff on Sweetness.

You Say that you find it hard to get your Wood Cut at Present. I am Sorry you will have to get along the Best way you can for now. I am in Hopes that befor a nother Winter Comes round and my Father and yours that sets High above all and that Governs the Destineys of Nations as well as us Poor Mortals, will Bring this War to a Close and Spair me to come home to you again. We will see if you and me can not get up a Wood Pile that will Astonish the Natives. You and your Gran Mother think you can Cut Down Faster than Angline and Lewis can Trim & Cut it up. The Truble is Lewis must Stop Braking is Arm. You waite till it gets well again and me help him a little.

You and Gran Mother will have to get up Earley. You have two Babeys to your House. I hear you have all the Musick you want at Present. I shouled think I am glad to hear that the Little Strainger[170] you have Taken is getting along so well. You must be kind to him, Faith, you have never told me what its Name is. Genral Buttler is well and Hearty and runing alone, you Say.[171] Give him the Millatary Selute and Present Arms to him and give him the Top of the Morning, Shake up that Arthur, and Kiss all the Babys for me and your Mother, Gran Mother. Help your Mother all you can and make as Little Truble in the House as you can, do all that you are Told to with a will and may Heven Bless you all and keep you.

From your Affectnat Father,
Charles W Sherman

---

[170] The Sisson baby, Virtue's nephew
[171] Charles B. Sherman would be about thirteen months old at this time.

Camp Stevens, Bayou Lafourch, La, Februry 13, 1863

Dear Wife & Chirldren,

I take great Pleasuer in writing theas few Lines to you hoping thay may find you all in good health as theas Leaves me at Present.

The Wether is very Plesent at this time, quite warm. White Clover is in Blow and Dandeliyons & the Willow Trees are Leafing and Natuer is making Prapperations to Come out in her Tallest Dress. She can Dress hear in the highest Fashions. She has not to go to Paris or London for Designs. It makes one think of the Garden of Eden whare our first Parents was and if thair was nothing Els[e] in the way of the of the Rebles, the Simple fact that it was wrong to try to Shut thair Northen Brothers & Sisters out alltogather from Enjoying this Splended Climate of Sun Shine & Flowers. We all have a Equal right to Come into this Garden and Enjoy ourselves and I have yet to Learn whare they have the right to Build up a Barier or Fence to keep us out of our Inheritance. At Present thay stand a good Chanc of Losing thair share and thay Deserve to be Driven out and Disenherited. Thair Crime is great and as things are goin now thay are taking some of thair Punshment in this Life. We know thair Punshment in the next World is Shure.[172]

Febeuary 15, 1863

Dear Mother & Father,

This is Sunday Morning and a most Beautifull Day it is. I felt this Morning that I shouled Like to go to Church but that can not be at Present. If I had being to home and Looked out the Window this morning and See the Snow Sifting along the Road, I might have thought that a Rocking Chair and a good Paper whouled be much Plesenter then goin out into the Cold. You know we act quite Different under certain Circumstances and that what whouled be Pleasuer at one time we whouled Consider Hard Ship at another.

I hope that my Chirldren will take Pleasuer in atending Church and goin to Sunday Schooll as thair young minds whouled get Strength and firmness and Confidence in Coming in Contact with the Rough and Smooth Edges of Socity. It will be of the first importance to them so thay grow up and go out into the World and mix with the Different Classes that go to make up Society. You, my

---

[172] There is no signature here; however, the overleaf starts a new letter to his parents.

Dear Parents, will try and guide them by the Experince that is only acquierd by a Long Life of Tryles and Trubles and Straing Vicisitudes that we Shall all meet with as we Jurney along the road that leads to Eternity. We have all got to walk in that Boundless Sea. No Travlier as ever returned to tell us of the Whrecks that Looms upon the ever Trubled Waters. All is Dark and the Clouds Drop Blackness; no sun to Cheer the Marener on is way.

We are still hear in Thibodeaux waiting for Orders. Our Genral has taken to himself a Wife and it may be that we shall Lose him. We hope not. Genral Weitzel is one of those men that men take to and Consider them a part of themselves. If all our Genrals that the Cuntry is Trusting thair hopes with are such men, as it has being our Luck to be under, this war whouled have being Brought to a Close before this time.

Genral Phelps was a Father to us. He was what you whouled Call the Soldiers Frend. Comissiond Officers and Shouldier Straps had to Stand [to] one side. When a Poor Fellow came to him for Redress, he was atended to right away. The Cut[t]ing Sarcasms that he Delt out to some of the Shouldier Straps was worse than a Discharge of Canister and maney will have Cause to rember him. I wish he was with us now. You whouled Laugh to hear him Talk. We laugh among ourselves when we rember the Droll Sayings that he used to get off to the men.

The Darkey Redgiments are Coming up. We have got to the 5th. Thair is and as being a good Deal said for and against it. The Line Officers of the White Redgiments think themselves above those of the Coulerd, but that will whare away in time. Thair is a fine Chance for the Goverment to meet the Trubles that will be upon them when the Nine Months men and two years mens time is up. Thay will not Enlist maney men from the Old Redgiments. Thay will want to go home. The new men want to get [out] of it more then we do, as we have got used to hard knocks and hard fare and we Look on the Poor Fellowes in the Light of so many Poor Chirldren that ought to have staid with thair mother a spell longer, but thay will come to it in time.

The 12th is Looked upon as the main stay in this Part of RebleDom and thay are no Discredit to the Nutmeg State. Coll Deming has not used us well, never Came to see us when he went home and alltogather he has not don the fair thing by us and the Boys will rember him if thay get home unless thay get too Tight.

Sam Wicks is Down to the City again. He may get is Discharg but it won't be at Present. The Boys do not think much of him. Thay think he Plays off and all such do not get much Sym[p]athy if thay are sick. You must not Let is wife know what I write as it whouled make her feel Bad and whouled do no good. You can tell her he is a little unwell, but nothing else.

Give my Love to Virtue and tell her to take truble right by the Horns and Look them right in the Face and thay will Flye away at the first Look, keep up a Cheerful Spirit and Put her foot down with a will, and Just tell them to stand from under.

Give my Love to the Chirldren, kiss them all for me and tell them that I hope thay will be good to thair Mother and Gran Parent. I send my Love to you and Mother and may Hevan Bless you all. The Pictuer of the Chirldren I keep by me and shall a spell Longer. Those that have seen it say it is a nice thing the Chirldren takes them all Down. Thay are Taken very good, couled not be Better.

Your Afectnate Husband & Son,

Charles W. Sherman

I send 5 Dollers in two Letters. Let me know if you get them.

Chapter Ten

Camp Reno, Brashear City, and Bayou Boeuf

Berwicks Bay, Brashuer City, Febuary 24, 1863

Dear Wife & Chirldren,

I take Pleasuer in writing theas few Lines to you hoping thay may find you in good health as theas Leaves me at Present.

Genral Weitzel has move his Brigade to this Place and the Chaing is for the Better as this is higher Ground and ought to be healther for us. We had Just moved our Camp to whare the 160th New York [was], and had Just got our Floors Down in good Shape when the Order Came for us to Pack our Knapsacks and be ready to move by 4 Oclock in the morning. Now that was a Little Tough, but it had to be don. We Marched to the Terebone Station[173] and thair took the Cars for Brashure City,[174] got thair About Dark and Lay Down for the night and Glad I was to rest. I was soon asleep. It was some Cold, but we do not get up so Soar as anyone whouled think we Shouled.

The Next Morning we took our Tents and Put them up. It was Washingtons Birth Day, the 22nd, that we moved. Allways on a Sunday when we do anything as though thair was no other Days to move on.

---

[173] Terrebonne Station
[174] Brashear City

Last night we Lost the Grey Cloud. She was goin up the Bayou Teash[175] on Picket Duty. Thay send a Boat up every night to Watch the Rebles and see that thay do not Come too Sud[d]en upon us. She had a Compney of the 75th New York for Sharpshooters on her. She run into a Snag and Stove a hole in her Bottom and the Captain under took to run her Back to the Depot and get her onto a Sand Bar so as to save her Guns. He reached the Bar but she Slide off and Sunk out of Sight. I went Down to the Place this morning. It is but a Short Distance from our Camp, but couled not Learn how many Poor Fellows was Drowned of the Crew. All the Soldiers got off. It was all Don so Sud[d]en that not a thing was Saved, onley what thay Stood in. I see some of the Crew Bare footed walking round. The Crew numberd some 80 men but how maney was Sucked Down by the Water when She Slide of[f], thay couled not tell me.

I had some Intrest in that Boat as She cared 5 Compneys of the 12th about Lake Pontchtrain, and up the Differant Rivers that Emty into Lake Pontchtrain, Looking for Guralas bands & she was a Old Mississppi Boat.[176] Comandoar Buchanan had fitted her up for a Gun Boat and was hevaley Armed with some of the Best Rifled Canon that couled be Procuerd and the Rebles have Being expected Down to Drive us away and we couled Ill aford to Lose that Old Boat at the Present time, but one thing Cirtain, if thair had being Less rum Down, the United States whouled have had one more Gun Boat this morning more than she has.

Febuary 25th

The Rebles Put one of thair Torpados Down the night befor Last to Blow one of our other Boats up, but we know how to take it up.

I recved your Last Letter with the Recept for that Box. I guess that all the things was in it and I have Mentiond them in a Letter that you must have got it by this Time. I shouled have wrote more but have not time.

---

[175] Bayou Teche
[176] This expedition was mentioned in the letter dated July 28, 1862.

Give my Love to Virtue and the Chirldren and Mother. I shall write more in my next. Accept my Love and Best respects, Dear Father, and write often.[177] Yours in Hast[e] as the Maile is goin sooner then was expected.

Yours Affactnateley,

CW Sherman

Brashear City, Berwicks Bay, La, Febuary 25, 1863

Dear Wife & Mother & Chirldren,

I recved your kind Letter of Febury 8th and was glad to hear from you and that you was all well. I am in good health at Present and feel thankfull that my health as being Spaird and that of my Wife & Chirldren.

We have moved our Camp and I hope we Shall never have to go Back, but Contineu on the move. This Point whare we are must be held, Cost what it may. We have got hold of the Richest Parts of this State and the Comand of the greatest Part of the Raile Roads and that gives us great Power to move, and the Bayous & Creeks, our Gun Boats will Clean out and hold. We have Lost one but thay are Building others at New Orleans.

The impression round hear is that Starvation will give Port Hudson and help give us Vickburge. Thair has got to be a great Amount of work to be don and no time to do it in, as I can see. If we have to waite till Spring the Rebles may get the Advantadge of us in Kentuckey & Tennesee and, in that Case, if the Rebles Can hold our Armey at Arms Length in Front of Richmond, thay will be Able to throw a Large Force to releve Vicksburg and make it quite warm for us at this Place.

Thay have Stoped recruting in this District for the Coulerd Redgiments, and thay must go up to Baton Rouge to Enlist for those Regiments. How Lincoln can Except a few Parishes in one State from the operrations of is Emancipation Proclamation and Put it in force in the Parishes ajoy[n]ing, I can not see.

---

[177] Charles often starts his letters off with a salutation to one person and ends it addressing another. This is a good example, as he has addressed it to "Wife and Chirldren," but ends it as if he had written his father.

I wish Buttler whouled come back. The Planters are geting Saucy and thay want him to keep them Straight. Thay Turned out in Large numbers to do Honer to a few Hundred Reble Prisnors that was a Leaving New Orleans to be Exchainged and Such things ought to be Frowned down and not be Alowed. The Sesch ought to have the Lines Drawen so Tight that thay can not Breath[e], onley with Difficulty.

This Cuntry whare we are is the Best that I have Seing and it ought to be filled up with a Differant Race of People. Thay have never realized the Blessings that Providence as Serounded them. It whouled do you good to see the White Clover that is up and Blowen out. It Comes with out any Truble. Maneuer onley Spoiles this Land.

We are Encamped near the Depot. Thay had ferrey Boats to Connect with the Raile Road [on] the other Side of the Bay that runs to Franklin and up as high as Shrevport. We have got to get that Part of the Raile Road but will have to waite till Vicksburge & Port Hudson is taken. Berwicks Bay is some 80 Mile from New Orleans and I do not see that I shall get Down to the City unless I get Wounded and get Carr[i]ed thair. Thay have Cleand up the Hospitals and moved out all that couled be moved so as to give the Poor Fellows a Chance that will be Brought down from Vicksburgs and Probley from Brashaer City. The Rebles are on the other Side. Thay Come down most every day with a Flag of Truce and our Scouting Partys meet thairs, but Seprate good Frends and that is Just how we shouled be if we couled get hold of thair Leaders.

Sam Weick is Down to New Orleans. I think he will get a Discharg if he lives long anuff. The Truble is with him, he is homesick and wants to come home and so the rest of us whouled like to, but I, for one, do not want to get home that way. And a nother I want a Sergents Birth and my Chances is good at Present if things work right.

You say that you see no Chance of our geting the Best of them at Present. Now, do not get disheartend, we shall Whip the Rebles and can do it any day if thay will come out of thair holes and give us a Chance. Thay have got to Come to thair Milk and take off thair Hats, those that have any, and Bow Down to that Old Flag that thay have Tryed to Traile in the Dust. If [we] can Crowed them for the next three Months, we can make them come in and Seue for Peace.

I feell Just as Ugley now as when I went away, and have never seing the first day when I felt that I whouled like to Serender to the Cussed Rebles and never shall, Let the War Turn what ever way it may. Thair is some to home, that if thay were Drawen up and a Equeal number of Rebles, I whouled Fier in to those that have Counseled giving up to Jefferson Davis first and the Rebles next. Thats Just how I feel and if we couled get hold of those Gentlemen that have Tryed to Weaken Uncl Abe when he was Trying to hold up the Stars & Strips, thay whouled find it was not Frends that had them.[178] We know that those Elections that have gon agains[t] the Administrations have helped the Rebles more than 50,000 men can make good to us. The Rebles sent Down another Flag of Truce to us giving us 24 hours to Clear out, but we do not know what that means, as thay will find out to thair Cost.

The Newes has Just come up from the City that the Ball as opend up to Vicksburge. The Rebles have Captuerd the Ram, Queen of the West, but thay will not keep her Long as our Tars will insist on having her Back again.[179]

Keep up your Curadge, Virtue. I hope to see you all again, but must do my Duty till this Reblion is Put down, wich we all Pray may be soon. Kiss those Babys for me. Kiss Mother for me and tell her to remember me in her Prayers. Shake up that Arthur for me, give my Love to the Chirldren. Those, or that, Pictuer, I got Captain Roche to Put in is Trunk for me with the Prayer Book as I did not want to riskque them in my Knapsack till we can get Settled again, and if anything Shouled happend to me, he will send them home.

May Hevan Bless you all and keep you all is the Prayer of your Affactnate Husband & Son,

CW Sherman

---

[178] Referring to the "Copperheads" who were Northern Democrats, (also known as Peace Democrats), opposed to the war, and who wanted to make peace with the Confederates. The term Copperheads followed from their practice of cutting the Liberty heads from copper pennies and wearing them as lapel pins or buttons, as well as from their opponents who associated them with the venomous copperhead snake. Delores Archaimbault and Terry A. Barnhart, "Illinois Copperheads and the American Civil War," Illinois Periodicals Online, accessed April 23, 2012, http://www.lib.niu.edu /1996/iht319615.html.

[179] The *Queen of the West* was sunk below Fort de Russy on February 14, 1863, raised, repaired by the Confederates, and put into service with CSS *Webb,* capturing the Federal ironclad USS *Indianola.* In April 1863, she was attacked by US Navy gunboats, set afire, and destroyed. *CSS Queen of the West, Civil War Confederate Naval Ship,* AmericanCivilWar.com, accessed April 23, 2012, http://americancivilwar.com/tcwn /civil_war/Navy_Ships/CSS_Queen_of_the_West.html.

Camp Reno, Berwick Bay, March 2, 1863

Dear Wife & Chirldren & Parents,[180]

With much Pleasuer I write theas few lines to you hoping thay may find you in good health as theas Leaves me at Present, except for a Sleight Cold that has got hold of me this morning, but will have to leave as soon as the Sun gets to work on it.

I recved your kind Letter of 18th of Febury and was glad to hear from home and that my Wife & Chirldren and Parents was in health. You must be Prospering thair and the War dose not interfear with the Increase of Stock.

Lewis has tuned Dog Merchant I hear. I am afraid that it won't be a Paying Bissness after he has rec[k]oned up the Cost of keeping and first outlay, but Dogs are higher with you then hear. Thay are below Par in the South. Thair is more Dogs hear than Inhabitans, but the Dogs we think more of than the People, and thay get more kicks then Crusts. You whouled think the Rebles was Coming Down on us with An Armey of Dogs if you couled hear them yelping nights when a Ordley Galops by some House and Disturbs the Slumbers of the Canine Tribe that keeps wach thair. But we will hope that Lewis may do well with his pups.

I am pleased to hear that the cow has come in well and that she is givin Down her Milk. A New Milk Cow on the Banks of the Mississpipi is a Small Fortune to the Owner at the Present time with our Troops as Costomers, as the Water is about of the Consistance and Couler of Milk and, by that means, it sells redley at a Dime Per Pint mixed with a Little Milk.

That Box reached me all Safe and the Contents I Distributed to the Boys in the Tent that was of Perishable nature. The Minetuers was all right and the Tobaco & thread, hot Drops; the other Bottle, what ever was in it was Brock. Thair was nothing taken out it; it was Nailed to stay. I thought I never shouled get into it. The Aples was Rotten and the Pie was Mouldey. I couled not make out what that was. The Puding was all right. Aples & Eggs is not the thing to send hear. One of the Corproals that is in my Tent had a Box of Eggs sent to him and thay was all Rotten, all though Packed in Salt & Saw dust. If you know of any one Putting up a box for any of thair Frends South, tell them to Pack with Dryed Aple.

---

[180] This letter is transcribed from photocopies.

Wicks' Box has Come and is in the Captain's Tent and Wicks is still Down to New Orleans in the Marene hospital. I sent him a line by one of our men that got his discharge as to the box, and it cannot go to the Hospital as thay will not Let the men Eat anything but what thay may think Proper, and asking him to come up if he can. I have not recved any word from him as yet.

I have heard that you was having one of the Mildest Winters North that has being for a long time. It dose not Look much like Winter hear. Our Drill Ground is a Beautifull White Clover Field and the Days Puts one in mind of June North, but we shall get Heat anuff soon to make up for this.

Captain Roche met with a Accedent yesterday that will send him home when he gets well. The Fact of it is our Commissond Officers take to Wiskey as naturley as a Cow dose to Cabbadges, or a Cat to Milk, and he thought a Horse was Just as good to ride on as going afoot. And, Carrying more Bricks in his Hat then the Regulations Alowes, he came off over the Horse's Head with more haste than grace and the horse kicked him in the Face, which did not improve is Beauty. And the Consiquances is that he takes up a Cot in the Hospital. I have heard that, among other antics he cut up, was riding over a Sergant of the 75th. Now the Regulations say nothing about Commissiond Officers Riding Down Non Commissiond Oficers and all to gather it Looks like a Court Martial and Being Casheierd[181].

Our first Leautenant that we Lost at Gorges Landing and has since being Exchainged and Joyind us Since, was under Arest at this time and it Leaves us Short of Officers. He was under Arest with our quarter Master fore Entering a Leautenant tent and Pulling him out of Bed and raising Ned.

Tell Edwin that I am glad to hear that he is doing something fore is Cuntry and that he has such good luck, but it is the other gender that we want at this time. Tell him that he must Try again, never do to give it up.

So Virtue has not to keep her Sister's Chiled for nothing. Well, that is as it ought to be. I couled not see the Beauty of keeping other's Chirldren for the Fun of the thing. I hope she will have good Luck with her Motherless little one.

I am glad that Lewis takes to his Books. I know that the Girles will try and do thair Best and Learn and he must not be Beat. Give my Love to the Chirldren and kiss those Babys for me. Keep up your Curadge all of you and Virtue, you must not get Down at no time, but Put a Cheerfull Face on at all time[e]s and

---

[181] A term for a dishonorable discharge

Places. The Rebles have not got me as yeat and for the Present I do not think thay will, but we know not what is in the Futuer and it is best that we shouled not. I send my Love to you all and do not forget to Pray for me, for I need the Protection of one that is mightly to Safe.

Your Affactnate Husband and Son,
CW Sherman

Camp Reno, Berwick Bay, March 3, 1863

Dear Chirldren,[182]

I received your kind letter and was Pleased to see the improvement you have made in your Composition and writing. Continue to Cultivate a habit of thinking and write your thoughts out on any Subject that Interest you.

Last monday Morning I was Put in mind of you as I went round Placing the Gard. One of the Posts was in front of a Small School House that is on the right of our Camp. The School Misstress stood in the Door, as I have seein them to home, waiting for the Chirldren to come. The Wether favord the Id[e]a, and it was the first thing that remined me of home Since Leaving.

Thair is no Inhabitans hear to Speak of, no men, onley a few Wemon and Chirldren. All gone to the War. The Streets Look Lonesom. You see no hapey Chirldren to Play in them, only the Sentinel walking his Beat.

Our Gun Boats are the onley Boats that is Ste[a]ming up and down the Bayous. This morning one Hundred men Left hear for the Point whare we Distroyed the Cotton.[183] The Rebles had Sunk some Boats Loded with Bricks to keep our Boats from goin up the Bayou and we did not move the Blockage at that time, but now we are goin and Cleer out this Section of Cuntry.

Genral Banks Came up this morning from New Orleans and a Forward movement may be looked for at any time. We expect to Bag the Rebles now. Thay have a Salt Mine up to Franklin and thay will make fight thair, if not before we reach that Point.

I shouled like to see you and hope to some time.

---

[182] This letter is transcribed from photocopies.
[183] The Gunboat *Cotton*

Theas Wicked men is Trying to Distroy and Brack up this great Cuntry to help forward thair own Private and Ambitious Ends, filling the Cuntry with Widows and Orphans and Covering the Face of this Beautiful Land with Poverty and Desolating the once happy homes of those that can not, or will not, be Drawen into the Reblion. If you couled see the great Distress that is hear in the once Welthy Planter's Home, as well as those of the Poorer Class, you couled realize the great Curse War is. You to home in the North have not felt the first Eavils of this War. I know that the Fire on many a Hearth Stone has gone out forever with us, but hear every Womon that you see in goin through a Town is in Mourning. Whare we have Lost one, thay have lost five; not in Battle all to gather, but by exposure and Dese[a]se. All over the South the graves of our own men lie Scattered, but thay have Lost thair Lives in a righ[t]eous Cause.

I hope you do all you can to help your Mother. She must have more work to do then She is able to and you can Lighten her Burden much, and your GranMother, you must be kind to and do all that She wants you to, and you must be kind to one another. Kiss those Babys for me, and your Mother & GranMother and Cheer them up. Sing to them the Boney Blue Flag. You have all the Dogs that you want to Play with now I shouled think, and a young Calf I hear. I shouled like to see it. Let me know in your next how your Hay Holds out and all the Newes. Give my Respects to Edwin & Harret and tell them to write to me. I send my love to you all and tell your GranFather that I am coming home Some time to Plague again.

Your Affactnate Father,
CW Sherman

Camp Reno, Brasher City, Berwick Bay, March 7, 1863
Dear Wife & Chirldren & Parents,

We have being having some more Mud, very Disagreabl to those on Gard, but we that did not have to go, we are in the Same Place with the Old Darkey, more rain, the more rest.

We do not see much of our Grey Back Neighbours, in Fact, thay are not half as Socible as we was led to beleve. Thair Picket is one side [of] the bay; ours, this [side of the bay]. Our Picket Boat goes up every night with a Compney of men to Repell Boarders as that is the onley way thay can take our Boats is by Droping along side in the night and Bording and then the Bayonet tells agains a Ships Crew. The Rebles have the Queen of the West and the Indianola taken between Vickburg and Port Hudson, and can take all of our Fleet if we run them Down one at a time.[184] It is time that kind of fun was Stoped, for like the Boys & Toad, it may be fun for the Rebles, but it will be Death to us. Thair is to be a movement soon and things are working round in such a way that thair must be Somthing don, more then looking on and waiting for Somthing to turn up. I hope that the next time we do move it will be to some Perpose and it must tell on us or the Rebles. Thair can not be any half-way work anymore.

March 13th

Since beginning this Letter, I have recved one from Henry and a Paper and have Answerd it. I have to write home if I do not get any letter & we are still here.

The Rebles come down and ride through the Deserted Town of Berwick that is on the other side of the Bay. Thay fierd on our Picket Boat as she was returning the other morning, but did no damadge. But in the Afternoon, as a Party of thair Cavlery was riding through as usual, one of our Batterys sent them a hevey Charge of Grape that Emted some Saddls and put the rest in a way to Put as much distance between them and our Parrot Guns as posable. It will learn them maners and to be Carfull how thay throw thair lead about. When we invite them to Shoot, which we shall soon, it will be time for them to put daylight through us then.

We are building a Fort about two mile above us that comands the Atchatchfalyou, Bayo Teash[185] and Grand River. The Rebles are above us at the Town of Franklin. Thay have fortified that Point with Earth Works and Rifled Pits & for Benefit in Grand Lake. Thair is an Island that has a Natural Salt mine and Salt Works and thay will try to save them.[186]

---

[184] On February 25, a dummy ironclad was floated down the Mississippi by the Union Navy causing the Rebels to destroy the captured ironclad USS *Indianola*. "USS Indianola (1862–1863)," Naval Historical Center, Naval History & Heritage, accessed April 23, 2012, http://www.history.navy.mil/photos/sh-usn/usnsh-i/indanola.htm.

[185] Atchafalaya, Bayou Teche

[186] Avery Island, Iberia Parish, Louisiana, is home to one of the largest salt mines in the world. "Avery Island Salt Mine (United States)," accessed April 23, 2012, http://www.aditnow.co.uk/mines/Avery-Island-Salt-Mine/.

Genral Banks is trying to Send a Force from Baton Rouge to head them off in that direction while Genral Weitzel takes them in the rear. We have heard that Banks is to Work on Port Hudson and that Porter had run is Fleet by the Batterys of Vicksburge.[187] The loss of two of is Boats by runing them Single down Convinced him that that was not goin to work and it was time he was doing something and that he was the same man that called to see them last Spring but whouled make a more lenghened stay at this time with the greatest Plesuer.

I see by the Papers that the Copperheads are to work pois[on]ing the minds of the People and trying to Weaken the Hand of Uncl Abraham and give all the Aid & Comfort to the Rebles thay can. If those men onley knew how we regard them, thay whouled not dar to sleep nights and we whouled like nothing better then to come home and Hang every one of them on the nearest tree. All the Regiments feel about so, and thay will bring a Storm upon themselves that nothing in earth was ever like it. The Rebles have don nothing to Injuer us so much as theas Peace upon any terms Party.[188] It whouled be delightfull to Charge on such a Party.

As thay are, the Rebles are looking fore a muss among us North, but thay will make but Presious little by it. We can take care of bothe Partys. Thay need not Flatter themselves thay will make anything. Thair Names will go down to Posterity with Bendick Arnol, whose Treson is handed down to us and our Chirldren as a Warning to all futuer time, and all Nations of men will Curse them for Deserting the Cause of Freedom in its hour of need. But the Star of the Worlds hope will not be Put out, but it will Shine with a Brighter light from being Partialy hid or Coverd by the Clouds of Adversity. Cheer up, it will never

---

[187] Union Rear Adm. David Dixon Porter. In 1862, he was involved in the expedition up the Mississippi to take New Orleans under his foster brother, Admiral Farragut. He later commanded the Mississippi River Squadron during the Vicksburg Campaigns, and his Flagship was the lavish *Black Hawk* aboard which he had a cow for fresh milk. Both the *Queen of the West* and the *Indianola* were lost in his fleet [mentioned here by Charles]. He ordered the hoax of the dummy ironclad gunboat mentioned previously to try to save the *Indianola* from being salvaged by the Confederates. Catton, *The Civil War*, 75; Donald L. Barnhart Jr., "Admiral Porter's Ironclad Hoax During the American Civil War," *America's Civil War Magazine*, Historynet.com, published online June 12, 2006, http://www.historynet.com/admiral-porters-ironclad-hoax-during-the-american-civil-war.htm.

[188] Copperheads

do to give it up, so give my love to the Chirldren and Acept a large Portion yourself.

Your Affactnat Husband,
CW Sherman

Camp Reno, Brashaur City, La, March 15, 1863

Dear Wife & Chirldren,

It is with much Pleasuer that I write that I am well at present and hope theas few lines may find you all in good health.

The time of the 12th Redgiment is half out and if Providance Spares us a few months longer, we shall be in hopes of geting to our homes again. We are having Beautifull Wether at this place. I cannot bring myself to beleve that I have gone through what you call a Winter, but it is fact. Spring will be with you with Flowers and grim Winter will have to unclasp is cold Icey hand from my Northen home and the Birds bring thair Music back to you and if it couled only Bring Peace along with its other Blessings, it whouled be one of the most Beautifull Springs that ever blesed Mankind. But we will waite till the good time comes, as come it will. You must keep up good Curadge and Cheer up. I hope that you do not Worry about me. I must stay and do my Duty till my time is up, but before that expiers we are in hopes of bringin the Traitors to termes.

The Newes came over the wiers this afternoon that Port Hudson had Serenderd.[189] We hope it may be true. It will onley be a question of a few days in any case. The vigrous mesuers that will be carred through by Uncl Abraham to fill the Union Armies must Convince the Traitors North and South that we are in ernest in this thing. Thair has being false hopes held out to theas Southron Traitors that thair whouled be Division in the Union camps to home and hear to such a degree that the victory whouled be Easey fore them, but the truth will come home to Jeff & Co[190] that thay have being sold and decived and that thair is no hope fore them in this World and thay know to a Cirtainty thair is none fore Traitors in the next. I have Just as much Faith of driving the Rebles to

---

[189] These were rumors, as Port Hudson was not surrendered until July 9, 1863.
[190] Jefferson Davis, President of the Confederate States of America

termes as I ever had and more for we are neare the end then many immadgin and may it come soon.

I am geting along slow. It is uphill work to one that as no frends. I stand first on the list for the next Promotion. I have being selected, am serving in the Colur Gard. The gard Consists of 8 Corproals and 2 Sergants and thair duty is to go out with the Colors and gard them. Thay are responsable for thair safe keeping in Action and it is a responsible Position and I trust I may prove faithfull to the Confidance reposed in me. It saves me from standing Gard nights and do not have to go to Battalion Drill but 3 times Per week at Dress Parade. Evanings we have to ware white Gloves and Sundays Inspections. It is one of the Best Gards in any Redgiment. You may think it is more Daingrous, but that is a thing no Sherman ought to think of fore one moment. It is the Rebles that must be put in mind of dainger when thay come near them and the same Power that as garded and Protected me so far is Able to Protect me thair as well as any whare els. It is duty first and last.

I hope you may have an Earley spring. Henry wrote me in is last letter that he shouled go down to you and help you Plant all you can, but he promises so much that I will think more about it after he as being down and fullfilled some of is promises.

March 22nd, 1863
Dear Wife & Chirldren,

Sinc starting this Letter, we have had lively times. The Fleet, or part of it, as forced thair way by the Batterys of Port Hudson. We lost the Frigate Mississippi, she got aground in turning one of the corners or bends and the Captain had to blow her up to save her falling into the Hands of the Enemy. The Admrils Flag Ship Hartford got by without a Scratch and is now above Port Hudson.[191] Genral Banks made a move into the Enemys Entrenchments at the same and the movement was all that was desierd.

Genral Kirby Smith with Genral Magruder[192] laid a very Preaty Plan to Bag Genral Weitzel, but he is not the Man to be caught by such Sofft Headed

---

[191] Adm. David Farragut's flagship

[192] It was Gen. [Alfred] Mouton, not Magruder, who was in on this plan. Various sources show Magruder would have been in Texas at this time. Subsequent mentions of Magruder in this paragraph have been substituted with "Mouton" in brackets. Lt.

Genrales as Smith & [Mouton]. Smith was to come in our rear by boats Down the Bayou Bafft[193] and [Mouton] with the Rams Queen of the West and Webb. The Queen of the West the Rebles took from us, theas with some other Boats, was to come down the Hachafalaya [Atchafalaya] which emptyes into Berwick Bay and give us fits in front, and Smith [was to come] down Bayou Baff at this Place the Rail road Crosses the Bayou. Thay was to burn that and that whouled Cut us off. We was informed of thair good intentions by some Deserters. This was on last Thursday. At night the Genral sent 3 Compneys of the 12th on some Cars with 3 Peices of Artillery down to the Bridge, some of the 75th N York on the gun Boat Calhoun up to the Fort to board the Rams if thay should come down and the Rest of the Brigade lay on thair Arms in line of Battle till Morning. No Enmy Came. The same aringement was made for Friday night. Compney K was orderd on Bord one of the Gun Boats, but was sent to get thair Knapsack, but found the Whole Regiment Packing up. Genral Weitzel had sent up a Flag of Truce to Franklin giving them 24 Hours to Clear out and at the same time had seven Traines coming from New Orleans to Move us back to Bayou Baffe. The Rebles can not get in our Rear at this Place and we can Atend to them if thay should be so foolish as to atempt Driving us from this Camp.

Sadurday Morning when we landed from the Gun Boat, what a Sight for us, not a tent standing and as far as you couled see was Cars loded with men, niger Wemon & Chirldren and not a Car for us, but after a time I found the Coulers and Climbed into that Car and we started fore Bayou Bouef and got off and we soon had a nother Camp laid out and our tents up. You ought to see the fences Come down, gardens laid open and Trod down. You think Considerabl of Pea Nuts to home, but we have to Tread them into the ground. Thay are Planted in Drills and look very much like Peas coming up. It is of no use to Plant this way for we have to get round and Gardens are of no use to us as we can not stay to get any good of them.

This Place is 8 Mile from Brashuar City or Berwick Bay. We have a strong Picket at Brashur City. We was not forced from that place but fell back to keep the Rebles from geting in our Rear. The Rebles are not Expected to come to

---

Gen. E. Kirby Smith was commander of the Confederate forces west of the Mississippi. De Forest, *A Volunteer's Adventures*, 80; Gabe Weaver, "Edmund Kirby Smith, Biography," Son of the South, accessed April 23, 2012, http://www.sonofthesouth.net /leefoundation/edmund-kirby-smith.htm.

[193] Bayou Boeuf, spelled by Charles "Bafft," "Baff," "Baffe," and "Bouef"

Brashuer City. The Cars run up every day with men. We have Brought every thing away, not a Piece of Board has being left behind and nothing as being distroyed. We had Built a fort that was left in good Shape, only the Guns was taken away.

This is a lovely Place.[194] All swamps and as full of Aligators and Mocasin Snakes as much more Poisinus and Deadly then the Rattle Snake as two things can be. The men think thay have had some Experince in Miscatos, [mosquitoes] but thay all own up thay must have being mistaken as this Sweet Place takes us all down in that Comodity. Thay are Paramount for Size and Beauty. We are not one half so much afraid of the Rebles as theas little Tormentors and the men whouled turn out quicker to fight then to go out Back after dark. I am in Clover as I have not to stand no more Gards till I get my Sargents Warrent and I hope that will be soon so that will save some Swaring on my part, I mean on account of Miscatoes.

I recved your last Letter of March the first as we lay on Picket on the Gun Boat Diana and was glad to hear from hom and that you was all well. I hope that I may be Spaird to see you all again and I trust and have Faith in that good Being that as wached over and Preserved me till this time, that I shall come out of this War all right and that Freedom and the rights of Nations to govern themselves will never be brought in Dainger any more on this Continant.

This Nation is passing through the Fier that is to Purefie it and make it stronger and Better. Thair is a Element to home of Barberisms, What the Copperheads call Democrcy, that is trying to get the uper hands of us at Present and it will make us more Truble if it is not put down with the Strong hand and I, for one, want to come home and Call on those men that are trying to Distroy me and give them five mineuts to Pray and then String them up to the nearest tree. I whouled not give one of them thair life. Thay have, and are trying to take my life by keeping me hear and telling the Rebles to hold on and thay will help them is giving the Rebles more Aid & Comfort then England or France can, but I must wait for the good time coming that will give us Peace & Plenty and Prosperity.

I am glad that those two Letters with the Check and money came safe. I couled do no better then send it that way. I got all the things that you sent me. The Pictuers, or Minetuers, I have all safe. I put the Prayer Book and Pictuer

---

[194] Tongue-in-cheek, to be certain

Case up with the Captains things for safe keeping when we move, as our Knapsacks recve hard usadge some times. I do not see but I must keep them. I like to look on those Chirldren, thay look so good and Healthy that it dose me good to look on them. I wish I had Mothers and Fathers but I hope to see you all some time.

Virtue you must keep up your Curadge and Cheer up. I am worth ten Dead Rebles as yeat and the Chirldren, sing to them. Have Mother shake up that Arthur and kiss them all for me. I send my Love to you all and Father, you must not let the blues get the uper hand of you, but keep up a stif uper lip. All will be well never fear.

Your Affactnate Husband & Son,
CW Sherman

Bayou Bauef,[195] **La, March 24, 1863**

Dear Wife & Chirldren & Parents,

We have beaing having some more Rain and mud and it makes us feel some blue. It is the most disagreable Place that we have being in. Genral Banks came up from New Orleans yesterday and stayed till night. What Conclusion thay came to, we know not. We have to keep open the comunications with New Orleans and have but one Brigade to Gard 80 mile of Raile road and fight the Rebles. We have three Gun Boats to suport us on the Bayous and Berwick Bay.

The night that we got hear the Rebles came down in some flat Boats to Burn the Raile road Bridge, not knowing that we were in force at this place and might have being all Captuerd but our Picket was green that was on that night and fierd too soon. The consiquances of thair hast[e] was one Cavlery Picket shot off is horse and two New York Soldiers Captuerd and a genral turning out of the Batterys to warm our frends if thay forced themselves upon us, but thay thought that thair welcom was too free to be sincer and backed out. Thair is some talk of sending the 12th to Brashuer City as Picket. I am willing to go any whare out of this mud.

---

[195] Bayou Boeuf

March 25th

The Clouds have gon and we are having one of those bright Cloudless days that are no whare els to be seing, only in under a Southron Sun. I have got me a bunk [mate] Sargent Lucas[196] sleeps with me, a young man that as served in the Englis Armey. He was first Sargent or Ordley Sargent of Company K when we left Hartford, but got Reduced in Camp Parepet for getting to much Beer down, but for good Conduck as got Promoted 3rd Sargent again, and he and me Chum togather.

The Rebles do not truble us and we have got another Battery sent us from Baton Rouge that gives us 25 Guns in the 4 Batteryes and the 3 Gun Boats can Bring 15 more to bare on the Enmey and if thay can Stand such a fier thay can do more then thay ever did befor. We have six Redgiments of Infantry and Banks is agoin to send us 15 thousand more men and with such a force we can Stand most anything.

Leautenant Col Coburn as being made Col of the 12th, Col Deming having resigned & gon home. Major Peck as being Promoted to be Leautenant Col and Captain Lewis made Major.[197] We have got things in working order and if every Regiment in the Service are kept in as good trim as the 12th thair ought to be more don than thair is, but it takes time to get in Working order. The 12th as found one Coll for Mayor for the City of New Orleans. The Leautenant Col has being Detached to Start and Put in Order & run the New Orleans and Opposalls [Opelousas] and great Western Railroad and Berwick Bay. It is the best apointment that has being made, was the apointment of Leautenant Col Colburn for that Place. He was a Practical Machinest and knowes is bissness as superintendent and is one of the Best Millitary men that Connecut as sent into the Field and it is through is Care that the 12th as got to be the Best Drilled Regiment in this Department.

Genral Weitzel ought to be a Judge of men and Redgiments and he selected the 12th for his Bodygard and sticks to us like a Father. He thinks the Union

---

[196] Sgt. William Lucas, Stonington, Connecticut. *Record of Service of Connecticut Men*, 496.

[197] Ledyard Colburn from Derby, Connecticut, Twelfth Regiment, promoted to Full Colonel on January 31, 1863, resigned June 29, 1864; Frank H. Peck, New Haven, Connecticut, enlisted as Major on January 30, 1862, Twelfth Regiment, killed September 19, 1864, at Winchester, Virginia; George Lewis, from Hartford, Connecticut, Twelfth Regiment, promoted on March 1, 1863, to Full Major. Ibid., 474.

safe as long as the 12th is in the field and it is about so. Other Redgiments [h]as men to blow for them but we have not, but that makes no difference when any thing is to be don. The 12th is the Redgiment that can do it. When such men as Genral Phelps Pays Complements to Redgiments and Buttler, thair must be some Cause. You may think that I am blowing, but it is simply the truth.

March 26th

This morning is Cool and Plesent. I have being walking up the Bayou and it looks very much like staying, trains coming and goin. We have Picked up any quanity of Dugouts and Sail Boats that as being Brought hear to keep them out of the Rebles hands. You whould Laugh to see what a looking asortment thay are, but this is a Wattery Cuntry and thay need some means of geting round in high Wattery times. It must be very unhealthy in the hot Wether round hear, but we do not expect to be hear this Sumer if things go only half right.

I hope Henry will come and help Plant all he can this Spring and I wish Virtue had a few good Sheep to run with her Cows as it whould help very much, but thay Cost so much at Present. Wool will Bring good Prices. For some years to come thair will be more Woolen Garments worn then Cotton, I think, and if thair was we shouled be more healthy then we are at Present. Cotton will be King no more in this Worled. His days are Numberd.

The Southron People are Suffering more then you can think but thay are kept down [by] the Iron hand of Millitary Despotism, and thair is no help for them till the Fedral Arms brake the Chains by which thay are held Down, but the time will come and may it come soon.

March 28th

More mud this Morning and I sopose we shall have to take it fore aspell longer. April and May is Wet, but the Sesonse are somewhat the same hear as to home. Thair as being 3 Steamers in and brought me no letter or paper and I expect one in every Streamer. Tell the Chirldren I want them to Write to me and tell me all the newes and how much thay have learnt this Winter and what thay intend to do this Spring. It seems a long time since I see them last, but my three years will come to an end and we live in the hopes that the War will come to a Close before our three years are up.

Give my love to Mother and tell her that I hope to see her again and Father. Tell Virtue to Cheer up and kiss that young Buttler for me and Shake up that Arthur and those young Ladys. I wonder if thair is room for them to get round. Give my love to them and tell them I expect them to lighten the Burden that thair Mother has to bare and do every thing thay are requested to with a Willing mind and the Task is half don. Lewis is Inspector Genral and we expect that he sees to everything and that everything is don to order. Give my love to Edwin and Wife, and see if thay have time to write to me and I expect him to Cast two Votes, one for me and the other for himself, for Buckinham and if he can Shoot that Tom Seymour for me he will do a great favor for me.[198]

Your Affectnat Husband & Son,
CW Sherman

Camp Mansfield, Bayou Baeufe, La, March 30, 1863

Dear Wife & Chirldren,

It is with much Pleasuer that I write to you at this time and that I am alive and in good health at this time.

A Sad desaster as befallen one of the Compneys of this Regiment which has Cast a feeling of gloome over the rest of us. One of the best Compneys Composing this fine Regiment has beaing Distroyed, or nerley so. As nearley as I can get at the facts, thay are as follows: The right Wing, Comprising 5 Compneys, was detailed for Picket duty at Brashaur City. Thay left Camp the 27th for Brashaur and entered upon thair dutys. On the Morning of the 28th, Compney A of the 12th, with one Compney from the 160th New York Voll, was ordered Abord the Gun Boat Diana. The Diana was ordered to go up to grand

---

[198] There was an election for Governor of the State of Connecticut that spring. The candidates were William Alfred Buckingham, Republican, and Thomas H. Seymour, Democrat. Buckingham was selected as a compromise candidate in 1858 and defeated James Pratt by a narrow margin. He was then reelected annually for seven more years, though the vote was very close in 1860 with Seymour as his opponent. Seymour sympathized with the Southern states' concerns and was opposed to the Union Cause. However, Buckingham received over 50 percent of the vote in every subsequent election, defeating Seymour more soundly in 1863. David O. White, *"William Alfred Buckingham, Governor of Connecticut, 1858–1866,"* Connecticut State Library, last modified June 2009, http://www.cslib.org/gov/buckingham.htm.

Lake and look in and make enquirys and find out if the Queen of the West made her aperance in the Lake, as she has being expected down most anytime theas last few weeks with other Reble Boats to Drive or distroy our Boats, the Diana & Estrala and Caloune.[199] The Diana was orderd not to go any further, but to return and report. The Caloune had orders to keep steam up and if she heard any firing to go to the Asistance of the Diana. It apears that the Diana went into the Lake and steamed through into the Hatchafalaya Bayou[200] that Emtys into the Teche and so down to the Bay. As the Diana came oposite a large Sugar House, the Doors was thrown open and two Peices of 32 Pound Cannon was let Drive and into the Boat. The result was the Serenderd of the Boat and 95 men to the Rebles. I have written more, full and Paticulers [to Henry] with a request that he whouled send the Letter to you.

April the 5th, 1863

I recved a letter from Henry with a Paper & after I started to write this letter to you and had Just time to Post it when I had to Fall in with the Right Wing and March to Brashaur City. The Left Wing with my Compney was all ready thair on Picket Duty and as I am with the Colors, I have to stay under the Comand of the Adjutant of the Regiment. We staid to Bayou Beaufe till all the Batterys had Crossed over the Raile road bridge, and the Trains bringing Genral Grover from Lafourch with is Brigade to hold the Bridge in our rear while we footed it back to Brashaur City. [We] went in thair so still that our own Picket did not know that we was thair till the Batterys came in. We were tierd that night, got our tents up again the next day, and are waiting till the time comes for us to move up to Franklin and from thair to Alexandra. We have a hard nut to Crack, but it must be don. The Loss of the Diana as being the meanes of geting us two more Gun Boats [which are] as much superior to the Kinsman and Diana that we have lost, as a Tea Kittle is over a Tea Cup.

---

[199] Gunboats USS *Diana*, USS *Estrella,* and USS *Calhoun*
[200] Atchafalaya

<u>April 6, 1863</u>

This Letter I have been writing some time and a Part of it I have sent to Henry with the request that he whouled send it to you.

We are Packing up again to night to be ready to cross the Bay at any Mineute. The time as come to move upon the Rebles. Do not be afraid, I shall come out all safe I trust, and do not worry about me. The same Power that has Protected me thus fare will Protect me in the futuer. It will be very warm work but we expect to make it short. I do not know as I ought to have writen to you at this time till I knew how it will be with me, but I had the Letter most writen and I thought that I whouled send it. It whouled be some satisfaction to me, if I shouled fall into the hands of the Rebles that I wrote when I had a Chanc.

Cheer up, rember that I am under the Colors and thay will be all safe. It will be a big Pile that gets them. Thair hands will not be in thair Pockets about that time. Kiss my Little ones fore me and keep up your Curadge. My Love to you all. I have no more time.

Your Affectnat Husband,
CW Sherman

Camp Reno, Brashuar City, April 7, 1863

Dear Wife & Chirldren,

We are still hear but our stay hear is short. Our Pontoon Train came last night. Our Regiment was turnd out to unload the train and things look like doing something when we do move, thay are raising the Gun Boat Kinsman that was sunk some time ago.[201]

---

[201] The *Colonel Kinsman* was originally named CSS *Grey Cloud*, and began the war as a confederate ship. It was captured at Biloxi by Union Forces in July 1862. It was rebuilt as an armed steamer and used by the Union Army, renamed the USS *Colonel Kinsman*. The name has been interchangeable with just *Kinsman*. It was in service in the Atchafalaya Basin in southern Louisiana before it sank in Berwick Bay on February 24, 1863, after striking a submerged log. Charles's letter of July 28, 1862, mentions their excursion aboard the *Grey Cloud*. It is the same boat that engaged in the previously mentioned battle with the Confederate ironclad gunboat *Cotton* in January 1863. Roland R. Stansbury, "Remember the USS *Colonel Kinsman*" (paper presentation at Young-Sanders Center, Morgan City, LA, August 21, 1999), http://www.youngsanders.org/youngsanderskinsman.html.

Thair is a string of Troops all the way from A[l]giers to this place. The Whole of Genral Banks Troops are coming by this way to go into the Red Rive[r] Cuntry. Thay have don all that thay intended at Port Hudson and have Shut up the Rebles thair and Cut off thair suplies and thay are doing a great Peice of Engineering Work above and around Vicksburge. The works that we are doing extend 500 mile. Thay Embrace three Distinck Plans eather of which will Reduce Vicksburge and if Roseencrans[202] can hold his own and Whip Brag[g], we think that the War is Virtuley ended.

Thay may hang out in some Parts in the shape of Gurrileas. We are in a c[u]rious Cuntry, but I hope we shall get in to a Dryr and higher Cuntry for I for one do not Fancy this wet and Mudey Place.

April 9th

We are off this morning with 6 Days Rations and it may be some time before I can Write again. Do not fear, I trust to get out of this all right. If so, I will write. Kiss my little ones for me. Virtue, keep up your Curadge, all will be well. Put your trust in One that is able to Preserve and feed you and Protect me under all circustances. I want you to kiss Mother and give my love to Father and accept a large Share your self.

Your Affactnate Husband,
CW Sherman

---

[202] Union Gen. William Starke Rosecrans

Chapter Eleven

Battle of Fort Bisland, Opelousas, on the Way to Port Hudson

. . . boat Diana,[203] that it was warm, you can guess, as the thunder of the guns at 3 & 500 yards started the Blood from some of our mens Ears & Noses.[204] After getting through the Cane field, the 12th was orderd to Lay Down in front to suport 3 Batterys and if thair is a Disagreeabl Place to any man, it is to take the fier from both sides. We had men killed by shell from our guns and, we being in fair sight, thay took great Plesuer in Droping Shell & Grape among and around us and thair Infantry amused themselves in seeing how near thay

---

[203] The date of this letter is unknown as the first page is missing. In it, Charles describes the fighting at Fort Bisland on April 12–13, 1863. This letter was written to his brother, Henry, on very small paper, and the pages were numbered. We start with page number two.

[204] USS *Diana* was a 239-ton gunboat built as a civilian side-wheel steamship. In April 1862, she was captured at New Orleans, Louisiana. She was then employed by the US Army as a transport. In November of 1862, *Diana* was transferred to the Navy and, that same month, took part in action against the Confederates, and also on January 14, 1863, at Brashear City and Bayou Teche, Louisiana. *Diana* was captured while operating on Grand Lake, Louisiana, on March 28, 1863, and was used by the Confederates to shell Federal forces at the Battle of Fort Bisland; that shelling is described here by Charles. She was later destroyed by Federal forces. "USS Diana, Civil War Union Naval Ship," AmericanCivilWar.com, accessed April 23, 2012, http://www.americancivilwar.com/tcwn/civil_war/Navy_Ships/USS_Diana.html.

couled come and not hit us, and I must say, thay did come unplesently near. It was a trying spot and thair was no help for it. The guns must be suported and somehow all the Battery like to have the 12th around. Then thay allways give us a Cheer. Our Boys lay down and take things Cool, wach the afect of Each shot and, if a good one, sing out to give it to them and go in, and you couled not help Laughing, I couled not, to hear the droll remarks of the men.

We had two days of such fun, but it was serious fun for some of the Poor Fellows. To tell the truth, it did me good to see the shell Piched into them Rebles. The Guns round whare I was got out of Aminition once, but thay was soon suplied. Each Cassion holds one Hundred rounds and at the Close of the Last day, thay had to go back 6 mile to fill up 8 again, so you can guess thair was some work don.[205] It was warmer than Antietam so the Artist of Frank Leslies Paper told some of our Officers.[206] He was thair, he mentioned several other Battles and Genral Banks said that it was the most Terific Firing he has heard or that has Being during this Reblion. Thair was some 60 Guns in full blast and all Rifled Peices. The Rebles fierd the Last gun. The first day we fierd the last one.

The second day and when it was over, I for one, felt Releved for such a strain on the nerves is not good. I will mention that I felt Better that night and slept Better then the first night, all though I got no su[p]per. The first night in moving Back for the night the 12th was on the Left and we came to a Large Dich some 8 feet Wide and 6 feet deep with 4 feet Deep of water. The Regiment came to a suden halt. No man fancies Wet Clothes to sleep in, to say nothing of mud and no fier, and as a Regiment is expected to follow thair Colors and the Line was some a head of us, I moved we wade through and in we went and Climbed out a nice looking lot of men. Those that went through after some hundred or so had got wet, the Order was given by the Left Flank and we had the Plesuer of seeing those that were not in the dich coming round Dry as soon as we got straightend out.

Genral Banks came up and Orderd a halt as he was goin to Chaing the Line so as to get out of range of the Enemys Guns which was giving us Particuler fits all

---

[205] Caisson—A two-wheeled carriage used to transport ammunition. *Merriam-Webster*, s.v. "caisson," accessed February 18, 2014, http://www.merriam-webster.com/dictionary/caisson.

[206] *Frank Leslie's Illustrated Newspaper* was the main competitor to *Harper's Weekly*. Faust, *Historical Times Illustrated,* 342.

the time. I sat down side of Banks and scraped some of the mud off me and whrung my stockings as he was telling the men that thay was not retreating and it was Little cared wether he was retreating or not. I was bound to get some of the mud & Watter out of my Clothes.

His Aperance to me at that time as he sat on is Horse was like some Old Farmer giving some instrutions how he wanted the Cattle tied up for the night. He has not a very Millitary Look or way with him, a Old Regulation Black felt hat with Broad Brim, no fether, Dark Clothes and White neck Cloth. My Father whouled make a better Looking Soldier than Genral Banks, but after all he has the Brain and I know that he is round when any thing is to be don and so far he has don it up to the Handle, to use a slang Phraise, and again he has a experanced and Capable Genral in Genral Weitzel. He was Buttlers Engneer and knows this Cuntry has he Conducted the United States Servey of this State and Trusted the Advance to his Brigade and we have come through safe to this Point.

You will see that the papers that Banks will get all the Praise and Genral Weitzel be barely mentiond, but the Boys hear know who dose the Work. You do not know, nor can not imadgin, how we Love that man. He is one of those men that makes no Parade to see him round Camp. You whouled not suspect that he was in Comand, no stripe or strap to show and he gos round so quietly. He will never have the men on gard Trubled by being turned out on is account. I have seing him under fier 5 times when it was warm, giving orders Just as Cool as though he was ordring another Wiskey straight, smoking as unconcerned as though it was a every day afair. He calles us is right hand. We Brought him out of a Bad Scrap[e] once.

I have not writen what I wanted. I have had no Paper and so couled not write when I Whouled. You must Acept it as the best I couled do. I have not tuched on half the things in my mind that I whouled like to. I cannot write to Virtue at this time as we are expecting to fall in soon. If this reaches you safe, Pleas mention it to Father & write to me as usal. The Directions are the same all though we are moving away further from New Orleans. Whare ever the 12th are, and I am a live, I shall recve what ever is sent. I have seen the want of such things as Paper and Tobaco and Watter we wanted very much on our last march but such things must be Put up with.

Give my Respects to Mr. Paul & Family. I recved a Paper from you in the Last Mail and a Letter from Father. I trust I may be spaird to see you all again and keep up your spirits. We shall get out of our truble all right. Never fear. That Conscription Bill suits us to a Charm. It is the finishing Blow in connection with

Freedom to the slave. I do not wonder the Democrats turn Republican, but I can not Put in what I whouled. Give my respect to Elvira and accept the same yourself.

I sent you a Leafe of the Magnola flower. Thay are in full Blow and thay look Beautifull and thay will scent a section where thair is a Orchard of them. When I see them in connection with the Orange Groves I fancey I shouled like a Planters Life. I am Just about Lazey anuff to live hear, but I sopose I shall not come in for one of theas Deserted Plantations as I have not the Dust to give Uncl Abraham and the Old man needs all that he can get.

Your Affectnate Brother,

CW Sherman

Write to Father if convenant and send Virtue and yours . . . I send you a part of the Magnolea Flower. It is about 8 Inche across when Blown out and smell Beautifull Cent. The Cuntry whare thair is a Orchard of them, thay are in full Blow at Present. On every Plantation thair is mor or less of them, but near the river thay grow Best. Thay are Perfectley White but turn to a Brown Color when dry. I have to write in Pencl but I hope you can make it out.

Opelousas, Camp in the Field, April 22, 1863

Dear Wife and Chirldren,

It is with great Pleasuer that I write theas few Lines to you using a Drum Head for a Writing Desk. We reached this Place night be for last after a two days fight with the Reble Genrals Mouton and Sibley. We Drove them from thair strong Intrenchments, captuerd thair Whole Camp Equipadge. It has beaing a runing fight all the way. Banks gave Genral Weitzel the Front all the way and if this Brigade did not have to use thair Legs, I whouled not say so. It was a forced march all the way. The Rebles Burnt all the Bridges and we had to Wade through Swamps and Creeks. At night I whouled throw myself down on the Ground and had to Lay thair for a spell before I couled get round to get anything to Eat.

I must refeur you to the Papers for an account of the March and it was a forced March of one Hundred & 30 Mile. We have baing resting at this Place two days. I have this Chance of Sending you theas few lines. I am tierd but hope to stick it through. I never see Blisterd feet till on this March. We have got into the Cuntry from whare the Enemy as baing geting thair suplies from. Thair Extensive Salt works we have got and it will all tell on the Rebles.

I recve your last two Letters on the March. I shall heed your kind Counsell. I was glad to hear from you and that my Wife and Chirldren were well. Give my love to Mother and Virtue. Tell them to Pray for me. It has been very trying for the 15 Days Past butt I shall trust in one that is mighty to save. Kiss the Chirldren for me. I send you my love to you all. When I have time I will write you more fulley.

Your Affactnate Husband & Son,
CW Sherman[207]

Opelousas, around April 22, 1863[208]

Dear Father & Mother,

Your last Letter that you sent, I recved from you, I got the night before we starded for Opelousas. It was Dark and I read your Letters siting between two Rebel Prisnors our compney was Gard that day of all that was Captuerd, thay was sick of War. Many of them was onley Boyes. In Chasing them up, many got off into the Woods. I know not how maney we took but thay must have amounted to two or three thousand. The Texans and Indans was all mounted and kept out of the way. We Pased lots of Cotton on fier. Thay manedged to Burn a lot of it. We had to march through burning Cotton in Places in getting into the town of New Iber[i]a, or New Town. Dead Rebles Lay round. Our Cavlery Charged on thair rear Gard and took one of Genral Syble[y]'s staff and came near taking him. Thay took one Hundred Prisnors and some of our Boys Brought in more after we came to a halt.[209]

I can not Answer you Letters in any kind of order. I got them all wet, but can make them out. You want to know how I get along with my washing & mendin; I have got to be quite handy mending stockings when I can get any yarn, and for washing my Shirts & Drawers. I have to whare them to keep my

---

[207] This letter is transcribed from copies.

[208] This letter did not have a date. It is estimated to be around April 22 based on content.

[209] This appears to be referring to the fighting at Fort Bisland.

legs from Chafing & thay are made of Cotton Flnel, and washing my Pants, I can Beat Virtue in using Cold Water. We have to keep Cleen when in Camp and on the March. I try to keep Cleen so as to Preserve my health. On this March it has being Tough as we couled not get Watter to Drink that was fit for a Dog and as for the Pest of Lice, I have seing anuff of them, but thay have Trubled me but little as I have a way of fixing them when any got onto my shirt, as I couled not avoid that if any of my Chums had them, and thay was Preaty thick after our long stay on the Transports below Fort Jackson. I never got one on me aboard the Transport has I took my quarters upon the top of the Cooks Galle[y]s. I was wet sometimes but never took any Cold and it was much healthey for me. My schooling on Ship Island had Prepaird me some what for going through the mill. It is the least of my Trubles is Lice, for three Weeks now we have had to be wet and hungry and Preaty well used up.

When we came hear this day, we have being having Rain with thunder & Lighting. Two Poor Fellows of the 75th New York that was on Picket Duty in front of our Camp was struck. One as Died from the effects of the shock. When it dose thunder and Lighten it is very sevear and we are not safe. If the Rebles are not trying to shoot us, one thing or a nother is taking us off. I do try to Put my Trust in that God that has Preserved thus far. I have Beaing whare I did not expect to come out of the fier with Life, but our Regiment came out with onley a few killed & wounded.

The 12th had to suport 3 Batterys and as a consiquence was exposed to a Terable fire. We Lay Down in front of our Guns and Lost men from the Bursting of our own Shell and thay Birst on Leaving the Guns. The fier of these Batterys Drew the fier of the Reble guns. We was Just in front of thair Intrenchments and thay couled see us, but Dare not Charge as that whouled have Brought us to our feet. Thay Raind every concivable missal upon us and around us. The wonder was that half of us were not killed, but Providance carr[i]ed us through safe. I never want to get whare thay can make it any warmer and I hope I shall not, not that I am afraid, but the Ring of 80 peices of Canon in a small space is awffull to say nothing of 20000 rifles, but Cheer up and Pray for me. Kiss them Chirldren for me. You see that I can not write what I whouled. This is the Last of my Paper. Give my Love to Virtue and accept the same yourselves,

CW Sherman

Camp near Opelousas, La, April 27, 1863

Dear Wife & Chirldren,

I am well at Present and Genral Weitzel is resting is Brigade and we needed it very much. This march was very trying to the men. It came very near finishing me. The last Day was through swamps as the Rebles had burnt the Bridge and we had to go along way round to get into the Road that leads to Opelousas. We was two days getting 27 miles.

We marched on Opelousas on Sunday Morning the 19th of April and we shall rember that Sunday the longest day we lived. It had raind all night and in the morning Banks Ordere a National Selute to be fierd in honor of the day, it being the Anseversay of the Battle of Lexington. We started at six in the Morning. It was raining anuff to wash us into the ground. The roads was Cut up with the Arttillery and the March of so many men in pasing through the Town of Saint Martins.[210] Every house had a flag of Truce. The streets was knee deep in mud & Watter. The men went through singin. The People must have thought it of no use to fight men that made fun of hard Marching, wet through and Coverd with mud.

About 3 mile the other side of the town, we halted and the way Fences Sufferd to make fiers to dry the men will be a warning to all futuer generations of Southron men not to get up another Reblion. We Camped that night 22 mile from whare we started in the morning which, under the Circumstances, was good Marching.

The next day we made Opelousas. It was onley seven mile but it took all the next day to get thair. We having to go round so far on account of the Bridges being burnt. We had to wade through one Peice of Watter up to our hips. If you want to see our March, you will have to get Frank Leslies Paper as is Artist Accompned us all the way and for a Acount of the Battle you can get all the Papers how maney numbers it will be in I do [not] know, but I shouled like for you to get them all and I shouled like to see them when I get home which I trust I shall.

The 12th has had to do Picket duty ever since we came out this Ground till yesterday when we were moved into line. We have Built Covrings from the sun & rain of the fence Railes. Whare ever a Large Body of men Camp, the first thing that suffers is the fences and a Large extent of cuntry as being laid open.

---

[210] Saint Martin Parish in southern Louisiana

No Crop can be made whare we go, the Land has being Planted with corn this year with some little Cotton. I send the Chirldren of few Cotton seeds in this Letter.

I had the Chance of seeing the 25th Conn the day Before we march on this Place. Thay are in Genral Grovers Division. I did not see Sissions. He was left sick at Bayou Baouf. G[e]orge Frinke was wounded in the Hand Selightle, nothing serious, so is Captain told me he was left in Franklin. Harry Dudley was left in Baton Rouge sick the day the Division started for Brashaur City. I saw Lt. Brainerd of Foxes Villidge and James Clark, Donahue Fisk. Thay was all well. The 25th got cut up some the morning we started for Franklin. The Cause I will tell you when I get more Paper and time.[211] Theas two sheets that I have sent you written in Pencl was sent to me by Henry. He was in New York and the Paper is some Dirty, but it is all I can do at Present. How long this Campaing will last, I do not know. We have Captuerd a Lot of Cotton and we are waiting while thay Collect all that can be of use to us. The Rebls that we have being after have got into Texas. Thay Rob[b]ed all thay couled, Drove off a Large lot of Cattle & Mules. We have mounted the 4th Winconsin on Horses as mounted Infantry.

Give my Love to Virtue and Chirldren. Tell them to keep up and all will be well. Give my love to Mother and accept the same, Dear Father. Thair will be a spell that you will not get any letters, but I couled not help it.

Your Affactnat Husband & Son,
CW Sherman

---

[211] Ira P. Sisson was from Stafford, Connecticut, and was mentioned in previous letters. He was perhaps a brother-in-law of Charles. Frinke was also from Stafford, was wounded at Irish Bend, and mustered out [discharged] August 1863 with the rest of the regiment. The only "Dudley" was William H. from Stafford—perhaps, Harry is his middle name—mustered out August 1863. This editor could not find a Lt. "Brainerd" or "Brainard," nor a Foxes Village, Connecticut—possibly George Brennan, Second Lt. from Stafford, wounded at Port Hudson. Clark, from Stafford. Adorno P. Fiske, from Stafford. The Twenty-Fifth Regiment engaged in its first real battle, April 14, 1863, at Irish Bend on the Atchafalaya Bayou resulting in ninety-six killed, wounded, or missing of about 350. All of the preceding from Twenty-Fifth Regiment, Nine Month Division, Company D. *Record of Service of Connecticut Men*, 791–806.

Camp near Opelousas, May 3, 1863

Dear Wife and Chirldren,

I recved your kind Letter of April 12th and was glad to hear from you and that you was all well as, Bless a kind Providence, this Leaves me at Present.

We are under Marching Orders a gain. We have stoped at this Place long anuff to get rested and washed up and Genal Banks as got Back from New Orleans and we must be on the move again, but whare, we know not. What we do, [we] must do befor the hot Wether comes in and Banks is goin to Push things in this quater so that it help Ends this War the sooner. I am willing he shall use me.

You mention my Being Color Gard as Daingrous. Well if thair no Dainger, thair whouled not be any honor and wemon whouled go to war and what kind of a World shouled we have then? And you ought to rember that Duty shouled Govner all that Bares the name of Sherman, and to be a good Soldier he shouled never question an Order but simply ask, whares the Enemy, then step to the front and do is Duty. Let it be what ever it may be. A stout Heart and a Clean Breast will all ways come out first. Best never fear. It is as you say, the Enemy allways want to get the Colors, the next thing is to get them. It [is] them Colors that we are fighting fore and it is that that has Brought us hear to Defend. The Rebles have set [at] them at night and we are hear to make them respect them when ever thay are willing [to] set them up again and thay float over every foot that ever belonged to the United States, then our Trubles End.

I am glad to hear that Spring as returned to my Northen home and that grim Winter has had to flee and take up is quearters in the Frozen North. We have being having a Delightfull spring Down hear, but War with its whide Desolation Distroyes the Blessings that Natuer gives this suney land. All through this Cuntry we have had to Distroy the fences and Crops. Thay had Planted the greater Part of the Land in Corn this year, but it will not help them. The Cattle wander over the fields and fier as used up the fence. Thay are Paying a high Price for the Priveladge of having thair homes made Desolate. When will thay Lis[t]en to reson and come to terms with us?

Genal Banks as Orderd all the registerd Enemys of the United States to Leave befor the 15th of this month under heavy Peneltys. We shall soon have the Whole of this state. We have found any quanity of Cotton and thay say our ocupation of this Part of the Cuntry is telling on Port Hudson [and] Vicksburg. I hope that we may get them, as it whouled nearly End the War. Admirl Faregut holds all suplies from the Red River Cuntry and Jefferson the first will find it hard to feed is Large Famley and may be induced to take the Oath to behave for the futuer. May the time soon come.

It is nerley a month we have being with out our Tents and Blankets and we want to get [them] so that we can Camp once more. Thair is a Town above whare we are called Washington. When we got hear thay sent two Peices of canon to Gard a Bridge that Crosses the Bayou above the town. Thay was masked. 500 Reble Cavlery charged on the Bridge Last friday to Burn it, but was opend on by the Battery and before thay couled get out of range, lost 35 men besides many wounded. It will be a lesson to them to let Bridges alone. Thay have Burnt anuff of them latley and Put us to a great deal of Truble in getting round them.

The Election in Connecut has Cheerd the men and Put new life in all of us. We have men that whouled have voted for Seymour if thay had being to home. Thay are mostly Irshmen and do not know any Better. It will has[t]en the End of this Reblion.

Thair is Large quanities of Corn in this Country of last years Crop that come handy to feed our mules & Horses. We Couled never starve them, with the Climat and Plenty of Corn & Beef & Salt, but by get[ting] hold of the Salt & Beef and corn we get to them. The People suffer for many things [this] year, Coffee thay have not had for months, Tea thay have not had and Clothing. Cotton Cloth is worth 250 Cent Per yard. The Cuntry is as bare of many little Nessaryes as a Desert and thair must be some Portions that suffer more than others. When Charlston falls, I shouled think the War nearley over as thay have got to the End of thair Conscription and, as Butler told the New Yorkers, we have not begun ours.

That Box that Mrs. Wicks sent her Husband, I took and Directed to the Marein Hospital, first writing to Sam to know what he whouled have don with it. He Directed to have it sent to him. The Captain told me he couled not get it and, after we moved to Bayou Beaff, it came back again and the morning that we Left Brashuar City for this Expedition, the Captain got me to Put his things away in a Large Comissary Building and that Box was among the things Put away. I moved it myself, but wether I shall ever see it again, I know not. How Sam is I know not, but tell her not to dispair, he will come home again. It is a good thing he did not come with us has the Hardship we have had to go through whouled have Laid him out. If I get a chance I will try and write to him or see him, but I am some 300 mile from him at Present.

Tell Virtue to keep up her Sperits and do the Best she can. We shall get through our Trubles soon and then for home and I guess I shall have got all the Soldering that I shall want for one Life. Tell Mother she must not have any bad Dreames about me and when I get home, I will try to be a better Boy.

Give my Love to the Chirldren and tell them to be good and help thair mother all thay can. I have four months wages due and have being musterd in twice and we Expect to get 4 month Pay, but when I know not. Virtue must want some green Backs and shall have them as soon as I can get them. Write as often as you can. I may not be Able to Answer it at the time. Give my Love to mother and Accept a large Portion yourself.

Your Affectnat Husband and Son,
CW Sherman

Camp on the banks of the Red River, May 13, 1863

Dear Wife & Chirldren,

We have returnd again to our Camp on the Banks of the Red River, 2 mile out of Alaxandra [Alexandria] and shall rest hear one day and then March for Port Hudson and see if we can not Bag the Rebles thair. We have Chased the Reble Texan Troops more then 300 mile. We fowllerd into the Pine Woods whare thay Promised to make a stand. What a grand Place it was. The Road runs some 20 mile through the Woods. Such Pines and White Oaks is not seeing every day.

We have found any quanity of Cotton, every House & Barn full. Not all gin[n]ed, Just as it was Picked. The Cuntry is all Planted with Corn, not much Cotton Planted up this way. Maney fields, you couled not see whare thay did End, and all so evan. Thair is many fields all Tasseled out at this time, Peaches, any quanity.[212] The trees hang full, but we was a little too Early for them.

The Rebles have all Put for Shreevesport, our Cavlery came upon thair Rear Gard. Thay was Crossing the Bayou on Raffts, and we shall go to Port Hudson and Vicksburge having Drove the Rebles out of this Part of the State. We must Drive them from the Mississppi and the way thay are doing things up

---

[212] Meaning the corn is tasseled out at the top

this spring, it looks as though the War must soon End this way. This Marching so far in this hot sun is using the men up fast. Thay have to be sent back. Our Regiment dose not muster 4 Hundred men and not so many more. Soar feet and sickness have Reduced us. My health is good, but I have all I want to do and some days I think I must give in, but have not so far.

Genral Hunter as come from Charlston with is men and a fleet of Iron Clads & Monitors and we are goin to Join him. We have the Rebles in Port Hudson and Vicksburge Cut off from thair suplies and that is what Banks has being doing with us and the next thing is to Bag them. I hope we may be suckcessfull. With the Mississippi in our hands the Reblion will be narrowed down to smaller limits. You to home are waching anxiousley for the End, but not more so than we poor Fellows down hear.

You are Planting, I sopose, at this time and I wish I was thair to see how you do it, but I sopose you are geting Proficient in the Farming line and think that what you do not know is usless to learn, is that not so, Mother and Virtue? But you hold your Horses, do not go too fast. This is the Cuntry to farm it in. Raise any kind of a Crop with out using any kind of Maneuer and I couled live here with Perfect impunity for if I was goin to have the Chills & fever, I shouled have had some Tuch of it. Maney of our men have being, and is now, sick with the Ague & Fever. We have being Camping out 5 Weeks with out any Tents and how much Longer we shall have to stay so, we do not know.

This is a Beautifull Cuntry. We have got away from the lowlands of the Mississppi and, for one, I shouled like to stay up hear, but that can not be. Our work is not don as yeat, and as long as thair is anything to do, I hope our Leaders will do it so that it will not have to be don over again. Thair is scarsley any White men left in the Cuntry, all gone to the War. Nothing but the slaves left and on the Rout[e] that we have Travled, thair masters run them off or what thay couled. You never see such Pleased and Happey men and wemon as theas Slaves are when we Passed the Plantations. Thay whouled Line the road or get on the Top of the Fences to see us Pass and Bless us in thair way, "I am so glad your com" and "we have Being Expecting you so long," "do anything for you?" Thair Masters run the Best of thair Stock & Horses and Mules into the Woods and theas Slaves whouled soon hunt them up and the finest was taken with a Slave that couled ride them and I fancey the Owners will not soon forget the March of Genral Weitzel Brigade as he Alowed his men to take everything that was good to Eat. He whouled allow nothing to be Wasted or disstroyed. The other Genrals whouled not Alow thair men to take anything. Our Camp mornings Looked as though Feathers was Cheap. Poultry suffer some. I have being Luckey anuff to get this Sheet of Paper, but have to write with Pencl. I hope you may be able to make it out. I can not do any Better for you at Present.

Give my Love to Mother and Virtue. Tell them to Cheer up. Our time is half out and the Look at Present is that the other half will be Cut down some, God helping us, it will be. I do hope that we may not meet with and Defeat any whare. Cheer up and Trust in Providence. Kiss my Babys for me. I never see any White Chirldren hear. I cannot write all I whouled. We expect to fall in the morning for the Work on the Mississppi. If we have to March all the way, it will be Tough. Write the same as usal.

Your Affactnat Husband and Son,
CW Sherman

Alexandria, May 16, 1863

Dear Wife & Chirldren, Father & Mother,

We move from this Place at 4 Oclock. It is now morning and I take this opertunity of writing theas lines to you. I am in good health at this time and hope this will find you all enjoying the Blessings of health.

The 12th has being doing Provost Duty hear for two days. We relevd the 6th New York, Billey Wilsons Lambs as they have being called. Thair time is out and they have left for home but the time will Come when we shall come home again, or what is left of us, and it may be sooner then we think and the sooner the Better.

You to home must keep your Curadge up. Tell Virtue never to dispond nor let the Blues get hold of her, but keep up a good Heart. I shouled like to send her some money, but can not at Present and we do not know when the Pay Master will Come round and see us. This is the 5th Month and how much longer the Campaing will last, we cannot tell. I sopose we shall get no Pay till it is over. You shall have it as soon as I can get it. I have a Bounty Check due but shall not get that till we can get into Camp again. You must do the Best you can till I can do better for you. It will all come right, never fear.

We are quartered in the Court House and we have helped ourselves to Paper, such as it is. Court Records and everything Else. You see that I am sending you a Letter on a Bill of Court fees and [just] so you can read it is all the same to me.[213]

This is a Preaty Place on the Banks of Red River. Thair is some Inhabitans hear but most have gon. We are on the Road that has suplied Vicksburge and Port Hudson with suplies & men. The Communication with Texas is Cut off and the Rebles can not get any help from thair, and now we must see if we can not Captuer the Whole of thair forces that is in those two Places. We have Genral Hunter with is Army from Port Roiyl and Charlston and the Iron Clad fleet with Dupont and between Faregut & Dupont with the Land forces of Banks and Grant and Hunter and Sherman and how many more, I know not, we ought to do something and we have don something.[214] So far we have Captuerd any quanity of Cotton; all of Last years Crop. The Texans in thair retreat Burnt some but we Pressed them too hard for them to stop and Amuse themselves much that way. Corn in any quanity we have got if the Goverment moves it with Horses & Mules and about all that the Cuntry contains. It is a Rich Cuntry up hear. It is all Planted by Jeffs[215] Orders with Corn and I hope Uncl Abraham will see that it dose the Confedrates no good when it ripens.

Give my Love to the Chirldren and tell them to be good to thair Mother and help her all they can. Before this Letter reaches you, I expect that the Last strong hold of Reblion in this state will be ours.

In Coming into this City the other night, thair was a Woman Crying and Wringin her hands. I couled not make out at the time what it ment. I Learnd since that this Regiment kiled her Husband and one son at the Battle of Gorges Landing[216] and she hoped we wouled not kill [her] other son. Little dose she think [of] the Widows & Orphans with us North, made so by such men as her Husband and son. Give my Love to Virtue and Mother and Acept the same your self.

Your Affactnat Husband and Son,

CW Sherman

---

[213] He is writing this on an actual form "Bill of Clerk's Fees due" taken from the District Court Parish of Rapides. Soldiers often used whatever paper they could find as supplies were scarce at times.

[214] Maj. Gen. David Hunter; Rear Adm. Samuel Francis Du Pont; Adm. David Farragut; Gen. Nathaniel P. Banks; Gen. Ulysses S. Grant; Gen. William Tecumseh Sherman

[215] Jefferson Davis

[216] This was the Battle of Georgia Landing, or Labadieville, in the Lafourche region on October 27, 1862.

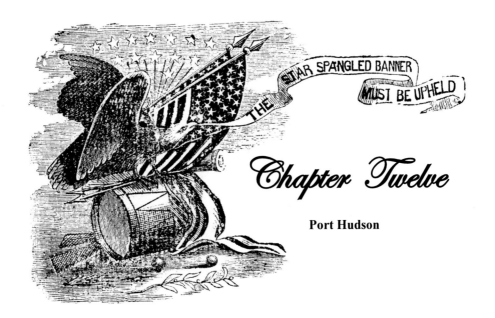

Chapter Twelve

Port Hudson

Port Hudson, June 1, 1863

Dear Wife and Chirldren,[217]

It is with Pleasuer that I write theas few lines to you at this time. I am well and by the Mercy of God, unhurt up to this time.

After two Months of sevear Marching and Counter Marching Genral Banks sent for Genral Weitzel to Bring is Troops to this Place. We have being under fier 9 days and the Place still hangs out.[218] We are in the Woods, having Driven the Rebles out of thair first Line of Works. We are on the Back side or rear of thair Intrenchments. Our line of Battle is seven Miles in length and We have completely serounded the Rebles thay cannot get out as Faregut as got them in front with is fleet and you know if he is a man to let them go that way or not. I am writing this Letter with the Reble bulets singing over my head and shell Droping round. We have silenced all thair guns on this side. Our Sharpshooters keep them away from thair Guns. Our line is some 60 yards from thairs. Thay have within the last 5 mineutes Shot one of our men. The Twelfth is on Duty to day as Sharpshooters. We shall be releved tomorrow. The Cuntry

---

[217] This letter is transcribed from copies.
[218] The Twelfth Connecticut was situated at Port Hudson by May 25. Gen. Banks ordered an assault on May 27. *Record of Service of Connecticut Men*, 472.

hear is very much like the South Woods, all Cut up with Ravin[e]s, onley on a larger Scale. The Rebles have Cleard or Cut down the Timber for about 200 yards on the outsides of thair Works and the Rebles first line of works was in the Woods. Thay made us suffer the first day in driving them into thair Intrenchments. The 12th has lost about 50 killed and Wounded. The Whole loss up to this time is 2500 killed and Wounded and how much more it will cost we know not. We have about 8000 Rebles shut up here and thay will have to give up soon.

I recved your kind letter of the 14th of May. We had just got releved by the 8th Vermont; it and the Bulets was singing lively. It was a Curious Place to get Letters, but we mind theas things but little. It is straing how men get used to Dainger. It is a straing life we lead at Present and full of Incidents, but I can not Jot them down not having the Paper & you tell me that Henry can not stay or help Plant a little this Spring. I shouled have thought that he whouled on Virtues Account but do not dispond, do the Best you can, all will be fore the Best and Trust in Providance, he doith all things well. Keep up a Stout Heart. You will have your Barn full and I Trust that I may see you and help you. I can not write as much as I shouled like to. Virtue I hope will not fret or take any more truble on my Account as it will not help me and will make her Daley Labor more heavy. Mother, I hope will not Worry herself. I have Passed through some Tough Times and the same God that as Preserved me to this Present time will Protect me still. I try and Put my Trust in Him who Goveners Individuls as well as Nations. I have seeing the ut[t]er nothingness of man when he is Brought to look Death in the Face and is Comrads is Cut down around hime. I do not want to discuradge you in anything but to look on things as thay are. You must call out all your Fortitude and Strength of will and it will help you and me to Bare all the Triles that we may be Called to Pass through.

Kiss my Chirldren for me. Give my love to them. I hope to see them again after a few more Months. Give my Love to Virtue and Mother. Thay must cheer up and I know thay will do the Best thay can under the circumstances Thay are Placed in. May God Bless you is the prayer

Of your affectnate husband and son
CW Sherman

Port Hudson, June 2, 1863

Dear Wife and Chirldren,[219]

We are still in the Woods waiting for our Mortar Battery to get to Work as the Intention is to give the Reble Works and Intrenchment a Tirable Shelling as thay will not give up the Place and Serender to us, knowing thay cannot hold out as thair hope of Reinforcements is Cut off some time ago. Thay sent seventeen thousand men to Jackson to help hold that place but Genral Grant Cut them up and dispersed them. How maney thair is inside of thair Line we do not know. Some say 8, and some 10 thousand. It may be more as thair Line of Works is extensive and could not be defended by a small force. Thay say that Faregut Spiked 16 of thair Guns on the River front. One Reason of thair holding out is thair is a large number of Paroled Officers and Soldiers with them and, as thay have Brocken thair Parole it is nattural thay Shouled want to save thair Neck. I want them to give up on Personle grounds. I am Rag[g]ed and want to get some Clothes. When we started from Brashuar City no one thought we whouled be gone more than 8 or 10 days and we Packed our Dress Suites in our knapsacks and took only our India Rubber Blanket and Over Coat. I Put a Shirt in mine and Pair of Stockings and, when we Left Alexandria I gave a Contraband is Brakfast, and, as he wanted to get away and go with us, I engaged him to Carry my things. I have never seen him from that Time to this. I expect he was Captured by the Reble Cavlary that hung on our rear. Officers and men lose thair things. Our Second Leautanant lost all of his things. Captain Roache lost everything he had by the sinking of a Flat Boat.

It is two Months since we left Berwick Bay and in that time we have Travled more then 500 Mile and then did not reach the Center of the State. Thair is not one in ten to home that knows the Extant of theas Southron States. We have not traveled every day. Some days we was Put through 35 Mile. The Wether is and has been very dry and warm.

The New Regements make us Laugh as thay come up. Thay tell our men how thay was Marched 15 mile a day, had nothing but hard Bread and Meat and Coffee. Some Complain how thay was put through 16 Mile and in two days had nothing but Soft Bread, and Pork and Beans, Coffee, luxuryes that makes our mouthes Water to hear them Mentiond; what we have not had for a long time as our teams couled carry nothing but Aminition and hard Bread. Fresh

---

[219] This letter is transcribed from photocopies.

meate we have had in any quanity, but it is Tough and I did not care anything about it. When I couled get fresh Pork I took that, but the Beef is to[o] Tough.

I hope in a few days to send you that we are out of our Trubles and can take a Little rest. Virtue must Put on a Cheerfull face and the good Lord that is over all will do what is Best for us all, if we only have Patiance and Curadge to meet our lot as men and Wemon.

[You] shouled give my respects to Edwin and is wife and Direct you[r] Letters the same as you all ways have. I can not write when I whouled, but when I can, and thair will be gaps in between my Letters but that I cannot help.

Your Affactnate Husband and Son,

CW Sherman

Port Hudson, June 7, 1863

Dear Wife and Chirldren,[220]

I am well at Present and whare I was when last I wrote in the Woods in rear of the Reble Works. We have Just got a Maile but no Letter for me. I got two Papers, one from Henry and one from Southbridge.

We have not got any further into the Reble Works then we got the first day that Cost us a Pile of men. Genral Banks has being making great Preperations to Shell the Works. We have 250 guns in Position and Mortars and tomorrow thay will open. It will be a terable Bombardment. The Intention of Banks is to Shell them 24 hours and if that dose not Bring the White Flag up, shell them till it dose.

We have had plenty of work since Coming hear; the Regiments detailing so many Compneys from each Regiment to Act as Sharp Shooters. The Reble Rifle Pits is Just in front of us and the Boys amuse themselves Shooting at everything that moves in the Line of Pits in thair reach. Our Batterys Shell them every few mineutes and when it comes dark, the Rebles Shell our Guns and us, but so far have don us no Damadge.

Keep up a Stout heart. I shall write again as soon as we have taken the Place. I have but a few mineutes to write this as the Maile leaves. Do not be

---

[220] This letter is transcribed from copies.

discuradged, all will be well. The 25th Regiment is Demorlized and unfit for duty. Thay have being of but little use and thay think of nothing but goin home. Thay are Encamped about a Mile from us. I have being and seeing them. Harry Dudley is well. Sissions is round, but has not done any duty for 3 mo., his leg as trubled him and the Climate. Donahue Fisk is Preaty well. He is not as fat as he was to home. The Regiment will be to home soon.

Give my love to the Chirldren and Mother and Virtue. Keep up, we shall get out of our Trubles if we keep faith in a good Providence and faint not. We have not got any Pay as yet. I have 5 Months Pay due and a Bounty Check of 10 Dollers. You shall have it as soon as I can get it. I have sent one letter to Willington Town and hope you will get it. Do the Best you can. I am in hopes that I shall see you all again and before my 3 years is up. The Battle has to Turn any day now in our favor and then it is all up with Jeff & Company.

My love to you all and may God Bless you all is the Prayer of your Affactnate Husband and Son,

CW Sherman

Cheer up, the Wether is Beautifull and Providence smiles on us and will fight for us.

Port Hudson, June 12, 1863

Dear Wife and Chirldren,[221]

I am well and in Good health this Beautiful June Morning. We are in the Woods in the Rear of the Enmys' flanks. We have them encircled with our Batterys but the genrale Bombardment has not begun as yet. Some of our Guns keep throwing shells into thair Intrenchments and our Sharpshooters keep Pecking away at thairs.

On the night of the 10th about midnight we whare waked up and told to roll our Blankets and fall in without noise as Orders had come to take thair Parepet. 4 Compneys from our Regement was to go forward as Skirmishiers and 4 from the other to be Governd by the movements of the 12th, the other six Companeys to act as reserve. Our line was to move forward all at the same time.

---

[221] This letter is transcribed from photocopies.

Our Boys had no more then Stepped over the Temporary Breastwork on our side, formed by the Ridge, then thay was opend up on by the Rebles in thair Rifle pits. A disadvantage our Boys labored under is it has being very warm and we was expecting rain and the Skies and the Whole Hevens was lightend up with Heat Lightning and showed our men to the Rebs Plain, but thay kept on. In our front the Rebles have Piled in the Brush and trees and it is next to imposable to get to them without losing hevaly. Having a large force to back us up, the Demonstration was made to Draw thair Arttilery fire so that our Batterys could work to Advantage. We cannot get a Shot from them now; it failed to Draw thair fire. The Rebles whouled sing out to our men to come on as thay was waiting for them and ask if we had any hard Bread and Confiscated Tobaco. We have have tobaco served 3 times to us that was taken from them.

Then the Rain came on and put a stop to the Murdring work and the fiering stopped to let the Thunder of Hevan Shake theas Old Woods. It was a Tirable night. The Wounded had to stay till daylight before thay could get thair Wounds Dressed. A shell from one of our Mortars Burst and cut a large tree down on the right of whare I was standing but it did no harm. Thair is being a large number of men hurt by shell from our own guns. The fact about it, this place is a hard Nut and it takes in a large Extent of ground and the Woods Plague us. You cannot see what the Rebles are doing. We want to find thair Batterys. Thair is going to be the most Tirrable Bombardment of the War to take Place hear. We have 300 Guns & Mortars redy to open on the Rebles.

I go out and see what is goin on and View the works; no one to ask me whare I am going and no duty to do but to Rest. I go and fier a few Shots at the Rebs in the Rifle Pit if I feell like it.

I have being down to the 25th today. Harry Dudley was well. Sisson and Fisk, thay will be to hom soon and I shall have to stay a few months longer, but that dose not matter much if I have my health. Thay will soon pass away and I shall feel a great deal better from the fact that I have don my Whole duty in this War. The Name of the 12th is a Tower of Strength hear in Louisana. The Rebles themselves respect us.

Banks wanted to take us out of Genral Weitzel's Brigade and give him a New York Regiment instead. Weitzel told him that he shouled resine is Comision in Vollenteers Serv[i]ce and go back into the Reguler serv[i]ce if he did so. Banks let him and is Brigade alone for he wanted Both. You cannot think how we like that man. He can lead us any Whare for we feel Perfect Confidance in him, and he in us, that no other man inspiers.

It is one of the Worst things to take a Genral away from his men and Put a strainger over them, for some Genrals can never get the Confidance of thair men. The Armey of the Gulf had Perfect Confidance in the Millitary Capacity of Genral Buttler, and it was an evil day that sent Genral Phelps home. He told the Officers that met at is Head Quarters that thay whouled see the very things that has come to Pass in this State that he predicted, and agree with him in the steps that he had taken. I know thair was a great maney that did not beleve him and thought he Payed more Atention to the Slave then to the White Soldier. He claimed that we shouled never put this Reblion down with the White Soldier alone and facts that have come under our own Eyes have proved the Old man was right.

On the right of our line is three Black Regiments and thay have fought as White Troops seldom do. Thay was Brought to the Charge 3 times running on the same day that we came into this place. The Rebles are afraid of what thay used to term "the dam niger." The nigers Can Beat them man for man. The Rebles Charged on them 3 times and the Coons, as we call them, Drove them Back and took more than 100 of them Prisnors. The Rebles, I have heard, took six of them and hung them the same day. The Coons do not give quarter if thay can help it. If any of the Coperheads say the slave won't fight thay tell the Truth, but put Uncle Abraham's Uniform on them and a Rifle in thair hands, all I have got to say is "Rebles keep from under." We have a Regiment of them as pointers and the way thay will work Digin Trenches, Cutting Rodes, we could not get along without them. We are raising nine Brigades of them and thay will be heard from some day. I have Being called a Black Republican and some of our Boys call me Horace Greeley. I Answer to that Name as often as to my right one.

I cannot continue on what I was writing for want of Paper. Give my love to Virtue, Mother, Chirldren and do not Worry about me. I am in the hand of a Kind Providance who will do with me as with him good. Cheer up and trust in the Mercys of that Providance.

Your Affactnate Husband and Son,
CW Sherman

Port Hudson, June 13, 1863

Dear Father & Mother,[222]

I recved your kind Letter of May 27th and was glad to hear that Virtue & Chirldren and you & Mother was well. I am well, thank the good Lord for is kind arm over me. I have not got Faneys Letter but it will come. I am very Sorry to hear that you have met with the Loss of the Old Cow. It is very unfortunate after Wintering of it and Just come in but do not take it to Heart, but keep up a Stiff uper lip and go right on. Something may turn up in the futuer to make you forget the losses that you Sufferd. It is to bad, but things will not allways whare a Gloomey aspect or look. Tell Mother to Cheer up and still trust in that good Providence that has brought us so far. Pleas do not worry but keep up a good heart.

I have 5 Months and 13 days Pay due and a ten Doller Bounty Check due which I shall send home as soon as I can get it. I know not when we shall get our Pay but soon we hope. We can not get it till this Place is taken and I hope it will be soon. I trust to come out safe. I do not want you to worry about me. I will send you as soon as I can. I have sent 3 Letters to Willington and you can look for them. If I had sent to West Willington, Frinks folks couled have brought them up, but you said Willington Town and I directed them thair. Do not truble about the loss of the Cow.

The Bombardment as begun and the Guns shake this Part of Rebledom as it never was Shaken before. The Rebs must suffer Auffully. Thay are Paving way into Port Hudson with Shell. If thair Leaders were not Drunk all the time, thay whouled have Serendere to us befor for thair is not a Goast of a Chance for them. The Prisnors that come in say that it Stinks auffley inside, we have killed so many of them, [along] with Cattle & Mules. The war is coming to a Close for we must and shall Win. Thay can Stave off the Day of Greife but suf[fer] Sorrow thay must. We are in Earnest down hear and mean to do the thing up in shape.

Do not be afraid and keep up a stout Heart, Virtue and the Chirldren will do all thay can to help you and I shall feel better when I can send you a few Green Backs. Give my love to Virtue and Mother. Kiss the Chirldren and Cheer up and do the Best you can. News will come North that will Put new life in the

---

[222] This letter is transcribed from copies.

Nation. Give my respects to all enquiring frends. The Battery shake me so that I can not think the beginning of the End is near.

Your Affactnate Son & Husband,
CW Sherman

Port Hudson, June 16, 1863

Dear Chirldren,

I recved your kind Letter to day and was glad to have you write to me and that a kind Providence has kindley wached over you and Spaird your health and that it is so well with you. May you all ways think of that good Beaing all the day and so Govern your thoughts and Actions, that is Blessing may rest on you. Be good Chirldren and Cause your Mother as little Truble as you can. Help her and make her Burden as light as Posable. Maney Cares She [h]as that you can help lighten and your kind Gran Parents, be kind to them. Age is Coming on and they can not Bare as much noise as you must make sometims. Be careful and not Anoy them. Maney things you can do for them and what ever thay ask you to do, do Cheerfulley.

You tell me that you have lost the Old Cow. I am very sorry to hear of her loss. She was so kind and such a good Cow. It was very unfortunate at this time. I am afraid your Granfather will blame me some on account of that water, but who whouled have thought she whouled have gone into that swamp. I all ways gave her Credit for more sense, but go she whouled and we must Bare the loss the best we can. Your Granmother feels bad about it, you must Cheer her and tell her that Providence will Provide. Many losses She has met with in this World. They are sent to try us, but the same God will give us Grace to Bare our tryles. Keep up a Cheerfull Countenance and will yet be well. I wish I couled send Money anuff to buy another [cow], but I can not.

Your Affactnat Father,
CW Sherman

Have not time to write any more at Present. Give my Love to your Mother, Granmother, and kiss them all for me.

Port Hudson, June 16, 1863

Dear Brother,

I have Just recved your two last Letters of April 29th and May 10th and was glad to hear from you.

We are in the Woods in the Rear of the Rebl Works and a Hot time we had Driving them out of thair first line of Rifle Pits. The 12th lost thair Major and fifty men.[223] It Cost us very Dear, but we have them serounded and thay can not get out. This is the Aufflest Cuntry to Drive Artliery out. It is all Ravins and was hevaley Timberd. The Rebs have Cut the Timber for about 500 yards and have throwen the trees every which way and thair Intrenchments is very strong.

Our Line extends 8 Mile.[224] We have 300 Cannon to open on them Mortars but we know not whare thair Guns are. Our Batterys have thrown any quanity of Shell into them and Dismounted all the Canon that we can see and have Charged on thair works 3 times, but have being repulsed. We tryed it one night to Draw thair Arttlliery fier, but failed. The 12th lost 35 Wounded and 3 Captains, 6 kiled. It was one of the Worst night that I have Experanced.

Sunday the 14th we made another Atack, our Brigade goin forward as Skirmshers. We started at two in the morning, got under fier about 4, Genral Pain Leading the Charge on the Left of us.[225] He was shot down a few yards from the Brest and we gaind the Brst works but was not suported, not anuff men getting into the Works at a time. The Dich on the out side keeping us back. The Rebs raking the Dich Both ways. After Daylight another Charge was made by

---

[223] Maj. George N. Lewis wounded on May 27, 1863. *Record of Connecticut Men*, 474.

[224] On May 27 at Port Hudson, the Twelfth Connecticut, (led by Lt. Co. Frank H. Peck), was a part of the Nineteenth Army Corps, Army of the Gulf which was commanded by Major General Nathaniel P. Banks. They were one of five infantry regiments in the Second Brigade of the First Division. The Second Brigade was headed by Brigadier General Godfrey Weitzel, and was under the command of the First Division and Major General Christopher C. Augur. "Union Land Forces at Port Hudson—June 30, 1863," accessed April 23, 2012, http://pth.thehardyparty.com /fed_units_6-30.htm.

[225] Union Gen. Halbert E. Paine was on the Union right flank for the May 27 assault. He was severely wounded in the leg at Port Hudson on June 14, and eventually had to have it amputated. His diary doesn't refer to which leg it was, however. He returned to duty commanding troops defending Washington, and reached the rank of brevet major by the end of the war. "Brigadier General Halbert E. Paine," accessed April 23, 2012, http://pth.thehardyparty.com/cmdrs/gen_paine.htm.

two Brigads led by the first Louisana. Col. Holcomb, he was shot Dead all most immeadately.[226] He was about the finest man I ever see. The Rebs Pun[i]shed us severley. We had to lay in the Sun in the Ravin all day and the Natuer of the Ground whiped us more then the Rain of lead thay Pouerd upon us. I can not say how maney we are short of. The most of our Wounded is with Buckshot.

It was a sevear day but we are in our own quarters again, a ravin, or one half of. The Brigade is on Duty night and day as sharpshooters. We can not muster 1500 men in the Whole Brigade. The 12th as about 250 men for duty and the other Regiments about the same. We shall get the Place, but it is goin to Cost some thing.

I wish you couled have helped Plant a little, but you know Best. If anything shouled hapen to me, do the best you can for Virtue, but I trust I shall see you all again with Gods Blessing. I try to trust in his Merceys. I have being spaerd to the Present time. We have hard nut [to crack] but a Stout Heart and a good Cause will Suckceed. I cannot write what I shouled but think of me kindley if anything goes wrong this time with me.

Yours Affactnatley,
CW Sherman

We are getting up a storming Party to take the Works. When I wrote this I was well. That night I was taken down.[227]

"The man that I work for at Webster sent for me to come and finish the house. I hope you will have good weather this week."[228]

---

226 Col. Richard E. Holcomb, formerly a major with the Thirteenth Connecticut, was in command of the First Louisiana. De Forest, *A Volunteer's Adventures*, 140.

227 These lines were scribbled upside down in the top and bottom margins of the first page, apparently afterthoughts. Here he mentions coming down with yellow fever.

228 Henry wrote these two sentences at the bottom of the page when he forwarded the letter to Charles's parents and Virtue. Henry's lines were across the bottom and up one side of the reverse side page.

Port Hudson, June 28, 1863

Dear Wife & Chirldren,

I take this Chance of sending you a line. We have not taken this confounded Place as yeat. It has Preaty much used me up. I am a little under the Cloud at Present, but shall be all right again soon.

This Place as used up a large number of men. Genral Banks is making the last Praperations, Bound to go in this time. The Fleet has given the Rebles a lively time, kept up a contineud Bombardment. 28 days we have baing under fier, have made 3 Charges and baing repulsed each time. One man inside of theas Works is as good as 15 outside.[229]

The Rebles have baing trying to take Brashaur City and distroy the Railroad, but have baing driven out. All the Troops baing hear, thay thought it a good time to over run the country but we shall be at liberty to call round thair way and make them a Visit.

I recved your last letter of June 7th and was glad to hear from you, but was sorry to hear that your health was not good, but hope theas few lines may find you good health. And Mother, I recved 3 Letters from Henry telling me that he had baing down to see you, but couled not stay to Plant. I was some disapointed but he knowes is own Bissness best. He says you whare getting along better than when I was to home. Henry said that he whouled come and get your Hay without fail. If he can do that, it will be a great help to you as help is scarce. I hope [every]thing will turn some for the better. It was very unfortunate that you shouled lose that cow at this time but such losses must be baurn with Cheerffullness and that will take away part of the Burden.

I am glad to hear that your Aple Trees look so Promising. I hope the Grass may tu[r]n out better then you Expect. Before this Letter reaches you, you will be getting your Hay and I hope you will have good luck in geting it in. Lewis I hope will be carfull and not get hurt fallen off the Hay, & that Lot back of the House, I shouled think whouled be a good Peice to Plant. It wanted Plowing, the Grass was all run out. That water you can take off and so do away with all fears of anymore truble on that account. Thair must be a lot of mud on the Bottom. I shouled like to see it after the Watter is let off to see how it looks.

---

[229] "Works" meaning "breastworks" which were temporary barriers, usually about breast-high, to protect soldiers from enemy fire. *Dictionary.com*, s.v. "breastwork," accessed February 18, 2014, http://dictionary.reference.com/browse/breastwork.

I know not when I shall be able to send Virtue any money. Not till this Place is taken and how much thay will Pay I know not. She must be in want of some. I hope Virtue will keep up her Spirits. It is Tough times my way and I am expecting this fight to come to a Close sometime. I am glad you have had your Minetuer taken, it was most time[ly]. That one of my Chirldren, I Put up in the Officers Mess Chest when we Left Brashuer City and that was left thair, Put away in one of the Buildings and we have never seeing our Knapsacks or anything since, but it is all saff and I shall send it home when I can get Hold of it again. Give my Love to the Children and Virtue & Mother and I hope I shall feel better in a few days. I have a tuch of the Janders or yellows,[230] and shall have to get along the Best way I can. Sick men can not get much Atention at Present, so many wounded men. Give my Love to Edwin & Wife and all Enquiring frends,

Your Affactnat Husband & Son,

CW Sherman

Port Hudson, Jun 29, 1863

Dear Brother,

I take this Chance of sending you theas few lines hoping thay find you in good health. I am a little under the Cloud at Present. We have baing Subjected to Preaty hard usadge and how much more we shall have to go through I know not.

This Place we have not taken up to this dat[e]. Our Brigade as baing under fier for 35 days and we are getting reduced in numbers. We have made 3 Charges on the Works but have had to give it up as to[o] much for us. The Gun Boats keep throwing those Old Stoves into the Rebles and our Sharpshooters keep the Reble works Coverd as by Death. Day and night we work on them.

---

[230] Yellow fever is spread by mosquitoes. It causes high fever, nausea, and severe jaundice—or yellowing of the skin—from the damage to the liver. In those days, it was sometimes referred to as "the jaunders." At the time of the Civil War, no effective treatment existed. *Yellow Fever*, accessed April 23, 2012, http://www.wtv-zone.com/civilwar/yellow.html.

Banks is making is last Praperations. When the next Charge is orderd I know not, but it will Come off soon. Every thing is nearley ready and it is bound to go in this time. Thay keep 5 full Batterys Harnessed up night and day ready to drive into the Works the moment a opening is made for them.

I have had a Smart Chance of Fevor and now I have got the Janunders and Yellows. I have not baing in any Hospital, but am taking care of myself in the Woods. Thay are oganizin a Select Storming Party of one thousand Vollenteers. I was one of the first that Put my name down, but have had to go to the rear and do not feell as though I couled Charge much. I can Just guide this pen and do not feell as though I couled rip things much. It do not take longe to Bring a man down and make him as weak as a Child, but I shall come up again and it may be all fore the best that I was taken down. Do all you can for Virtue and help get the Hay, if Posable.

We have lost Brashure City, the Rebs hold it. When we left on that March, we Packed our Knapsacks away in some Buildings and we Learn the Rebs made a dash across the Cuntry and tore up the Rail road Track, but failed to burn the Bridges but thay Captuerd our Knapsacks and all that was in them. The Goverment will have to make it all good to us again and thay will have a Chance to see our Faces again after we have Cleend out this Place.

Your Papers Come Preaty reguler to me and I get reading anuff of one of those Papers to last me a week. I am Pleased that you shouled rember me so often. All ways write if you do not get any from me, for it is not any time I can write. Rember me to Alvira and all Enquiring frends.

from your Affactnat Brother,
CW Sherman

when we get into Port Hudson, I will write you how it looks.

Port Hudson, July 2, 1863

Dear Chirldren,

I recved your kind Letter of June 13th and was glad to hear from you and that you were well. I have baing off Duty 3 Weeks and do not intend to do any more till I feel better. I am not Sick anuff to go to the Hospital. I have had the Jaunders and am coming round all right. You need not have any fears about me. I take no Medcin and do not need any.

The Bombardment of this Place go[e]s on and Banks says that he shall Celebrate the Fourth [of July] in Port Hudson. He has got up a Storming Party of Vollenteers. Thay are all ready and tomorrow morning the Asault will be made, so thay tell. My Name was down with the first but that night I was taken with some thing like the Pleursey and I did think I shouled go under, but a Blister and some Pills Put me all right, but left me weake and thay can take Port Hudson with out me. Thay will have to.

This has baing a Costley undertaking for us. So far we have lost 5000 men killed & Wounded. The Papers do not Put the loss so high.[231] Thay never tell the truth in that respect. I can count nerley a Hundred that I have seeing Shot and Wounded right by me and around me. I am geting sick of so much Blood. I have had some Narrow Chanceys. I have had Rifle Balls pass through my hair and have Put my hand up to see if a lock of it was not Cut of[f] by the Bulets.

We are Close on the Rifle Pits of the Rebles so that our Boys talk with them. The Rebs apear in good Condition, do not look as though thay lacked food or that thay are on half rations. We know thay have Plenty of Corn Meal and one steame Grist Mill that is in the Town that we can not get at. We have Burnt Large quanities of Corn that was stored and one Grist Mill. The Rebs use small Hand Mills to grind thair Corn. We can hear them in thair Rifle Pits grind thair Corn. After Dark, the firing Ceases and all is as still as Death unless the Rebles try to bring any Canon to bare on us, and then the stillness is Brocken by our Guns Picking Shell into the Reble works, or whare ever thay can see any thing moving.

We have not given the Rebs one moments Peace since we Closed around them. The Mortar Fleet sends thair Comp[li]ments nights in the shape of 13 & 15 Inch Shell and the Gun Boats make them step round lively, and taken all togather it must be much Plesenter out of that Place then in it.

The Rebles have tryed to get up a Diversion in our rear several times, but did not make out much. The Negro Regiments fight like so many Devles. Thay have taken lots of Prisnors and don good service. We whouled rather have one Brigade of them than all the nine Months men that has baing sent to us. Thay are worth more. What whouled some of my good Coperhead frends do or say to me when I tell them that the Niger makes a better Soldier then the White

---

[231] The losses to the Twelfth during their forty-two days of fighting at Port Hudson were 111 casualties. Blaikie Hines, *Civil War, Volunteer Sons of Connecticut* (Thomaston, ME: American Patriot Press, 2002), 151.

man? The reson is thay are fighting for thair liberty and that makes a great Difference. The nine Months men think of nothing but goin home.

The 4th Massachusetts threw down thair Arms the other day. Thair time was out the 18th of this Month, but Genral Banks wants them to stay till after we have taken this Place. He gave them one hour to resume thair Arms or go to the Tortugas for 3 years and thay thought it best to go on duty again.[232] It makes things worse to have Regiments Act so. Our Three Years Regiments are geting reduced in Numbers and the Goverment must do something to fill up the Old Regiments.

The Hot Wether is up on us and we have not got through with this Campaign. The Rebles have taken Brashur City since we have baing hear. We had a lot of Sick men thair. Thay took and Paroled them. Our People set fier to the Building whare our Knap Sacks were Stoard and Burnt them up. We all lose our Dress Suites and Woolen Blankets and I am afraid that my Pictuer is gone up. I had Put that in the Officers Chest and that was Stoard with the other things.

Our first Leautenant Francis was on the Gun Boat Diana when she was taken and he was shot through the Brest and thay said he couled not live. The Rebles Carr[i]ed him to Franklin and when we went through that Place we left a man to look after him and he got so that he couled Walk round. Since then the Rebles have Come Down and taken him again. The Old man, Rodman Darrow, that was taken with him got a boat and got Francis into it and got a Negro to row them to Brashuer City. He took the Chest and Carr[i]ed it to New Orleans and got a Furlough for ninty days to go home, and wether he has taken the Pictuer or not, I am unable to say or find out at Present if he has taken it. You can get it from him. If he did not take the Chest with him, it is in it, all safe. Do not truble about it till you know it is gone.

You will have begun your Haying before this reaches you and I hope you will have no Truble in getting you[r] hay. Henry will Come without fail, I think. We was Mustard in for the third time first of July. That will give us six Months Pay, but when we shall get it I can not say. I shall send it home as soon as I get it. I can not do it before. I know that you want some Money and it is wrong to keep us so long without Pay, but Genral Banks though[t] that he whouled Put an End to Reblion in this quarter before Paying us.

---

[232] United States military prison on Fort Jefferson in the Dry Tortugas, west of Key West. "History…," Dry Tortugas, Fort Jefferson, accessed April 23, 2012, http://www.fort jefferson.com/history.htm.

Chirldren, I shouled like to see you, but must waite some time longer. I shall be spaird to Come home again. Keep up a stout Hea[r]t and do all you can to help your Mother. Kiss your Mother & Granmother and the Babys for me. Tell them not to fret or worry about me. I am in hopes to see you all again. Some thing will turn up this summer to let me off, I think.

Your Affactnat Father,

CW Sherman

Chapter Thirteen

Port Hudson to Donaldsonville
to Camp Reno

Port Hudson, on Board the Empier Parish, Mississpip, July 11, 1863[233]

Dear Wife & Chirldren,

I am well at Present and hope this may find you in good health. This Place Serenderd to Genral Banks the 9th of July with 6000 Rebles besides 2000 sick & Wounded. If thair were a Happier lot of men then we was, it was the Reble Soldiers when thay Learnd that Genral Banks was goin to Parrole them and let them go to thair Distant homes. We have Regiments hear from Alabama, Texas, Virgina, Mississipip and most every other State in the Southron Confederacy.

The News of the Serender of Vicksburge to Genral Grant came down the River on the 7th. He gets 27,000 Prisnors, 126 field Pieces and 76 he took from Grege and Pemberton in May.[234] He gets 130 Large Seige Guns. How many

---

[233] *Empire Parish*

[234] Confederate Gen. John Gregg, under orders from Gen. Joseph E. Johnston, lost to the Union Army under the overall command of Maj. Gen. Ulysses S. Grant at the Battle of Raymond on May 12, and at the Battle of Jackson, Mississippi. on May 14, 1863. Lt. Gen. John C. Pemberton commanded the Confederate Department of Mississippi and East Louisiana. The May conflict referred to here is the Battle of Champion Hill on the sixteenth, which was a pivotal battle in the Vicksburg Campaign. Grant defeated Pemberton's army east of Vicksburg, and opened the way to the eventual siege and the surrender at Vicksburg. Vicksburg

Guns we get, I am unable to state at this time as we spoilt quite a number and what I have seeing are Monstars, 10 & 11 Inches and one 13 Inches. Theas are mounted on the Water Batterys and taken all togather, this Place dose not Come behind Vicksburge and Naturaley, it was a Stronger Place.

We told the Rebs that Vicksburge was ours, but thay was hard to beleve it. As thay was nearly out of Provisions, and the Newes that we told induced them to Put up the White Flag and thair officers and ours got together and, after one days Talk, Genral Gardner Serenderd the last Stronghold of Treson in the SouthWest and fore the first time in two years, the Father of Waters runs free from the Rocky Mountains to the Gulf of Mexico. The Western men can not complain. Thair River is open and thay have the Satisfaction of Forcing thair way down and through the Reble obstructions that had baing Put in thair way to force them to Join the Southron Confederacy as the Price of the free uses of the Father of waters.

I hope that the Armey of the Potomac will do something this Summer. If thay will onley Captuer Lee and scatter his Armey. Why, the Reblion is down and we couled come home.

We are Encamped at Donaldsonville with 15,000 Rebles under Dick Taylor, old Rough and Readys Son. We have them Serounded. Brigadier Grierson, with his Illinois Boys, is on the outside of them and Genral Weitzel with our Brigade and Pain[e]'s are after them.[235] We are in no hurry. Thair is a Skirmish goin on with them as I am writing. Our Pickets have baing firing for two Days at the Rebs. Thay are in a cornfield.

We expect to Summer a few miles from whare we was last Winter. Genral Weitzel has said that we shouled have the best Camping ground between hear and Thibodeaux. Thats about 40 mile from hear. The Iron Clad Essex with the Richmond have Just Droped Anchor opersite our Camp and things look more lively and Cheerfull to us after baing shut up in the Woods from the 27th of May to the 10th of July.

National Military Park, National Park Service, "The Campaign for Vicksburg," accessed April 24, 2012, http://www.battleofchampionhill.org/trail/index.htm.

[235] Union Brig. Gen. Benjamin Henry Grierson was most noted for a Cavalry expedition in April–May 1863 that severed vital telegraph and rail communication lines between Vicksburg and Confederate commanders in the Eastern Theater. Tim De Forest, "Grierson's Raid During the Vicksburg Campaign," *America's Civil War* magazine, September 2000, published online June 12, 2006, http://www.historynet.com /griersons-raid-during-the-vicksburg-campaign.htm.

Weitzel says that his men shall have thair Pay if thair is a Pay Master in New Orleans. He has sent down for one and you shall have some. I do not see how you have got along without any so long, but I couled not help it. It will not be so again.

I hope you will have got through your Haying before this gets to you and I hope you will have good Luck with your Crops and may Hevan Bless you all. Tell Mother to keep up. I am in hopes of seeing her again. Give my love to the Chirldren and Father and tell him to write often. We had a Mail to day and I did not get any Letter. Henry Sends me the Tribune about every Mail. Give my Love to him and Accept the Bigest slice your self.

from your Affactnat Husband,
CW Sherman

Donnlsonville, July 17, 1863[236]

Dear Wife & Chirldren,

I recved your Last letter of June 30th and was glad to hear from you and that it was so well with you. I am Preaty well at Present.

The Summer is goin and for one, I do not realize that it is so late in the Seson. We have baing knocking round so much and the work we have had to do has knocked time and day and night all askewe with me, but the Rebles have Cleeared out of our front and what Arraingments Genral Banks has made to Cut off thair retreat, I know not for cirtain, but rumor says thay are Preaty Extensive. Grant is helping to some Extent, so we hear. Genral Banks is working night and Day with the Small means that he has to do with. He ought to have 30 thousand more men than he has. We had to give up the Teishe [Teche] Cuntry as all the Troops that Banks had was needed to Port Hudson and the Rebles thought that, by geting in Banks rear and Threatening New Orleans, it whould Draw part of is forces from that Place and releave the Rebs, but he let them work and get in this Cuntry and the moment that Port Hudson Serrendered he sent for Transports to Carry our Brigade with Dudleys and Paines to the very spot that the Rebles was and he has been Colecting the means to entrap theas

---

[236] Donaldsonville, Louisiana

Texan Troops. Thay are all mounted men. Brigadier Grierson is after them with 2000 Cavlery and he will give them a nother Taste of Yankee Pluck and daring.

Banks has raised a Brigade of six thousand Union men from New Orleans. Thay are up the Rail road some where in the Naiborhood of our Old Camp on Bayou Beauff and we have Chainged our Camp for a better one and may stay here a short time. The Coll Peck as just put on a Camp Garde and that is some Intemation of how things are. We expect our Pay in this Place in a few days. It may be any day after this.

Things has a more Cheerfull look to us now. We are out of the Woods and rifle Pits. It is the most trying place to put men. The Tribune of June 27th discribes our Situation to a Charm. The Corospondent is speaking of Vicksburge. Thair is a incident in that paper that I see one Just like it, that is the Sharp Shooting Duel, onley with this Diffearance – our man Shot [h]is Sister's Husband, [h]is wife's Brother. His Name, Charles Constantain. The Rebles recognized him the morning we went in and [h]is Sister waiting on thair wounded and went and told her that the man that Shot her Husband was thair. She came to see him and it was her own Brother. The Coll as given him a short furglough to take her to New Orleans, [h]is wife is down thair.

Kiss the Chirldren for me. I can not write anymore. The Mail goes in a mineute. Give my Love to Virtue & Mother and Accep the same your self. I will write again and more fulley if we stay. Keep up your Speirts. The Newes is cheering from all quarters and this Reblion is goin down.

your Affectnat Husband
CW Sherman

I am sorry I have no more time.

Donnlsonville, July 20, 1863

Dear Wife & Chirldren,

I wrote to you on the 17th and the Envlope was not what it shouled be and I shouled like to know if it gets to you safe. I had but a few mineutes to write as the Maile was goin and if I lost that Steamer it whouled be some days before another one whouled be goin. I hope that you all to home will put up with any small difficultys or delays in geting letters from me. If this place is to be our

Camping ground the rest of the Summer, I shall have more opertunity of writing to you reguler.

We are Camped on the right Bank of the Mississipip in what was a Cornfield when we came, but it as disapeard. I know not if we shall get any Tents. We have not had any Since Leaving Brashuar City. We put two rubber blankets to gather and get some small sticks and make a Shade for two to get under. Whare Fences are Plenty, we can extempor[i]ze quite a Shanty. To Look over our Camp as we are at present, any one whouled think that we was the most folorn and helpless Crowd of men that you whouled wish to see. The men when off duty amuse themselves in Cooking thair Hard Tack as thay call our hard Bread. Thay make curious dishes with it. Our Camp is in what was a City, but now thair is but few Houses Standing.

The Rebles whouled fire on our Boats goin up & down the River, all though told that we whouled burn the place if thay did not stop and one night, to make the Lesson more impressive, some of our Gun Boats Shelled the Place and Burnt it. Any one that never see Shells thrown in the night can form but a feeble Id[e]a of the Distructive and Granduer of the Sight and the auffull Power of shell.

I have had all the experince I want in the Woods. You never know when you are safe. Thay cut the Largest Oak trees of[f] and the Top comes tumbling down upon you. The affect upon ones nerves in the night or day is not sedative. We Lost lots of men by our own Shells Bursting as soon has thay left the Canon and the Peices fliying among the men that were Suporting the Battery.

I see by the Papers that great Credit is given the Black Regiments in the differant Charges that was made on the Reble works. It is all deserved. Thay did thair duty like men and better than some White Regiments that I couled name. The Rebles are very Bitter against them and, as one told me, thay did not care about our using them to dig, but Puting a Rifle in thair hands is the hardest Cut that we have given them. Thay show no Mercy to them when thay fall into thair hands and it is time the goverment was doing some thing to Protect the Black Soldier. When the Rebles took Brashuar City, thay caught 8 Black Soldiers. Thay drew them up in line and Shot them, and thay will Continue to shoot as long as the Goverment remains mute. I wish Buttler was hear. I think he whouled find out a way to Put a stop to this wholsale murder. The Rebles can be made to respect the usadges of war, to say nothing of the Humanity of the thing.

The Papers Put the Loss of the Black troops to high. Thair actural loss alltogather was 300. The Papers put the loss of one Regiment at 600 men. That is not so. That was written fore Affact or for the Northren Market. The truth will do Just as well as to strain it. The Black Regiments are left in Charge of Port Hudson with a few nine months men. Thay are of no account. Banks is goin to send them home by the way of Vicksburge. I wish we was goin now, but the time will come.

You wanted to know my Captains name. It is Capt James D. Roche of Westerly, R.I. He came out hear as First Leautenant. Capt Abbot goin home Last Summer, he was made Captain[237] and Sargent Major James L. Francis made first Leautenant. He was a Showey Officer with any quanity of Asurance & we lost him at Gorges [Georgia] Landing in our first fight, was sent North, came back and was Shot & taken Prisnor on board Gun Boat Diana. He was not on duty, but away from his Regiment & Compney. He was retaken by us when we went up the Teash [Teche]. The Rebles recaptuerd him and Paroled him. He has Brocken is Parole by runing away from the Place whare he was put and has gone home again on a ninty Days Furllough, but it is not likely he will come back to us again.[238]

Most of our Regimentle Officers are coming home on Furlloughs. 3 Captains that was Wounded has all ready gon. Major Lewis of Hartford is goin or will as soon as he can.[239] He was Shot through the Shoulder on the 27 of May as we was forcing the Rebles back into thair Intrenchments in the first days fight. We miss him very much and hope he will come Back to us again.

Two Leautenants the Rebles have taken off with them and all togather our Regiment will need to Come home and recruit again. This Brigade Last Fall when we started for this same Cuntry whar we are to day, Numberd 3500 hundred men. To day it Numbers 1150 men. The 13th Connecut had as maney men as the Whole 5 Regiments that Compose the Brigade. If we have not Sufferd one way and another, I shouled like to know.

---

[237] Edward K. Abbot, Norwich, Connecticut, resigned August 20, 1862. *Record of Service of Connecticut Men*, 495.

[238] Sgt. Maj. Francis died October 26, 1863. Ibid., 495.

[239] Maj. Lewis returned as a Colonel to the regiment in October, just before the Battle of Cedar Creek. See the letter dated October 14, 1864.

<u>July 21st</u>

We have recved Marching Orders to go some whare and to have 10 Days Rations with us, so we are not goin far but it will Put off our Pay so much the longer. It seames as if we shouled never get any more money.

It is very Gratifiing to hear from hom and that all are well. We are not suffincantley greatfull for the many Blessing that our Father in hevan as Serrounded us with. We are to apt to forget his Mercys to us.

As you say, if I shouled have written if Wounded, but so far I have Escaped unhurt. It is all most all ways fatle to be wounded very severley. In this Climate the lack of Ice is the Great Truble, but it is to be hoped our fighting is about over. Thair is a Reble forc[e] in this Cuntry, but this Brigad will not be in the front, will give some of the other Brigads a Chance. We have been in the front fore 3 Months and it is most time we took some rest, but we can not tell to a Cirtainty whare we shall be.

It was my luck to see the first Boat through from Saint Lewis loded with Cattle for the New Orleans Market. After more then two years & half, Bissness is again geting into its usal Channels and we hope never more to be interrupted. Since that first Boat came through thair has been quite a Number through.

What Affected me most was a Sight of the Hartford & Abbross Just above Port Hudson the morning that we got in.[240] Thair thay lay as if nothing had been the matter. When I thought of the Stream of Fier thay had to Pass through to get up by those Tremendous Battery whare I was, it was the greates Wonder that thay got by without beeing Sunk. The riskque thay had to run and the amount of work that had to do after thay got through, no one can conceive. With Visiting the Place thay had to Patrole the Mississipp for more than 300 Mile. She as Just gone up the River.[241] Thair is a great deal of Intrest atached to that Boat with its Gallant Crew & Commander that no other Boat can inspier and thay are all deserving the highest Praise.

---

[240] Adm. Farragut's flagship, the *Hartford*. On the night of March 14–15, Adm. Farragut passed the Rebel batteries at Port Hudson with these two ships, the *Hartford* and *Albatross*. He attacked the forts with his entire fleet, but all were repulsed except these two vessels. The *Mississippi*, grounded, was set on fire and abandoned. Mark Hudziak, "Admiral Farragut Passes the Port Hudson Batteries March 14, 1863," Iron Brigader, accessed April 24, 2012, http://ironbrigader.com/2011/02/09/admiral-farragut-passes-port-hudson-batteries-march-14-1863/.

[241] Referring to the *Hartford*, Farragut's flagship

I know that you are anxious to hear from me, but it is out of my power to write Some times. That Box that Mrs. Wicks sent her Husband, the Rebles got when thay took Brashuear City. Thay got all of our knapsacks and all the Officers Baggedge. It was all stoard in the Buildings thair. Thay took an immense amount of Plunder. Some Reble is wharing my Dress suite, but what I feel most, I lost my Warrent that Coll Deming gave me, but it can not be helped. We shall have the Place back again soon, but that won't restoar our things. I know not if the Goverment will make it up to us. We can get along without the Dress suite as it will save us some extra work.

I have not writen what I want now. Tell Virtue & Mother to keep up, all will yet be well. Give my love to them. Kiss the Chirldren and tell them to be good.

your Affactnate Husband and Son

CW Sherman

Onboard the Cresent City, July 25, 1863

Dear Wife & Chirldren & Parents,

I am once more Abord a Stransport waiting for Orders.[242] We left Donlsonville on the Afternoon of 23rd and Steamed down to New Orleans & Anchord opersite the City. Whare bound, we know not. The 12th & 13th Connectcut are Abord and we are some what Crow[d]ed. The Wether is very hot and we can not go on Shore and we have no Money if we couled. The Boats come off to us with Soft Bread, Watter, Mellons & some can induldge, to the rest of us, it is very Tantlizing. How much longer thay are goin to keep us without Money I know not, and you must be in want of some, but things will not remain so much longer.

Thair is not much Chance of our geting much rest this Sumer. We have got to open the Lafourch Cuntry and recaptuer Berwick Bay & Brashurar City and theas two Regiments has been selected to take the Rebles in the Rear, but we do not move as though our leaders was in much of a hurry. It is Great Punshment to us to be kept on a Small Stransport with no Protection from the Sun. Our

---

[242] Steamboat *Crescent City*

Officers are a Shore as much as thay Please, Drinking and Enjoying themselves, giving no thought for us, how we are Stowed away, or any thing Els but thair own Private Presious Selves. The men have lost all respects for thair Officers and it is most time the War was Brought to a Close.

I for one whouled like to get out and come home but I must serve my time I sopose. I shall make one efort to get a Furlough. Captain Roch is coming home on a Furlough and if he will give me a lift, I think I couled come. It is a considrable of a undertaking to get your Papers, even if the Coll will give his help and 40 Days is the limite of time and 20 Days must be Consumed in goin & Coming. If I couled get a cirtificate from home frome some Doctor that my Wife was Failing and Sickness, I might Posable get a discharge, but shouled have to lose my Hundred Doller Bounty as I have not served two years, but some thing may turn up yet. Captain Roches Father is to work in Stafford, so he told me, and if he comes home I shall want him to Call on you. He told me that he shouled go to Stafford to see is Father thair. Some men that can get home without much Truble and others can not. If you couled Act on what I have writen in regard to a Cirtificate, Large Famly of Chirldren that whouled be left. It must be all straight forward so that thair couled be no Truble. I do not know but I may be writing foolisness, but I am sick of this War and the way we are used.[243]

We came near having a Serious Accident last night. We have some Mules & Horses on the lower Deck and thay got loose. Thair is two Compneys of our

---

[243] Charles goes through a bad morale period in the summer of 1863—he's been sick and the troops haven't been paid for seven months. He eventually bounces back with his grit and fighting spirit; getting paid helped a lot towards perking up the men's disposition. De Forest references the same problems with the paymaster who apparently arrived in Donaldsonville the day after they left on the *Crescent*. He, too, was broke and hungry. According to De Forest, the purpose of this excursion was "to cut off the escape of Dick Taylor across the Atchafalaya," but they arrived too late. He also mentions the loss of their baggage when the Rebels burned the sugar warehouse where their belongings were stored. Charles goes into more detail on this in the following letter of the twenty-ninth. De Forest ends by saying, "A soldier is not a hero in fighting alone; his patience under hardship, privation and sickness is equally heroic; sometimes I feel disposed to put him on a level with the martyrs." It was too bad Charles could not have heard those words at that particular time for he may have felt more appreciated and less "used." As previously mentioned, De Forest was a Captain in the Twelfth Connecticut. He was not in the same company as Charles, and occasionally they were not on the same duty, but it appears that most of the time they were in the same place, at the same time. *A Volunteer's Adventures*, 150–1.

men in one End, the Rest are stowed all over the Ship whare ever thair is room to sit or Lay down. Theas Confounded Mules made such a noise and the men that was down with them, that it waked us up on the uper Deck and the men that were nerest the Paddle box jumped off into the River. A Boat was lowerd and 4 picked up and thair is two missing. One of them the Ordly Sargent of Camp and Named Thomson, a fine fellow. He had Just got Promoted. It was very Lucky the Boat was at Anchord. If we had been goin every one of them whouled have been Drowend as the Boat whouled have Sucked them under.

It is wrong to Put so many men on a small Stransport. We cannot Lay down in any Comfort to say nothing of our many discomforts other ways. You will think that I am Whining or finding Fault unessarley, but that is not so, and get out of this Armey I will if I can Honerabley, but not otherwise. I know that Virtue is Worring her self and if you can get up a Paper without Exciting Suspicion, you know what I mean, and I think Mother is Smart anuff to get it. Send it to me and I will use it. It is all fair in war and thay use us so that I feel Justified in trying to get out of it. If such a Paper was got up Proporley and sworn to befor a Justice of the Peace, it whouled hold Weight. Please do not Worry your selves about me for I am no worse off then others, but I feel some things more than others.

The Newes from the North is more Cheering then it has been and we down hear hope the North will turn out and make the Captuer of Lee and his whole Armey Shuer. We see nothing to Prevent Mead or any other Genral [from] Distroying the Whole of the Reble Armey and so Put an End to this War. Thair is no need of it runing six Months longer.

Our trubles are over. We started at noon today on our Jurnery down the River. We have to go to the Mouth of the River befor we turn. It dose not interst me as much as it did one year ago. The Mississipip is higher then it was last July and truley it is a Noble Streame. No Wonder the Indian, in a Figuertive and Flowery Language, Called it the Father of Watters. It is as Mudey now as ever. I can Drink it now with out making any Whry Faces and glad to get it. It is the best Watter in this state but that is not saying much. I was in hopes of being on its Banks this sumer as we have Sufferd for the want of Decent Watter but to all Aperances that is not to be.

In coming down the River from Donalsonville we Pased our Old Camping ground Camp Parepet but it did not look Nattural. The trees was all Cut down. Orange groves that we had left with thair Red Fruite had all disapeared and Houses like wise. Everything that obstructed the full Sweep of the Death

Dealing Canon had been removed, such is the Fruits of War. Thay are Bitter but those that Sow the Wind must reape the Wirlwind and the Southron People are reaping as thay have Sowed. Is that Scriptur for you?

We reached the Mouth of the Mississipp about Dark and in Grim Silence was Uncl Abrahams 3 War Dogs riding at Anchor. We took on a Pilot and Put into the Gulf. We soon found the Difference between the Easey motion of a Boat on the River and the open Sea. We are laying at Anchor waiting for a nother Piolot to take us over a nother Bar. The Wether is very fine but warm. I am well and if I was Easey in my mind, shouled Enjoy it much but all things will turn out right if we only have Pactence [patience]. I can not contain my self when I see things go as I have seeing them. I know not how you will take the Sugestions that I have throwen out, nor how far you can carry them out, but you can look it over and if you can make it Feasable, do so, but be shuer that it is don right as that will save me Truble. Give my Love to the Chirldren and Mother and all Enquiring frends,

your Affactnat Husband,
CW Sherman
Gulf of Mexco, Transport Crescent

Camp Reno, Berwick Bay, Brashaur City, July 29, 1863
Dear Wife and Chirldren, Parents,

You will see by the Heading of this Letter that we have recaptuerd this important Place again with out fiering a Shot. As soon as the Rebs found that thair Old Enemies, the gun Boats, was coming to Pay them another visit thay did not lose much time in Puting as much Distance between themselves and us as thay couled. It was unfortunat we did not catch them, as I am afraid that thay will Truble us this Summer as much as thay can and I for one do not care about Chasin them all over this state, as we have had Marching and Fighting anuff for 4 Months Past, and since we left this Place last April, we have made a compleat Circul of the Cuntry.

And while we was at the Seige of Port Hudson, the Rebs gathered in our rear to the Number of 20,000 to theraten New Orleans or make a Dash on us at Port Hudson, but thay found that Banks was Prepaird for them thair, so thay made a Raid into the Lafourch Cuntry, Burnt some Small Boats and Captuerd this Place with 1500 men and all our Camp Equeapadge and all our Knapsacks and the Officers Baggedge that was Stoard hear.

Banks had made a Canvalcent Camp hear for the Sick & Wounded men and had a immense quanity of Stoars hear of Evary kind. All of it fell into the Hand of the Rebs. We have not a single thing to bless our selves with, onley what we stand in and I am about as rag[g]ed as I wish to be, but thair is no help for us till the Rail Road is opend once more so that we can have Comunications with New Orleans.

The Rebs Burnt all the Bridges and two Trains of Cars and two Engines and raised the Old Nick genraley so that the 12th and 13th will have to hold this Cuntry till the Road is open. We hear the Rebs have Intrenched themselves again and about 14 mile above us, or whare thay was last spring, and Sunk some Boats in the Teash to prevent our Boats geting up [it]. But I recon thay will get out of that when we start for them, and I hope with Better Luck then we had Last Spring as Genral Grover let them get by him after Genral Weitzel had Forced them out of thair Intrenchments. After two hard Days Fighting, we made shuear we shouled get them, but by the Blunder of one man our work was throwen away and we onley got some 3000 of them by forced Marching. It makes me Ach[e] to think of those Hot Days and dustey Roads and the way we was Put through.

We have no Tents as yet and have to get what we can to cover us and keep the Rain & Sun off us. I have a Peice of Cotton Cloth that I Brought from Simsport[244] that I strech over some sticks and bring the sides down some what like the Roof of a House and a Old Door put up on some more sticks to keep me off the ground and all to gather I have quite a house, Ventolated to kill, rather to[o] much so when the Wind s[h]ifts the Rain in, but it is the Best we can do. Some Put up Shanteys but I do not Fancey them as thay will Leak and are not Breezey anuff in a hot day.

I do not know when I can get this Letter off. I have two written now, one to Henry and one in pencil that I wrote on board the Transport.[245] You must be geting over your Haying if Henry came down as he Promised to. I hope you have had good Luck with your Summers Work and that you may have a Bountifull Harvest and make your selves as Comfortable as you can. I shall do

---

[244] Simmesport, Louisiana
[245] The previous letter of the twenty-fifth on the *Crescent City*

the Best I can, but when I shall be Able to send you any Money I know not. It dose not Look very Promising at Present. This is the 7th Month since we have seeing any money and how you have got Along with out any, I can not see. I hope that Banks will not keep us much longer without our Pay.

He is sending, or goin to, his Pets, the nine Months men, home by the way of Vicksburge. I do not hear the question asked now, are you a Soldier or a nine months man? Some of those Regiments goes home with a Beautifull Name. The fact about it, thay ought to be ashamed to Show themselves. I Notice in some Papers some Tall Lieing in the shape of Puffs that thair frends Put in the Papers in regard to them, but thair is maney of us that whouled fancey goin home with them.

The Wether is Lowery this Month and we having been used to a more Active life then we are Leading at Present, makes us feel dull, cut off from the rest of the Brigade and can hear no newes of what is goin on out Side of our own Pickets.

Leautenant Col Peck of our Regiment is in command of this Post at this time. The men and Officers do not like him. Our own Col has been detached from the Regiment since last fall to take Charge of this Rail Road and put it in good Order. He has the same work to do now has he had last fall onley more of it, as the Rebs took up the Ties for miles and Burnt them this time so that it will take longer to get the Road in runing Order.

This time the Rebs made Shure of geting New Orleans while we was away but got disappointed and it wont be Posable for them to try it again with any Prospect of suckcess. The Texans say thay will never come into Louisana again to help them. Thay have got all the Fun thay want, Long Marches and no Pay. Twice thay have come but have had to retreat Back. Thay did get some Plunder this time, but the Q[u]een City was the Prize thay came after and have had to give it up as a bad Job, and if thay couled have seeing the String of Gun Boats Anchord opersite the City, thay whouled have thought that thay might as well go home. The Gun Boats have nothing to do now but Polece the River & unless Banks moves on Gavlstone [Galveston], as that is in his Department, or Mobile but he will have to have more Troops then he has at Present

That pictuer I have all safe. I am the onley one that has saved thair Dargarietypes [Daguerreotypes] or mineteurs. Leautenant Francis, when he got away from the Rebles, took the Chest, his Clothes and took it to New Orleans and left it thair and when we came by New Orleans in coming hear our Second Leautenant Allen went ashore and got some of his own things and Brought the

241

Pictuer to me and I shall send it home when we get Paid off. I am glad the Rebs did not get it, as thay cirtainley whouled if Francis had not taken the Chest away, as everything we had hear, the Rebs got and took away with them. The Pictuers the men had of thair frends to home, [the Rebs] Put in a pile and Danced on.

Virtue and Mother must keep up a good Heart and make the Best thay can. I know thay will without writing it. Kiss those little Plagues you have thair to home for me. Tell them I think of them often and wish I couled see them but must wait a spell longer. Tell them that I want them to be good and do all thay can to help thair Mother. If you shouled send me any thing, Pleas Put up a Hanchife.[246] I want one the worst way. You couled send me one in a Paper don up Tight.

your Affacnat Husband and Son,
CW Sherman

Camp Reno, Brashear City, Berwick Bay, La, August 2, 1863
Dear Wife & Chirldren, Parents,

I recved your ever welcom Letters, Fancy withe the Pins, and was glad to get them. I recved Henrys Paper. It all came in the nick of time as I was wishing for some thing to read. I was glad to hear of the wellfare of those that I often think of and long for the time that shall make me once more a Free Citzen and the right to go whare ever I Please with out being brought to a halt and the enquiery, "have you a Pass?"

We are still at this Place waiting for the Road to be opend and the Bridges to be rebuilt. The rest of our Brigade is at Thibadaux and we hear have been Paid off, but we shall have to wait till the Brigade Joins us, or we them. We know not which but for one I whouled rather stay hear then go to Lafourch. It is healther hear. We being but 17 mile from the Gulf and the Land is higher and when we left last April it was geting to be quite a Bissness place, but now the still ness of Death reigns hear.

---

[246] Handkerchief

I Notice in the Tribune a peice of fiction put in by some one that knew better, or Els it was for afect. We never had 30000 rounds of Cannon Ammunition hear and do not beleve thair has ever been 300,000 Dollers worth of suttlers storse in the State at one time, and the Slaughteard Negros, I never heard of. Thay did shoot 8 Negro Soldiers at Bayou Bauffe, and kicked and Cuffed the Negroes most unmercifulley. That I do know as we have two or 3 that belonged to our Regiment that was Captuerd thair and when thay found that we were at Donlsonvill, run away and Joind us again and thay whouled be likley to know the fact about it. The Rebs got a rich haul and much good may it do them. We got Port Hudson in exchaing for our Clothes and we are Satisfied if thay are but whouled be better Pleased if Dick Taylor whouled give a nothe Call while we are hear.[247] I have heard that thay Promised to be back in a fortnight, but am afraid thay wont keep thair word, not but I have had anuff of Powder & lead, but maney of us whouled like a recpt for thair lost Knapsacks.

I am glad you have taken hold of that Frink and trust it may do him good but thair is not much Prospect that he will reform. I hope he will not do you any under hand Injurey. I was in hopes that you whouled not have any more truble with him, but he still showes the Cloven Foot and I sopose he will Contineu to till Suden Death overtakes him.

I am Sorry to hear of the Contineued dry wether as it will Injuer your Buckwheat and that is the Cheapest Crope you raise all things considered. I hope you will meet with no Difficultys in geting your Hay. I shall Contineu to send my Letters to West Willington if you think best.

It was a wonder that so maney of us Escaped from the Seige of Port Hudson as whare our Brigade was Posted was in the most Exposed Place. For 42 days a Perfect Shower of Rifl Balls was around us. The men was struck down walking about and Laying down. No Place was safe but thanks to a kind Providence I was Preserved through it. The 14th of June was a Perfect Buchery. The Rebs had us at a great disadvantadge. One Captain of the first Louisana Colerd Troops was shot on the 27th of May and the Rebles kept is Body Coverd by thair Rifles and he was not Buered till Last week. The Rebs whouled not let any one come near him till the 8th of July. His frends in New Orleans gave him a Publick funnrell. We had men Lay out for 3 Days wounded, with out food or Watter. It was the most Dredfull time thair. We thought we had Devils to deal

---

[247] Confederate Maj. Gen. Richard "Dick" Taylor, Zachary Taylor's son

with and I for one was surprised I did not find the Cloven Foot on them when we got in. We shall never have such another time.

Give my Love to Virtue & Mother and the Chirldren. I shall try to write as often as I can. Never fear but thair may be times that you wont have any Letters but thair will be a reson for it.

from your Affactnate Husband and Son,

CW Sherman

no sign of any Pay yet thay may get through this week

Chapter Fourteen
Camp Life in Brashear City, Marching to Franklin

Camp Reno, Brashear City, Berwick, August 7, 1863

Dear Wife & Chirldren, Parents,

I take this opertunity of sending theas few lines hoping thay may find you all in good health as theas leaves me at Present.

At last the long looked for Pay Master as come and handed over the green Backs. We got Payed off Just at night and has I couled not go down to the City at Present, I gave the Chaplain 65 Dollers, as he his a Agent for Adams Express, and the Express & Insurance was two Dollers but it was the Best I couled do. We know not a day, but we may have to fall in and Money is what I do not want round me or I shouled have sent it in different sums in my Letters. I have kept some littl as I want some Butter and I shall want some to send the Minetuer home with my own when I can get away to the City. I beleve I have told you in one of my Letters that it was saved, it beeing down to New Orleans when the Rebs Sacked this Place, or it whouled have went the way of the rest of the things.

I feel vext to think thay got my Corporals Warrent as it came from Coll Deming, not has I ought to think very much of him. The Regiment feells hurt that he did not come and see them befor he went away. I all ways kept [the warrant] in my Knapsack to Defend my self if by any Chance I shouled get into Trubl, be Court Martialed, as I have the same Privladge as Comissiond Officers, onley my Pay his not as much, but I have not thair responsability. Do not read what I have writen in regard to myself as thay might think I was Egostical but all of us have more or less Pride.

The Road is Preaty much Finished and then we shall be all right. I hope you got along well with your Haying. I hope this war will be Brought to a Close befor another July comes round. You must all keep up your Spirits and take things as you find them. Let the World frown if it will. Take Heart and try it again.

Things is very high to home I hear, and I can not think how Virtue has gotten along without any Money for such a long time but Mother must have helped her. I hope and Trust I may come out of this War with my life. If I do, Providence helping me, I shall try to make the rest of the Jurney of Life as Plesent as I can for my Poor Old Father and Mother. I do want to see them and have thair Blessing befor the Angel of Death calls for them and thay have to take that last long Sleep that all of us must take, young and Old.

Those Lines that you sent me whar very Preaty and thay give me strength to do my Duty as far as in me lies, Providence helping me. Virtue I hope dose not worry about [me] but try to think that I am mearley gon a Short Distance from home, be back again in a short time. Sing to young Buttler and amuse her self shaking up that Arthur, and by the way, he looks mighty Glum as he sets in the Chair as though he whouled like to know what that Masked Battery was Placed in his way for. Buttler looks as though he did not care a fig for all the Rebs in Rebldom. Fany is very Nattural. Everyone that has seeing her take her to be Older then she is. Angline is her Perfect self. I can see her Just as well as though she was Present. Lewis lookes as though he was Tempted to Laugh but restrains him self. I shall hate to Part with the Pictuer but I will not run no more riske of the Rebs geting it and Stomping it underfoot as thay did so many others a Short time ago.

20 men go down to the City this morning, two from a Compney, have a Pass for 4 days, but it takes one day to go, one to come back. I shall call on Sam Wicks when I go. He has not gon home, or Captain Roch told me so. Captain James D. Roch goes hom by this Steamer and will go to Stafford. His Father is to work thair. I wish you couled see him. He has a Fourlough for 40 days. His Father is to work on Stone Work at the Springs. Give my love to the Chirldren and Virtue & Mother, and Edwin & Wife, and all Enquiring frends and may Heaven Bless you all is the Prayer of your Affactnate Husband and Son,

CW Sherman

I have sent the Money to Rockvill for various Causes, yours Truley

Camp Reno, Brashear City, Berwick Bay, August 11, 1863

Dear Wife & Chirldren,

I have recved your kind Letter of July 26th and was glad to hear from you and that you was all well. I am well at Present. The Jaunders has left me but I have some billiousness about me and shall till the Colder wether comes Along.[248] The Doctors can do nothing hear if any one is sick, nothing but Bleu Pills, quinine, and then you need not be Alarmed about me. If the Rebs do not slip any Lead under my Ribs, I think, with the Blessing of my Father in Hevan, I shall Turn up in Old Connetcut one of theas days. Have Faith in the goodness of that overruling Providence that has Protected me till the Present and Preserved my Wife and little ones and you, till this Present. We will hope for the best.

I am glad you have got your Hay in, [even] if it is light. I trust your Winter may not be as sevear as thay have been and that you may have anuff and to spaier. I am glad that Henry came down and helped you. It made the otherwise hardest time fore the Farmer more Plesent and your Burden lighter. I sopose I shall be no whare in the Hayfield again after the Doughtly Deeds of you and Henry and the French man, but you waite till Lewis and me get to work behind you.[249] I do hope that your Buckwheat will be a good Crop as I hear that Flour is very high and other things that you have to buy.

I have sent 65 Dollers to Virtue by Adams Express. It Cost me two Dollers but it is the safest way. I couled not do any [other]. Hope it will come safe. I sent it to Rockville and the Letters to Willington. You can guess why I sent the Money to Rockvill. The Pictuers I have safe with me and as soon as I can get some Clean Clothes I shall try and get down to New Orleans and send mine and the other home, and I hope I shall Follow soon, but can not tell when.

---

[248] Biliousness—"A term used in the 18th and 19th centuries pertaining to bad digestion, stomach pains, constipation and excessive flatulence . . . The quantity or quality of the bile was thought to be at fault for the conditions." "Definition of Biliousness," MedicineNet.com, accessed April 24, 2012, http://www.medterms.com /script/main/art.asp?articlekey=19438.

[249] "Doughty"—marked by stouthearted courage; brave. [Middle English, from old English dohtig] *The Free Dictionary* by Farlex, s.v. "doughty," accessed April 24, 2012, http://www.thefreedictionary.com/doughty.

[Sam] Wicks has gon I hear, and I am glad of it fore his Wife and Chirldren's sake. He has never smelt Powder, but when the Wiskey was down you whouled think that the Best thing for the Rebs to do whouled be to get out of his way. I do not want such goin to war as that. We have had to much of that kind.

The Rail road is not opend all the way through but will this Week. We expect the Rebls have not Cleard out of the Lafourch Cuntry and we hear thay are Cut off from geting into Texas and thay have to stay, but how that is I know not for a Cirtainty. We are safe from them all though thay out Number us by 6 to one. I do hope things will take such a Turn this Coming Fall & Winter that the War will be brought to a Close and we Poor Fellows be allowed to step out of the Harness. I have written one letter Pointing out how I think I couled get out of it, but great Care whouled have to be used. You can do as you think best.

Give my love to the Chirldren and Virtue & Mother, and take a large share yourself and may Hevan Bless you all is the Prayer of your Affactnate Husband & Son,

CW Sherman, LA

Camp Reno, Brashear City, Berwick Bay, August 14, 1863
Dear Wife & Chirldren, Parents,

I take this opertunity of sending you theas few lines. It has been some time since I have had a Chance of Writing from Camp, having had to write when I couled which was not all ways under the Best of Circumstances. I hope we shall Enjoy more Leasuer and quieat then has been our lot for 6 Months Past.

You to home must try to Enjoy as much of life as you can. Do not Fret at what can not be helped. Thair is more of Joy in this Worled than we give it Credit for. If we will onley look around for it, it lays with us to Pick out the Suney Places and let the Cloudey ones alone, thay will leave us and we can Easely for get. If we will only look on the Bright Side of things, and let the Dark and Gloome side for those that love to go through life with thair Head Down and looking as though it was a great Sin for to Bring them into this Worled. The tru way is to hold up your Head, look the Worled right in the Eye and if thair is any impedement in the way, Close your Ranks, Shut your Teeth, give your Visor a slight Pull down, Just a nuff to Shade your Eye, and Charge Bayonets, Charge home and the Day is yours.

I have been under the Cloud some myself and have felt as though it whouled be a Releif to lay down and take that long sleep, but Duty called "Charley get up and Put your Harness on, give them a nother Trial,"[250] and I have felt better and Stronger to meet whatever was in Stoar for me. It is no use to grive over what can not be helped. We must all be up and doing or we shall be left behind and instead of our beaing in the front Rank, we shall be found in the Rear with the Stragleurs and those that have Shirked thair Dutys in the Great Battle of Life. Thair, I think I have written you a homley on what we should do. What we should not do I will leave to a nother time.

Thay have got the Rail road finished. The Trains came all the way through yesterday Bringin Genral Weitzel and Staff and thay Burnt some Powder in Honer of the occasion. I was told thay had a small time in one of the Cars & I am glad the road is in Working Time once more, as it will give us some soft Bread. My Teeth are giving out Eating so much hard Tack, and we shall get a Paper from the City every day now and so find out how the World is going.

The Coll is letting two men from a Compney go down to New Orleans at a time. That takes 2 men off for 4 days. It takes one day to go, one to come Back, two in the City. I have not Been down as yet having no Clothes to go in. I shall try to send my Pictuer if I can get it taken, not that it is so very Hansom but for Contrast and Variety.

The Wether is hot. Thats the word - non of your half way warm days but such as thay get up down this way. Give my love to Edwin & Wife and tell him that I get few letters from him. Give my love to Mother and tell her that I often think of her and wish I couled see her but the time will come. Kiss those Babys for me and tell them to be good Chirldren and do what thay can to lighten the Burden thair Mother has to bare. Give as little truble as Posable. I hope your Celler may be full and that Hevan may Bless your labors and all of you with health and Contentment is the Prayer of your Affactnate Husband and Son,

CW Sherman

P.S. One of the Sheafers of Willington, his given name I do not know, he was Ordley of Comp D, was Reduced to the Ranks for Cowderdice or Shirking from the fight on the 14th of June when we made that last Charge on the Reble

---

[250] This is the second instance in which he calls himself "Charley," so one could assume that is his nickname and how his friends and family address him.

Works.[251] I am sorry for him. He has a Son in the Band, a nice young Fellow, but hope that he will do Better. I send Uncl a letter this time. I have sent all my letters lately to West Willington thinking you had got through in Rockville. Sam Wicks must be to home. How he got away I guess he will not tell.[252] I can not use the same means. It was no place for him hear and he shouled never have come, but I am glad he as got away. I have not seeing him for a long time. If you see him give him my respects. I should fancey coming home myself, but must Hold my Horses a spell longer. Keep up your Heart, Virtue, things are working round in such a way that this War may be Closed up sooner than we may expect, but we must.

Camp Reno, Brashear City, Berwick Bay, La, August 19, 1863
Dear Wife & Chirldren & Parents,

It is raining hear to Day and it was what we wanted very much, for the heat was geting opresive and the Misceatoes was having to good a time with us. The Rebs got our Misceato Bars and may thay never know rest as long as thay keep them. We have to Builde fiere in our Camp Streets when it Comes Dark and let the Smoke Smoather us and our little Tormentors, but thay are not so Small, faith, thay are big anuff to Perice through any quanity of Clothing. Some of the men Claime that thair Shoes are no Protection from them. I do not wonder that Southron Chirldren are few and Small, for if thay are not Carred off Bodley thay must be Sucked to Death and the great Wonder is that thair are any Chirldren raised at all. And Flies you may think that you have anuff but where you have one, we have five Hundred. Thair Bite Brings Blood. If Jeff

---

[251] There are four Shaffers listed in Company D: Leonard, First Sgt., reduced to ranks on August 2, 1863; Emory H., Sgt. reduced to ranks (detached) on April 1, 1863; Frank S., Corporal; and Daniel J., Corporal, reduced to ranks March 17, 1862, promoted July 1, 1862, reduced to ranks April 1, 1863. It appears the father referred to here would be Leonard, since he was reduced to ranks in August 1863 and was a First Sgt. or Orderly Sgt. A family tree on www.ancestry.com shows the family with Leonard as father, Emory H. and Frank S. as sons, and no mention of Daniel. *Record of Service of Connecticut Men*, 482.

[252] Samuel Wicks received a disability discharge from Company K, Twelfth Infantry Regiment Connecticut on July 28, 1863. Ibid., 497.

Davis thinks this Cuntry worth fighting fore, I do not, that is for a man to take Comfort in it.

August 19th

A Sad day this as been. Our Second Leautenant Allen of Ledyard, one of the kindest hearted men and a Braver one thair is not in this lower Worled, tryed to take is own Life. He has been in Sick for some time but has tryed to keep up. He was the onley man among all our line Officers that the men respected. He was a little out of his head last night and one of the men staied with him till morning. He got up as usal and went out Back of is tent to the Sink and after Brakfast, he was not to be found. I, with a number of the Compney, went out to look him up but couled not find him. We looked all the Fornoon and into the afternoon. At last one of the men found him with his Jackknife open and his Throat Cut and it apeard that he had tryed to open the Vaines in his arm, but thay do not appear to have bled much. Thair is little hope of is recovery. It is very unfortunate that we did not find him Earler in the day. We all had great Confidance in him and the men loved him like Brother.[253] He was all the Compney Officer we had, Captain Roche having Just gon hom on a Furlough and Francis our First Leautenant is at home Wounded.

We buerid one of our number to day, a old English Soldier that had Served in India. Two more of the Compney was taken to the Hospital this Week. A great many of the Regiment is Sick. I am in Preaty good health at Present, having got rid of the Janduers with out Medcin, havin taken nothing but one Dose of Salts and a Bleu Pill.

The Wether is Wet at Present and Cooler. I hope we Shall go down to the City, that is the talk at this time. We do want to go some whare and recruit. Thair has been quite a number of Deaths in the Regiment latley. Now the men have money thay get things that dose them no good and not being in the habit of Eating such

---

[253] The incident is mentioned in *The Military and Civil History of Connecticut*, with mention of his bravery, and his being held in high esteem by the men. De Forest mentions it also in *A Volunteer's Adventures*: "In an insane access of country fever he had committed suicide." He also complimented Lt. Allen as having distinguished himself at Port Hudson by "his cool gallantry." Croffet and Morris, *The Military and Civil History of Connecticut,* 514–5; *A Volunteer's Adventures*, 152–3.

things, it has a Bad affect on them, but men are worse than Chirldren in some respects, for if thay have the means, thair is no govering them.

I hope that money will reach you Saff and I wish it was more, but you must make it go as far you can. I understand that we shall get two Months more soon and then the Paymasters agoin home to Spend thair Thanksgivings and not come back for four Months and my Thankgiving may be in Mobbile for that Place must come next.

Thair is two Divisions of Genral Grants Armey in our Old Camps, Camp Parepet and Camp Kearney, geting ready to look in upon the good City of Mobile. For whar ever Uncl Abrahams Boys want to raise the Stars & Stripes, neather Principalitys nor Powers in the Earth or under the Earth can Prevent them, and Jeff Poor man as looked is last on Allibama. The lines are drawing Closer and tighter round the Booted Southron Confederacy. Before this Letter reaches you Charlston and Savanana will be ours and if the north will onley Roll up the Conscripts and Strengthen Mead and Genral Foster at Charleston, we have Crushed the Reblion and Roszcrans and Burnsides can com up through to Richmond and Pick up the Pices.[254] I hope that we shall have no more Falling Back, but keep the Ball in motion. It is for the men of the North to say wether we shall come home or leave our Bones hear. If thay will onley turn out at this time as thay Whouled to a Fier we are Saved, the Cuntry is Saved, the War Brought to an End and we Poor Fellows can have a Joliffication with out geting into the Gard House. Thay must bare in mind thay must not come down this way with long faces for thay will not be tolerated. We want them to Bring all the Fun thay can, for thay will need it and a light Heart, but I can not give my Advice for nothing and Shall keep the rest for my Self for I need it all.

Your Potatoes are geting ripe and I hope thay may be free from the Rot. I shouled like to get some of them. We get non and I feel as though it whouled be good to set down to a good meal of Such food as is Spread on your Table, but the time will come never fear. Give my love to the Chirldren and kiss them for me. I send my love to Virtue & Mother. Tell them to bear up, all things will Come right if we have faith. I send my love to you Father and may Hevan bless you all is the Prayer of your Affactnate husband and son,

CW Sherman, La.

---

[254] Maj. Gen. George Meade; Maj. Gen. John Gray Foster from New Hampshire; Maj. Gen. William S. Rosecrans; Maj. Gen. Ambrose Burnside

Brashear City, Berwick Bay, La, August 25, 1863

Dear Wife & Children & Parents,

I have recved your kind letter of August 10th and was glad to hear from you and that you was all well as this leaves me at present.

Our Regiment is about used up since the men have been Paid off thay have been taken down Sick and quite a number have Died. The 12th is onley a Skeleton of what it once was. We have sent home six men to Bring us some of those Luckey men that have Drawen a Prize to come and Join thair Brethern that have Born the heat and Burden of the day. Thay ought to Consider themselves highly honerd to be Alowed the Privileege of Joining the Old Armey of the Gulf. Thay ought to know that thay never come to thair Manhood till thay step into our ranks. That day will be the Proudest of thair Lives.

You speak of the Defeat of Genral Banks, that is all Southron Bragg. We never come any whare near the Rebs but thay Cut and run. Thair aint Southroners anuff in Louisisana, Mississipip and Texas Combined to Whip us and as to Dick Taylor, Green, Mouton & Magruder, thay whouled not waite for two Small Regiments, the 12th & 13th, to come up with them.[255] That was all the Force that Genral Weitzel sent to recaptuer Brashear City from them. We did not have a singl Battery to help us. Thay take us Prisnors, what a livley time thay whouled have doing it, no thay will let that Jobe out.

I am thinking you want to know if I carey a Musket. I do [have] a very Preaty Enfield Rifle, and my Duty is with the help of 7 more Corporls which form the Color Gard to see that the Stars & Stripes are kept up and kept to the Front, but in Battle we do not Fier unless the Colors are in Dainger. We have to reserve our fire till thair is Dainger of the Enemy getting to near us for Safty and then we Just Blaze in thair Faces. We get no Extra Pay but have Cirtain Privleeges, when thair is a Vacance in our differnt Compneys, we stand next on the Roll for Promotion. My Chances are good for a Sargent Birth. Our Captain

---

[255] Brig. Gen. Tom Green was instrumental in the capture of Banks' depot at Brashear City that contained all of their supplies and possessions. James McPherson, *Encyclopedia of the American Civil War: A Political, Social, and Military History*, ed. David Stephen Heidler, Jeanne T. Heidler, and David J. Coles (New York: W. W. Norton & Company, 2000), 878.

is to home. The first Leautenant is Wounded and our Second Leutenant has, under a fit of Insanity, Cut is Throat. Our first Sargent will get a Leautenants Birth and that will make a opening for me. Two of our Sargents are on Ship Island Prisnors of War. It is uphill Work to get up unless you have Strong frends. My Place is Better then a Sargents Birth in some respects. I have no Gard Duty on the March and in Camp have every night in Bed, if a Spruce Board can be Called a Bed. It is all I have to Lay on.

The Rebs got our Blankets, Knapsacks and we have had non given to us yet and Blankets we Shall not get unless we Draw them but have Over Coats instead, so thay tell. The Truth is we have had a Rough Time. I know not who is to Blame for keeping us so, but Blame rest some whare, either with our Coll or the Quarter Master. No Tents nor anything for Comfort but I get along Preaty well and do not worry about me. Providence will Preserve me. It might be Better and it might be much worse.

4 men in Each Compney have been Alowed to go home on a Furlough for 60 Days. We Drew lotts to see who shouled be the luckey ones. I was not one of the Fortunat few, but if Captain Roche had been hear I shouled have been on my way home at this time as he Promised me that he whouled get me a Fourlough, but I shall try. I have been Waiting fore Coll Peck to Come back. If he will give me recomend to the Brigade Sergon to give me a Cirtificate of Disability, I can get hom and if he will not, I can not Come. Do not think of my coming for a great maney have tryed and been refused, and it may be my Luck, but I shall not Cry my Eyes out if I am Disapointed. I have got used to Disapointments.

I am glad you got your Hay in in good Shape and that you was Able to be thair your self and that Henry did not Disapoint you. If he couled not stay himself, he found a man that couled do the Work. I hope I may be thair myself a nother time to see you swing that Hook.

The 25th Regiment is to home by this time and I know nothing of thair beaing Cut up. I know that it whouled take a great many such Regiments to Amount to much and the less thay have to say of thair Feats this way the Better.

Give my love to the Chirldren and Virtue and Mother and may Hevan Bless you all is the Prayer of your Affactnate Husband & Son CW Sherman.

I have sent Virtue 65 Dollers and you must have got by this time. Write me if it came safe. Rember me to Henry if you see him and his Wife, Edwin & Wife and all Enquiring frends.

yours Affactnatley
CW Sherman

Brashear City, Berwick Bay, La, August 29, 1863

Dear Wife & Chirldren,

You want to hear that I am well. Well I never was better in my life all though thair is many sick at Present, but I think the worst is over as the Wether Chainges and we draw nearer to the Fall. It is very warm in the Middle of the day but quite Cool Evanings and in the night a Blanket whouled not be to much. Some of the men have Drawen Blankets but I shall not at present. If the Goverment can not make good what we lost I am not goin to Pay them for one. At present I am thinking that the United States is geting Stinge and using us Poor Fellows quite mean in not making up to us befor this what we lost. I do not know but I shall see you soon, if so I will write.

I have writen you about our Second Leautenant Stanton Allen Cuting his throat while laboring under a fit of Insanity. We did what we couled for him but we couled not save him. He has gon from us to that other Worled. We must not Judge him for we know not how soon our turn may come to try that unseeing Path. We put him in a large Box and sent is Body to New Orleans to be Emblamd and Put in a Matlick Coffin to send him home.[256] I made Aplication to be alowed to go home with the Remains. I had no Officer to aply to. The Coll has been down to New Orleans for some time and I went to Captain Dickson of Compney C. He his the Color Captain and with him I have been Detailed for the last six Months as one of the Color Gard. I told him my Story and he has kindley Enterceeded for me with the Major for me and he has Promised to forward my Case to Head Quarters, and I hope thay will favor me. It is next to impossible to get Furlough at Present. Thay was goin to let 4 go from each Camp but thay have returned the Papers Disaproved and that is knocked in the

---

[256] Fisk Metallic Burial Case, patented by A.D. Fisk in 1848 and manufactured with modifications, such as the Fisk Model 3 whose improved form was patented in 1858, and remained in production well into the post-Civil War era. Dan Sumner Allen IV, "The Mason Coffins: Metallic Burial Cases In The Central South" (paper presented at South Central Historical Archaeology Conference, Middle Tennessee State University, Jackson, MS, September 20–22, 2002), PDF e-book.

Head and thair is no chance of my getting a Cirtificate of Disability from the Sergons. I do not look Pale anuff and my Chance whouled...[257]

September the 1st, 1863

I have not had Permission to Bring the Body of the Leutenant as yet. He will have to be kept till next Month on account of Sanatary resons and the 12th is under Marching Orders, but whare we know not. I will write soon and let you know. I hope thay will let me go home with the Leautenant as it is my onley Chance unless I whouled get Wounded severley wich I can dispense with and feel Just as well without a Ounce of Led in me.

Give my Love to the Chirldren and Virtue. Keep up your Spirits. Charlstons ours and Mobile will be soon. Genral Weitzel is expected to Show off is Brigade that way and luck will Follow us under him.

Your Affactnate Husband,
CW Sherman

Brashear City, Berwick Bay, La, Sept. 14, 1863

Dear Wife & Chirldren,

You will see by this Letter that we are Back again to Brashear. We spent some 7 Days down to Algiers and then was orderd Back to this place.[258] The Expedition to the Sabine Pass Sailed with out us,[259] and for one I am not sorry

---

[257] He apparently got interrupted here, as this sentence is not finished, and he starts again on September 1.

[258] The Twelfth Connecticut went to Algiers on September 2 in anticipation of joining the Texas expedition; however, the transport selected was not seaworthy and, before a substitute could be found, news of the failed assault was received and the regiment returned to Brashear City. *Record of Service of Connecticut Men*, 472.

[259] The battle of Sabine Pass took place on September 8, 1863, as the Confederates turned back a Union attempt to invade and occupy part of Texas. Gen. Banks sent some 4,000 soldiers and four gunboats under the command of Gen. William B. Franklin to try to gain a foothold at Sabine Pass where the Sabine River flows into the Gulf of Mexico. The Confederate Fort Griffin, under the command of Lt. Richard W. Dowling with a force of only forty-four men, was a target, but it managed to force the Union to retire and to capture the Union gunboat *Clifton* when it ran aground. The *Sachem* was

as it Ended Badly for us.[260] We shouled have been on board the two unfortunate Gun Boats that the Rebles took, the Seventy fith New York was put on them as Sharp Shooters instead of us and, at this time, I shouled be a Prisnor to the Rebs instead of writing this letter to you. I can not tell you so much of the Desaster as the Papers will give you, but as Genral Weitzel had Comand and his Brigade was thair, except the 12th C V, I knew that you whouled be anxious to hear from me and I am well at this time.

I have heard nothing as yet of my Aplication to be Alowed to come hom with the Leautenants Body when it is fit to be sent and my Chances are small I am afraid, but I shall endaver to do my Duty just the same.

Grants 13th Armey Corps is hear and a Part of the 9th, Burnsides Old Comand and we are rather Crowed for Room with so many men. Thair is to be a big time this fall and we know not how soon we may move. The Expedition to the Sabine Pass has returned and our Brigade is Down to Algiers and we may be on duty on the line of the Mississipip and not go with the Western Troops, but it is all in the Dark has yet, in fact I do not know who is in Comand of the Western men.

I hope I may hear frome that Money I sent Virtue soon, has it was sent on the 4th of August and now it is the 14th of September. I do hope it will arive safely. I put it into the Chaplains Hands in less than half an hour after beain Paid. He is a Agent of Adams Express Compney and took it down to New Orleans the next morning. I send you a Pictuer of three of Compney K. It was taken for Julius Pasco[261] of Wharehouse Point[262] and he gave it to me to take care of it for him. We were over in New Orleans at the time when we heard that the 12th was on the Cars for Brashear. The Grass did not grow under my feet

---

also exploded by cannon causing the *Arizona* to retreat when it could not pass the *Sachem*. The fourth gunboat, the *Granite City,* also turned back in face of the accurate artillery of the fort. Captured were 300 Union prisoners along with the two gunboats. Alwyn Barr, "Sabine Pass, Battle of," *Handbook of Texas Online,* accessed February 19, 2014, http://www.tshaonline.org/handbook/online/articles/qes02.

[260] Meaning the Union

[261] Julius Pasco served in Company K, Twelfth Infantry Regiment Connecticut from February 1862 to February 1864 when he was transferred into Company B, Twelfth Battalion Infantry Regiment. He was mustered out on August 12, 1865. *Record of Service of Connecticut Men*, 497.

[262] Warehouse Point, Connecticut, is where his uncle and aunt, James and Elizabeth Derrick, resided.

much till I found myself in Camp. It was after Dark, the Regiment was all Aboard the Cars and I had Just time to get in when the Train Started and Julius Pasco was left behind and his Pictuer with me and I take this means of sending it to his Mother and Sister at the Point. Please send it to Sarah Derick as his Sister works in the Mill and I want it to go to his home without Fail.

Your harvesting will be on your hands before this reaches you and may it be Bountifull and you all be well Paid for your labors. Keep up your Heart, never give in to disponding thoughts. All may be well, this War may come to a Close sooner then we may think. The Rebs can not get the Line of the Mississipp never again and with out that thay are Down, no hope for them. We may have some Fighting down hear but we shall get the Better of them in the End.

Cheer up Mother and Father I trust to see you all again. Kiss the Chirldren for me. I do not know has I shall have a home long anuff in one place to get into my Old habits of thinking but I will try to write whar ever I may be.

Your Affactnate Husband and Son,
CW Sherman

Berwick City, September 18, 1863

Dear Wife & Chirldren & Parents,

I have been waiting to hear from you once more be for we leave this Part of the Cuntry for good. The long talked-of Expidition for Texas is Actuley underway. Genral Weitzel Crossed his Old Reserved Brigade to this side of the Bay on the 17th and we are to have the Advance. We are on the same ground we was on in April last. The Brigade is not what it was, but he sayes he will Comand it as long as thair is men anuff to Carry the Colors. I am still thair for one and shall stick thair.

When we came over yesterday the 114th New York was sent out as Picket. In the Afternoon some Reble Cavlery Charged on them. Thay fell Back about half a Mile. The Genral was waching the move and orderd the whole line under Arms. One of our Batterys threw a Shell among them and that spoilt the fun. Just out side the Picket is a Shugar Mill with 500 Barrles of nice Sugar and our Boys all have a Sweet tooth and will run any Risque to get it. He [the General] road up to the Picket and seeing a lott of men round the Mill enquired who those whare. Beain told thay were some of the Brigade after Sugar, well thay desarve it, says he, but do not let any more out to night as we couled not tell what might hapen, but in the morning thay can go again.

On our last March through this Cuntry, Chickings & Pigs sufferd some but this time a half of what is left this time will not be much. Thair is a Big Pile of men this way. The 13th Armey Corps that was Genral McCellerands, Genral Ord Comands it now,[263] and how much of the 19th Army Corps gos, I know not but Genral Weitzel has one Division of it. We have a long March be for us if we go from hear to the Rio Grand. I shall have a fine Vew of this Contested Cuntry if nothing hapends to me, which we will Trust in a kind Providance to Protect and save me from all harm.

I recved a Letter from Henry in the last Mail and he told me that he had writen to you to get some Cloth and make me some Clohes to send to me. I am sensible of is kind intentions towards me and thank him, but I do not wish you to send me anything but two Dark Blue Woolen Shirts and Tobaco as I have Drawen a Pair of Pants and a Blouse, and I am not goin to have any more Clothes then I can Carry Conveanintly as we shall all ways stop long anuff in Places to wash up. We was hard up this Summer, but that couled not be helped I sopose, as it was Difficult to get food to us and some days we had to go Short. I asked Henry if he couled send me two good Shirts and some Tobaco I shouled feel indeted to him, a Pair of strong suspenders, Ink is our Principl need and as we are goin on a long March, anything else at this time whouled be out of Place.

September 19th

The Wether as Chainged quite Cold. It nips us some but it will help us that have had a Tuch of the Swamp Fever. I, for one, feel quite Differant.

---

[263] Maj. Gen. Edward Otho Cresap Ord, United States Army, was a West Point graduate. He was severely wounded in 1862, but returned to command in 1863 and had commands in Louisiana and in the Shenandoah Valley. He took over command of the Thirteenth Army Corps on June 19 from Gen. John A. McClernand and moved the Corps to Jackson, Mississippi, after the surrender of Vicksburg, and was moved then in August to New Orleans and the Corps saw duty in Texas and Louisiana. Catton, *The Civil War*, 312; "Edward Otho Cresap Ord, Major General, United States Army," Arlington National Cemetery Website, last modified September 17, 2005, accessed April 24, 2012, http://www.arlingtoncemetery.net/ecoord.htm.

September 21st

The grand move through the Teash [Teche] Cuntry has begun. Genral Weitzel, with the first Division of the 1,2,3 Brigades takes the Cande. The 12th is in the 3rd Brigade. We moved yesterday 5 mile and Camped and last night our mail came and I recved your kind and Cheering letters of September 2nd and Faneys kind letter. Tell her that I was much pleased with her letter and the kind words of Cheer it contained. I am glad that you are more hopful of the futuer and that Virtue feels more reconciled and that we must Trust in a kind Providence for life and Safty through the many Daingers that we must be Called to pass through. I shall do my best to keep up and do my Duty. Never fear, I shall not Desert. I wrote that letter through low spirits, Cramped up on a small stransport, but I feel better and my health is good.

I am glad that the money got home Safe. I know you must be in want of the money and hope it may do you good. I wish it was more. Do the best you can and Providence will help us through. Let Sisions have his child, if he can do better by it than you, which I Dout very much.[264] I do not know what to say to you, Father, About Potter. I wish I couled send you a Hundred Dollers to Pay him. I do not want you to Part with your Stock & Hay, but I hope you will not be Oblidged to give him a nother Morggage and that he will not force you to Pay till you can see a way to. I recved your Papers and the Handchiff all safe and the little Currle from the Genral's[265] little Currley Head and a Preaty Currle it is and long; may those Currles Wave in the Breeze and Sun. Tell Lewis I am Pleased that he is trying to read and Angline that she is trying to write. Tell them to stick to them Studys and thay will suckceed. I send my love to you all. I can not send you letters now reguler as we are on the move but you can write Just the same. The Mailes will follow us whar ever we may go.

Your Affactnate Husband & Son,

CW Sherman

---

[264] This would be Virtue's sister's baby, last name of Sisson, whom Virtue took in months earlier. It seems as though her sister has died, and the widower wants to take the baby back. If Ira Sisson of the Nine Month 25th Connecticut Regiment is the brother-in-law and father, he would have just recently returned home; however, the first names of the sister and brother-in-law have not been definitely determined.

[265] His pet name for Charles Butler Sherman after General Butler. Charles B. would be about twenty months old at this point.

Camp in the Field near Franklin, Sept. 27, 1863

Dear Wife & Chirldren, Parents,

It as trubled me to get a Sheet of Paper & Ink to write to you, but I have made out to and hope theas few lines may find you in good health as theas leaves me at this time.

We moved our Camp forward 15 mile yesterday and the day was very warm. It made quite a number of the men Sick. We may stay hear a few day for Orders. I hope we shall not have any forced marches. We are on the same line of march that we was on last Spring.

Tel Harry Dudley that Pigs begin to Suffer some, but Chickins are Scarse. We have had very Stringent Orders read to us about Straglin & Entering Houses, but if thay can keep the men from Adin to thair Scant rations from Rebl Stock, thay will do more then is possable.

Genral Weitzel was goin out to look at the Picket the other day and met a Soldier with a Goose which he was tryin to hide under is Blouse. He had twisted the neck but not anuff to keep it from kickin. The Genral see how matters stood and when he came up with the Soldier he Sung out, "my man, you had better give that goose a nother twist to keep it still!" Genral Weitzel is a man and a good Genral and is willin to have the men help themselves as much as thay can use reson in it, not to waste any thing. In our last march, men Shot Cattle Just to get thair Toungs and left the Carcas to stink. Now he dose not alow such wast as that and it will not be repeated.

It is reported this morning that the Rebs are moving down to meet us but it may be only rumor. Thay will get whiped in any case and what is the use of thair undertaking to stop us. The Old Flage must wave and thair rag come down.

In one of your letters you spoke of Dick Taylor capturin 6,000 of us. Now we have never been able to have him stay long anuff to make is acquaintance. He is great on Wiskey and making Retrogade movements. He was so Drunk[266]

---

[266] There were obviously a lot of rumors floating around the different camps, however, it was discovered that Dick Taylor suffered from rheumatoid arthritis. The attacks from this disease would leave him incapacitated and crippled for days. During the Seven Days Battles in 1862, he was unable to leave his camp and command his brigade. Perhaps these attacks contributed to rumors of heavy drinking. "Richard Taylor," The New Texas Handbook. http://www.angelfire.com/tx/RandysTexas/page70.html;

when he Captuerd Brashear City last Jun that he couled not sign is Name to the Paroles of our men and it had to be don by one of his Aids,[267] and every one of the men are on duty again except the nine month that have gone home. The Paroles were of no use as thay have to be Signed by some Genral, and that simple thing give us 40 men to our Regiment that we couled never have had the use of again till thair time was out.

I hope that you will keep up your Spirits and never get down Hearted. You will be gathering your harvest about this time and I wish I couled be thair to help you. The Fiealds hear are all growen up to Weeds. The Houses all Deserted Preaty much and decay and ruion marked on this land. You whouled be Surprised to see the amount of wild Stuff that is on the Fiealds hear. We had to march in line of Battle over them last Spring as the Rebs were in our Front and we had to be . . . .[268]

Richard Taylor, *Destruction and Reconstruction, Personal Experiences of the Late War in the United States* (London: William Blackwood and Sons, 1879), 112, PDF e-book.

[267] As mentioned in this letter, it was Taylor who reaped the benefits of seizing the stores at Brashear City in June when the depot containing their supplies and knapsacks was captured. The spoils included twelve guns, 32s and 24s, "small-arms and accoutrements, and great quantities of quartermaster's, commissary, ordnance and medical stores." These supplies were in such abundance as to serve for the Red River campaign of 1864. Ibid., 185–186.

[268] This letter is missing the rest of its pages. There is a gap from this letter dated September 27 until October 22. *Record of Service of Connecticut Men* mentions the march to Opelousas where the regiment remained until late fall when it went into winter quarters in New Iberia. *The Military and Civil History of Connecticut* puts the timing of the return to New Iberia in November. Charles states in the letter on the twenty-second of October that he and six others were left at Franklin, as they were not well enough to march. *Record of Service of Connecticut Men*, 472; Croffut and Morris, *The Military and Civil History of Connecticut*, 515.

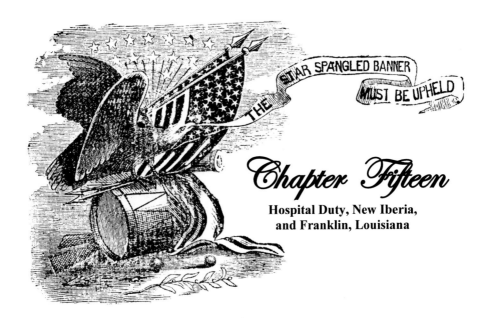

Chapter Fifteen

Hospital Duty, New Iberia, and Franklin, Louisiana

New Iberia, October 22, 1863

Dear Wife & Chirldren,

You may think I have forgoton you, but that is not the case. I am not with the Regiment, but back at the Genral Hospital. I got left at Franklin with some 6 others of my Compney that was not well anuff to March,[269] and when that Hospital brock up and moved to this Place, those of us that were well anuff was put on the Boat and sent on to our Regiments. We did not reach New Iberia till late in the Afternoon and I, being the onley noncommissiond Officer in our Squad, had to hunt round for Rations for us. We expeced to find the Brigade Camped some few miles out of New Iberia but found thay had moved forward the day befor and was some 40 mile a head of us. Some of the men couled not March and I found Amblances for them to go to the Hospital. It was Dark again. I got them started. It was some 4 mile to the Hospital and I felt some tierd, got about a mile outside of our Picket and went off the road into the Praiere and lay

---

269 *The Military and Civil History of Connecticut* quotes a soldier's letter to home in which the soldier states that August and September was spent in "one of the most unhealthy localities in Louisiana. Nearly all the regiment was sick at Brashear City; so that the fall campaign was entered with less than 200 men for duty, and with nearly three hundred in the various hospitals of the department." Croffut and Morris, *The Military and Civil History of Connecticut*, 515–6.

down for the night thinking to get to our Boys before thay started in the morning, but the Amblance Train started by light that morning and when I arived at the Hospital whare thay had Put up the night befor, I found them gon. The Sergon in Charge gave me some Brakfast and, after a few questions which he Put to me, told me that I couled not go on as he wanted me to stay with him, and has the Hospital was Just starting and every thing had to be put in Order. I had my hands full. I had to go and Forage Pots and Stoves to Cook with, get Neurses to look after the sick, Dig Graves, make Head Bords,[270] Draw Rations for 250 sick & Wounded men, see that every man had what he wanted, and get the roomes sweeped Cleen and other things too Numerous to mention.

You think I am Joking but that is the last thing I shouled think of doing. I have seeing to much Suffering to Joke. I have not so much to do now but it is anuff. I have to Buery the Dead & Draw the Rations and Polece the Hospital and go after forage.

I do not want you to write to me any more till you hear from me again as your letters go to the Regiment and I do not know when I shall get them and to write to me hear, I might not get them as I might not be hear.

I [am] Preaty well and hope this may find you all in good health. Give my love to the Chirldren and accept a large share your selves one and all. I shall write more full in my next.

Your Ever Affectnat Husband and Son,
CW Sherman

New Iberia, October 28, 1863

Dear Wife & Chirldren, Parents,

By good luck, our Chaplain called into the Hospital on is way to the Regiment today. He has been home and was Just returnd and, as he Looks after the Mailes for the 12th, he had the Maile with hime. He kindley looked it over for me and 3 others that is away from the Regiment, and by that means I got your

---

[270] Grave markers. This term is used also by Sgt. Larkum in his letter to the family in October 1864.

two Letters of the 5th & 12th of October and two Papers from Henry. Those are the only Letters & Papers that I have had for some time. He will send me my Letters, if any, when he gets up to the Regiment.

I was glad to hear from you and that you was all well and that the Genral[271] gets along so well and takes after you. I do not know as he couled Imitate a Better man or one that couled set him a Better Example, unless it was myself. I have some Conceit, you perceive, Soldiering has not taken it all out of me yet, but it has Learnd me some Rough Lessons.

I recved all your Letters and the one that Fany wrote. I have never answerd Fanys Letter but will when I get time. That Pictuer of 3 of us, I thought I explain in the Letter that I sent with it, it belongs to Julius Pasco and I hope his Folks will get it has my Honor is at stake if any thing shoueld befall it. I shoueld think that you might make out that one of the three was your Fathers Son. I sent mine in the Parcl containing the Chirldrens and I am glad thay got home safe, so that in the time to come, if I shoueld fall into the hands of the Rebles, thay wont have my Wife & Chirldren. I shoueld like to have kept it but my Wandering life that I have to lead whoueld not admit of it.

That Cider you speak of will not do me any good has I shall have to stay my three years as things look now. If I couled onley stay in the Place I am in at Present the Rest of my time that I shall have to serve my Uncl Samul, I shoueld like it and thair is no knowing, but I may. I live well hear, have given up Soldiers Rations and begin to fill my Clothes and couled manedge to get along the Rest of my time esay for I am Just Lazey anuff to Boss a few men and do things up Brown. You think you have to work hard now, but wait till I get home. I will give you a lift. It will come Preaty Tough to go to work my self. No more calling on Black Bill or yellow Jack or Aunt Diana to do this or that.[272] Sometimes I think I shoueld like a cuple of Hundred Nigers and some of theas fine Plantations whare I couled lay back under the Orange Trees and smoke my Havanas, not a Care in life as the Poet says, let the Wide Worled Jog on as it will, we will be free and Easay.[273]

---

[271] Young Charles Butler Sherman is about twenty-two months old at this point. Charles is referring to his father as the man the child is "imitating."

[272] "Aunt Diana" reference is to the gunboat *Diana*. Yellow Jack is yellow fever. The Rebel uniform had a gray hat with a black bill so he likely means a Rebel soldier.

[273] These last few sentences are obviously tongue-in-cheek, but as hard as Charles has toiled, one can imagine he would be daydreaming of a life of leisure about now.

Still I wonder how Lilebridge[274] likes Paying 600 Dollers, that Drawes on his Patriotism some, and Edwin, how did he feel when he came so near being a Bold Soldier Boy?[275] I am glad he got out of it as he did, has one Sherman is anuff to serve is Cuntry at a time.

Give my love to the Chirldren and Mother & Virtue. Tell them to keep up a Stout Heart and Pile on the Wood for a Cold Winter is coming on.

That Box you speak of that Virtue has sent I have not got. I spoke to the Chaplain about it, he told me thair was non for me. He had a list of all the Express Matter that was at New Orleans for our Regiment. It may come in the next Steamer. We expect to move down to New Orleans soon and I shall have a Chance of seeing to it my self if thay keep me. The Chaplain will look out for it for me, has he gets all the Boxes that is sent to the 12th himself , and he knowes whare I am. I shall stand a good Chance of geting it. I did not want you to send me anything till I knew whare I shouled be, but I guess it will be all right. Take no truble about it.

---

[274] Burnham Lillibridge is mentioned in more letters in 1864. He was a friend or neighbor from Willington and is listed in the 1860 Willington, Connecticut Census as being fifty-four years old and a farmer. He had two sons—Truman C., age twenty-one, and Sherman, age seventeen. There is a military record for Sherman, Eleventh Regiment, Company B, transferred to Battalion of Engineers, October 1862. None could be found for Truman (see next footnote). "United States Census 1860," Census Place: Willington, Tolland, Connecticut, Roll: M653_80, Page: 601, Image: 343, Family History Library Film: 803080; *Record of Service of Connecticut Men*, 440.

[275] "The Conscription Act of 1863 also permitted two means of escape for those drafted men who could not obtain an exemption for health or hardship. Anyone who paid a commutation fee of $300—the yearly wage of a common laborer—would be excused from the draft call in which he was chosen, though he might be drafted again in the next levy. The man who wished to secure permanent exemption could simply hire someone who was willing to enlist as a substitute in his place. These clauses, and particularly the commutation provision, provoked many to object that the conflict was 'a rich man's war, but a poor man's fight.'" The figure of $600 used by Charles means that Lillibridge paid the commutation fee and also hired a substitute. Lillibridge may have paid for his son, Truman, to avoid the draft since his other son Sherman had already enlisted. William Marvel, "A Poor Man's Fight," *The Civil War's Common Soldier*, nps.gov, accessed April 24, 2012, http://www.nps.gov/history/history/online _books/civil_war_series/3/sec2.htm.

The Fall as been very Beautifull so far, but we are having a little Wet Wether at this time and we need it very much as this Summer has been very dry and the Water Tanks are low.

Yours Affactnatley,

CW Sherman

Kiss the Chirldren for me and let the Genral run and Enjoy himself.

New Iberia Genral Hospital, November 4, 1863

Dear Wife & Chirldren Parents,

I am still well and doing well and hope this letter will find you all in good health. The Armey is still Camped hear and to all apearance will Winter hear. The Cold Wether still holds off and that Suites me to a Charm, but if I couled get home this Winter, I whouled run the Risque of Freezing. But when we do get a Cold North East Storm it makes us think of Over Coats but such wether dose not last long. The Gardens was in a healthey a few days ago. Cabbages was growing & Turnups, and in as much Security as if it was Sumer. The Flowers in Bloom and it put me in mind of Summer to hom, but a untimley Frost Cut things and put an end to many Plants. Such is life in youth, life and the Futuer looks bright, all Sunshine and Flowers, but as we advance in life our hopes wither and we gather dry leaves instead of Flowers, but our hevanley Father has Planted in mans Nature hope so Strong that it sustains him all through the Jurney of life, till the last Closing of lifes great Problem.

The 12th Con was Paid off the other day and I thought it was most time that I shouled look on Uncl Abrahams Pictur as it looks on the Green backs that the Paymaster brings round with him and see how a few of them whouled affect me. I find that the ownership of a few is good for the health and have sent 40 Dollers of them to Virtue to make her laugh and my sixth Bounty Check, which is good for ten more and that makes fifty Dollers. I have Directed it to Willington Town and hope to hear of the safe arival of the money and hope it may make you all the Happier. It dose me good when I can send any thing home during my Absance to the Regiment.

The Medical Dirrector of this Department Promoted me to be Asistant Steward of this Hospital and sent in my Name to Genral Banks to have me Detailed from the Regiment and that is one step in my favor. It entitles me to a

Goverment Horse and Rations for the same, besides insuring me good keeping and a good Bed to lay on as long as I am in the Service. I never asked much, but that is better then I expected and I feel very thankfull for my good luck and hope it may continue. The Compney was glad to see me when I was down to the Regiment and when thay hear of my good fortun, I have the Satisfaction of knowing that every man among the many that I have been with, will wish me luck. If that is not Braggin I do not know what is newes.

I have not much to write and I hear but seldom from home, how the war is goin or what the prospect is for this winter. I do hope that Richmond may be taken and the Rebls forced to give the war over. I do know that the Rank & file of the Confederates are heartly Sick of the war and want to go home. Thay have had all the Fighting thay want, and a nother winter Campainge will bring them to that last dich thay talk so much about and the sooner thay get into it the better it will be for them if thair is only Dirt anuff to Cover them so the Dogs wont find them.

I want Virtue and Mother to make themselves as Comfortable for the winter as thay can. I shall often think of them and the Chirldren and Pray that no harm may come to them. You must see that Master Lewis dose not get onto that Pond till it is Froze hard anuff to bear up a Horse. I sopose it will be most imposable to keep him off the Ice and I am willing that he and those young Ladyes shall Enjoy themselves, but not to neglect thair Studys or run into needless Dainger. Please let them get into the Snow and tumble as much as thay please for I cannot. My Slaiding down hill days are over and I beleave that a little fun is healthfull faith. You whouled think I did if you couled onley have been in the Tent that me and some 7 more occupied. Was not that tall times? The Captain used to think that it was not alltogather a Moddle Tent but I am out of it at present and am leading a steady life. Give my love to the Chirldren and accept a large share one and all.

C W Sherman
Assistant Steward
Genral Hospital New Iberia

New Iberia, November 13, 1863

Dear Wife & Chirldren,

You must excuse my not writing to you oftener as I have had so much to do that I couled not; nights I am to tierd. I am still at this Place doing all I can to help the Poor Fellows that is sent hear from the Front. As soon as thay get so that thay can help themselves, thay are Passed down to New Orleans and others sent to the Hospital. We have two hospitals hear.

The 19th & 13th Armey Corps are Consolidated. The 19th is Genral Banks Troops. The 13th is Genral Grants. Eastern & Western men are Fighting this Campaing to gather. Thay are Camped some 50 mile from this Place and are waiting for the Rebs to come down upon them. You must not sopose that our men are Idle. Thay have Skirmishes withe the Rebs every Day and our Caverley have a Beusey time on Picket & garding Waggon Trains.

I fare Preaty well hear, Better then any time since leaving home. I am geting to be quite a theefe and it wont do fore me to come home fore I might take things that do not belong to me. I have to do the Foragin for the two Hospitals. I have the Bigest Team in Town, 5 yoke of Oxen and 6 or 8 Contrabands for Drivers and if Corn and Chickings come in my way, thay suffer. When I first went out on the Praiere I felt lost. No roads, nothing but Cattle Paths to guide ones self from one Point to another and small Farm Houses. The Praiers is Coverd with Cattle & Horses and no Owners as far as I can see. If Uncl Sameul & Uncl Abrahams Boys Suffer for Fresh meat the fault layes with themselves. Goin on foot is simpley westing time & Shoe Leather, for all you have to do is to throw a Lasso over a Horse's head and then run the Risque of your Neck for a day or so and your mounted with out throwing your Green Backs away in a Horse that may be stole from you be for morning. For Horse Flesh, as the Darkeys express themselves, is mighty unsartin hear.

We are throwing up Brestworks about two mile out of town. We must hold this Cuntry, Cost what it will. The Rebs are in force in our front. Genral Verbadge is in Comand of this Place.[276] The Pickets Caught one of the Citizens goin out of the lines with a Invitation to the Rebs to come down upon us and the Citizens whouled help them. The Genral sends for the Provost Marshall and gave him Orders to take very man and Put him to work on the Fortifications so

---

[276] Since there is no "General Verbadge" or anything close to that, he most likely means "verbiage" as in an excess of words; in this case, verbal orders are in command.

as to keep them out of mischiff. Men that never did a Days work in thair lives have had to take the Shovle and the Hoe with Nigers and do something for thair Cuntry.

It was a good thing and it may save us from a fier in our rear. The Bayou runs up above this Place. All our Commissary Stoars comes up on Boats from Berwick Bay. The Rebs have any quanity of Gurilles out and thay thought of taking our Boats. Thay fierd into one that had a Gard of Colerd Soldiers, Wounded 3, but killed non. We have them at the Hospital. Thay are doing well. The Gurilles are Preaty thick. It is all I can do to get out of the lines now to Foragge as it is not safe. I hope you do not truble about me for I am doing well and have good Rations and shouled like to stay but cannot tell what may turn up.

The wether is Beautifull, Just the kind to Brace up the sick & Wounded men. You must be having Cold Wether and a little Snow by this time. Cheer up and trust that I shall be to home again some time. Providance has been very kind to me and I feel thankful that it is so well with me at this time. It seems more like home to me to set down under Cover once more.

I do not know when I shall get any Pay again has my Captain refuses to send my Discriptive List, but if the Doctor is a mind to have me Detailed, he can get it for me.[277] You must try to get along till I can do something for you. It may be soon. I have 4 months Pay Due me and a Bounty Check, if you have not recved one, has I left it with one of the Boys to get it and send it to you for me. I hope you will not want for anything till I can send my Pay. I know you must be in need of money to get things for the Chirldren.

I get but little newes where I be of the War, and how things are goin on. I know but little of the Fight or how the Battle is, but trust we are wining, holding our own will not Pay. We must get ahead.

Give my love to the Chirldren and tell them thay must not for get me if I am away Down South in Dixie. I send you my last Pass that is given by all Provost Marshalls in the South to all Prisnors and all that have to go out of our lines. I have to get one of them most every Day. Tell Virtue she need not get

---

[277] A descriptive list, or roll, documented the volunteers. It was a form that included vital statistics such as name, age, height, complexion, color of hair and eyes, birthplace, occupation, period of enlistment, promotions, demotions, etc. "Descriptive List and Account of Pay and Clothing," in Virtual Exhibits, Item #406, accessed April 24, 2012, http://sos.ri.gov/virtualarchives/items/show/406.

marr[i]ed, she must wait anothe[r] year, [278] for I shall cirtainley Turn up some time and Father & Mother must Bare up and Carry the Burden a spell longer. I shall be thair to help the Waggon along. Cheer up and Trust in Providence. I send my Love to you all and may Hevan Bless and Preserve you all is the Prayer of your Affactnate Husband & Son,

CW Sherman
Genral Hospital, New Iberia

I have Just got that Box and was much Pleased with it, but do not send me again as you can not tell what I want most.

New Iberia, Genral Hospital, November 22, 1863

Dear Wife & Chirldren,

Having a few mineutes to my self, I thought I whouled Indite a few lines to you. I shouled like to give you a Orange that a frend has Just rolled across the Table to me, but as it wont keep, I think that I shall Eat it myself. You may think that is one way of showing my kindness, but it can not be helped.

At this time I am well and in Better condition than at any time since coming into this Delightfull Clime. This is sunday and one of the most Beautifull Days that you ever saw. We do have nice Wether when it is in Seson and that is most of the time. The Cold is not what the Natives represent it to be. I have never seeing Ice since I have been hear, but have felt the Cold more then at any time to home.

The 19th Armey Corps is Just below Town Strung along the Bayou Tash [Teche]. The other night Genral Carr surprised a Texan Regiment that was out scouting and was coming into town.[279] The next morning, having been informed that we was gon, he took 120 of the Beautyes and whouled have taken the whole Regiment, but 6th Missure [Missouri] had to go some two mile further then the rest and did not Close up in time and the rest of the Grey Backs got away, but it was a good thing, as it was. Thay was a Miserable looking lot of men Dressed in every thing under the Sun. Thay did not look as if thay whouled set the Mississipp on fier, but thay made some truble.

---

[278] Tongue-in-cheek. This last phrase is eerily prophetic, even though he meant that he had one more year left of his three-year enlistment.

[279] Brig. Gen. Eugene Asa Carr

I guess you might write to me. I shouled have got your letters and I do not know, but I made a mistak in writing to you in the way I did, not to write to me till I knew whare I was, but at that time we all thought we was goin into Texas, but the Armey did not go any further then Opelousas. Now thay have returnd and my Brigade is onley 4 mile below and I hear that Weitzel is goin to Winter hear and in that case, I couled get my letters. My Captain and Coll sent for me to come back to the Regiment, but the Sergon in Charge requested them to let me stay a few days longer. The Hospital is goin into the other hands the first of next month and I do not know that I shall stay, but I shall try to be retained. I know that thay like me hear and my quarters is much better than in the Regiment and I know the Differance between hard Tack and Soft Fodder which is considerable of an Item. If I stay this Winter hear, my time will be drawing to a Close.

How things is Progressing I know not, but the Newes hear is that Banks is in Texas and has Captuerd 5 mile of Cotton and the Union men are flocking to the Old Flag by Thousands and Banks is getting on and Subduing the Reblion at a great rate. I have not seeing the Union men that thair is so much talk about in this State. I do not know but thair may be some. I have to see the first one. I hope this may find you good health and that this Crule war was over and we poor Fellows on our way home again.

Give my love to the Chirldren and accept the same your selves from your Affactnat Husband & Son,

CW Sherman

New Iberia, November 29, 1863

Dear Wife & Chirldren,

I have just recved your two last letters of October the 27th & September the 20th and was glad to hear from you and that you was all well and that you was doing so well. You speak about some money that I sent. I sopose you mean the bounty Check. I was not cirtain that it was sent as I have not seeing the Compney for nearley 3 months and thair must be another Bounty Check due soon.[280] I hope thay will Pay the Regiment off whare thay be at this time, so that I can Send a nother 50 Dollers or so, for a Cold hard winter is be fore you and you must want maney things for those young Ladyes and Jentlemen that you have with them, faith, I shall not know them if I have to stay my 3 years. That is if my Life shouled be spaird so long, which I trust it may.

This is Sunday and a very cold day it is for this place. The Colerd Jentlemen are nearley Froze and thair White Brothers are put in mind of thair Northen homes and large fiers and Smiling Faces that used to gather round the Old home Stead and Earth Stone, but time Flies fast, the longest day has a Ending, and our time will be out soon. I am still at the Hospital and have Snug quarters, but how long thay will last is the question I can not Answer at this time, but do not take no truble on my acount.

I was sorry to hear that mother was still trubled with that trublsome Pain. I was in hopes that it whouled Leave her as the years came round, but that dose not seame to be the case. That Pictuer that I sent is not a veary flattering one, but I was not so bad off as you imadgin.[281] I did have a Shirt on, if you do not see it, if you will unbutton my Blouse you will find a Shirt. But those Shirts, Virtue, that you sent me was Just what I wanted. The Paper and Envlopes came [in] handy. The Paper was stained some, as you will see, but I can make it go, but it dose not Pay to send Boxes out hear, the express Charges to much for so small a Matter. We love to have things come from our frends to home. I hope thair will be no nesseity of sending many more. I for one whouled much rather come home myself and get what things I need, but our Officers have a paculear Notion of theas things, but we shall get the better of theas Shouldier Straps some day and it will be a longe day before I shall carry a rifle for the benefit of those Cowderdley Whelps that get the benifit of our Sufferings and Triles and never get the first word of commendation from them. Thay have Payed men 3 & 500 Dollers for doing nothing. The men themselves, if thay will tell the truth, will say that thay never earnd thair Salt, but the three years men have never had one Doller Added to thair Wages. It may be all right but for one, I can not see

---

[280] In reality, he was with the company on the twenty-seventh of September according to the letter "in the field near Franklin." That would make it nearly two months at the New Iberia Hospital, not three.

[281] It is likely that the photograph of him that appears in this book is the same that he refers to here, as it is the only time he mentions having one taken in his uniform.

the Point. Thair has been a great whrong don us and it must remain as a Stain on the Towns & State.

You complain of my not writing oftener but I couled not. Thair must be some time between my Letters, but I may have a better Chanc of keeping you informed of my whareabouts if things goes well with me. You onley Tantelize me with Naming your Cider. I can not get to it but you may drink all you can for me. I have not tasted any [in] so long that I shouled like some. I am glad that you have got your Crops in and that your Crops have turned out so well. I hope to be with you by this time next year, if not befor.

I was sorry to hear of the Death of Samule Fenton. I shouled like to have seeing him, but is race and Jurney through Life is over and don. I have recved your Box and this is one of the Sheets of Paper. I am glad you sent that Minetuer to that young mans frends. He was fast to get it and intrusted it to me. I have not heard from Henry for some time, not for 3 months. I have got 3 Papers from him.

The young men to home have quite a lively time. The differant Colls keep them moving and takes off thair loose Chainge, well it Suites me. I hope Uncl Abraham will keep them Dodgin till thay are Brought up to the ring. It whould do them good to live on hard Tack and that with good Marching, bad Watter, and night Picketing.

But I must bring this letter to a Close. Kiss my Babys for me. I will write again soon. I hope to recve your letters more reguler and may this Winter pass off without any more Truble this way. Give my love to Mother. Tell her I shouled like much to have a Chat with her. Tell Virtue I am geting along well at this time, but thair is so maney Chainges in this Millitary life that one dose not know how it will be with one from day to day, but I shall trust Providance for the futuer and be thankfull for the Past. I send my love to you all and may heven bless and Protect you is the Prayer of your Affactnat Husband & Son,

CW Sherman

Genral Hospital, New Iberia, La

Genral Hospital, Franklin, La, December 20, 1863

Dear Wife, & Chirldren, Parents,

It is with much pleasuer that I write theas few lines hoping thay may find you all in as good health as thay leave me at this time. I have been Detailed and sent to this place and I find my self in good quarters and hope that I may not find my self in any worse during the remainder of my term of Sirvice.

We are on our last year and that gives us more pleaseaur to do our dutey then if we was on our first or Second year of probation. Soldiering is all very well on paper, but the romance of the thing weares off after a time and Camp life gets to be to much of a good thing. But I have made out to pass two years and hope that the rest of my term may pass as plesentley.

We have hopes that the Goverment will take some Action in regard to the Old Troops and let us go home next June. I wish our frends couled see Genrle Buttler and find out wether thair is any Chance of our getting home at that time, for thair will be truble if we are kept longer then the first of June. One consideration, if no other ought to govern our Officers, is the time of the year. You can not Disband Soldiers who has been for such a length of time in such a Climate as Louisana and send them to thair Northen Homes, with out losing one half of all that get back, if taken north any time after September. June is the proper time to bring us back. Just look at the nine months Regiments, how thay rot[t]ed after geting home and thay had a Easey time hear. I think I have made out my Case to my satisfaction, if I faile to Convince the Powers that Rules in Washington, it will not be because my Notion of what thay ought to do was not right. I wish I couled just see Uncl Abraham a few mineutes. I think he whouled come round to my way of thinking for the Old Jentleman has tru Notions of what is right and thats more then can be said of some that have Rented the White House of us, for I am one of the Manegers of that Machine and shall go in for Uncle Abes runing it 4 years more on his own acount and make as much as he can, for he has had but little time to enjoy him self this terme.

I hope Virtue and Mother will do all thay can to make themselves comfortable this Winter and pile on the Wood and keep the Old House warm. And those young Ladyes & Jentlemen that you have with you, let them go [at] it while thay are young, but when thay are at Schooll, thay must atend to thair Studyes and learn all thay can, for now is thair time to qualifie themselves for the dut[i]es of Life. The more a man knowes, the Easeir it will be for him to get along through life. If I had a good Bissness Education, I have Chances every day to better my Condition, but I can look out for my Chirldren. I hope I shall live to see them doing better than I can ever hope to do.

This is the Cuntry for Gorge Derick.[282] He couled get is 15 Hundred Dollers and found and more by waching is Chances. Thay need good Penmen and men with some Knowledge of Bisness in most all the departments of the Goverment. If Henry will oneley come hear, what a pile he couled make, beat your California Gold Mines all to Peices.[283]

Just wait till this little row is over. If I do not get the Green Backs, then I whouled not say so, but keep up your Curadge aspell longer. We are goin to have such times after this Storme that you will think the Meleanum [Millennium] as come and that good time spocken of in the good Book, thats the time for you. Just hold your Horses, you will be all right when you are seting under your own Orange and Fig Tree. If you couled only see it, it is so nice with a Dozen or so of Colerd Jentlemen to waite on you. You need not think that I am goin to work anymore, that is played out. It might do once, but not now. I have been waited on so long that it will be nessery for my comfort to have it continue. It is nesseary for my health to be Laze and do as little as posable. Please make a Noat of it, as you may be asking me to Cut a little Wood, or Bring a Pail of Water. Such little things are very anoying and you must bare this in mind. Do not Laugh at this Letter, as that is not Proper.[284]

Give my Love to that young Jentleman Called Lewis and those young Ladyes and the Genral. You may Kiss him and, in fact, if I couled get to them, I do think thay whouled get Shook up some!

My Love to you all,
CW Sherman, La

---

[282] George William Derrick, son of Charles's aunt and uncle, Elizabeth and James Derrick. George was born in 1843 in Massachusetts, married with three children, and was listed as a traveling cutlery salesman in the 1900 Massachusetts, Middlesex, Cambridge city, Census. "United States Census, 1900," index and images, *FamilySearch* (https://familysearch.org/pal:/MM9.1.1/M9RB-QL5: accessed 16 Feb 2014), George W Derrick, Cambridge city Ward 2, Middlesex, Massachusetts, United States; citing sheet, family 440, NARA microfilm publication T623, FHL microfilm 1240657.

[283] Charles's brother Henry spent two years, from 1852 to 1854, in California during the Gold Rush days.

[284] This passage with his fantasy plantation, being waited on, and too lazy to do chores is a good example of his sense of humor.

Ceeder Creek, Oct, 12th 1864
Shenandoah, Valley, Va

Dear Wife & Chirldren Parents
we are still camped hear but
how much longer we shall be
allowed to Desacrat this secaid
Soil by our presence I know not
the Rebs came down in great
Wrath yesterday and if the mouse
that mad a noise could have
thought that our time was short
but Sheridan made a few
moves that took the conceit out of
them we got ready for a warm
time I can not say the weather is
warm it is very cold up hear in
the Mountains all the Troops was
moved and Massed in the Woods
when it came night but our
solitary Brigade and one Battery
of six guns we was left to the
Tender Merceys of the I Wrathfull

Background is the letter from October 12, 1864

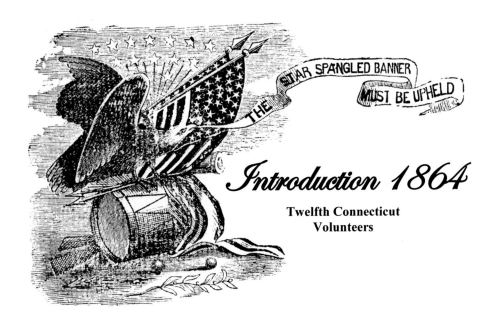

Introduction 1864

Twelfth Connecticut
Volunteers

The end of 1863 and beginning of 1864 was a time of re-enlistment for the men in the regiment. The following order, complimenting the regiment, was issued by the commanding general of the division:

Headquarters First Division, 19th Army Corps,
New Iberia, La., Jan. 1, 1864
General Orders No. 2. – The Twelfth Connecticut Volunteers, Lieut.-Col. F. H. Peck commanding, having re-enlisted, will comply with Special Orders No. 1, from headquarters 19th Army Corps, and proceed to New Orleans.

The general commanding the division thinks it due to this regiment, and to the lieutenant-colonel commanding it, to express his high opinion of its good conduct, whether in the face of the enemy or in camp, and especially the promptness with which it has come forward to re-enlist under the first call of the President of the United States.

The regiment is the first that has been called upon under the law. It has set a good example. The country, and the authorities which represent the country, will not fail to honor the Twelfth Connecticut.

By command of Brig-Gen-Emory
Frederick Speed, A. A. General[285]

Towards the end of January, the regiment headed for a thirty-day furlough in Connecticut on board of the steamer *Mississippi*, arriving in New Haven on February 12. There, and in Hartford, they were honored with receptions. The regiment received the news on March 19 that their furlough had been extended for twenty days.[286] After spending some days in camp in Hartford, they once again sailed for Carrollton, Louisiana, on May 8.[287]

From there, the regiment was ordered to Morganza, which was north of Port Hudson, to aid in Gen. Banks's Red River Campaign. It was attached to the Second Brigade, First Division, Nineteenth Army Corps, Brig. Gen. McMillan commanding. However, by the time the Twelfth arrived, Banks's campaign had failed and the Nineteenth Corps returned to New Orleans before being sent to Fortress Monroe, Virginia. From there they went to Washington, DC, to City Point, Virginia, to Bermuda Hundred, back to Washington, DC, and finally joined Maj. Gen. Philip H. Sheridan in his Shenandoah Valley Campaign on August 7. The regiment had traveled over 5,000 miles in three months![288]

The Twelfth, as part of the Nineteenth Corps, traveled from town to town in western Virginia and western Maryland, fought valiantly on September 19 in the Battle of Third Winchester, (also known as the Battle of Opequon), in the Battle of Fisher's Hill on September 21–22, and in The Battle of Cedar Creek on October 19, however it suffered such terrible losses on that day (170 killed, wounded, and captured) that the Twelfth Regiment was disbanded, its survivors being transferred to a battalion of six companies.

---

[285] Croffut and Morris, *The Military and Civil History of Connecticut*, 516.
[286] Ibid., 524; De Forest, *A Volunteer's Adventures*, 159.
[287] Croffut and Morris, *The Military and Civil History of Connecticut*, 517.
[288] *Record of Service of Connecticut Men*, 472; *Annual Report of the Adjutant-General of the State of Connecticut for the year ending March 31, 1865* (New Haven: Carrington, Hotchkiss & Co., State Printers, 1865), 257.

Chapter Sixteen

New Orleans, Home to Connecticut, Back to Louisiana

New Orleans, La, Janury 21, 1864

Dear Wife & Chirldren,

You may have thought it Straing that I have not written to you before, but Straing things are happening every day. I thought I was all right fore the rest of my time, but it was not to be. Captain Roche Droped upon me one Sunday morning with the information that the Regiment was goin home and that it had Enlisted for 3 years more, if the war lasted that length of time, and that I must go with him to the City to be turned ove[r] if I did not go in for 3 years, and down I came.

The Comanding Genral has been Pleased to give the Prefrance to the 12th on account of its great Services and the Patrotism of the men. I did not fall in immeadatley. The bounty of 800 Dollers was some temptation. I took time to look the thing squear in the face. If the war shouled Close this year, I thought I should be Sorrey that I did not help my Self to some of the Bounty, and if it contineued 3 years more, it whouled help me beare the Burden & heat of the day. I can not say that I have not had anuff of Soldering. I have all that I want, but the Newes of the Vollenteering of the Old Regiments will have a good affect on the Rebs. It shows them that we mean to stick to them like Brothers. Thay may not see the Point.

I know that you whouled like to see me out of it, but I must be Discharged honorabley, or not at all. You whouled not like to have me stay hear like a Sneak and the Regiment having a good time. 30 Days are a short time to stay with ones

281

frends after so long an absance, but if others Sneak and Shirk thair duty, thats no reason that a Sherman should. I hope you will take it kindley. This Crule war will not last for ever. I have been Preserved so fare and I have Just as much Faith that the same kind Providance will wach over and Protect me in the futuer. We are getting ready to come hom for a Short fourlough and Recruit up and take some other Field. We have given one State to the Union, or helped, and we can give one more Star or keep one in the Union. Please do not make your selves uneasey on my account. We was in hopes that the Reblion whouled have been Crushed befor this, but we must not look back after once taking hold of the Plow. We shall turn the Tables yeat, and one other reson why we ought to hold on is this, Uncl Abraham as not once turnd back from the first start and it is our duty to Soport him through thick and thin.

Give my love to the Chirldren and do not be discouradged. Light will shine through the Storms that now Cloud the way if we onley have faith and Put our trust in that Power who rules above and among the Chirldren of men. I send my love to you all.

Your Affactnat Husband,
CW Sherman

Wallingford, April 21, 1864

Dear Wife & Chirldren,

I am not well, but must see this thing through. I got to Hartford and not suspecting any Dainger, and having to waite 3 hours, I went up into the City and was stoped by 2 of the Invalid Corps with, "got a Pass?" Not having such a Doccument, they Politley requested my Compney to the Provost Marshales Office & thair I found the 12th was under a Cloud, but that wont last long as we expect to go to the Pet Armey of the Potomac, as they have for 3 years been trying to get into Richmond. They couled, if they had any one to show them how, and their hope are going to be realized.

The Powers that be, and that amuses them selvs by stoping all men that have blue Clothes and ask them inconveant questions, concluded to let me go as I was the onley honest man that was in the City. I got to this Place and found the Regiment Quarterd in[a] Brick Building that had been used for a Factory.[289] In a Day or so the Captain fixt my Pappers and I gave him the Cirtificate that Doctor Newton gave me, but it will do me no good.[290]

I can not get a pass to go to Hartford to get my Bounty, as the Coll as gon to New York and has forbiden any Passes to be given till he gets back. But it will all come out right yet. I shall do all I can and not make any truble for my self. You must not truble your selvs about me. I shall turn up sometime. Thair is a great many of the men sick with Chills & Fever.

Do not write to me now as we do not know how long we shall stay hear. Thair will [be] something turn up. Do the best you can. I shall write to you again soon and be able to see my way more Cleer. Give my love to the Chirldren and accept the same yourself and keep up a good Heart.

> Your Affactnate Husband,
> CW Sherman

Fair Haven, April 28, 1864

Dear Wife & Chirldren & Parents,[291]

I write you from this Place since sending you from Wallingford. I have been in the New Haven Hospital and was used well fore a few days. Last Sunday the Regiment had Orders to go Abord the McCllend Stransport for New Orleans and they Arived by the Cars Sunday Noon.[292] The Stransport was waiting for them, having came through from New York to take them, and all the Sick that was Able to move was Orderd to Join the Regiment. The Doctor came round and Picked the men out. He said that he Shouled not send me but sent me to get ready. Thay said that I was not fit to go but had to Obay Orders and I got on board the Stransport at Dark night, and such a Crow[d]ed Steamer

---

[289] This letter is written at Wallingford, Connecticut, where the regiment was housed waiting further orders. Charles had been on furlough February, March, and part of April, so there were, of course, no letters during that time.

[290] Since he mentions that he is not well, one could speculate that the doctor gave him a "certificate of disability," or something similar, that would excuse him from his service, but it obviously wasn't accepted by the captain.

[291] The first part of this letter is transcribed from photocopies.

[292] USAT McClellan – US Army transport

it never was my luck to get on. Thair was not standing room to think of, having to stay for 12 or 14 Days in such a Crowed was more of a Punshment then I thought my Sins Called fore at Present, and to make it more plesent, thay Brought 75 Conscripts fore us and put aboard, and such a Godforesaken lot of recruts it never was my lot to see. If we have to Fight the Rebs with such Matairel [material], we shall fail.

When we got to New York, 7 of them got away by one means and nother. We Droped Anchor and a number of our own men came aboard during the Day that had been left, and then thair was a rumor that the Small Pox was on board and more was made of it then need to have been. The captain refused to go to sea with us Crowed has we was fore fear of what might be to pay when we got into a Warmer Climat. That was good news to us, and at last thay came to the conclusion of bringin us Back and hear we are at Present in the conscript Camp and in the best quarters we ever was in, and the longer we stay, the better for me.

When I was in Wallin[g]ford, I tried to get away to get that money, but it was no go. I had the fever and Chills every day and then, when I went to New Haven, I counted on getting away, but thair I was confined to my bed till last Sunday night, and then it was all up, but recond I shouled make it all right when I got to New Orleans.

Now I am waiting to see the Chaplin to see if he will help me or can. Do not take any truble on my account. It will all come right. Try and get along till I can do some things fore you. The Officers are out of Money and thay may Pay the Regiment before we go. In that case I shouled [send] something. I do not feell much like writing, but shall get along some how.

Do not write till I know whare I be, for at present I can not tell whare I am 24 hours[293] at a time. I want Mr. Brooks to write and Send me some Papers, for in our Wandering life thair is not much to interest me, and in Camp, when the Maill come in, to have nothing is like being shut out from the rest of the Worled.

I hope, if have any Frends, thay will not fore get to remember that a kind word makes the Soldiers Heart light and his hand Strong, and he can go and put is Shoulder to the Wheel and lift with a will.

I want you to give my best respects to Mr. Brooks' Family and kiss that young Buttler and all the Chirldren. Virtue must Cheer up, it is only for a short

---

[293] The completion of this letter is from an original page.

time. She must do what she thinks best, it will come right. I want you to let me know if you get all my letters & when you do. Let me know if you get all my letters and when you do.

Your Affactnate Husband and Son,
CW Sherman

Fair Haven Conscript Camp, April 30, 1864

Dear Wife & Chirldren, Parents,[294]

We are still hear and this being the last day of the Month we are Musterd in for Pay. The talk is that we shall be Payed next Week and then I shall be Able to get my back pay and Bounty. I have tryed every possable way to get away, but it is no go. I see the Coll yesterday, and he said that he whouled see Capt Roche, and that may be the last of it till I get to some US pay Master. Without thair help, that is one of the worst Featuers of this Millitary life, you can not get Justice don, and in this War thair has been a great Deal of unnessary Suffering through having so much red tape. But it is for only 3 years unless sooner shot.

<u>May 2nd</u>

This is a Beautifull morning but I cannot enjoy it. I do not feell well. I have not been to the Doctors lately but must go to get excused. The Capt found fault yesterday because I had not been; not with me, but with the Ordley. Thay can not do me no good, but I am expected to do Duty if not excused.

We was musteard in the last day of April and thair is some talk we will get our pay this week. I hope so as Virtue has no money.

Thair is some talk of keeping this Regiment to take recruts to the differant Regiments in the Field, but thair is no telling what we shall have to do. I can see no way of geting home at present but thair may [be] some thing turn in my favor yet. We must have Faith in all things.

It was a good thing thay took us out of the McClland. It whouled have went hard with us if we had continued on that Steamer. We did not have the

---

[294] This letter is transcribed from photocopies.

small pox to any extent, only 3 or 4 cases, but it whouled have spread when we got to a warmer Climate.

I hope you may have good luck with your Farming this year. I do not see the use of Virtue having a Cow and having to Buy Hay all winter and get no milk, as that is a little to much of a good thing. But I expect Mother and Virtue to get along without any Beckring. The Chirldren, I hope, will go to School reguler and learn all thay can.

If you write, Please Direct to CW Sherman, Comp K, 12th CV, Conscript Camp, New Haven. I send my love to you all. Kiss the Chirldren.

Your Affactnate Husband and Son,
CW Sherman

Conscript Camp, New Haven, May 5, 1864

Dear Wife & Chirldren, Parents,

We are still kept hear and can no more get out then though we was Prisnors. I am waiting for a Chance to get that Money. You must get along as well as you can. It will come sometime. I am not well, but I whouled not have you think that I can not help my self. I can, but I do not feel well anuff to do any duty, and do not but I shall be all right some time.

Yesterday was the day the Govnor took his Oath of Office and the 12th formed Part of the Escort.[295] I did not go. The Regiment did not feell flatterd as Col Peck whouled not Alow them to get any refrashments for fear that some of the men whouled get away. We have some 600 Conscripts hear. 6 of ours tryed to get a way the night, one was shot Dead, 3 Captuerd, 2 got away. The frends of the one Shot Subscribed 75 Dollers, Bought a Beautifull Matalic Coffin, and sent his Body to his frends. It is with quite differan feellings his frends must recve thair Dead then though he had lost his life in the discharge of his duty, but such is life.

Thair is a Prem[i]um of 30 Dollers Paid for every Recrut shot trying to desert. We are geting into trublsom tim[e]s, but thay must soon end, as thay get Bitter every day. How soon we leave, I know not, but thay say next Monday.

---

[295] William Alfred Buckingham

You must worry about me. I am in hopes that I shall do well yet. If we go so soon, I shall try to let you know.

I wrote to Henry this week. I have not writen to Uncl as I have not felt like writing, but shall get to soon. Let me know how you are geting along and do not faile to write often, and I shall be happy to recve Letters from any one els. Tell Mr. Brooks that he must not for get to send me a paper some tim[e]s and not to for get a letter some tim[e]s. I shall not for get his kind treatment, or the kindness of his Famley to me.

We are kept very stricked hear. I never was lied [to] so be fore. That is [the] one and onley cause that makes me wish I was some whare els, but the truth, this is the best Place I ever was in so far as Accomidation is concernd. I couled stay hear very comfortable the rest of my term of Ser[v]ice, if I couled onley get a Pass to come home once in a resonabl time.

I want Virtue to get what ever she and the Chirldren wants, but the next thing she must have some money, and Mother, you must let her have what she wants till I can send some, and money, if you have it. I do hope you will get along comfortable and as well as you can. Tell Father he must keep up a good heart. Give my love to the Chirldren and them two Ladyes must be kind to one another. I will send Lewis something for I did not use him right the morning I came away. I did not kiss him. I was afraid to see him Cry and I owe him some. He must be a good Boy and not make his mother no more truble then he can help.

My love to you all,
CW Sherman

Conscript Camp, Sunday morning, May 8, 1864

Recved Orders to fall in 7 A-M. All hands Packing Knapsacks, all in a Hubbub. The Long Roll Beat at 10 A.M. line was formed, Marched to the long Wharfe where the Steamer Travlear was waiting for us to take us to New York.[296] Be for we got to the City proper, 7 of our Conscripts Jumped over Board and Swam ashoar. We was near the Shore at the time. Thair was a Gard over them at the time.

We was soon Aboard the Stransport Merrimack of 2000 Tuns, and we was told thair was Bearthes for 900 men, but we failed to see them. Thair might

---

[296] Steamer Traveler, perhaps

have been room for 900 men by Stowing 4 men in a bunk. That was how thay counted. After waiting on Deck till after dark, the 3 Left Compneys, ours included, had the Pleasuer of staying on deck. Any one that never had the fun of a deck Passadge can form no Id[e]a of the disagreablitys of life on a Stransport. But we are only Soldiers, food for Powder, and, as some of my frends on Villidge hill whouled say, glad of it, stay to home, what bissness have you down South burning & Stealing.

As I was giving you some of my trubles, I looked round for a place to lay my Blanket for the night. I found a Boat that was half over the deck and it crawled through my Wool that was Just the spot, as the Boat whouled keep the men from treading on us in the night. Every Soldier, if he is anything, will all ways have a Comrad to look after thair Comon plunder and Sargent Lucas wanted to Chum with me. We are togather now having some tender Ham that was served out raw as time had don that. It had a very strong Smell that put one in mind that Noah went to Sea once up on a time and that he must have had Salt meat and that the Hams must have kept well to last to my time.

But we was not Alowed to Flatter ourselves on our quarters. Thair was a Watter Barrle on the opersite of the Deck and soon thair was a young Missispp runing under our Blankets and we had to Serrender and Beat a retreat with the honors of war. Our case was geting desperat and some thing must be don, and down Aft I Charged and found a Beautifull Place and was soon laid out with the Cirtainty of having to Cleer out sooner or later. Some of the men lay and Cursed the Ship Captain and every thing genraley, and wished the whole Crowd in a much warmer place than Louisana, and that is needless. Our worse fears was more then realized.

Monday morning the 9 had a Beautifull Shake with fevor and again [at] night, had moved 3 tims, and finally found myself in a Bunk in the Hold whare for 8 days I lay having a Shake every other day. I wished my self back to America. The Bunks was made to hold 4 men, but was not large anuff for 3 men, all though thay cramed 3 into them.

When we got into the Gulf it was to warm for me. The Sun came down as though we had not Just left our Cold New England Hills. Our Conscripts do not Jump over board now. 11 got away from us from the time we left the Conscript Camp and Started down the Bay, one stabed another monday morning.

<u>May 15th</u>

I have been very misarable and sick so far, but we are nearing the Land of the Orange & Magnolia, Suney Skies and Bayou Watter & Miscatoes. We reached the Crescent City at 5 P.M. and Anchord 2 mile above the City, much to the Chagrin of the men who were thus cut off from geting Ashore.

About 10 that night we all thought we was all goin down. A Steamer, loaded with Wood & Stors for some Point on the Texas Coast, under took to run across the Bowes of our Boat and manedged to run into us, tearing away her Smoke Stack and other wise Injuering herself, Just like the Wemon when thay are bound to have thair own sweet way. Thair was some noise on board our Boat and two more of those Aposales of Liberty, called by way of distinction, Conscripts, who Jumped in the darkness from our boat into the other Boat and we did not know, but She was sinking. I say Bulley for the Conscripts. I expect to hear of some of them Wading the Gulf of Mexico.

We got on Shore about 9 AM May 18th and went one mile to Camp Kearney and the Regiment stacked Arms about 25 rods from the Banks of the Father of Watters. The River keeps with in her Banks this Spring. It is very plesent to wach the great rush of Watters and see the imense trees & logs go rushing toward the Gulf and the ever Chaingin Curent, first up, and then down. The water is quite Cold at this time and, as it is all that we can get, we make it go, but it seames that it is bringin down the Rockey Mountains for I do not see whare so much dirt can come from.

<u>May 20th</u>

3 days we have been in Camp and hot ones thay have been. Thay get to us. Thair are a large number of Troops hear. Banks is up to Simsport, having fell back from Alexandra, after Burning that City he has got away with is Gun Boats.[297] The Rebles sunk 4 for him and Captuerd a Stransport with 600 men.

---

[297] The Red River Campaign began in March of 1864 and continued through May. The Red River's waters were much lower than anticipated, which compromised the movement of gunboats with troops and supplies. Maj. Gen. Richard Taylor was leading the Confederate opposition. The capture of Shreveport was the objective by the Union forces, however, it was an unsuccessful campaign; they never reached Shreveport, but were forced to retreat to Alexandria. Because of the low water levels, ships were in danger of being trapped and not being able to retreat; however, "luckily for Banks, Joseph Bailey, the chief engineer on General Franklin's staff, had some experience of

The feelin against him is very strong. You have not had the truth in regard to the losses that the Rebs have inflicted on him. He got to within 29 Miles of Shreveport, the 13th Armye Corp in the Advance, and expected to get thair that day. He sent 400 Waggons with 8 days Rations in Advance with 6000 Cavlery and 2000 Infantry. The Rebs, 30,000 strong, was waiting for him.[298] The 19th Armey Corps was 6 mile in the Rear. The Rebs opend on the Cavlery and forced them to retreat. The Infantry s[u]ports was not strong anuff and thay had to retreat. The Waggons Blocked up the road, and the Artlery not beening able to get by the Waggons, had to be left and the Rebles Captuerd the Waggons and 6000 men. I get my information from them that was thair. 27 Canon was among the spoils after the Sacond days fight and the Armey was falling back. Banks came riding down through the line with is hat off. Thair was some 500 Reble Prisnors and thay Cheerd Banks, telling our men that thay whouled not Shoot Banks as he was the best Comissary thay ever had.

How things will turn with us this Sumer, I know not. We are waiting to hear of the fall of Richmond, may it be soon. Be of good Cheer, Virtue. I am waiting to get my Pay. The look is good at this time. You must be in want of some with them Hungry Mouthes that is around you. It will not be long that I shall be away. I hope, and if it was not for hope, what shouled we do in this Worled of Chaing. Keep up your Heart, all of you. Kiss those Chirldren for me. I shouled like to have them go to Stafford this Sumer and have thair Minetuers taken again.

I must Close this letter. I cannot write long at a time. I do not feel like writing, but will try to let you know how I am geting along. Please direct your Letters as usal. May Hevan bless you all and keep you. Give my Respect to all enquiring Frends.

From Your Affactnat Husband & Son,
CW Sherman

---

dam building. In the first half of May he built a series of dams of different types, and was able raise the water level above the dams sufficiently for all of the Union ships to escape." J. Rickard, "Red River Campaign," Military History Encyclopeadia on the Web, September 3, 2007, http://www.historyofwar.org/articles/wars_red_river.html.

[298] The assembled Union forces were, in theory, to number 42,000, but this number never materialized. Steele's 17,000 Arkansas troops were not able to play a significant role. Taylor had about 11,000 men at Mansfield. Ibid.

Camp Near Carrolton, New Orleans May 23, 1864

Dear Wife and Chirldren, Parents,[299]

We are still camped near the Father of Watters and the Old man still rolles down with Perfect looseness, and to me, he seems to rejoyce now his Fetters are brocke and he can Carrey what ever is a mind to Flote on its ample Bosem. This sense of Freedom it imparts to the logs and the way thay go Dancin & bobbin and nodin to you, as much as to say "don't you wish you couled come along and have a Spree with us down in the Gulf? It whouled be very cooling & refreshing theas hot days." It is warm, some whouled call it a little to much of a good thing. It gets to me.

The night that we camped hear thay served out some more of those Shelter Tents and thay are no protection unless Coverd by our Blankets. Thay will do very well on the march whare it is imposable to carry larger tents for the want of Transportation. We are kept in with the us[u]al Camp Gard that Col Peck allways puts on the moment the Regiment Stacks Arms. No getting out with out a Pass and those are limited to so many in a Compney.

May 24th

Recved your letter of May 8. Was sorry to hear that you had been Sick. You must write more Plain; you wrote that Mother took the same complaint that you had and Died, and you did not tell me that Lewis had been sick. I gathered that from Henry's letter. I recved one from him and a Paper. I hope that Alvira will not put to much on Faney, but give her all the Chance she can to learn. I do not know how Virtue will get along with out her as she was of service to help her with work, but we will hope for best.

It was a good thing to get two Porkers if thay will not cost more then thay are worth in bringin them up. I think that Pork will be high next fall and it is meat that we can not go along with out. We down hear have more then we know what to do with. I can not Eat it nor thair Salt Horse and hard tack is my Abomanation. It is tough for any digestion. I do hope you may have a good Seson and good Crops.

---

[299] This letter is transcribed from photocopies.

We hear of Grants Sucesses and hope that he will be Able to make Lee Serender with what Army he has. That is the onley thing that will tell in our favor. Mearley getting the works and the City will not bring the war to a Close if Lee is allowed to get away with the Bulk of his forces and take up some other Strong position whare he can collect the scatterd rements of the different Corps and make another stand. The State of Gorga is full of places that can easely be made too strong for us to take with a great Sacrefice of men.

Genral Banks has come down to the city and we hear that the Rebs have turned thair Faces Texasward. Banks Brought off his Transports & Comodor Porter got his Gun Boats out of Red River. The Expedition was a dead failure and the ground will have to be gone over again. I do not want to go up through that Cuntry. I have been thair and was satisfied. Thair is some talk that this Regiment will go to New Orleans for Provost duty. The Cle[a]nest and Best Regiment will go thair. Thair is to be a revew to see which can out shine the other. Our Boys are Burnishing and Cleening thair Rifles and the Prospect is that we shall win.

I send my love to you all. Tell Virtue not to get to rich with her Loom. I shall be able to send her some money soon and the other will be all right. Kiss the Chirldren for me and I hope Angline and Lewis will Learn all thay can.

Your Affactnate Husband and Son,
CW Sherman

New Orleans, Camp Carollton, June 3, 1864

Dear Wife & Chirldren, Parents,

I am still alive and feel some better but weak. The Wether is hot to us. Theas smal Shelter Tents that we have, beaing so low, the Sun Shines right through them and we are Camped in a open lot with no Trees near to get under in the heat of the day, and anyone with the Fever as I have had it every other day, makes it a great worse, but it is all in 3 years.

Fany sent me a letter. I have not Answerd it yet, she told what She had to do. One thing was to Milk a Goat as her Aunt had to weane that young Sherman and bring him up on the Bottle.[300] She told me that She had wrote home but no one had Answerd her letter. Now that must not be. Some one must [answer] her letters.

Things must be looking plesent round you at this time. I shouled like to get out of this heat and cool off in your mialder Climat. It is the heat of the day and the Dews of night that put the Seeds of Sickness and Death in our ranks.

The Regiment is furnishin a large Gard. One party acts as Gard on the Jackson Rail road to Manchac Pass and another on the Carrolton New Orleans road, besides the reguler Camp Garde. The Campain is over for this Summer. I do not hear of anything goin on round hear at present.

We in Camp talk over the Virginea Campaing and look anxiousley to see the Union Armey in the Reble Capital. The Veteran Regiments are returning and the Cavlery are Drilling and thay are quite beusey orgnizin the Artilery and geting ready to Strike some whare.

The Old Settlers say that this is goin to be a Sickley Summer down hear, but we must trust in Providence. We are in is hands and he will protect the right. All the men that did not r[e-]enlist have been Orderd to report to the regiment and are all with us at this time. Thay have isued some new Springfield Rifles to our Regiment and turnd in the Old Enfields. It will make the Regiment look better and give the men more work to look after them.

The Paymaster started to Pay us off, but stoped on account of some of the Pay Rolls being whrong and I shall be unable to send Virtue any Green Backs this time as the Mail gos tomorrow at 8 O'Clock AM. I sopose she want my Board Bill paid. It has been runing long anuff, but Virtue, I will make it all right some time. She shall have a nuff to have one fourth of July. The Bount[y] Check, she must get that Dress with, not go about as though she had no frends. I am not gon under yet. I hope you may have good luck with your Farming this year. I have not been so I couled write latley, or I shouled send you more. You must all look on the Brightest side of things and trust in a good Providence that over rules all things for our good. What looks Dark to day will be Bright to morrow. I shall try and send you a few lines every week when I can.

---

[300] Henry and Elvira had a baby boy, Dwight, on the fifth of February. Fanny was the oldest child of Charles and Virtue and is almost fourteen at this time. She had gone to help Elvira. From Henry's letters to his parents during this time, it appears as though Elvira was having some health problems after the birth of their son. In the following letter to Fanny, Charles mentions Elvira's sickness as well.

Give my love to the Chirldren. I hope thay are Learning all thay can. I send my love to you all and may theas few lines find you all in good health.

Your Affactnate Husband & Son,
CW Sherman

New Orleans, Camp near Carrolton, June 6, 1864

Dear Daughter,[301]

I recved your kind letter of May 15th and was pleased to have you write and that you was well. At the time I recved you letter, I was down with the Shakes & Fever and the heat of the day was so great that it made it worse for me, but I am better now. The Shakes have left me and I feel better then I have for 4 months past. I couled not answer your letter till now. We have been having Thunder Storms and a great deal of rain for the past 8 days and it looks as if it was goin to continue Stormey.

I am sorry to hear that your Aunt as been so Sick[302] and that the Baby is goin to be trublesome. You tell me that you have a goat to milk so that baby may have milk anuff. I sopose that the Goat dose not give you much truble. I have been in Towns in this State whare the Inhabitants, or People, had nothing but Goats. Thay went in large Flocks, or heards, in all Southron Towns. The Streets are full of them, and quite large some of them are.

You hope that I might remain in the Conscript Camp till this Crule war is over, but it was not to be. And it whouled not be right for me to remain inactive at this time when the Goverment is calling on all her Sons to the rescue, when one more effort will Crush this wicked Reblion and Peace onece more with her Olive branch shall cover this Land and the wearry Soldiers return to thair homes and no long roll disturbe thair rest.[303]

You have some fears that Henry will be Drafed, but I hope not. Drafted men are of no use and it is much better to Pay for men then force them. Unwillin men are onley a Saurce of weakness. We must trust to that Providance that doeath all things well. I have had very tryin tims, but have been Preserved

---

[301] Fanny
[302] Elvira was Henry's wife.
[303] Roll call

through them and Shall trust the same Power, that as looked over and brought me out safe, to the end.

My Dear Daughter, you are away from home and I expect that you will so conduct your self that your frends will have no cause to complain. Other influnces will be brought around you and you cannot be to carfull of your self. Your Speech and deportment will be weighed and Straingers are hard Judges, very little will be excused on account of youth. Much will be requierd of you. I want you to learn all you can and youth is the time to fit ones self for the Dutys of life. You couled not be in better Hands then your Uncl & Aunt and you must pay them proper respect. The Sabbath school I know you will atend and much is to be learnd thair to fit you fore life in this world and the Worled to come.

You can write to me as often as you can and it will improve you in Composition and you must try to improve in writing. Make every letter better then the preceding one. Write to your Mother as often as you find time. It will be easyer for you to write the more you practice. I must close, wishing you health and as much Happeness as falls to the lot of us poor mortals. May Hevan Bless and gard you is the Prayer of your Affactnat Father

CW Sherman

New Orlean, Camp near Carrolton, La, June 8, 1864
Dear Wife & Chirldren, Parents,

I am in truble as I shall have to disapoint you all this time through the Blunders of Captain Roch[e]. I had counted on sending two Hundred dollers home this Mail, but shall have to waite, how long I know not. If the Goverment settles up once a quarter, I may get it sometime in July, but I shall not count on so earley a settlement.

I have writen to Henry to let Virtue have what Money she may need. I do not want her to want for anything and I know that Henry can let her have all the money she may want. She will only have the biger pile when it dose come, but Father will feel the disapointment, but I couled not help it.

The Difficulty of my not gettin the Money at this time was through Captain Roch[e] not puting it on the Pay Roll. The Pay Rolls are made out in Duplicate. One is sent to Washington and one is kept by the Pay Master and thay couled not Alter one Roll with[out] the other, and that one was sent to Washington. You must get along the best you can. Henry can let you have all the Money you may want till I get my Pay. Cheer up, it will all come right.

I have wrote a letter to Faney and one to Henry and am waiting for a letter from home. We have had 10 Days of Rain with Thunder & Lightin and it as made it quite mudey and theas small Shelter Tents do not keep our things dry. I feel much better then when I left home, but I am weak yet and theas hot days dose not help one much.

You have Summer with you now and things begin to look Cheering. I wish I could lay under one of those Maples and take the cooling Breeze that comes off the Hills, but that can not be. I shall keep perfectly still the remainder of my time in this Worled if I get out of this safe. I have had all the travile and do not care if I do not see all that is in this Worled. I want rest. It makes me sick of the war when I think of those things that some call men to home who have Lengthend this war by word and deed.[304] Thair is more Rebles in the States that Profess to be Loyle then thair is hear and thay go greater lengthes to help the Southron Reble then the same Class will do hear. Of the two, the Southron Reble is the most Christain, although his hands are red with his Brothers Blood.

Please let me know how you are geting on and what Henry sends, for what he dose, I want hime to do right away so that I may know, for I shall not be easy in my mind till I know that Virtue has 50 Dollers above what she may owe and Henry can do it. I am afraid she may want and that must not be. Tell her that the Pile will all [be] the Larger by having to waite, all though it may be inconveant at this time, but I hope that things will work better for the futuer.

I send my love to you all and kiss the Chirldren for me. I can not write as I whouled, I have had 3 Letters to write and I do not feel like writing so much at one time, but shall send you every week if I can.

your Affactnat Husband & Son,
CW Sherman, La.

---

[304] Copperheads

New Orleans, Camp near Carrolton, June 14, 1864

Dear Wife and Chirldren, Parents,[305]

We are still Camped in this place in the mud. It is some worse than your Pig Pen. It as rained every day this month and theas swamps are full, driving out all kinds of Snaks that come and take up thair quarters with us in our Tents, but thay are counted Rebs and get killed. It is not plesent to have Toads Jumpin into your bosom and on you, but you can not keep them out and thay will hop in the night. Great Cuntry this, but needs Fencing in.

I am waiting for a Letter from home. This makes the 5th I have sent and am thinking that it is most time I shouled get one. It trubles me to think I can not send you any Money and I shall be anxious till I hear from Henry and how much he can let Virtue have till I can send some. The Goverment is goin to settle up the Clothing account every quarter and those that are inde[b]ted to the Goverment must Pay up. Then maney of the men will not have anuff coming to Pay having over drawn thair 42 Dollers allowed them, and I may get my Pay then as some of us will have some thing coming to us on acount of Clothing. I have all ways had to Pay, but this year I am inside of my acount with Uncl Abraham. I know he wants his Boys to dress well if we do not save a Cent.

June 17th

I have been waiting for a letter but must close this without one. I am getting quite well and feel better than I have for 4 months and hope this may find you all to home enjoying the Blessing of Health, for non of us know the value of health till we have lost it. I am the worst one in the world to be sick. I have gon on duty again and our Regiment is goin on Detached Service. We are goin to be broken up, one Compney goin to one Place, and a nother hear and thair. The Genral in comand of the Defenses of New Orleans is Genral Roberts[306] and he has taken a great likin to the 12th and the Col has trimed us out with white Gloves and Shouldiers Scales.[307] As we take the place of the Regulers, we have to conform to the Regulations. If Hartford did not think much of the 12th, Genrales that have seeing service says that we are the best

---

[305] This letter is transcribed from copies.
[306] Gen. Benjamin S. Roberts, Nineteenth Corps
[307] Metal "epaulets"

drilled, Cleavrest Regiment in the Department and the People like it if thay do kick over thair Stands, but thair is hard work to be don and we can do it.

Please give my respects to Mr. Brooks and ask him if his Brother thinks of cuting Grant & tell him he may cut Banks Head off for he was the Whrong man sent to the wrong Place, but it is our luck in this war.

Give me all the newes when you do write. Keep up your Spirits and kiss those Chirldren for me. Mother you must see that I get more letters and do not forget to Pray for me as thay give me Strength to do my Duty to my Frends & Cuntry. I send my love to you all and may Hevan bless you all is the Prayer of your Affectionate Husband & Son.

CW Sherman

New Orleans, Camp near Carrollton, June 23, 1864
Dear Wife & Chirldren, Parents,

I recved your Letter of May the 31st and was pleased to hear from home, but the pleasuer had some Alay[308] when I thought of your sickness and the Suffering of the Chirldren, but I hope you are all well at this time. Virtue and Mother as had a hard time, but in this Worled thair shall be trubles and Sickness, Pain and Death, but Mother and Virtue must Cheer up, beter times Coming.

We have not moved yet, are waiting for a Boat. The rumor is that we are goin to Memphis, but thair is not much to depend on theas Camp Stories. We have packed up our Dress Seuites and whatever we do not want to carry. I take my Rubber and over Coat and Shelter Tent with a Chainge of Drawers & Shirts & Socks, and that is all that I can carry. This Marching is what I do not like, but Uncl Abraham as this little Job on hand and we must do as the Old man sayes like dutifull Chirldren.

The saile up the River will be refreshing, as the Banks are Clothed with a Dress of such Beautifull and ever Chaingin Color, that it is hard to beleve that wars desolating hand is to work to mar the Beauty that other wise whouled be a Joy and a pleasuer to us. But so it is in this Worled. The Great giver of life

---

[308] "Allay—to subdue or reduce in intensity or severity." *Merriam-Webster*, s.v. "allay," accessed February 14, 2014, http://www.merriam-webster.com/dictionary/allay.

Creates and serounds man with [h]is bounty and Scatterd Blessings in [h]is Path and man gos to work like a spoilt Chield and distroyes what was made for his Benifit and to Cheer him in is Jurney through life.

I do hope my health will be spaird to me as I stand a good Chance to go through Mississippi and Tenneessee (I guess my spelling is not quite the thing, but I can not get Websters unabridged). Memphis is 800 Mile up the River. We are to Reinforc my Name Sake, Genral Sherman, and when he is informed that I am with him, he will [be] like Paul when he came in sight of the three Tarvans,[309] Bless Uncl Abraham, and take fresh Curadge and I Pity Johney Reb when we Both go into them. Thay will find Jordan a hard road to Travle but the fun will be all on our side. Never fear.

If you couled onley look in on our Camp you whouled see mud and wonder how it is the men are not all sick. It as rained every day and when we left a week ago, most of us had a board or something to keep us out of the Mud. My Chum is Shaking at this mineut. I have Just coverd him up in his Blanket.

When we came back onto our old Camp ground, everything was gon, not a nuff to make a fier, everything taken away, the Col having given it to a man for the use of a Barn to keep is horse in. And we have to lay in the mud like so many Pigs and we shall leave this Place with pleasuer and the sooner the better. If we was in the woods we couled soon[310] fix ourselves from the damp ground. The way is this: we Cut 4 Sticks with Crotches and about 2 foot long and drive them into the ground, 3 foot apart one way and 6 foot the other. Then cut 2 sticks 6 feet long and 2, 3 feet long and then you have your frame. Then go to work and Cut a nuff 3 feet long for your bed, then put some Brush on and spread your Ruber, and you have a bed that Puts Feathers out of sight and never needs shaking up, and when it gets hard, Just turn over and rest. It is one of the healthest beds as you have plenty of Ventelation and the Rain dose not afect it and dose not find hidin places for Bugs. Young People that are Just starting in life will find that a great saving can be affected by Just studyin the way our Boys keep house. And Bording House keepers couled learn something to thair

---

[309] A village on the Appian Way, south of Rome, where St. Paul was met by Christians from the capital. "The believers from there, when they heard of us, came as far as the Forum of Appius and the Three Taverns to meet us. On seeing them, Paul thanked God and took courage." Acts 28:15, *The Wesley Study Bible* New Revised Standard Version (Nashville, TN: Abingdon Press, 2009), 1366.

[310] The letter transcribed from originals ends here and is completed with copies.

advantadge by suplying thair Boarders with Uncl Abrahams Rations, givin them plenty of Salt Horse and Hard tack, and if thay couled onley get some Goverment Coffee, thair fortune whouled be made. Good Cleer Watter is not nessary in decocking a Cup of Coffee.[311] The nearest mud hole will answer and if thair shouled be a few Polley wogs or a peice of half decayed Mule meat that has been thrown in when is owner has don with him, it will put the requ[i]site flavor to it.

I shall keep you advised of our travles, but I am so far a head in letters that you will have to put in and write more then you have. I have recved all your letters. The one you sent to Fairhavan and the 31st of May. I am enjoying good health at this time and if I couled get the same living as to home, shouled be able to snap my fingers to most men, but one can not keep up and feell well at all times. If I had known that I shouled be placed by the carelessness of those over me in the Position I find my self, I shouled have let Henry have but 50 dollars if he couled have got along with that, and you and Virtue the other 200, but Henry will do what is right and let Virtue have what money she wants and Potter will keep still till I can get my Pay. I am sorry that I couled not do as I wanted. I have written to Henry stating how I am placed and you will hear from him befor this reaches you. It will be all right some time, but I never can have any respect for one man that is over me, rum made all the trouble. You need not have any fear that I shall drink any thing stronger then a Glass of Beer. I can not taste it; the smell of it makes me sick. Captain Roche ought to be Court Martialed and be made to Pay me for the time & expense that he put me to when I was to home, but I must put up with the short Comings of others. I have written one letter telling you how I am with respect to my Pay and you will be apt to get this and that togather. I have explained how I couled not get my Pay and Bounty and how Virtue is to get out of the Difficulty. I must Close. Tell Virtue I am sorry to hear that she has not got quite well and to let me know how much Henry sends her. I send my love to you all and kiss the Chirldren.

From your Affactnat Husband,
CW Sherman

---

[311] Decoking—to remove the carbon deposits from an internal-combustion engine. His wry sense of humor at work again. *WritersEvents*, s.v. "decoking," accessed February 19, 2014, http://www.writersevents.com/Words_Starting_with_D/deckle _edge_decoying/decoking_definition.html.

New Orleans, Camp near Carrollton, La, June 28, 1864

Dear Wife & Chirldren, Parents,

We have not gon up the River as yet, but expect to today. We have been under marching Orders 10 days and have started twice, once for the want of a Boat we had to return, and the next time the Shaft Broke and toar one mans Arm all to Pices and kiled one horse, and we then had to drift down again to our Camp and hear we are again. The Boats are taken up moving troops and 8 Boats was burnt at the levee, as you have herd or seein by the papers, and the want of them is felt at this time.

I am well, this Climate agrees with me. I do hope I shall have my health for thair is small Chance for a poor Fellow down hear if you once get down. I am speaking of this Regiment. Thay will not send you to the Hospital till you are past help, or so near it that thair is small Chance for you to get well. A Surgon said to me once, thay keep you men in camp till you are dead and then send you to the Hospital to be buried, and it is true.

Thair was a Maile come aboard the Boat as we was leavin but nothing for me. I do wish you whouled try and write oftener. I recved a paper from Henry after I got back to camp. It may be all for the best that we did meet with accident at this time, as the Rebs Sprinkle a few Rifle Balls over most of the Boats that have Troops aboard.

Three times, inside of 12 days, we have had to Brake up camp and the poor Whites that live hear carry of[f] every stick and stake so that we have to go some distance to get a nuff to spread our shelter tents. I had to go 3 mile to get 3 pices of Board to put up our tent. I went into one yard whare it looked as though I shouled find what I wanted. The Place was owned by one of the Smartest Lawyers that his State affords and [I] sent a Colord Indavidual to hunt his Master up and when he was gon I took a look round and thought I shouled like to be a Southron Planter, and do not wonder thay want to keep up a institution that helps them to live in such luxery. After a while, the Propriator came out, Dressed in a nice pair of white Pants, Shirt & Straw hat and Patent leathers. He looked decidaley cool for a hot day. I made my Salam to him and we soon were on good terms.[312] He did not invite me into Brakfast, or take a smile, but we soon hunted up what I wanted and after a nother Sallam, we parted. I did not know who he was till afterwards, but it whouled not made no difference as we must have what we want. We can not make free with fences down so near the City & it was human Natuer to wish to swap places with my frend, for I was tierd and hungery. I do not wonder that thay fight for such a land, all though the Cause is bad.

Pleas let me know if Henry let Virtue have any Money. I have wrote to him to let her have as much as she wants till I can send her some. I do wish that it was settled. Give my love to the Chirldren and accept the same yourselves.

Your Affacnat Husband,
CW Sherman, La.

---

[312] A salam is a "salutation or compliment of ceremony in the east by word or act; an obeisance, performed by bowing very low and placing the right palm on the forehead." *The Free Dictionary* by Farlex, s.v. "salam," accessed April 24, 2012, http://www.thefreedictionary.com/salam.

Chapter Seventeen

**Traveling
Times Ahead**

Dear Wife and Chirldren, Parents,[313]

I am well and hope this will find you all well and Contented. This Place is 180 Miles above New Orleans. Thair is, and has been, a large number of troops at this Point, but some are goin away. We are under Marching Orders at this time, but whare to we know not. The first Division is Orderd away and the 12th is in that and first Brigade, so that you will know whare we are. When you see the Name of Brigadier Roberts you will know whare I am. We left Carollton June 29th. It was with regret I left that place, sweated myself most to Death in getin to the Boat, Part of the time wishing the Southron Confederacy in a warmer place then this is, but that whouled be needless. We was Stowed in us[u]al like Pigs, heads and Points in the Sun on top of the Hurrican Deck to Cool. Had a fine vew of Both Banks of this Magnifance River. It was a Beautiful day, if you couled keep cool, and enjoy the Panarama that was spread out befor us as we steamed up the River. Every thing so plesent, excep a though[t] of getin a sprinkling of lead as some of the Boats have been honored with such atentions from the frendley inhabitans that do not live on the River. I couled not

---

[313] This letter is transcribed from photocopies; however, it is missing the closing page.

realize but we was on a Picknick excursion. The Plantations whare under Cultovation, but did not see the large gangs of slaves in the fields that was to be seein 2 years ago with thair Drivers with those whips. I wish you couled see them.

I shouled like to have some men that do not live more then one thousand miles from Vilidge Hill tied up and make them feel how pleasant it is to be cut up with whips and then washed down with Salt Brine. That whouled be light Punshment to what thay deserve, but thair time will come.[314] But that condition of Southron Socity, thanks to Jeff, the first is don away for ever.

The Slave is a free man to day with a good Springfield Rifle in his hands, or a large number of them, and thay must help Carve out thair own Freedom with thair Strong right hands and Stout Hearts, and when once asuerd of thair Independence, he must learn to fit himself to maintain what as cost so much of the best Blood of the Cuntry, to say nothing of the Vast Det that has been incurred to Carrey out and make Shuer of his Independence to all coming time. His white Brother is Payin his Det that has been owing to him and will be leaving the Colerd Race in det to all future time as Thomas Jefferson, the immortal Framer of that Constitution that we had been living under for nearly a Century, truly said, that all men was endowed with cirtain inalienable rights among which was life, Liberty, and the Persuites of happeness. It is our great Privaladge to see this day, to see the realization of the fact that was first Put in writing and form by the Great Virgi[ni]an nearly a Century ago. I say that it is our Privaladge to see this day, may our Chirldren maintain with thair good right hands and Blood, if need be, the Great truths that thair Fathers are transmiting to them. May thay defend and see that thair Chirldren recves the Legacey that has Cost so much.

---

[314] Referring to the Copperheads

On Ship's Transport early July, 1864[315]

. . . we are Passin Port Hudson, but everything looks different. It is held by Colerd Troops. You can not see the place from the river on account of the Bluffs, or high Banks. I thought of the Hartford and Albertross that, for two months, was cut off from the rest of the Worled and stuck to the Rebs like thair evil genuse, never givin them a moments Peace. Thair days was pased in wachfullness and thair nights in fear of that 200 Pounder Parrot that the Hartford Carred.[316] It was worse than Gilmors Swamp Angle[317] that disturbed the security of Beauregard and that put him in mind that Uncl Abraham was after him.

Morganza Bend is full of troops and more coming. We moved twice the first day, which is not plesent. We had Just got our tents up when came orders to have t[w]o days rations Cooked and be ready to move at a moments warning. The men had been racing round all day plundering Camps where the troops had been and was fixed up for House keeping, when we had to fall in and stow ourselves on another Boat. Three Regiments was on the Boat we was put on, and room was not over plenty. The Cinders flew in a Perfect shower from the smok stack. We lost one man that night through them. Someone waked him up & toled him is Blanket was on fier and he Jumped over board and that was the last of that poor fellow.

We got down to New Orleans on the 3rd of July and we got a Maile. I recved your letter of June the 19th and was made Contented, more so then I have been for some time. I was glad to hear that you was all well at that time and that Virtue had a Cow and that you was doing all that you couled to make her happy.

I wish that I couled send you that Hundred Dollers but Virtue shall have that Board Bill. It ought to have been Paid befor, but I couled not get it, but some of it she shall get soon. Our Pay Rolles was sent in yesterday and, has we

---

[315] The opening page of this letter is missing, but content of this letter and the letter of July 7 places it beginning on the way back to New Orleans and ending on about July 4.

[316] Referencing the Siege of Port Hudson in 1863

[317] The heavy eight-inch, two-hundred-pounder Parrott siege gun, which was called the "Swamp Angel," was used to shell Charleston in August of 1863, with Union Maj. Gen. Quincy Adams Gilmore in charge. It went into history as the most famous Parrott gun. Jack W. Melson, Jr., "Famous Cannon & Mortars," Civil War Artillery, accessed April 24, 2012, http://www.civilwarartillery.com/cannon/default.htm.

are goin out of the Department, we expect to get Paid soon. I shall be able to send one Hundred Dollers cirtain. I wrote to Henry to send Virtue some Money.

I thank Mother and you for your kindness to the Chirldren. I know that you do all you can for them and if my life is spaird, I will try to make it as esay for you and Mother in the Decline of life. I know your Jurney through this worled has not Been as plesent as some, that thair has been more thorns then Roses and that the Pathe has been rough and hilley, but we will trust that God that has Brought us so far, and whose care of us as follered us from the Cradle to the Present time. I am sorry to hear that you have had a dry June. We had a wet one down hear. I wish I had some of that Milk for it whouled be good hear. I am glad that the Chirldren will have a nuff Milk for it will do them good.

I do not understand how Faney did not stay any longer with her Aunt & I hope that Henry will be able to help you get your Hay, for help is so scarce. You need not truble about me, for I am quite well and feel better then I have fore a year. I felt very uncomfortabl when I was to home and did not Enjoy myself, not a bit, but it was the Climat that put me so much out. I feel that I must come home in the Summer to get over the affects of this Climate. Thair is a large Expidition fitting out hear, but whare to is a secret. All that I know, we are in it.

I send my love to you all. Keep up your Curadge. All will be right yet. Give my love to the Chirldren and kiss them Babys for me. Tell Buttler that I love him as much as I do Arthur and that I make no differance between them.

From Your Affactnat Husband and Son,
CW Sherman

New Orleans, July 7, 1864

Dear Wife & Chirldren, Parents,[318]

We have not left up to this time but have orders to fall in at 5 O'Clock this P.M. We have been waiting for Transportation. Our Destination is a Secret. Genral Roberts has taken the A Tents from our Officers, and thay must take Privat fare as no Transportation will be allowed them. The Caverley & Batterys have gon. The impresion is that we are bound to our Old Comander, the man

---

[318] This letter is transcribed from copies.

that waked up Jeff Davis by Knocking at the Back Door of Richmond, but it is all Guesswork as nothing is known whare this Expedition will strike, but it is my Privat opioin that we shall give Mobile a loud Call to return to the Bosom of Uncl Abraham and not be wandering in the Desert of Secession, but to return to the true Church and not Sin anymore.

The fourth was a Dul[l] day with us, but not so dull as last fourth. We had to be Shuer a larger Selute thair then hear that day and the Mortar Boates Treated the Reble Genral Gardner to a biger Dose of 15 Inch Shell. I did think the Loyle People of the City whouled have had more Patrotism and showed it by Fier works in the Evaning, but except a few Rockets, that was the extent of the Celebration and we was kept in Camp, no Pases beain given on that day except on Bissness. Those of us that have Stripes can Pass any Garde and go whare we please, but having no Green Backs my self, I contented my self by writing a letter to you and promising myself quite a tall time when we have put down this Reblion. For one, I mean to have a Jolification and keep it up long anuff to pay me for having to forgo the plesuers of Home on that day. May the great giver of life and all good in is Great Mercy bring this Crule War to a Close and cause the Olive Branch of Peace to Spread over this desolated land before a nother year rolles round. I hope you to home had a good fourth and enjoy your selves and let care slide, make your selves comfortable. I was in hopes that we shouled get Payed befor we went away but it wont be long now before we shall get some green Backs.

Virtue, I thank you for your kind wish that I couled [have] some of your surplaus milk. It whouled make our Shoe Leather that is dealt out for Coffee to us tast[e] Palatable to us and I couled soake my Cakes in it, that is if I shouled live long a nuff to have them soak through. I for got to get my Teeth filed and put in order be for I left home and feel the loss of sharp Molars when I try to grind a Cake, but I will wait till I come home again.

Give my respects to Mr. Brooks and family and all enquiring frends. My health is good and you must not truble on that account. I can Eat my Rations and take in as much Mississipipi Mud in the shape of Mississipipi Watter as is good for me. I send my love to you all. Tell young Buttler that I love him as well as Aurther. Kiss them for me.

From your Affactnat Husband,
CW Sherman, LA

New Orleans, July 8, 1864

Dear Wife & Chirldren, Parents,

We are on board the Alabama the 2nd, not the Pirate Alabama. We are laying off in the river waiting for a Crew. The Present Crew has Struck for higher wages. We have been waiting for a Boat and now we have one, we can not get away for the want of help. This is how the world go[e]s, when it is not one thing, it is another. But if we are wanted very much, it may disaraing the Plan and we meet with disaster and defeat, but we will hope for the Best. This Boat is Built half River and Lake, but can not live in a hevey sea, so that we know we are not bound to Fortress Munro for we couled not get by Cape Hattras.[319]

Things remain quiat and we have nothing to stire our Blood or wake us up, but may have more then we want or that is good for our health. The Rebs are Colectin at differant Points. Grant and Lee are Pounding one another and Sherman hunting Johnson in Gorga,[320] and Banks down hear is Sweatin and, as it has apeard to me, is taking it as Cooley as it is posable with the Sun Shining as hot and melting as it is posable to. And we poor Devils are like so many Chickins that is all ready Picked and waiting for some one to stick us onto a Spit and rost us.

The Mississipipi gets Mudeier and dirtier. I think thay are seeing how much filth it will bare, what with Dead Soldiers, nigers and Mules. However our Drink ought to be good.

As we was going up to Morganza Bend, we met a Dead Soldier floting face down wards in the Watter with is Knapsack on. He must have fell overboard from some Boat and he may stay in the River any length of time, for human life is not thought much of in theas times. By one of the Wharves whare we had been geting

---

[319] Fort Monroe was a military installation in Hampton Roads, Virginia, overlooking the Chesapeake Bay. Andrew Lawler, "Fort Monroe's Lasting Place in History," smithsonianmag.com, July 5, 2011, http://www.smithsonianmag.com/history-archaeology/Fort-Monroes-Lasting-Place-in-History.html?c=y&page=2.

[320] Gen. W. T. Sherman fought a lengthy campaign against Confederate Gen. Joseph E. Johnston's Army of Tennessee, and attempted a direct assault on June 27, 1864, at the Battle of Kennesaw Mountain, Georgia, in which Sherman suffered heavy casualties. In July, Sherman continued his drive toward Atlanta. John D. Fowler, "Battle of Kennesaw Mountain," *The New Georgia Encyclopedia,* last modified January 10, 2014, http://www.georgiaencyclopedia.org/articles/history-archaeology/battle-kennesaw-mountain.

water hear was a dead niger tied by the Arm to one of the Spiles and left to float. He fell in some 3 days ago and thair he must stay, I sopose.

This life aboard theas Stransports is the most trying. We do not get room to hardley set down and as to laying down, that is a Siance onley acquierd by long practice.

July 9th

We reached the South West Pass this morning, sailing under Sealed Orders till noon when it was found that our destination was Fortress Munro. We do not care so much about whare we was goin, but whouled liked to have had a better Boat to go to se[a] in. This Boat was built in new york to run between Mobile and Galvastone, but not to stand the Sea. It will be all but a Mericle we get by Hattras, but we must hope for the best. It as run the Blockade 24 times and was Captuerd last October and now is put to a beter use. It is taking one thousand Stout Hearts to Buttler and if that back Door dose not open to thair knock, thair is no Virtue in New England Knocks. The men are well pleased to know that we shall stand a Chance of beaing onc[e] more under the man that makes opertunitys, not waiting for opertunitys, to make History for himself and the luckey men that are under him and the Nation whome we serve.[321]

Stransport Alabama, July 12, 1864

We are off the Coast of Gorga at this time in a state of Starvtion, or so near to it that we do not know the differance. The Tub that it pleased the Powers that be and that governs us at this time and that sent the 12th C.V. to Sea in, as not sunk yet, but that was not thair fault, but is owing to a good Providance that has sent us Plesent Wether.

We are on short rations of Water, and such Water. To Judge by the Smel & Strength of it, it must have been Pumped out of Noahs Ark from what Leaked in, in that Wet time, and been Preserved for the use of 12th C. V. If any town in that Good Old Land of steady habits, Hansom Wemon, and Fat babys had a

---

[321] The letter transcribed from original pages ends here and is completed with transcription from copies of the remaining pages.

Sink Hole that smelt one half as bad, it wouled make it self libale for damadges, but any thing is good anuff for Uncl Abrahams Boys when thay get them away from the Old man.

This Old Basket that was thought good anuff to take the Best pile of men that ever left thair homes to help Crush out the Seeds of Reblion and Treson, are piled like Pigs for the Slaguter from 3 to four feet deep to swelter and sweat and may be Contract Deases that thay will carrey to thair Graves. This is no over drawn state of things. Company K is stowed alongside of the Engine room & Boilers in a space not more than 8 feet whide. The front rank taking one side, the rear the other, and to lay down you have to take your opersite Naiboes feet to nurse and if it shouled hapen to be one to whom Water is an abomination, the contact is far from agreeable. But we shall get out of this soon, if we have good luck, in 3 days from now.

July 14th

We are nearing Stormey Cape Hatteras. We have had to heave to to day 3 times so that Uncl Abrahams Bleu Jackets could come on board to see that it was all right. Thay keep a pretty sharp look out for Blockade runers and, as we have to run in near the Shore, we run into the Gun Boats of Willmington & Gorga, South Carolina Coast. We are getting along nicley on Short rations and get in Fighting trim by the time we get to Fortress Munro. The Boat rolles Beautifulley, drawing but 4 feet water. The Wheels or Paddles, Play one at a time, one beaing out the Water and the other one in, very pleasant indeed goin to Sea in a Tub. I expect to be Floted back to New Orleans on a Shingle when thay get through with us this time.

July 15th

Well, hear we are on the Potomac making the best of our way to Washington. We reached Fortress Munro at 4 P.M. and then was orderd to Washington as the 19th Army Corp was thair and I shall Post theas Letters from thair, but you must not send till I send to you as I do not know where to Direct you to write till I know.

I am well and any Letters you may have sent to New Orleans will find thair way back. Give my Love to the Chirldren. Tell them I am neare[r] home then when I was in the Swamps of Louisana. The Capital is all safe and the War most over. We are hear.

Your affactnat Husband & Son,

CW Sherman

Washington, July 16, 1864

Dear Wife & Chirldren, Parents,

We have arived safe and in the very nick of time. Never was troops needed more than at this time and by all accounts, we shall be under fier in a few days. One of the Regiments that started with us from Morganza, the 47th Pensalvane, landed hear and was under fier the same day. Lee seems to be bound to give us truble this summer, but do not truble about me. I shall do well anuff.

We have had a tough time coming. I made shuer we shouled go down off Cape Hattras and it was no Idle fear. I did not let on that thair was any dainger, but looked my chances over of swiming ashore. One Boat that started 2 days befor we did has not arived. She had 6 Compneys of the 15th Main[e] on board.[322]

<u>Sunday the 17th</u>

We are camped 7 Mile out of the City. We arived in Washington about Noon and found the Citzens anxiousley looking for us, as the 19th Army Corp that was on the way from New Orleans was expected some days befor we did get hear, but as we did not Sail togather, we did not arive hear togather. The Boat that brought us did not sail as soon as expected for the want of a Crew as no one did want to risqu themselves on her, but we knew nothing about it and Soldiers are expected to know nothing but obey Orders.

---

[322] Indeed, six companies of the Fifteenth Maine Regiment, under Col. Dyer, were on a "small, awkward, incommodious low-pressure steamer named the Exact..." They encountered a gale off the coast of Hatteras on the fourteenth, which put them in peril for two days, but when it abated they continued on to the Fortress Monroe, arriving four days behind the others steamers from New Orleans that had left at about the same time. Henry A. Shorey, *The Story of the Maine Fifteenth: Being a Brief Narrative of the More Important Events in the History of the Fifteenth Maine Regiment* (Bridgton, ME: Press of the Bridgton News, 1890), PDF e-book.

We are camped inside of the brestworks, that Portion that protect Washington from the South. The Rebs made a bold dash for the Capital, but was sent back howling.[323] The Citizens turnd out 11 thousand strong this time and formed the first line of Battle. How many we lost, I can not find out. We lost 47 Officers kiled & wounded and the Privats must have numberd some Hundreds, but what the Papers Put our loss at, I do know. Our Corps is in Pennsynlvania and we know not what we shall do.

<u>July 18th</u>

Well, hear we are in the Chesapeak Bound for Fortress Munro & City Point. We was doing very well whare we was, 7 Mile out of the City, but orders came for us to report Back to Washington and back we had to go. The Sun was hot and it soon had us plasterd with the dust. We was taken to the Washington & Balttemor railroad Depot and I never took the Harness off with greater pleasuer. The Coble Stone that the Streets are paved with made our feet soar and lamed us some. Gorgetown Joins Washington, and 7 Mile of such Marching whouled [give] any one tender feet.

Everyone wanted to know what Regiment it was and how many men we had as the 3 Compneys of the 13th Main[e] that come out with us made the Regiment look large. Thay are atached to our Regiment for the present. We was taken to the Soldiers home in the Rear of the Capitall, a kind of yard with two long Sheds parted off. After stacking Arms we took some of the Dust out [of] our eyes. We was told that we shouled have some sup[p]er and we was treated to a Bowle of Coffee and one Pice of Bread and Cold pork. The Coffee I liked, but I get all the pork I want and more, too, and the large slice that was on my Bread spoilt my Hunger, and I was all Jaded out as we was Marched further then was nessary to show the good People of Washington what kind of Regiments the good Old State of Connetcut had turnd out to Protect the

---

[323] Lt. Gen. Jubal Early with the Army of the Valley, and under orders from Lee, led an advance on Fort Stevens reaching Washington, DC, on July 11, 1864; however, he realized the Union positions were being reinforced and decided to withdraw to Leesburg, Virginia, crossing the Potomac at White's Ford, thus ending his attack on Washington, DC, on July 12. "Jubal Early's Raid on Washington, DC," Georgia's Blue and Gray Trail Presents America's Civil War, last modified January 5, 2008, http://blueandgraytrail.com/event/Jubal-Early's_Raid_on_Washington_D._C. ; Flood, *1864 Lincoln at the Gates*, 193–208.

integerity of the Union and teach Rebles in Arms to respect the Lawes and the rights of all.

We lay down that night thuroghley tierd and Just got to sleep when we all waked up to pack up and March. Very plesent that, for our bones Ached, but we was soon Marching through the now silent Streets, we knew not whare.

After[324] marching some 4 miles we were halted and most of the men was soon asleep on the street. In a short time afterwards we found ourselvs on board a nother Boat bound for the James River and Buttler, we sopose, as we have not got to our destination yet.[325]

July 19th

Passed Fortress Munro some time in the night. I was up at the time and the sight was very preaty from the number of gun Boats, stransports with thair light shining. All Genral Grants suplies come to Fortress Munro and Buttlers and it takes a large number of Boats of every discription to bring suplies to such a large number of men that is now on the Sacred Soil of Verginia and more acoming. It strikes me that this Regiment as don some tall travling lately, some 6000 miles. We have been rushed into Verginia and Maryland through the Capital twice and are now on to Grants Slaughter Pen as thay call it.[326]

You must get ready for a draft, for the men are needed and thay must come. Thair will be some growling among the frends of Jefferson Davis, the first that is among you, but thay will Howle more if thay compell Grant to send a few of

---

[324] Beginning here, two pages from copies make up the middle portion of this letter.

[325] "I had just laid down for the night on my blanket in the open court when another order came; we must pack at once, take a transport for City Point and join the army before Richmond. So here we are, cluttering the cabins and decks of the *Winona* and sleeping as much as possible in order to kill time and hunger." During this month, the regiment was ordered back and forth between camps south of Washington on the James River and then back to Washington again. De Forest, *A Volunteer's Adventures*, 162.

[326] This term references a key part of the 1862 Battle of Fredericksburg where the fighting was so intense that it became known as the "Slaughter Pen." Approximately, 5,000 men met their fate. After witnessing the carnage of the battle, Robert E. Lee made the famous quote: "It is well war is so terrible . . . otherwise we would grow too fond of it." The 208-acre Slaughter Pen Farm was purchased by the Civil War Preservation Trust in 2006 for $12 million. "Civil War Preservation Trust Announces Campaign to Save Slaughter Pen Farm," press release March 29, 2006, http://www.civilwar.org /aboutus/news/news-releases/2006-news/civil-war-preservation-trust-1.html.

those Regiment among them that have very little Pity for Whinein, Cryin, Blubering men that have given so much Aide & Comfort to the Rebs. How delighted thay whouled be to give them a call. How a Prick in thair rear whouled make them tread up to the Tune of the Coperhead Lament. I can write no more now. We are at City Point goin to the front.[327] Yours in haste, more to you later.

Your Affactnat Husband and Son,
CW Sherman[328]

I did not send this when I closed with my Pencle. We did not land at that Place but came up a few mile further and we are in Camp now with the rain coming down. This is the disagreable [part] of Soldierng. We are Camped 2 miles from Fort Darling on the James River and Glad we are to get on land once more and rest our bones. General Buttlers Head Quarters are about 2 mile from us, but wether we give him a lift or Grant, we know not, but hear we are and Johnny Reb will have cause to repent of the day that he meets the 12th C. V. in Battle aray. Wont thair be mourning in the Reble Camp? It Strikes me that thay will run against a stone wall and get hurt.

I shall come out all right. Never fear. Do not truble because I am hear. My Chances are Just as good, and the same God that as Preserved me till the present time is Just as Able to return me safe from the Fier. Keep up your Hearts, and think that I am in the Path of duty and tryin to do my best to put an end to this strife which I couled not be if I was at home. We hear the Boom of the Batterys from hear, and that gives me the asuarance that some one is to work.

Kiss my Babys for me and tell young Buttler that I am with his Namesake in virgiani. My love to you all. I cannot get that Letter that you wrote last. I

---

[327] City Point (now Hopewell), Virginia, was located at the meeting of the James and Appomattox Rivers. It was the site of General Grant's headquarters. A river port, City Point had become the logistical hub for operations against Petersburg and Richmond. Emmanuel Dabney, "City Point During the Civil War," *Encyclopedia Virginia*, last modified January 3, 2012, http://www.encyclopediavirginia.org/City _Point_During_the_Civil_War#start_entry.

[328] End of two copied pages; original pages follow

sopose that thair was one on the Electic Spark that the Reble Pirate Florada Captuerd and you can Direct your letters to:

Charles W. Sherman, Compney K, 12th C.V.[329]
19th Armey Corps
Washington D. C.

Bermuda Hundreds, Virginia, July 21, 1864

Dear Wife & Chirldren, Parents,

We are still at this place not having gon to the front.[330] We are waiting for the rest of our Brigade to com up. Troops have been coming every day and the 9th C.V., 26th Massachusetts, [and] 75th N. Y. left us last night for the front and we may go any Mineut.

We are Camped on the west Bank of the James River. Fort Darlin[g] is to the right of us, some 12 mile from hear. Petersburge is 7 miles South East of us. We hear the Picket fiering frome hear. Petersburge is in a Valley. Grants Works extend a long distance. How many miles of Earth Works, I have not heard. We have Batterys on a range of Hills on this side of Petersburge. The Rebs have thair works on our front and Works in the rear of Petersburge and Batterys

---

[329] On July 10, 1864, it was reported in the Columbus Carolinian (South Carolina) that the steamship *Electric Spark,* bound for New Orleans, was captured by the Rebel steamer *Florida.* The mails were being transferred to the *Florida,* and one of the officers of the *Florida* stated that the *Electric Spark* would be burned. The passengers were transferred to the British schooner *Lane.* "The Pirate Florida," *The New York Times* Archive, July 12, 1864, http://www.nytimes.com/1864/07/12/news/pirate-florida-privateer-our-coast-half-dozen-barks-schooners-cap-tured-near.html?pagewanted=all.
[330] Bermuda Hundred, Virginia, was incorporated in 1613. It is located at the southwest edge of the confluence of the Appomattox and James Rivers, opposite City Point. This area was part of the Bermuda Hundred Campaign fought in May of 1864. Gen. Butler, leading the Army of the James, threatened Richmond from the east, but was stopped by Beauregard's Confederate forces and retreated into his fortifications at Bermuda Hundred. Flood, *1864 Lincoln at the Gates,* 99.

placed on some Hills in the rear of Petersburge so that the City is placed in a tight place betteen two fiers.

Grant can take the City any time, but couled not hold it till the Rebs have been driven out of thair works in the rear. Grant is taking things Coolley, when the News was brought to him of the Reble Raid into Maryland & on Washington, he lighted a Seagar and told the Aide that Maryland & Washington must take care of themselvs, he was after Richmond, and hear he will stay till Richmond is ours.

The Rebs do not lack for men as yet as every whare we show ourselvs, thay are found in sufficient numbers to make the movement as livley as you please. We must have more men if we are ever to suckceed. Having to strech from river to river, we can not use all the men we have. We must be Strong anuff along our whole front to resist a Charge from the Rebs as thay can mass thair men and Brake through our lines. And we must have men and Batterys that can not be used onley under cirtain circumstances, all though thay are on the Ground and a Battle beaing Fought right under thair Eyes. This is one reson we have not been able to reap all the advantadges that have been thrown in the way of the Union Armys. To make the blow affactive that Grant is about to deliver, he must have more men, all though it is given out that he says that he as men anuff to Whip Lee on any Ground that the Reble Genral may chose. It dose not Follow that Grant can captuer the Reble Armey evan after Whiping them. To do that, he must have fresh men Captuerin a few when the mass of the Enemy gets away to take up new Ground and make another exhausting Fight for the Atackin Party. This is the reson that we have not made more Progress in Crushing out this Reblion. The means used have not been large anuff for the end aimed at, and the Union Armeys have had to go over the same ground agan.

What quaking thair will be when that Draft that is orderd takes place, for I do not imadgin that Uncl Abraham will get 500,000 more men by Bountys by September. How plesent for those poor fellows that have been paying thair 300 Dollers & thinking thay whare out of it and others in less Sums, but[331] "Jentlemen, you must come. This hangin back is played out. Pleas fall in and Dress to the right. You will feell better when you come in contack with your Betters that have been takin the load off your Shouldiers and carring it for you

---

[331] In the following, Charles imagines his speech to those trying to dodge fighting for the Union.

till the present time. The Cakes are better now. You will have escaped the Wormey ones that were our lot to Eat, to say nothing of that Mule meat. You will be taken by the hand and learnt, in a short time, various tricks that you whouled have went to your Graves with out the Knowledge of, and thay are very nessary for you to know in order to make respectable men and good Citezens of you, for non of you will have the Brass to pretent that you Posess those Virtues, all though you have impudance anuff for any thing that helps you to lead uesless and Vicious lives. Come and redeem yourselves so that a Curse rest not on you for Deserting your Cuntry till now. I do not wish to Flatter you, but your Education as been sadley neglected and it is time you whare doing some thing for yourselves. And your Southron Brethern have been wondering whare you was. We want you to make thair acquaintance. It will disabuse your minds of many of these false opinions that you have been laboring under. It will like wise be of the greatest Benifit to you to learn the different Geografical featuers of this Land. You can see for yourselves what a differance a few hours labor will affect in the formation of the ground, but I must not tell you the modious operandi. Come and see, you will not regret it, but found fault with me that I did not tell you the Beautyes of Soldierin. Do not let this opertunity slip by uninproved."

Virtue, I do not know when I can send you any Money and how you have gotten along till this time, but I couled not help it. Others have been to blame in this matter that shouled have don thair duty by me. I went to the Coll about it yesterday and he sent for Capt Roche to know the reson that I did not recve my Bounty & Pay. I told you what to do till I couled get this thing straightend out and I hope you did as I requested, or Henry did for you. I can not but think he must be in a situation to let you have anuff to get along with. If you have not recved any money from Henry, you must have been short of maney things that you wanted, but keep up your Heart. Better times coming.

Do the best you can for those young Soldiers and the Ladyes must not make any more truble nor cry thair Preaty eyes out if thay have to wait for thair new dresses a spell longer. Tell them I often think about them and wonder what thay are doing, but I know thay will help thair Mother all thay can and put up with difficulty. We can not have what we want at all times, but it as not been my fault that you have went short, but it will be all right if we only have faith in our selves and trust that God that as all ways Protected us till the present time, will Provide fore us in the futuer. I will keep you advised of my whareabouts and as letters ought to go and come sooner hear than in the swamps of Louisiana, I shall expect more. Give my love to the Chirldren and accept a large share yourselves.

Your Affctnate Husband,

CW Sherman, Va.

Camp Near Chaing Bridge, Maryland, July 30, 1864[332]

Dear Mother & Father,

I have thought of writing a few lines to you hoping thay may find you both in good health. I am well, except [for] a little Cold that I contrcted coming from New Orleans, as my Compney was Baked & rosted by beaing piled near the Boilers and that sweated us so much that I thought we was under Homepathic treatment. The effects was not benifical to me, but my health is good and I feell well.

You must have felt disappointed about that Hundred Dollers, but I couled not help it and it as been a source of truble to me. I have don all that I couled to get it straightend out and I told Captain Roche that if I did not get it soon, I shouled not do any duty, for it was wrong to keep me out of it so long. But we must take things as we find them, trusting all things to him who sees all things and that will Protect and feed us, if we onley will trust him.

My Wife and Chirldren, you have helped them when I couled not, but have tryed to make araingments with Henry to let Virtue have some money till I couled send her some, but it apears he has not don any thing as yet. It is not useing me right, but I can not get at the reson that I have not heard from Henry, for if he had writen I must have got his letter and, in any case, he might have writen to Virtue or you and stated the reson. He promised to see your Hay got

---

[332] The Chain Bridge crosses the Potomac River and was originally constructed in 1797 to allow the transportation of goods from Virginia to Georgetown, Maryland. During the war, the Union Army fortified areas around the bridge to defend against Confederate access to Union held territory. Conversely, it was used to invade Northern Virginia and seize Alexandria. Ron Baumgarten Blog, "Chain Bridge: Commuting Through History, Part I," A DC Lawyer on the Civil War (blog), June 6, 2010, http://dclawyeronthecivilwar.blogspot.com/2010/06/chain-bridge-commuting-through-history.html.

in in good shape, but you do not give up in Small matters, and I hope you will get through now.

Since I sat down to write theas few lines, I have had Orders to be ready to move at 5 O Clock with 4 days Rations in our Harvesacks, but whare we know not. I will State hear that the Goverment is owing me, at this time, 340 Dollers United States Bounty, one 100 Dollers Old Bounty, and 20 Dollers Back Pay, and Pay from the 16th of Febuary to the 30th of July and that if any thing shouled hapen to me and you do not hear frome Captain James D. Roche, to write to Coll Frank H. Peck Comanding the 12th Regiment Co Voll and he will see that every thing is righted. I do not write this to Alarm you, but that every thing may be straight.

Do the best you can for Virtue and the Chirldren. I will write you when we Camp again and kiss those Babys for me and Virtue, you must keep up a Stout Heart and never say die. That is not the way to get through this World, to be faint Hearted if the road is rough. Give my love to all the Chirldren and my best Prayers for all of you from your Affactnate Son,

CW Sherman, D.C.

Camp near Chain Bridge, Maryland, July 30, 1864

Dear Wife & Chirldren, Parents,

I am enjoying the best of health, never felt so well no time that I rem[e]mber since Joining the Armey and did not Join then for any love of this kind of life, but be cause I loved Peace and quietness and, faith, I have onely helped kick up a biger Muss then thair was before, but the Calme that follows the Tornado is sweeter than the light ruffling of Natuer and I shall enjoy it the more from having been out in the Storm.[333]

We are Camped near the Potomac and you can not think how plesent it is to us. The Waters are so soft and coolling that I can not think how I ever couled enjoy, or think I did, the Mudey Waters of the Father of Waters, and to Drink the Beautifull Spring Waters of theas Hills is more then I ever hoped to or dreamed of. It is health

---

[333] It is interesting to note that in the letter to his parents on the same date, he mentions having a "little cold," but here says he's "never felt so well." One must wonder if he isn't exaggerating a bit for his wife's sake.

and life hear and the Land that we have left was nothing but D[is]ease and Death and how we ever lived to Bring our Bones away beats me to tell, but thair may be some thornes and Stoney places for us hear, but taken all togather, I whouled be pleased to spend the short term of my 3 years or the War hear. The Rebs love this Place, or thay whouled not be so loth to leave and go to a Straing Land, but Grant says thay must be Picking up thair traps and Household Goods and the quicker thay are on the move, the better for me.

We are Camped nine mile out of Washington and the Cuntry much Broken up with Ravins & Hills and what I have seein of it is no wonder the Rebs have made such a good Stand. The very Natuer of the Ground as been a host in its self in favor of the Rebles and Uncl Abrahams Calls for men have never been large anuff to make up the differance of position, all though maney to home of the lukwarm, faint hearted half Reb and half Coward, have thought we have had more then anuff to put down this gigantic Reblion and save thair little mean and Souless Bodys from the fatagues of helping us in our need.

Fanney, you must tell Ark Fisk that thair must be some gross misunderstanding in is saying that I whouled not voat for Uncl Abraham if I couled have that Privlidge. Dose he, or any other Copper Head in the good old State of Stadey habits,[334] sopose that the man that Shoulders his Knapsack and Rifle to Fight for Law and good Order whouled not voat for the man that as never flinched or deserted is Post, and that stands as a strong Bulwerk between the Constitution and the Libertys of a free Nation on the one hand, and the disloyle Crew that whouled distroy those Blessings that have been handed down to us from a former Generation? Perish the thought that I couled so far forget the Teachings of a Hampden, a Russell, a Jefferson[335] and the long line of great and good men that have gon befor us to light the way for those that whouled, in a humble manner, try to walk in thair footsteps and follow thair Teachings all though thay shouled walk ever so blindley. May those that

---

[334] Connecticut, the "Land of Steady Habits." *A Dictionary of Americanisms on Historical Principles,* ed. Mitford M. Mathews (Chicago: University of Chicago Press, 1951), 954.

[335] John Hampden (1594–1643), an English champion of liberty who lost his life during the English Civil War; William Russell, First Duke of Bedford, English Civil War; Thomas Jefferson. David Plant "John Hampden, c. 1595–1643," last modified September 24, 2008, http://bcw-project.org/biography/john-hampden; David Plant, "William Russell, 5th Earl & 1st Duke of Bedford, 1616–1700," last modified October 6, 2009, http://bcw-project.org/biography/william-russell-earl-of-bedford.

misrepresent the thoughts and Actions of others look more serchingley into thair own Hearts and thay will see the C[o]rrupt fountain from which springs the Poisens that distroys thair own happeness and Enjoyments. To all such I say, Purefie the Fountain.[336]

Camp near Frederick City, Maryland, August 2, 1864

Dear Wife & Chirldren, Parents,

I am well and better than I thought I shouled have been if I had known what a time I was goin to have when I wrote to you last. I told you we was orderd to be ready by 5 Oclock to March with 4 days Rations, but the Orders was Countermanded and we fell in with 2 days Rations and to March back to Washington and take the Cars for Baltomore. What the People must have thought to see our Brigade back again.[337]

We got to Washington about 10 Oclck and was Packed as usal like Cattle for the Market. It was my luck to be detailed to Pattrole the Streets to pick up stragglers. After that duty, the Gard was tucked into a Car made of Sheet Iron and placed near the Head of the train and then we got under way and travled all night, or what was left of [it].

It was a long train, 5 Engines and some 150 Cars. We took the Balltomore & Ohio Road and then we knew we was after those Raiders that had pulled up some of the Railes and Burnt some Bridges on this Road.[338] At day light we

---

[336] This letter is incomplete and is transcribed from copies.

[337] The Twelfth was indeed being shuffled back and forth around Washington before finally being transported to Maryland, then northwest Virginia by the end of August, where they went back and forth some more. "The Twelfth Connecticut is traveling to and fro in quite mysterious and astonishing fashion...Back again, and without knowing why, in the defences [sic] of Washington. We were to have taken part in some movement at City Point, but of a sudden we got orders to go aboard a transport . . .Well, we tramped down the Shenandoah Valley, and we tramped back again." [notes in the book mention that this alludes to Sheridan's march to Strasburg and back. Ed.] and "Here we are, nearly back to Harper's Ferry . . ." De Forest, *A Volunteer's Adventures*, 161–167.

[338] Confederate Lt. Col. John Singleton Mosby led the Forty-Third Virginia Battalion in guerrilla attacks on Union railroads, wagon trains, outposts, and pickets in western Virginia from February 1863 to the end of 1864, finally disbanding April 21,

starded again, but goin slowley as we had to Put out Skimshers in front of the Train and on each side of the Road. Some times we had 3 Regiments out at a time, for the marks of the Southron Raider was thick, but we got along with out Accident and with out meeting a single Reble. The People was pleased to see us along the road. It was a Rough Cuntry we went through, as hard and Stoney as any road in the Northen States, and more so for the Road was graded with Stones Broken up, the same as thay do in the Old Cuntry, to fasten the Ties down. To see the large heaps of theas Stones Broken up fine put me in mind of the same sight that I rem[e]mber to have seeing in England along the Roads.

The State of Maryland is very Hilley and Broken and the soil of a light Collor and full of stone, small, none of those large Boulders such as in our land. The Quarres are of eather slate or a kind of Rotten Quartz and the People Stack thair Hay & Grain in large Ricks, no Barns of any Size did I see, but thair is some nice Farms hear and we passd lotts of grass cut and some tumbled. We got out [of] the Cars 2 mile from Frederick City and went into Camp. Had just put our tents [up] when the order came for us to fall in and protect our Waggon train.

The train and one Battery went by the Baltermore Harpers ferry turnpike and the Gurialley Moseby was after the train. It had not come up and the men had nothing to Eat and we couled not afford to give our Grubb to the Rebs and off we went, not knowing how far we shouled have to go. We came up with the train at midnight and found it all safe with a gard of 300 Cavarlay and that put us all in good spirits, but to lay in the road, our Clothes wet through with Sweat. I do not think that my Mother whouled have known her Son or that Wife that took me for better or worse whouled have found me much the worse that night. The dust was coated all over us and no Chance of washing with out goin back some distance and we was too tierd for that, and had to make the most of our luck.

The men was hungray and we had to March back with the train and did not start till the sun was up, and it came out very hot and the men fell out [of] the ranks and couled not be kept in. The Horses droped in the road and couled not be brought along. I stood the Press very well and, as I wanted Watter very much, I kept goin till I found some and got into Camp about 2 hours befor the Regiment and did not feell any the worse for the March.

1865. Jeffry D. Wert, *From Winchester to Cedar Creek, The Shenandoah Campaign of 1864* (Mechanicsville, PA: Stackpole Books, 1997), 147–156.

This morning I went and washed my Clothes, but the sun did not come out so I couled [not] wash my Pants and, as we may move any moment, I do not want to be caught with my Pants wet. I neve have and I get them dirty anuff with out traveling with wet Pants. We have funey times. We do not know a mineut but we may be goin some where or other, and my expearance is that we do not know.

Since writing this Letter I have fell in and Packed all my Traps and been in line to move, but Just as we went, orders came to brake ranks and hear I am finishing this letter. I have washed my Pants since and I guess I shall manadge to get Cleen again. Virtue can get a good living by taking in washing when I get home and set me to washing, for I am perfect, can beat any woman or Number of Wemon, not but thay can beat us at most household matters, but I can beat them in using Sope & Watter.

The News is not incuragin from Petersburge and Hunter is falling back and we are colecting all of our Corps at this Point.[339] Whare we are, is the Point the Rebs cross over into Maryland and the Ground we [are] on was Fought over 20 days ago by Brakenridge and his Rebs and he got the better of our Forces. Thay had to retreat and the Rebs run whare thay pleased till we came, and if Genral Lewis Wallace had had this Corps, the Rebs whouled not have been in the Shenodaha Valey at this time.[340] The Rebs came upon him with 5 to one of ours, and Wallace had to retreat, but that days Fight saved the City of Washington and gave us time to come up.

You to home did not realize that six thousand men on theas Hills fought 20 thousand men all day, but couled not save Chamberburge from beain burnt,

---

[339] Gen. David Hunter was in command of the Army of the Shenandoah in May 1864, defeating Maj. Gen. William E. Jones at the Battle of Piedmont at the beginning of June and then to Lexington where he burned VMI; however, he was defeated by Lt. Gen. Jubal Early at the Battle of Lynchburg on June 19. Grant then brought in Maj. Gen. Philip Sheridan to effectively take over the campaign. Flood, *Lincoln at the Gates,* 178; Scott C. Patchan, *The Last Battle of Winchester, Phil Sheridan, Jubal Early, and the Shenandoah Valley Campaign, August 7–September 19, 1864* (El Dorado Hills, CA: Savas Beattie, 2013), xvii, 12–13.

[340] Maj. Gen. Lewis "Lew" Wallace fought on July 9, 1864 at the Battle of Monocacy, part of the Valley Campaigns of 1864 with only a 6,000-man force under his command. They were defeated by Lt. Gen. Early, CSA who had some 14,000 troops; however, they were able to delay Early's advance towards Washington for an entire day, which gave the city time to organize its defenses and thereby repel Early. Confederate Maj. Gen. John C. Breckinridge also led troops in this battle, hence the reference from Charles above. Flood, *1864 Lincoln at the Gates,* 189–191.

nor the City of Frederick from Payin 250 thousand Dollers to save the City from the flames.[341] The County of Frederick is more loyle then any County North, and has suffere some on that account. This state has furnished 28 Regiments to the Reble Armey and 20 Regiments to the Union cause, so you see, the state is rather more inclined to favor the Reble Cause, but the state is considerd in the Union, but Union Bayonets onley keep the State in the Unon. I dare not tell you what is hear in the Woods hid frome the Rebs. We whouled be but to[o] happy to make them acquainted but the time is not come. The Rebs are bound to strike for Washington and then thay will be surprised with the sight that will be shown to them. Thay think that we have all our best troops round Richmond and that thay will onley have to contend with New troops. I shall have more to say about theas Hundred days men in my next [letter].[342]

Do not be alarmed about me. I am doing well, onley whouled like more Power to Grants Elbow. Give my respects to all enquiring frends and kiss those Babys for me.

Yours truley, my love to you all,

CW Sherman, Maryland

---

[341] Chambersburg in south central Pennsylvania. In 1864, it was invaded for the third time when cavalry was dispatched by Lt. Gen. Jubal Early, CSA, from the Shenandoah Valley. A large portion of the town was burned on July 30 under orders from Brig. Gen. John McCausland, CSA, for failing to provide a ransom of $500,000. Ibid., 245.

[342] In April 1864, the Governors of Ohio, Indiana, Illinois, Iowa, and Wisconsin proposed to Lincoln to provide 85,00 more volunteers into federal service for a period of 100 days to provide short term troops that would serve as guards, laborers, and rear echelon soldiers to free more veteran units for combat duty. Lincoln immediately approved the plan. Ibid., 65–66.

Chapter Eighteen

On the Move to the Shenandoah Valley

Dear Wife & Chirldren, Parents,

I write to you from this Famed place. Whare I shall bring up in the End, I cannot tell. You have heard of Flying Artllery, well this is the Flying Brigade of Infantry.[343] I have been in 5 States of this Union since leaving home this spring. Been or Traveled over 10,000 Miles and it is most time to bring up some whare. I was flattering myself of geting some rest when we Camped at Monocacy Bridge, but thair is not much to be depened on in this Campaing.

Last night I recond on having some rest, having had no sleep for 3 nights having been on Picket for that time, but Orders came to be ready to move in 5 mineutes and have 4 days rations of Hard Bread in our Harvasacks and we was on the move in no time. And after wadeing Monocacy River, which was very plasant, to say nothing of stayin or sleeping in our wet Clothes, at two O'Clock was waked up and orderd to take the Cars, and at six in the morning was in

---

[343] Flying Artillery is also referred to as "horse artillery," meaning the faster moving mounted artillery batteries. James Morgan, "'Mounted But Not Mounted,' The Confusing Terminology of Artillery," originally printed in the *Camp Chase Gazette* (1990), Civil War Weapons, last updated February 16, 2002, http://www.civilwarhome .com/artilleryterms.htm.

Harpers Ferry and such a place I never looked on. It is Grand, Such Mountains of Rock. It is the Strongest place that I have seein and I do not wonder that John Brown secleced[344] it for is Stronghold.[345]

We was Marched up the Mountain to what is called Maryland Heights and Camped. Had just got our tents up when we was Orderd to fall in and we was taken two Mile further and Masked in the Brush. Just such a place as the side hill down in the South Woods,[346] as Johney Reb had showed themselves and we wished to give them a surprise if thay came on as was expected.

We put up our tents for the sacond time, and coverd them with Brush and thought, as we went to sleep that night, how plesent it whouled be to stay thair a few days, but such was not the luck for us. When we waked up in the morning, the Regiment was gon, having moved off. In the Rain that was falling, 4 of us had gon a little way back and put up our tent and as the troops fell in with out the Drum, we was not disturbed and if I had waked up in Old Conct, I shouled not have been more surprised. Thay had gon about one hour and we was soon after them. Coming down the Mountain I wonderd how I ever got up [it]. I rem[e]mberd that I thought that my Knapsack was loaded with stone in Climing up, but the geting down was nearley as bad. When we got to the Road, we saw our Corps Climbing the Hill on the Harpers ferry side and a long line of Troops Crossing the Pontoon Bridge. We 4 was soon on the other side and Climbing the Narrow streets of the Town. I was looking round for the Engine House whare John Brown made his stand, but not having any one to tell me, I had to be satisfied by looking on the Burnt Ruins of the Goverment Works and the delapadated condition of the Houses, for this place shows the ravages of War, Burnt Buildings, shot holes in others, and fences gon. It looks as though hard times had visited it.

We found our Corps about 4 Mile out in line of Battle and Just in the Entrance of the Shennadoah valey. We have the right of the line, the 8th & 6 Corps have the Left, and he must be a bold Reb that undertakes to come on our front. The Batterys

---

[344] Selected

[345] John Brown was a militant abolitionist, and was an integral part of the Underground Railroad and was most famous for what was to be called "John Brown's Raid" on a government armory and arsenal at Harpers Ferry. He was eventually hanged on December 2, 1859, at Charlestown, having been found guilty of treason against Virginia. Faust, *Historical Times Encyclopedia*, 82–83.

[346] Referring, perhaps, to a hill at home in Connecticut

are Just Back of us and thay have a Cleer sweep for miles right and left. We moved our tents twice that day and it is not plesent to keep moving when you have got to Camp, but it as been part of the Program to have theas little things atended to.

At night we got a Maile at 9 oclock after we had turnd in and I was pleased to hear from home after so long a time. Not having any Candles, we made small fiers to read them by and promised ourselvs to Answer them in the morning, it beaing Sunday, but we was orderd to get ready for inspection and I had Just got to writing when we was given the usal five mineutes to pack up and March. After waiting a spell, most of us put up our tents again and hear I am trying to finish what I had began.

The Letters that I got was dated the 2nd of August and I see that you have had a trying time to get your Hay. I am pleased that Lewis is so handy and takes hold good, but you must be carefull that he dose not hurt himself. He is to young to be straind yet. Tell him I am pleased with is Conduct and hope he will continue to do is best. I am in hopes to be with him some time when this Crule war is over.

I was sorrey to hear that Virtue as been so sick and you have not told me of it till now. I see through it. You did not want me to know and it was as well that I did not. Tell her that I am glad that she is better and tell her not to worrey about me. I shall do well, my health is good and if I am not Marched too much.

The living as not been much latley, hard Bread and not half anuff of that and no meat. When we got to this place the men went round and gatherd some Bones and rosted them. Thair is plenty of meat in Harpers ferrey and the reson we do not get more, I know not. I have to tell the truth, Genral Hunter as been marching & fighting is men in this department with out any thing to eat and the Rebs have beat him and the reson is the men have been starvd and Ill used. He as had men fall out [of] his ranks and lay down to die because thay have had nothing to eat and the men have come back and seeing thair Comrads dead by the road side. Thair is regiments that started up the Shenanodah Valey this spring 800 Strong that, to day, can not muster 200 Rifles. The Rebs and starvation have reduced them down and it is not to be wonderd at that the Goverment can not get one single man to r[e-]enlist from such Regiments. I have not seeing theas things but have them from the Mouthes of men that have been through it and that knowes whareof thay speak. I do not write this to have you think that I am goin to go through the same usage, for I wont, but thair is some thing wrong some whare, some thing that can be put right.

I am Glad that Virtue as some Money, if it has been a long time coming. You did not tell me how much Henry let her have. I shouled like to have known and how he is geting on. I may not have any Pay for a long time yet, but you shall have it as soon as I can get it. Tell Potter that it is not my fault that he as not had it befor. He will waite till you can Pay him. I am anxious to have you Pay him as soon as we can get the means and have that off your mind.

I do not know as I shall have time to Answer Faneys letter now, but will as soon as I can. She must have a saprate Letter. By your letter, I understand that Mr. Brooks sent me one, but I have not recved it. I have writen him one from Washington. I send you all my love and may Hevan Bless you is the Prayer of your Affactnat Son & Husband,

CW Sherman, VA

Camp Near Harpers Ferry, Va, August the 7th, 1864

My Dear Daughter,[347]

I recved your kind letter of the 2nd of August and was much pleased to hear from you and that you and the Chirldren was well and that your Mother was geting better. You must not let her do anything till she is quite well and, mind you, keep me posted how your Mother gets along and those Babys.

Tell Aruther that I did not mean that he shouled be Spanked, but kissed, and that Buttler, how dose he get along? Dose he Chase the Cattle round and pull the Cat about? Lewis, he takes the Lead in Governing and directing the Working of the Estate, as Mr. Sunderland Calles it.[348] I shall be getting Jelouse of him, he will be Cuting me out of my Swath and laughing at me, I sopose, but such things must take place, but I shall give him a race some day [even] if I get the worst of it.[349] Tell him he must save himself and not do any thing beyond is Strength till he as don growing and if he takes care of his Body, he can grow up a Strong, healthy man and is mind must be Cultivated at the same time with his Body. One must help the other and in the same proportion, one must not get ahead of the other. You must help him all you can as well as inform yourself. You must mind your own strength and not go ahead to much, but what ever you do, learn to do easley and without effection and show. Do all you can for your

---

[347] Fanny, who turned fourteen in July of 1864
[348] Perhaps a neighbor or friend
[349] Meaning his son, Lewis, not Mr. Sunderland

GranMother, she is growing Old and can not do as she whouled.[350] She as been a good Mother to me and GranMother to you.

I have been knocking about hear to day and some whare els tomorrow, some tims have had some thing to Eat, and some tims not. You whouled have laughed to have seeing me and 20 other men 2 weeks ago to day. We was in a Iron Car on the Ohio & Baltamore rail road goin after the Raiders that had been through a portion of the state of Maryland & Pensylvania. The Sun came out very hot and we had to go slowly for fear of Acident as the Rebs had torn up the railes a few days befor. The Sun heated the Iron Car and we poor Fellows though[t] we was going to be rosted. It was the hotest ride that I ever took and do not wish for another.

It was a rugh, rug[g]ed Cuntry that we went through. We pased Numbers of State Quareas,[351] and one place a Cuntry School House whare the good People was met on that day. It put me to mind of home very much. Sundays are the days the most work is don in this Contest and it is no wonder we do not have more luck in our undertakings for the same work might be don on other days, but thair is no Sunday in the Armey. I am glad to hear that you have a good Sabbath School and that you can go with your Sister & Brothers. May you be made the means of much good in this life, for thair is much that you can do and Angeline, she can help you. I want her to write to me. She can if she will only try. If it comes hard the first time, it will be easeir the second time and now is the time to learn to write maney . . .[352]

Shenenadoah Valley, August 13th

Paper is scarse with me. I have no more so you must excuse torn & Dirty Paper and no chance of geting any at this time. August the 13th are Camped near As[h]by Gap, the 6th, 8 Corps in front. We are waiting to fall in. Hard Bread all gon, no Coffee, we are all feeling how good a Paile of Water whouled be to us.

---

[350] His mother, Sarah, would turn fifty-nine in 1864—perhaps considered old in those days! However, she lived to be eighty years old.

[351] Quarries

[352] This letter is incomplete.

August 20th, 1864, Shenenadoah Valley

Dear Wife and Chirldren, Parents.

We recved a Maile last night about 11 Oclock. Beaing on Gard I went and Brought that Part of it for our Compney, waked up the Captain, and got my part of it and went my way rejoycing for a small fier burning and read my letters by the light thair of. I recved your favor of the 11th of August & Faney's of the 9th, one from Henry.

We are camped 12 mile from Harpers Ferry, having fallen back to this place to await the Atack of the Rebs, if thay see fit to come on. We gave them a hard Chase, but couled [not] Bring them to a Battle. Thay [are] keeping to the Mountains, expecting that we shouled follow them and get hansomley thrashed for our pains, for thair intention was to draw us from our suplys and away from reinforcements, while thay couled get any quanity of help by raile Road and so out flank us and get to our rear and, in that case, we shouled be in a tight Place, but Genral Sheridan did not fancy that state of things and has fell Back to this place as we can Fight Longstreet or any other Street that Lee can send against us.

I was glad to hear from home and that you was well and that Virtue was getting better. I am well and in good health, but Dirty, Hungray and Rag[g]ed for Sheridan put us through in a way that astonshed some Regiments, but we had been thair befor and took it as every day afair, but it was a tugh March and many more is before me yet. Sheridan is a man of Bissness and the way he crow[d]ed the Reble Genral Earley was a Caution to the Butternutts, but thay was rather too smart for us. Some times I couled not see what we was doing. The People to home know more about our movements then we do. That thair will be another Big Fight this fall and the Question is, who shall hold a full hand of Tr[i]umphs, the Rebs or us.

I take it for granted that you will do better in your new Position for you must be qualified to take charge of Weaving and to do good service to those who employs you.[353] Thair will not be much made off the Farm this year on account of the Drouth,[354] but you must take it all for the best and trust Providance still and have faith that all will ultimateley be well. It has looked dark to you, and the futuer you have all most dispaired to look forward to, but take Curadge, the Sun will Shine yet. Let the Clouds look ever so dark and

---

[353] Assuming this reference is to his father, Thomas, who worked at a woolen mill in Rockville, Connecticut.

[354] Drought

stormey. Virtue will be owing you anuff to Pay Potter and the Money you shall have soon. I want some for I can not get a Chew of Tobacco and whouled give my best respects to the man that whouled send me anuff money to Buy a Chaw. Close the war or give us tobacco, for the Mountains Air have given us ravnious Apetites, can Eat anything.

If it was not for the Cornfields, we shouled Suffer much, for it is imposable to bring up supleys for a large forc operating in this Valley. Mosby Burnt 90 Waggons for us. He came through Snickers Gap, four mile from Bereyville and Cut off the Waggons, Shot the Contraband Drivers, the Gard ran away. Thay was Hundred Days men and had not smelt Powder. It was a loss to us. Thair was a large amount of stoars aboard. That Mosby is a Brick. The day that we fell Back to this Place, he rode into Genral Emorys Head Quarters with 20 men and got away again, but he will be taken yet and I hope soon, for he is a great truble and makes his appearance when least expected and cannot see how it is to be prevented in[355] this Mountainous Cuntry. Thair is so many Gaps that we can not shut them all up and thay know every by Path and road. It is the large Armeys that we can get at, if not to strongley intrenched. We must have more men and that in such numbers that we can bear down the Rebs by Weight and, for one, I do not want any loop hole for men that is Drafted to get out of. If we are to suckceed, we must Captuer one or more of the large Armeys that the South has now in the field. Till we can do that, we have a hard and laborious Work befor us if this Goverment can not put a large and well equiped Armey in the field under some one of the Present Genrales that the Soldiers have Confidance in, saperate from any thing that is now in the field. To take Linchburge and so Isolate Richmond and the Reble Armey that is now defending the Reble Capital, and have what Troops that Grant can comand cooperate with such a force, suckcess whouled be cirtain and the End so anxiousley wished for atained. Till that can be don, it is all up hill work and suckcess depends on some one of the Rebl Genrales making some Fatal mistake, which is not likley that any of them will do this year, but we must not dispaire nor give it up.

---

[355] The first part of this letter is transcribed from copies. Starting at this footnote placement are transcriptions from original pages.

I feel all beat out some times and feell my Faith put to sevear test, but rest and food gives me strength and on the Morrow I am ready for another Pull. So must we still keep our shouldier to the Wheel and lift again.

Give my love to the Chirldren and tell Faney that I shall write to her as soon as I can for she must have a saperate Letter. As long as she trys to give me all the news and she improves in her writing, and she will suckceed if she trys. Tell her that I shall look for longer Letters and she must take her time in composing them. Practice makes Perfect.

I send my love to you all, hoping that Reble Lead may still go whide of the mark.

Yours Affactnatley,
CW Sherman, Va

Shenendoah Valley, August 14, 1864
Near the Blue Ridge Mountains

Dear Daughter,[356]

I recved your kind letter of the 4th of August and was pleased to hear from you and that it was so well with you. I am well at this time but have had a tough time. The Wether as been very hot, and the Roads dusty and not having raind for a long time the Streames all dried up. It as been bad for man and Beast and it as beat me out some times. We have lost many men by the heat and Horses. How many times did Visions of a cirtain Well and the Cool Waters that was in it come up before me as I Marched along Watering the road as I went by the Sweat that droped of me, but no Water couled I get. This campaing will be rem[e]mberd by some of us years to come.

I am glad that your Uncl as been down to see you and that your Mother got some Money of[f] him, but the Amount was small. She ought to have taken more for I am afraid that it will be some time befor I shall be able to get any Pay. Your mothers bill, with your GranMothers, will be more then she think she will beable to Pay. If I do not send her money soon tell her that she need not fear, the Green Backs will be along soon, and that she must not Work till she is

---

[356] To Fanny

Perfectley well, and not to take any more truble or let any thing Prey on her mind but to Cheer up and let the Whide Worled Wag as it will. She must be free and Easy.

Still she knows nothing of what People have to enduer hear. The most Fruitefull Feilds that the hand of man as Cultivated, Orchards full of Apples Disapear and nothing but a Whide waste and Desolation is left behind the march of Invading Armeys. Wells Pumped dry, Fences torn down and every living thing gon. Oh, if the White liverd Cowerdley Peace makers to home,[357] those that have up held the Rebs in thair Deeds of Violance & Reblion, couled but see thair Work, for it is thair work and thay cannot Crawle out of it and tell us that thay tryed to put a stop to this distruction. I, for one, know that it is thair doing and the Sin Lays at thair door, for thay have held out false hopes to the Rebs.

It was a good thing that your Mother Bought Flour, for I have heard that it was very high and used to think how she whouled get along without Money, but she found frends to help her along and she will never fear. Sugar is past Buyin by what I hear of. What [I] hear this dry seson will be bad for you all, no Grass or Hay and but little Buter will be made this summer. Your Pigs do well and I am glad to hear that, for Pork will be scarse & high this fall.

That Steermaster, or Bull Drivers as thay are called in Western Louisisana, is a good Trade, for I expect that a cirtain young man, one Lewis W. Sherman, will be taking up a Ranch in Texas. And he is fiting himself to Govern Wild Cattle and he can not know to much about this kind of Bissness. And I am glad that he takes a liking to, and has a aptitude for out Door Work and a life in the open Air is the life for Kings. Tell him that I am Pleased with the good account that I hear of him. I shall try and do some thing for him sometime. He must be carfull and not get hurt.

Your GranMother thinks that travling is good for a Persons health. Well, it is to a cirtain extent, but any travling as been to hurt some one or get fits my self and the Sound of Uncl Abrahams Cannon as been in my hearing for some days Past, and the Sharp Crack of Federal & Confederate Rifles, but I have burnt no Powder my self yet, but expect to anytime in every 24 Hours or any mineut, but hope that my luck may stay by me when the time dose come.

---

[357] The Copperheads

I have recved that letter that Mr. Brooks sent me and sat down and Answered it. Give my respects to him & Famley. Kiss GranMother and the Babys for me and forty kisses for your Mother. My love to you all from your Affactnat Father,

CW Sherman, VA.

Camp Near the Shenendoah River, August 15, 1864

Dear Wife & Chirldren, Parents,

I shall try to give you a glimpse of the March we are on up the Shenendoah Valley to drive of[f] the Rebs that have had the Range of this Valley to Forage in.

The Rebl Genral Earley is at Whinchester with thrashing Machines and is trains are out Picking up the Wheat and otherwise feeding the Rebl Armey that is around Richmond. As long as the Rebs can go into Maryland, Pensylvania, and the Shenendoah Valley and get supplies, so long can thay carrey on this War.

We have 25000 Caverley under Sheridan and the 6th, 8th, 19th, 2nd, 5th Armey Corps. How many men in the Differant Corps, I can not tell. Thair ought to be 5 Divisions in a Corps and 15000 men in a Division, but thair are not that many men in none of the divisions. I am in the first Division of the 19th Corps and thair is but 8000 men in it, so I can not tell to a Cirtainty how many men thair is in the Valley at this time. I hope thair is anuff to make this Campaing affective, for it is most time that some thing was don to Put down this Reblion and bring this war to a Close for many of us are getting Wearey and tierd of this kind of Life.

August 10th

Fell in at 5 A.M. for Whinchester. The day was very warm. The men fell out fast and by Noon thair was as many men out of the Ranks as in. Water [is] Scarse & bad. We Pased through the Town of Charlston,[358] 8 Mile out of Harpers Ferry. This is the Place whare the State of Virgina Meted out Vengance to John Brown. It is a Poor Built Dirty looking Place, as all Southron Towns are. The Houses are Shaded by Trees in the Principl Streets.

---

[358] Charles Town

When our Colum got into the Town, it halted to let Sheridan and is Bold Riders Pass and a long Colum thay made. At the spot whare our Regiment was halted stood the Town Pump and thair had been detailes of so many men frome each company sent forward to fill Canteens & some of the F.F.V.'s[359] had Put Dirt of a cirtain Natuer on the Pump handle so we shoueld not get any Water. The Boys felt the Insult Put upon them, and a move was made to Put that Pump in Working Order by Braking the Handle of[f] and throwing it into the Well. Soon the Platform followed it. The Iron Dip[p]er was thrown in and then the Well was half filled with stones, the Band of the 8th Vermont giving the First Famleys of that Place the Tune of John Browns Souls Marching on. If the Old Man couled have seen the long line of Armed men standing, in the same streets and befor the same Court House, whare he was exhibited to the Gaze of the Croweds of Chiverley that Flocked to see the man that single handed, or nearly so, frightend the Whole State of Virgina, and the Bold Govner thair out of thair wits, he whoueld have been willin to have Died a thousand Deathes for the good cause, for this War is Simpley John Browns Fight on a larger Scale or National-lized.

As I look on it, it was a Grand Sight and, for one, I felt John Browns Knapsack grow lighter, and my Faith Stronger, in the ultemate Triumph of the Right of man to himself and the Great Principl that every man was and is Born free and Equel, with cirtain inainble rights among which is life, Liberty and the Persuites of Happeness. But to accomplish this we have to Pass through a rough time.

When we reached Camp that night, some Compneys Brought but few men in to stack Arms. Our Compney stacked 9 Rifles out of 60. I was out my self. 35 men was reported Dead and a great maney spoilt by the Heat for duty. It was tough.

August 11th

Fell in at 5 A.M. with out any thing to Eat and no time to eat a hard Bred. This day was spent in Flanking the Rebs and Whinchester. We was marched through the Corn fields & Woods in line of Battle, Sheridans Caverley on Both wings of the Line, Skirmshiers in front to feell of the way. It was a grand sight to see the longe Colums of men with the Different Batterys in between the differan Brigades, the 8th & 6th Corps giving the Rebs good Union Shell. The

---

[359] First Families of Virginia

19th Corps out Flanking the Rebls and at Noon the Rebs fell back and Whinchester was ours.[360] The Line of March was due South. In the afternoon we making for the Blue Ridge and As[h]bys Gap to cut off the retreat of the Rebs. This day suffered much for Water. One third of the men stragglin got to Camp after dark and was soon asleep.

August 12th

Fell in at 5 A.M.. This was a Tirable hot day. We feelling the heat more on account of not having had a nuff to Eat and weakness and not water anuff. The men fell out the Ranks, Ambulances all full before 8 A.M. with sick & Beat out men. This day the Road was over Hills and Mountains. It was a hard road to travle. I beleave the Ridges that we went over was Coverd with small Pines.

The Cavlery Skirmshed with the Rebs all day, Driving them steadley before them, Capturing some & Waggons. The talk is that we shall Shut them up, but thair is some work to be don first. We do not Captuer 40,000 men without truble, but the look is that if thay will stay whare thay are, we shall fetch them yet. This day was a Sneezer, but hear we are and the Stragglers coming up got to Camp about Dark, men coming in all night. It was a good time for the Rebs to have given us a Charge, thay whouled have taken the whole Corps, for thay couled not have made any fight.

August 14th

Fell in at midnight and was kept out in the rain. It rained Just anuff to make it mudy, but not anuff to raise the Streames & Springs. The Day [was] Cloudy and warm.

I got your Letter this morning of August 4th. Genral Emory took a spie today and he was hung at 12 OClock today.[361] He was with our Suply Train. It was Atacked in the night a few miles back as it was coming up. This man tryed to get away and he was Arested when brought into Camp. He was searched and

---

[360] The Battle of Third Winchester, sometimes known as the Battle of Opequon, was not fought until September 19, 1864. The mention of Winchester on August 11 was merely a preliminary skirmish and strategic maneuverings by both sides. Wert, *From Winchester to Cedar Creek*, 30–31.

[361] Brig. Gen. William "Old Bricktop," Emory commander of the Nineteenth Corps. Ibid., 20.

Documents found on his Person showing the strength of the Differant Corps & Batterys, and whare found, and names of the Differant Comanders. He Confessed. He was Put on a Mule, Drove under a tree and left till Dead. The Rebs hung one of our Spies on the same tree a few days befor.

The 6th Corps, who is feelling the way, took some Prisnors and among them was one of our men who had Deserted. He will be hung tomorrow morning. That is to good a fate for such.

August 15th

Turned out at daylight, Lay on our Arms waiting for the Johneys and after a time was dismissed to make our Coffee and those that had Water soon had thairs. Those that had non had to wait till a Pass was Signed by the Coll and the men goin out in Charge of a NonComissoned Officer. Men are not Allowed to go whare thay Please, but thay get away, Pick green Corn & Apels and so Eake out thair hard Bread.

August the 16th

Fell in at midnight for a Skedadale to Winchester. The 12th C.V., 31st Massachusetts taking the Amunition train in Charge. Got to Winchester at six the next morning, staid thair that day, Put up our Tents and rested.

August 17th

Fell in at 4 A.M. for Snickers Gap. Marched through the Town of Winchester to Bereyvill. The Day very warm. Pased the Waggon train burnt by Mosby. He Shot all the Negro Drivers. Got to Bery Vill at Noon, moved at dark. The Brigade goin on Picket duty formed line of Battle and went to sleep on our Arms with out any Super, was knawed with hunger all night, but thair was no help for it.

August 18th

Was moving in the Grey of the morning, rain falling, no Brakfast, was halted two mile out of the Town to let the train pass, the men trying to stop all Waggon that had hard Bread on Board till the General Promised that 3 mile further we shouled have Rations served to us. Had a Wet time geting the 3 mile, was Masked in a Beautifull Peice of Woods and got 3 days Rations, Coffee & Bread. Rested hear 4 hours, made fiers, the men goin after Green Corn to rost. I couled not help Laughing to see McMullen try to Beat the men from the Waggons that morning.[362]

Fell in at noon, McMullen with is Staff around [the] road to the Head of the Colum knawing a Rosted Ear of Corn. He is a Brick. He sees to the Comfort of his men and he has given our Officers fits for Neglecting thair men and one he sent home. He is not Choice in the Words he uses to them and thay deserve it. Thay Get it often and thay cannot be put in mind to often of thair dutys to the men under them. Genral McMullen is a thick set, strong built man, Bullnecked, Square Chin and not of a Amiable disposition when Crossed, but he is a Bulley man and he as the Bullest Brigade, the same that Weitzel had with some slight Chainges, and it is ready at a moments Notice to deal out Union Shell & Shot to any quanity of Rebs that may come in thair way. Thay all need the Medecin and will get it in large doses and questions asked; sad will be the day thay meet McMullens Bulleys in Battle Aray. McMullen makes is Quarters with the 12th which showes that he is a sensable man.

August 18th

Remaind two days till the 8th & 6th Corps came up, the Rebs fowlling our Cavlery Preaty Close but doin no damadge.

August 21st

Orderd to fall in at 12 noon, got to Charleston[363] at 3 P.M., halted in the Street till the Ambulances Pased with the Wounded and a train having some Prisnors on borde. In Passing one house, the Waggon stoped a few mineutes while one of the Prisnors was recognized by a Middle Aged Womon who Wring her hands and took on. Wether it was her Husband, I couled not find out. We went to the Rear of the Town and Put up some intrenchments, using two fences and filling up with Corn Stalks & Stone. Had Just gotten to sleep when we was

---

[362] The Brig. Gen. assigned to the Second Brigade in the First Division of the Nineteenth Corps was James W. McMillan. Ibid., 310.

[363] Charles Town

orderd to fall in and march to Harpers ferry. Got thair about 4 in the morning, Skirmishing goin in quite Brisk.

August 22nd

We are 4 mile out of Harpers Ferry; the 8th & 6th Corps throwing up Brest Works. The 19th Corps Masked in the Woods to suport Eather Corps. The Rebs are bound to try thair Luck in geting into Maryland & Pesylvania, fiering quite heavy at times. We was almost drowned today by a thunder Storm, the first that I have seeing this Sumer. It stoped the fiering. Orderd to keep ready to move any mineute.

August 23rd

Still in the Woods. The Rebs intrenching themselves and we. Thay want to Cross the Shenendoah River or the Potomac and Genral Sheridan Bound to keep them from so doing. How it will terminate, time will show. I understand that our Cavlery Burnt the Wheat Stock, Cut down all the Corn and Burnt all the Houses that no one was living in, and the Rebs must be in Large force to come down the Valley at this time.

Keep up a good Heart. I shall come out safe. We will trust Providence still. Give my Love to the Chirldren and kiss them for me. It will all be well soon. I send my Love to you all with the hope that we shall send theas Rebs howling Back to thair K[e]nnels. I remain your Affactnat Husband & Son,

CW Sherman

We are Puting up strong intrenchments and Wo[e] to the Rebs that undertake to come over them. Good Cheer to you all.

Camp Near Harpers Ferry, August 26, 1864

Dear Angline,

I recved your kind letter of August 20th and was glad to hear from you and to know that your Mother was getting better. You & Faney must help Cheer her up and make her Work as light as you can and tell her that she must get well, as we are goin to get Richmond and Close this Crule War.

We are doing a big thing hear and the Rebls will have to retreat and then our time as come to give the Crushing blow. The Goverment sent us 6000 more Cavlery yesterday so that Genral Sheridan will have a forc of Cavlery to throw onto the Reble rear when thay commence thair retrograde movement up the Valey that will overwhelm the Rebs.[364] We count as cirtain the retreat of the Rebs from our front.

Thair was heavy fiering on our right all day yesterday. The Rebs tried to cross the Potomac at Shepherds Town. The rumor is this morning that we Captuerd one thousand waggons from the Rebs. We waited till thay had got fairley in the river and then gave them Union Shell and round Shot. Thay got fits and will get fits till we get them into thair Kennels again or Captuer them.

If we couled onley get the men this fall, we couled whind up this muss or make it biger or larger. Turn out those faint hearted men that have been hanging onto thair Wifes Apron strings. It is time that thair Cheeks shouled be manteled by the Blush of Shame to be known to be hangin back, at this time, when thair Cuntry is holding out its bleeding hands asking for help, and the Blood of thair Fathers & Brothers Crying from many a Bloody field for Vengance on thair Murders. How thay can dare to walk abroad in the Sun light knowing that thair Naiboars & frends are Battling for thair rights, and hangin on With the Grip of desperation to the good cause saying, we will never give up, even if we are desearted and lef to fight it out alone. Are thair homes any better than ours? Do thay love thair Wifes and little ones more then us that thay hang round thair hearth Stones? No, that is imposable, thay can not and do not love thair Famleys and Cuntry with the same love that we do, or thay whouled be in the ranks with us Shouldier to Shouldier till Victory Crowned our eforts and Peace once more shead its Gentle Blessings around us.

May heavan guide our Rulers aright and strengthen thair hands to still do the work that is requierd of them, may the Nation come up to the high Standard that is requierd of it. Let the Nations see that we can govern ourselvs and maintain the rights of man and free Goverment, free Speech, free Schools, and be free men in every Sense.

You must write often and try to do the best you can and you will be able to write better every time. Tell your mother that I am sorry that I cannot send

---

[364] Possibly J. Howard Kitching's 6,000-man Provisional Division horse artillery, engaged only at Cedar Creek. Wert, *From Winchester to Cedar Creek*, 186, 313.

her any Money at this time. Henry wrote to me that he wouled let her have money at any time and she must call upon him till I can do some thing. I hope it may not be long. It as been very hard for her to get along. She must keep up her Curadge and have a faith that it will be all well yet. All is quiet on our front to day except a few Shots now an then from the Skirmish Line. You must Cheer your GranMother and Mother. Kiss them all for me, from Your Affactnat Father,

CW Sherman

Camp near Charles Town, Va, August 31, 1864

Dear Wife & Chirldren, Parents,

I am well at this time and hope this will find you all in the enjoyment of the Blessings of health and as much of contentment as falls to the lot of Mortals placed in the position we find ourselves in theas trublesome times.

I have Just been Musterd for Pay, but when that Indavidual called a United States Pay Master will make his aperance and Gladen our Eyes by the sight of Uncl Abrahams Green Pictuers, Vulgarly called Green Backs,[365] I can not say, but sooner then I expected. I think we must wait on the Powers that be and Patiently wait.

We have moved out of our intrenchments at Halls Town, the Rebs having fallen back on the 26th. Genral Sheridan ordered out Crooks Brigade or, more properley, a Brigade of Crooks Western Virgian troops to Captuer the Rebl Skirmsh line suported by some Cavlery in which thay succeed, but it Cost us over a Hundred men.[366] The Fiering was hot for a time. Our Brigade was under Arms to suport them, but lost no men.

---

[365] Greenbacks got their name from the color of the ink used on one side. "Greenback," however, was a term with negative connotation in the mid-1800s, because they didn't have a secure financial backing. Because of this, banks were reluctant to give customers the full value of the dollar. *Investopedia.com*, s.v. "greenback," accessed April 24, 2012, http://www.investopedia.com/terms/g/greenback.asp.

[366] Maj. Gen. George Crook, Sheridan's West Point roommate and close friend. In August, he took command of the Army of West Virginia, sometimes referred to as the Eighth Corps under Sheridan's Army of the Shenandoah. He led his corps at the battles of Opequon (Third Winchester), Fisher's Hill, and Cedar Creek. Wert, *From Winchester to Cedar Creek*, 20, 80, 132,183, 310.

The Rebs Fight Savadge. This year thay are geting Cornerd up Close. If we couled onley have 200,000 men to reinforce Sherman at Atlanta and Grant before Petersburg and give Sheridan anuff to make up for what men are leaving him every day whose time is out. 200,000 men whouled be more than anuff to do all that is requierd, and finish up Lee, fore he is in that last Di[t]ch that we have been looking for during the Last three years. We have found it, and one more effort put forth with a will to finish up this Reblion; it couled be don and we know it, and all of us return to our homes before the first of Janaury.

And if I am kept from home through the Backwardness of men that are at home to day and have to go through a nother campaing, and the Nation put further into Det, and our Burdens made heav[i]er through them, I, for one, whouled like to have the Soldiers, when we do get home again, to hang the Leaders that have Counsled the Poor trash that have helped them to bring us to this Pass. I say, put fier to thair homes for thay are only a disgrace to Manhood and Natuer Miscarred when it Produced such Abortions of things miscalled men. I whouled no more allow such mean, contempable things to come into a home of mine then I whouled a Copperheaded Snake, that thay are so Aproprately Named.

After we have the Reblion by the throat, all that we ask is a few live men, no Dead Beats, men that know thair rights and knowing, dare defend them. That is what we want at this time. If we cannot get that Class of men, do not send any. Money can not Fight the Southron Soldir today, nor men Bought by Money can not Fight Bob Lee. We want cooll, calculating men, for we have to Deal with desprate Ruind men, and a Cool Head and Steady hand is needed now more then at any other time Since this Wicked Reblion was forced onto us. May the Curse of the Widows and Orphron and Fatherless Chirldren Whose homes have been made Desolate in this Crule War, for ever rest on those that hang Back at this, our time of need. The Nation can not realize thair opertunity that is now before them, or we shouled not find ourselves in the Position that we do to day. Can men to home have watched the moves that have been made this year and not comprehend the fix the Rebs are in? Grant has out Genraled Lee, and the Southron Press says that Sherman must be moved from Atlanta, and Grant pushed back from before Richmond or it is all up with them, and unless thay can do those two things to say nothing of the Truble that Sheridan can make for them hear in the Shenendoah Valey.

The question to be decided now is men, befor the Winter Sets in, other wise the Advantadges that we have in our favor at this present will be thrown away and the South will be able to recover it self, and another great waste of life will have to be incured again, and so on indefantley till one side or the other will have to give up from want of Matairal and exhaustion. Who want to contemple such a state of things? The Election of Uncl Abraham will Aid us and show the Southron Leaders that the North intends to continue the War to the Bitter End and that, if thay are determed to carrey it to that Extrem end, thay have as determed Leaders to Fight and men as thay can bring on. But thair is no nesseity existing at this time for Carring it so far. If the People whouled onley turn out now, all further Waste of life and Tr[e]suear can and might be avoided and the War brought to a Glorious termination, a result that we have been Prayin and Fighting for, for 3 long years and the Olive Branch of Peace once more Cover this Land that has Pased through such a Fiere Ordeal and Bloody Civle War and the Great truthes and Principles that we have been trying to Demonstrate and uphold with our lives and Blood, if needs be, shall be strengthend and take Deeper Root and be held more Sacred by our Chirldren for all coming time.

We are 3 mile from the Town of Charles[367] and have this Place Intrenched, the 6th Corps on the extream right, the 19th in the Center, 8th on the left. Our Regiment have a Position in front of a Peice of Woods and the Compneys are detailed in turn to Chop the Timber Down, throwing the Tops towards the front whare an Enemy might be expected to come on, on the inside, on the Edge of the woods, in a Wheat field. We have thrown up our Defences the Length of the Regimental front and have made it Preaty strong but how long we shall remain in theas lines, we know not.

In coming through Charles Town the Second time, we halted in the Streets and the 8th Vermont Band gave the Sweet Inhabitants thair of John Browns Souls Marching on. Just as you go into the Town from the Harpers Ferrey side, stands the Residence of Genral Hunters Brother who is in the Reble Armey. It was a fine Place, but Hunter caused it to be Burnt. I shouled have said the Burnt Remains of the House. It is a warning to all Traitors. It is one of the evils of this War that Brother Fights Brother and Fathers, thair Sons. The Horro[r]s of this Civle War will never be Told and, if Told, whouled not be beleved, but an end to theas things will come sooner then maney expect and the sooner, the better.

---

[367] Charles Town is now in West Virginia.

Keep up your Hearts thair to home. Tell Virtue that I shall expect to hear that She has fulley recoverd her health sooner and that I am in hopes of beaing Able to send her Money Anuff to help her out of her difficultys and She can go on a Spree. I send my love to you all,

your Affactnat Husband,

CW Sherman

Camp near Charles Town, VA, September 1, 1864

Dear Wife and Chirldren, Parents,[368]

We are still Camped hear. The Waggon train as been Orderd up. We started with 3 days Rations in our Havarsacks and the Train was sent to Harpers Ferry, but the look is that we stay hear a few days, and then we may fall in at a moment's Notice. The face is we know not whare we are onley for a few hours togather. You have heard a great deal of the Shenendoah Valley. We have been Whiped out of this Valley every time that we have Atemped to hold it. Banks & Millroy, Freemont, Hunter and every one of our Genrales that have gon above Winchester have been out Flanked and thair Waggon Trains Cut off. Thair is so many Gaps to hold that it is imposable to stay in the Valley unless you can hold all the outlets and can have each Collum strong anuff to Fight its way. This is a great Wheat growing Region and the Rebs have all ways fed themselves from it and we have never been Able to prevent them.

Sheridan as Acted the most prudent part of any of our Genrales, avoiding giving Battle to the Rebs as nothing couled be gained by it unless he couled, at the same time, Cut off the Retreat of the Rebs. Thair as been a good deal of Skirmshing and Arttillery Practice, with some loss of life between the Cavlery. Earley has 30,000 Cavlery hear.[369] What Sheridan's Cavlery force has been, I know not. I have heard that it was 25,000. I know it is a big pile of Horses and riders. Some of them are Armed with seven Shooters or repeating Carebines besides thair Revolvers, and it makes those Regiments that have them very Affective. Thay are loaded quick and, under favorable Advantadges, can not be

---

[368] This letter is transcribed from photocopies.
[369] These numbers are, of course, greatly exaggerated.

beat. Thay have a Shooting Machine at Bermuda that I see thair fore Batterys.[370] It was 26 Rifle Barles on a Pair of Wheels and did open like a Fan. A Caisson was Attached the same as for Cannon and was Breech Loaders and thay must be very distructive to Infantry. It was a New thing to me never having heard of them. I shouled hate to have to face a Battery that had one of them Attached.

I have told you that we have been Choping. I find that I can not Chop much; the Axes are Clumsey and heavey and the Helves too long, and the kind of life that we have been leading as unfitted me for hard labore, and I do not think that the Goverment whouled get much work out of me in that kind of Labore. It is the most Splended Timber that I have seeing, except that in Western Lousana and the Red River Cuntry. Thair is no Brush in the Wood and it [is] more like some Park in the Old Cuntry then the unaided work of Natur. If Mr. Brooks couled onley have the Wallnut timber that we have Cut down he whouled be Independantly Rich. I never see such Wallnut Trees and so White and Cleer, no knots or limbs till you get to the Top. It looks Wicked to cut such Trees down, but Millitary Nessasity demands the Sacarifice and the most Beautifull Estates in this State is ruined.

The grass Crop has not been half gatherd this year that is in the Valley as far as we have been. We have Marched for hours across the most Splended Grass, most of it being Heardgrass, and the Clover fields looks as though the Crop had been heavey but was all Burnt up by the Drouth. It looked Wicked to see so much of the Gifts of a kind Providance left to Rot and waste. At some Points whare we have Camped, thair as been large Wheat Stacks, which the men whouled get to Lay on, and the most Beautiful Wheat. The Distruction of this Crop as been very Large. The Rebs had Carred off a great Portion of this Crop, but the lower Portion of the Valley thay had Just begun to gather this grain when Sheridan led up into the Valley. At one Place we came upon one Squad of Rebles in a open field to work with thair Tharashing Machine and Captured the whole lot of them. The Aples Orchards hung full and had not been disturbed till we came through. Thair was not maney Apples left on those trees. Some was ripe, but green and Ripe Sufferd alike.

I shouled like to live in this state. I have felt so well since I have been hear. You do not know how good I feel in this Climate. I have been loaded down so long with that Poisenous Bile and Swamp Fever Contracted in the swamps of

---

[370] Bermuda Hundred

Louisana, and my system as shook off the Poisen and made me feel lighter and 20 years younger. You can never know the Dead weight that I had to carrey about with me all day long in Louisana [and] when I was to home with you last Spring or Winter, I do not know which, for I was more dead than Alive and time I knew but little about. You must have noticed that I was weighed down with some thing besides a Guilty Contiance and to have this weight gon and to feel that you are [an] alive man is so good. Man must go through the same experience that I have to realize what good health is. I used to think that I enjoyed good health, but I must have been mistaken; must have taken the Shaddow for the Substance. You ought to see me put my Pork Ration away for we have been fed on the Abomanation of the Jewes lately, and it has been my Abomanation till I got to this state. My Cakes I relish more then I thought possible once, excep when we get a Box of Bugge[y] ones. The wormes in theas is a Mysterey to me how thay can grow to such a size. Thay do not improve ones Appetite and it is most time those Cakes was Played out. The Coffee is about the same. I believe that Wallnut Shucks, Baked and ground, goes to help make up our Coffee Ration. Fresh meat we do not get much of and then but small Rations, but it is Meat different from what we used to get in Louisiana. In that Texas Beef thair was not Greece anuff to Greece a Pair of Shoes.

This is the first of Fall and the Campaign not ended yet. What the results of this years Work will be I can not decide, but still hope that something decisive will yet be accomplished in our favor. But the End is not yet. It as been the grandest Campaign that the Worled has ever seeing from the number of those engadged, and the result of a suckessfull termination of the Campaign whouled be the cirtain distruction of Lee's and Johnson's Armey, and the uter Anialation of this Wicked Reblion, and the Truimph of the Cause of right Justice and Christianaty. We must still have Faith and trust in the final Truimph of the Union Arms. If we do not meet with the success that we look forward to, and shouled faile in some important Points, we must still keep up our Faith and strength and try again; no compromise with Traitors, no Patched up Peace lible to be broken at any time. When we have a Peace, we will have one that shall be lasting and Shuer. It shall be as shuer as the Sun's rising and as strong as the Everlasting Hills and Mountains that Bind theas States together that some have Claimed was Sunderd, but what God as Joind togather, the mear Proclamation of Poor Mortal men can not Sunder.

September 3rd

I hasen to Close this letter for as we was turnd in for the night, Orders came to be ready to move at 3 in the morning. I recved a Head of very nice Tobacco from Henry, I sopose, for thair was no Name; it was very acceptable. I am well. Give my love to the Chirldren. I send my love to you again. I remain your Affectnat Husband and Son, CW Sherman, VA

Camp Near Berryville, VA, September 7, 1864

Dear Wife and Chirldren, Parents,[371]

I am well and hope this will find you in good health. We lef our intrenched Camp Near Charles Town on the morning of the 3 of Sept. and felt our way to this place. I wrote to you on the Second but couled not send it till the 5th. I sent Henry a letter at the same time thanking him for some Tobacco.

The March on the 3rd to Berryvill was not trubled by the Rebs till Late in the afternoon when thay tried to outflank the 8th Corps, but Genral Crook was too maney for Johney that time and the 19th Corps coming upon Crook's right gave Johney fits. The fiering was heavy. The Second Brigad came into line Just at dark, but did not fier a Shot. We lay under a fence waiting for Johney to come through a Piece of Woods. Just on the edge of the Wood the first Main[e] Battery was Masked and the Johneys whouled have been astonished if they had come through thinking to outflank the 8th Corps on the right, but thay did not come and thair is more of us for duty this morning then thair whouled have been if that flanking move of Earley's had been Carred out. After dark the Rain came down and we had to take a Soaking. It was a Bad night. In the morning we went to throwing up intrenchments. We have 3 lines of intrenchments to this place, but how much farther Genral Sheridan can go up the Valley and intrench himself I cannot know, but not much further as we shall run the risqué of beaing outflanked as the Valley widens as you go up. This intrenching is done in the night so that the Enemy can not see what is goin on till it is to late to interfear, and then thay have the fun of Chargin those works, or fall back themselves, and the Yeanks, as thay call us, have a free range of this country and whare we go

---

[371] This letter is transcribed from photocopies.

we make Cleen work of the Crops and fences. Some of the Rebs Pull the wool over our Genral's Eyes by Claiming Protection at the lines near Charles Town. The first Conct [Connecticut] Cavlery wanted some Hay, but the owner whouled not let them have any. The men took some. Then this good Union man sent for the Coll who putt a Saftey Gard on the Property, but in the night the Barns took fier, but no one knew any thing about it. Of course, the Gard did not do it, as thay never do such things, but when morning came thair was the Ruins of a young Arsenal. Piles of Guns Barles and locks that this good Union man kept to supply Mosely's Guriallas and that is the way we have a force in our rear Cuting off our supply Trains. They are Peacable Farmers as our chums go by, but the moment that we are by, thay are off on Horse back Picking up our sick or Murdering them, for it is certain death to the taken Prisnor hear in the Shenadoah Valley. Thay spair no one. The Truth will never come out of the many Atrocitys that has been Perpatrated on our poor fellows that have fallen into thair hands.

We have been having a Cold North East Storm, but it has Cleard off this morning and the sunshines warm once more. The Trains came up yesterday with some hard Bread and Pork, Coffee and thay have gon back again.

The day after we got to this Place, Captain J. D. Roche got tight or Beastley Drunk. We was under Orders to be ready to move at a moment's warning. The Rebs was reported Marching down on us in two Lines of Battle and my Compny Commander was Laying gloriously Drunk in the Colls Quarters, having gon down to him to report one of his men. We had to March with out him and he is under Arest. It is not the first time that he as committed this offence and I hope that he will be sent home has he is a Perfect Bloat. We are getting the Pay Rolls ready and if we stay hear a little while we shall get our Pay. It is most time that I recved mine. I have spoken to the Coll about it and I must not be kept out of it no longer or I will carrey it [to] MacMullen and he whouled not be Choice in his Language to some of them.[372]

Give my Love to the children and all enquiring frends. I send my love to you all and hoping to write again soon. Faith, I think I do write often anuff for I have sent quite a number of letters lately.

From Your Affactnate Husband and Son,
CW Sherman, VA

---

[372] Major General McMillan, US Army

Camp Near Berryvill, Va, September 12, 1864

Dear Wife & Chirldren, Parents,

I am well and hope this will find you all in good health as I hope the Cool wether that you must be having at this time will be benifical to Virtue and she must look up and be ready to give one Cheer, for the fall of Richmond is near.

Sherman has got Atlanta and Grant is about ready to astonish Lee by coming into Richmond and asking Jeff Davis for Quarters for the Union Armey. What a bright Morning that will be when the Stars and Stripes Flutter in the Breeze and wave over the Reble Capital. That day will as cirtainley come as that the Sun will shine after a Storme. You to home must have more Faith, more confidance in the final Tryumph of the good cause. After so maney dark days, the Clouds are lifting and the Reblion is drawing to a close. The last Act in the peice is about to be played. The Curtain will drop and the vast Audiance that have been looking on will retier to thair homes and the Actors in this Play will leave the Boards, and, for one, [I] shall never want to return. A quiat life is what I delight in, but couled not be alowed to enjoy my self and so have gon in for a Row and Muss Genraley, but the scene is drawing to a close.

I hope the next Sixty days will tell wether I stay 3 years or not. Please tell my Copper Colerd frends to home that thay get maney a Hearty Curse and that thay will not be forgotten in the years to come. If thay onley knew that thair Southeron frends look with contemp on them and for the course thay have persued during this war. Thay have respect for the men that comes Boldly out against them, but for such sneaking, Cowardley things as thay are, the Reb will accept thair aid insofar as it gos to help them but, at the same time, dispise the sorce that it comes from and the motive that promps them so to act.

If a Rable raid couled onley be made through cirtain sections of the Northen States, my Copper frends whouled be delighted to have a Party call on them for Contributions for the good cause that thay represent. Thay whouled be surprised to have a Order to thair good Womon to Just set the Table with the Best the House afforded and. after satisfieing the wants of the in[n]er man, to see them Cooley help themselves to what was left. Thay whouled see thair Chickings knocked over and Gobbled up. and if thair was a fine Horse in the Stable it whouled be led out and such small Articls as silver spoons, Cleen Linin and what small Chaing thay might have about them whouled be Borrowed, all for the good of the cause. How surprised thay whouled be if told to hunt up what Sheep thair might be on the Place, and Cattle, and told to drive them a few miles on the road, and if thay made any fuss about it, how Astonished thay whouled be to recve a few Kicks and Cuffs for thair unPatroic Conduck. How the Scales whouled drop from off thair eyes when beaing left with thair House & Barn on fier and strip[p]ed of every thing thay had in this world and thay left to reflect on the straing situation. I think thay whouled come to the conclusion that thay had made one Grand mistake in the great question that is about to be decided. This is no over drawen Pictuer, it is not up to the truth and the naked reality of the experince of Thousands of men whose Predelections was. and have been. with the South in this War of Principles. and it is a great Pity that thousands North couled not be Converted to our side by being put through the same experance. for nothing els will ever convince them, but that thay have been right and we in the wrong, but the end will come. The Reblion is in its last Gasp and the final Strugle is coming. Give us a few more men is all we ask to finish up Lee and the Southron Confederacy.

At the same time we have been having a Cold rainey spell and we have been put in mind that we was not in Louisisana, but I have been in luck having had a over Coat that I picked up on the march up. The Wether was intenseley hot and the men threw away thair Clothing, but I kept the over Coat and have been more than Paid for carring it. My other one is in Harpers Ferry with a New Miscato net that I brought from Louisan but have had no use for it. If we do not go back, I shall send it home if I can get a Chance with some thing els.

I am glad to hear that Virtue is geting better. She must not give it up, so I am expecting to be Paid now every day, if the Rebs will keep still anuff. I hope to get the whole Amount and that will more then Pay my Board Bill with Interest. I want it Paid, it as been runing a long time and I Guess that She thinks so too.

I was sorry to hear that Mother was still trubled with that Pain that has caused her so maney sleepless nights. She must not truble about me. I am in hopes that I shall return to see you all again. The Same good Beaing that has Protected me till now will still Preserve me through what ever daingers I may have to pass through. I try to trust in is Mercy and goodness that he will Bring me safley through and return me in safty to my home again.

I hope that Faney may not hurt her self in trying to help her Mother. I am afraid of her sometimes. Give my respects to Doctor Newton. When I left home I did not expect to keep him waiting for his honest Pay. He tryed to help me and

I thank him for what truble he took in my case. I have been put to much truble through having a Drunken Captain. I hear that he has resigned, but he shouled not be allowed to get off so easely. He ought to be sent home in Disgrace, for he has been a Disgrace to the Union Armey and a Disgrace to the Compney that he Comanded and I hope justice will be meated out to him.

Father, you say that you feell discuradged some times and well you may, but do not give up. I will be with you again and the way we will make things smile will be a caution to all unbelievers. Keep up your Heart, all will be well yet. Why, I have pased through anuff and seeing anuff to almost make me forswear my kind, and some times I think I will go off into the Woods and never see mankind again, but that dose not prove that thair is no good in this World or that all men are uterle lost. We must take things as we find them and make them better if we can. If that is not posable, Fight it through and return Blow for Blow.

I think that Edwin is doing all he can for the Cuntry of his adoption, no man can say that he is not a Patrot, for he is doing all he can to keep our ranks full. I say Buley for Edwin go in and win. The Wemon of the Cuntry are in a healthy condition and that gives me hope of finaley Pulling through this truble. Give my respects to Mrs. Edwin Sherman, tell her she is doing Nobley.

I must close. We are laying on our Arms at this time, the Cavlery having gon out for a Muss and we have to keep ready to Back them up. Earley is at Winchester, a few mile in our front and we are waching him. Give my love to the Chirldren and kiss them all round for me. I send my love to you all.

Your Affectionate Husband and Son,

CW Sherman

Shenandoah Valley, Va.

Camp Near Berryvill, Va., September 16, 1864

Dear Wife & Chirldren, Parents,

I am well and hope this will find you all well. We are still Camped in this last intrenched Position that Sheridan has taken up in the Shenandoah Valley. We are waching the Johneys under Earley and the Reble Genral will not get away from us as easely as he has from the other Genrales. He has sat down in the Lower Part of the Shenandoah Valley. Sheridan has steped on Earleys Coat tailes and he can not get up without geting his Coat torn or, in other Words, Lee whouled like to get Earley back to himself again, but the question is, can he get back all right with Sheridan on his flanks and rear? I am thinking that suden destruction will find him if he is looked after Sharp and he will be.

We have moved our Camp and the impression is that we shall stay hear some time if Earley stays in the same Position and then we may move any moment. If Grant couled onley have that 100,000 men that he has asked fore, he couled carrey all before him, but I am afraid that the time will Pass by and the Winter be upon us befor the men can be put in the Field and we kept over into another Winter.

I was in hopes that Richmond whouled be ours by this time, but it will come. It can be taken at a moments Notice, but it whouled Cost us to maney men and Grant wants to Bring a Shortness of Rations to bare for the Rebl Armey and strengthen himself with more men and we must have to be reinforced so as to extend our lines.

September 18th[373]

I am on Picket this Sunday Morning on the outmost line and have to keep both Ears and Eyes open if we do not wish to visit some other part of the Southeron Confederate States. We was fierd on twice last night but no one was hurt.

The day is Beautiffull and still. The differant Regimental Bands are Playing and every thing full of life and it is hard to make one beleave that we are in the field and in the face of a Sleepless Enemy, but so it is. I have wished may times when Sunday has come round that I couled onley go to Church and rest. It has looked so plesent to go to Church and feel that no one can molest or disturb me. I do want to Pull this Harness of[f] and lay down and rest.

When will the time come that we can come home and Enjoy ones self? This Soldiering is not the life that I couled take pleasuer in. Nothing but a Sense of Sterne Duty compelled me to take up with this kind of life. I did not enlist

---

[373] Charles had written "19th"; however, Sunday would have been the eighteenth. Considering the events of the nineteenth, this editor has taken the liberty of changing the date above for accuracy's sake. Also, "From the 3rd of September up to the 18th we remained quietly among our fieldworks around Berryville." De Forest, *A Volunteer's Adventures*, 171.

for Honor or that I liked a wandering exciting kind of life, but a sense of duty to the Cuntry of my adoption and that no man couled do my duty fore me. If the Chances of Battle shouled consigne me to a Soldiers last resting place, I want you all to rember that duty called me and that a Sherman must all ways be in the front, ready when called on to strike for his God and Cuntry. You know that I consider that it ought to be a Pleasuer to every man that deserves the Name of a Freeman to be all ways ready to uphold his rights let them be endanigerd from what ever cause thay may or might be.

We are waching the course of the Peace Party[374] and I can asuer them, from my own Knowledge, that thay have lost Thousands of Voates in the Armey that thay whouled have been shure of if thay had not been so willing to give the Rebs all that we have been Fighting for, for the last 3 years. McClleand Stock went down so low with the Armey that it never will be brought into the Market again and Honest Old Abrahams Stock went up with a rush.[375] No other kind of stock will sell hear in this Market. Thair never has been a Candadate run for the Presidencey that will, or has had such a over Whellming Majority that Uncl Abraham will get. My Coppery frends to home might as well Save thair Powder for thay will be Whiped so badley that thay will run Howling to thair Kennells and never be heard of Again.

We know to a cirtainty that Jeff Davis is holding out hoping that thair will be Deversion made in his favor North, or that a Chaing in the Present Government will be afected so that thay will give him all that he askes for, for he knows that he is Whiped and cannot Blind the Southeron People much longer or keep them from a true state of thair condition, that this reblion will Play out this Winter and that thay can not recruit any more men or bring another Armey into the field besides what thay have all ready and that is Whasting away fast.

---

[374] Copperheads

[375] George Brinton McClellan was the Democratic candidate for the presidency in 1864, although he rejected the party's peace platform. He was a Union general, Commander of the Department of the Ohio in 1861, and subsequently commander-in-chief, USA. Having been relieved of his supreme command in March 1862, he retained command of the Army and Department of the Potomac. His Peninsular Campaign in April 1862 failed and most of his troops were reassigned to the Army of Virginia under John Pope. After Antietam, he failed to follow Lee's troops across the Potomac, missing a prime opportunity, and was removed from his command in November 1862. Flood, *1864 Lincoln at the Gates*, 37, 282.

Some have a Notion that the waste is all on our side, but that is not the case. Robert Lee, Genral in Cheef of all the Confederate forces now in the field, can not muster one hundred and fifty thousand men saprate from what Hood has, and one William T. Sherman will give a good acount of them soon and all that we want is a few more good men to lengthen our lines and Bob Lee is gon up the Spout and all the hopes of a Southron Confedracy gon with him.

Keep up your Hearts all of you a short time longer and you will see me coming home, having don my Duty, that is we will hope so, and then for a Glorious time. I have writen a letter to Charles P. Rider of Willington town. Give my Respects to Mr. Brooks and Famley. Tell him that those Papers he sent, one came safe and that the cause Prospers. Kiss those Babys for me and my love to them all,

your Affactnat Husband and Son,
CW Sherman
Shenandoah Valley, Va.

Chapter Nineteen

The Battle of
Third Winchester[354]

Ashbys Gape, Shenandoah Valley, September 21, 1864

Dear Wife & Chirldren, Parents,

I have written you one letter of September 18th,[377] but could not send it as we brock up Camp at 2 OClock Sunday night and moved on Earley at Winchester. It was a hard days work, from daylight till after Dark we was to Work on the Rebs. The Fier was very heavey. I am not trubled with the Head Ach, but the noise of the Canon, Musketry and the Bursting of the Shells was truley Auffull.

We lost heavley the first 4 hours of the Fight. Our Coll was Killed by the Bursting of a Shell.[378] He was Just on the Left of Comp K, about 10 feet from whare I was. The Rebs had a Battery that was Raking our line and in front thay had it all thair own way for some time. I can not enter into Paticulars now. The Skirmishers are at work now and Just in our front.

---

[376] The Battle of Third Winchester, also known as the Battle of Opequon, was fought on September 19, 1864. Opequon was a creek near Winchester.

[377] The mention here of the letter written on September 18 confirms the correction to the date mentioned in a footnote of the previous letter.

[378] Col. Frank H. Peck was mortally wounded while leading the regiment into action by a shell bursting overhead. The command then fell upon Captain Sidney E. Clark, Company F. De Forest, *A Volunteer's Adventures*, 182; *Record of Service of Connecticut Men*, 486.

I am well and not a scratch on me, but it was the Lords mercy that saved me that day. The 19th Corps kept up its Old reputation and won Prais from Old Campainger in this Valley. Thay say thay never see such fighting don before.[379] The Rebs was Astonished. Thay have had it all thair own way befor this and to be Whiped so hansomley from thair own Ground that thay have allways fought on. The 19th took the whole Brunt of the Reble Force till noon when the 8th Came up on our right and comenced flanking the Rebs. It was a Beautifull Sight to see our Line some what in the shape of a half Circel Advance and such Cheering and yelling as we went on the dubble quick.

The Rebs brock and run and thay was followed up from that time till dark. 35 hundred Prisnors was taken at that time and 9 Peices of Artlley. The Town of winchester was filled with the Reble Dead and Wounded. We followed them up to this Gape, got hear last night and are waiting for the 6th Corps to come up. Averlls Cavlery are in our front and thay will Atend to the Rebs when we get them agoin.[380]

We have no Compny Officer with us. [First] Leauteant Gorge Stedman was Killed and we did not know it till one of the men went back a little ways for something and thair he lay on his Back with a Bulet hole through his head.[381]

We lost 2 men Killed, and 8 Wounded in Comp K. Our Captain is under Arest and has been Court Martialed, but we know not what will be the

---

[379] The Twelfth Connecticut and Eighth Vermont distinguished themselves in this battle holding off enemy forces ". . . just beyond the western fringe of the Second Woods. This pair of stalwart regiments, for the past two hours, had maintained their line. . . No commands in the XIX Corps had fought more courageously or steadfastly than these New England units." Charging left into the trees, these two companies followed Thoburn's soldiers chasing Gordon's overmatched confederates. "Such was the deciding movement of the battle. . ." Wert, *From Winchester to Cedar Creek*, 88–89; De Forest, *A Volunteer's Adventures*, 187–88.

[380] Brig. Gen. William W. Averell's Second Artillery Division joined with Brig. Gen. Wesley Merritt's Division and delivered a crushing assault of the Confederate flanks and center. Wert, *From Winchester to Cedar Creek*, 97; De Forest, *A Volunteer's Adventures*, 189.

[381] In addition to the loss of Stedman, Lt. Col. Lewis, who was injured at Port Hudson, did not return to the regiment until October. See letter dated Oct. 14, 1864; First Lt. George W. Stedman from Windham, Connecticut. *Record of Service of Connecticut Men*, 496.

Sentance.[382] He is with the Regiment and his Conduck may have some favorable bareing on his case. He is no Coward but up and Dressed under fier.

Give my Love to the Chirldren. I shall trust in the Merceys of a kind Providence to Carrey me safely through. The Papers will give you more information of the days Battle then I can at this time. This writing under fier is not favorable and I may have to fall in any Mineute. Keep up your Curadge, all will be well. The Union Armeys will soon put this Reblion down and we have a Bulley Comander in Genral Sheridan. The men Love him and I know that he will Lead us to Victory. I wish I could write to you more fulley, but can not. Give three Cheers for our suckcess on the 19th and we will send you more Cheering news soon.[383]

Your Soldier in the front,
CW Sherman

Harrisonburg, Shenandoah Valley, September 26, 1864

Dear Wife & Chirldren, Parents,

I am well and Safe thanks to a kind Providence that has Protected me to this time. When I wrote to you last I was laying under fier in the Town of Strausburg.[384]

The Rebles had a Strong Position and the 19th was formed in line of Battle to the Right of the Town, and on a range of hills. We lay thair that day under fier, developin the Strength of the Enmy, the Batterys Shelling the Position of the Rebs, our Skirmishs line in front. The Rebs was in Rifle pits on the Hills in front. The 19th was not engaged.

---

[382] Capt. James D. Roche was "under arrest for something but present to fight." De Forest, *A Volunteer's Adventures,* 187.

[383] The Battle of Third Winchester was considered an important victory in the Valley for the North, but was also "the largest and bloodiest battle ever fought in the Shenandoah Valley." Early retreated to Fisher's Hill, twenty miles south. Patchan, *The Last Battle of Winchester,* 474.

[384] The previous letter, written on the twenty-first of September, briefly describes the Battle of Third Winchester on the nineteenth. In this letter, he describes it in more detail. The letter written September 27, Chapter Twenty, describes the Battle of Fisher's Hill, which was fought on the twenty-second.

The 1st Division is Comanded by Genral Dwight and the Corps by Genral Emory. It was our division that turned the fortunes of the day at Winchester. It was Dark and Blue when our Division went into Battle that day. The Rebles, having repulsed a Charge of the sacond Division, and had a Cross fier on us, we lost our Coll the moment the word was given to Charge.[385] A Aide on Genral Sheridans Stafe rode up to us at that moment and sung out, 12th Conn follow me, Waving his Soword and in we went and the 8th Vermont on our left, and saved the 11th Ind[i]ana and 24th Iowa. We took thair Places and thay went out. The Rebs was in a Belt of Woods in our front.[386] We gave them a Volley and the Order was given to lay flat on the Ground while the 1st Main[e] Battery got into Position, thay not being Able to Work thair Guns till we Coverd them from the fier of the Reble Sharp Shooters and we did give the Rebs the Lead.

At the first fier of the Rebs, our first Leautenant Gorge Steadman was killed. Two men was shot dead and 8 wounded in my Compney in a few mineutes. We fierd all our Amunition away.[387] Genral McM[i]llan on the right of the 12th gave the Order to Charge. Coll Thomas of the 8th Vermont rode to the right of his Regiment and our left Joine his. The Coll sung out to our Boys, Come on Gallant 12th and 8th Vermont, and such a yell and Cheer greeted him as we brought our Bayonets to a Charge and rushed onto the Rebs. Thay couled not stand Vermont and Connecticut at that time and thay showed us thair Backs.

We followed them through the Woods and at that moment the 8th Corps came up and Joind our right, the 6th on our left and if that was not a Sight to Cheer our hearts as the whole line advanced on a Charge. The Lead and Shells was thrown fast. The Rebs Brock. We had flanked thair works. The Cavlery Bugles sounded a Charge and on thay came and Cuting right and left. The Rebs did some tall runing, but the Cavlery was on them and the Battery that had killed our Coll was ours and 2000 Reble Prisnors.

---

[385] Col. Frank H. Peck

[386] This was Gordon's division in the Second Woods. As previously mentioned, the Eighth Vermont and Twelfth Connecticut bravely held their line in the field between the First and Second Woods. Wert, *From Winchester to Cedar Creek*, 84, 88.

[387] "Our men recommenced the file firing and soon shot away their few remaining cartridges." Also, ". . .160th New York as a replacement for the Twelfth Connecticut, which had no ammunition." De Forest, *A Volunteer's Adventures*, 187; Wert, *From Winchester to Cedar Creek*, 89.

The day was won and all we had to do was to keep them moving and, faith, I thought that if a Shell or Bulet did not bring me down, duble quicking of it whouled. It was a Glorious day, but Bloody. The Rebles couled not understand how thay got Whiped. Thay had been driving the 6th and 8th Corps and soposed that thay couled drive any thing.

Thay give the Credit of the day to the 19th and say that we beat all thay ever see. The fact is, we never Allowed them to Drive us and we did not come to Virgina to be whiped. We came to Shove the Constitution through the Southron States and Earley was the first that we aplied it to and we have kept it before his Eys for one Week. Night and day he was kept moving.

I told you in that last letter that when we got to work on him, he whouled go up and, faith, he has gon and we are ready to explain that Document to any other Reble Genral that wishes to be Converted back to the faith of his Fathers. It has been a hard time for all of us. Sheridan kept his Cavelary moving and we Infantry have had to keep within suporting distance.

The Papers will give you the Paticulers of our movements. We have got up to Harrisonburg. It is a Preaty Town and is the home of Averrill, one of our Cavelery Genrales. We are resting hear for two days while our Cavlery hunt the Cuntry through & we are bound to Staunton and that is 25 mile from this town. I have just heard that our Cavlery have enterd that Place. We have been told all the way up by the Rebl Prisnors that we whouled never get to that Town.

The Houses here are full of Reble Wounded and in fact all the Houses on the Road to this Town have more or less of them. This is the first defeat that the Rebs have sustaind in this Valley and the only Victory that has been well followed up by us during this war.

I have seeing some Beautifull Sights these last 6 days that can not be beat. I have seeing 3 Armey Corps in line of Battle and all moving has one man on the Reble Armey and the thunder of the different Batterys with the Sharp Crack of thousands of Rifles. Men falling every mineut is a tirable and Auffull sight, the Ground that we Charged over I never shall for get. The Rebs had repulsed one Charge made by Birges Brigade of six Regiments and the Dead and Wounded lay thick.[388] The Devels had begun to strip our dead, but we soon put a stop to that work. I see one great Burley Reb lay dead with 3 of our Dead

---

[388] Brig. Gen. Henry Birge. Apparently, Birge led a "hasty and tumultuous advance," but was repelled by CSA General Gordon who drove them further back and recovered what ground was lost by Evans. De Forest, *A Volunteer's Adventures*, 178.

men, Bundles straped on his Back. He did not get away with his plunder. One sight that showed the Affaction of a dog for his Master - a Dead Reble and his dog siting on his Body. Our Boys, in goin by, tryed to call him off, but he whouled not leave, only run a short distance and run back again, Whining to the Body.[389]

The day at Winchester was a day of Horro[r]s and many Widows and Orphornd Chirldren will long rember that day. I feel thankful that my life was Spaird and I hope that the many Merceys that have been Shown me will make me a Better Citizen and Husband.

Father, the morning that I wrote to you last we was drawen up and the Presidents thanks read to us and the Order of Genral Grants to have a hundred Guns fierd in honor of our Victory and then five mineutes to get ready to go into Action. Very plesent News to be told of a Voat of thanks to us and the next mineut to be told to get ready to be Shot, but such his the way.

I am goin to write to Henry to let Virtue have what ever Money she wants, for I can not see when we shall get Paid. If we can keep the Ball in motion, it is our duty so to do. Give my Respects to Mr. Brooks. Tell him I gave the Rebs 65 rounds for him and I hope did some good. My love to you all,

your Affactnat Husband and Son,

CW Sherman

Harrisonburg, Shenandoah Valley, September 26th, 1864

---

[389] This story is also mentioned in a history of the Eighth Vermont: ". . . the attention of the regiment was attracted to a strange scene;—a dead rebel lay stretched on the ground and in front of him sat a little brown dog, trembling with fear, bolt upright but facing square to the front, faithful unto death. Not a bayonet or a foot touched the faithful creature; the line of steel parted and the human wave rolled on through the woods, leaving the little sentinel undisturbed in his death-watch." G. G. Benedict, *Vermont in the Civil War, A History of the part taken by the Vermont Soldiers and Sailors in the War for the Union, 1861–5,* Volume 2 (Burlington, VT: The Free Press Association, 1888), 155, PDF e-book.

The illustration on the facing page was drawn by James E. Taylor, special illustrator for Frank Leslie's Newspapers. It appears in the following publication: Louis Shepheard Moat, ed., *Frank Leslie's Illustrated History of the Civil War*, (Mrs. Frank Leslie, NY, 1895), 446, PDF e-book.

SHERIDAN'S CAMPAIGN—AN INCIDENT AT THE BATTLE OF WINCHESTER: A FAITHFUL DOG WATCHING AND DEFENDING THE DEAD BODY OF HIS CONFEDERATE MASTER.

Chapter Twenty

Battle of Fisher's Hill and Maneuvers Leading to Cedar Creek

Harrisonburg, Shenandoah Valley, September 27, 1864

Dear Wife & Children, Parents,

We are still Camped at this Town. Our Waggon Train has come up and, not knowing when I may have a Chance of writing, and we expect a Mail by this Train, I thought that I whouled Jot down some of my experance these last 10 days.

On the morning of the 20th September we Marched from Winchester to Ceeder Creek, 16 Mile.[390] The day was very warm and we was Fatagued from our days work on the 18th & 19th, and we felt that a days rest whouled be good, but no rest we found. The Troops Marched in 3 lines in the Lots, or on each side of the road. The Cavelery and Arttiley taking the Road with the Ammunition train Bringin up the rear.

This is the Order of March, the 6th Corps, the 19th the Center, and 8th Corps on the right. In this order the differant lines of Battle can be formed with out Confusion. We reached Ceeder Creek and went over. The Rebs had Built a new Bridge over the Creek, having burnd the Old one when we followed them up some few weeks ago. Our Cavlery Pushed thair rear Gard so rapidley that thay had not time to distroy the Bridge after them.

---

[390] Cedar Creek, Virginia

Some 3 Mile beyond our old Camping ground we Camped for the night. We was Massed in or on the Edge of the Mountain, so the Enemy shouled not know whare to throw thair Shells has we did not know but thay might Shell us in the night if thay knew. After our line was formed for the night, the men went down the sides of the Mountain to make thair fiers [to] boile thair Cups of Coffee, as no fiers are alowed under such circumstances in sight. It was a difficult task to go down the sides of the Mountain to get water and get back again. No Path and so steep that if you lost your footing you whouled be Dashed to Peices at the Bottom. This is the kind of Cuntry that we are to work in and well have the Rebs chosen thair ground to Fight this Reblion out, but we are Equel to the Work befor us has thay begin to find.

In the morning September 21st we enterd the Town of Strausburg.[391] It is the same kind of Town that all southron Towns are. Thay have a Old delapidated look has though time had stoped with them. The Land oridginaley belonged to the Washington Estate and the home of the Rebl Genral Lee is hear. It sufferd some from our Boys. Lee is a distant relation of the Washington Famley.[392]

The Position of the Rebs here was very strong and how we was going to get them started again, I couled not see. We lay in line of Battle hear all day & night of the 21st till the morning of the 22nd when we fell in at 3 in the morning and went further to the right and flanked some brest works of the Rebs, we Chargin them and driving them out into the Woods and after them. It was a Puzzele to me how we got through those Woods and up the side of a steep Ravine. One thing I know, I wanted Breath when I got to the top. After geting the line straight again and formed anew, we moved further into the woods and halted when the Order was given to throw up Brest Works and nothing to do it with, but we got Railes & Stones and by goin back to the Rebl Works we found anuff to start with. After a time some Axes was served out and with some Picks

---

[391] Strasburg, Virginia, is at the northern end of the Shenandoah Valley on the North Fork of the Shenandoah River.

[392] "Robert E. Lee married the granddaughter of Jackie Custis who was Washington's stepson. Lee was also GW's third cousin, twice removed, since both men were descended from Augustine Warner, Sr. and Mary Towneley Warner (GW by way of their son, Augustine, Jr., and Lee by way of their daughter, Sarah)." Courtesy Frank Grizzard. *History of the George Washington Bicentennial Celebration*, Volume II, Literature Series (Washington, DC: George Washington Bicentennial Commission, 1932), 643–688, quoted in "George Washington, 1732–1799," The Papers of George Washington, accessed April 19, 2012, http://gwpapers.virginia.edu/history/faq/washington/.

& Spades we made our Position strong. We had two line of Works 4 rod apart. Then we cut all the small stuff down in front of us so that we couled see the Johneys good befor thay couled get to us.

After the work was don, it took about 4 hours for the work, the 6th Corps was moved further to the front and our Battery shelled the Rebl Rifle Pits. Then the Skirmish line was strenghend and was orderd to Charge the Pits, which thay did in Stile, the Rebs geting up and runing Back, our Boys after them, Cheering one another on. Our Batterys took possession of the Hill that the Rebs had left has it gave them great advantadge.[393] The Skirmish line beaing moved a mile further to the front and from that time till dark our Batterys shelled the Rebl lines.

Just befor Dark, the 12th was ordered to March, but whare we did not know till we got into the town of Strausburg. When we found that we was on Picket duty after the Gard for the night was stationd, those of us that was on reserve made fiers and prepaird to lay down and rest from the labors of the day and wait for our Cooks to bring our rations to us, as we was out and the Train had come in with Hard Bread, but thair was no such luck in store for us that night.

About ten OClock orders came to fall in and the News that the Rebs had left and was leaving and we must put after them. A night March is the most trying March you can put a soldier to, but it must be don and we fell in, took the road and such a road it was, filled with Bagadge Waggons and Arttlery, Ammunition trains. It was slow geting along, Ordleys & Staff Officers Galloping along and then the Chances of beain rode over was preaty cirtain. After a time we got by and reached the Pass that the Rebs had Fortified with much Labor and felt so Confident of holding, but the 8th Corps Climbed the Mountain on thair right and Flanked them and the way the Rebs got up, took the road again was a caution to all unbelevers in flank movements. We took 22 Peices of Canon and any quanity of Ammunition and Prisnors by the hundred.

---

[393] Although Sheridan's troops again defeated Early's at Fisher's Hill on the twenty-second of September, the skirmishes and battles in the Valley were not yet over as Sheridan moved his troops to Harrisonburg and ordered his cavalry to destroy the valley's crops, burn barns and mills, and leave virtually nothing to sustain the confederate troops. The CSA cavalry was determined to harass them. On October 9, Sheridan ordered an attack and Rosser's CSA cavalry fought Custer's US cavalry at the Battle of Tom's Creek. The US cavalry was decidedly victorious. Rosser and Custer, ironically, were friends at West Point. Wert, *From Winchester to Cedar Creek*, 135–164.

We had to halt and let a long string of them pass that our Cavelery had Captuerd and all that night we was after them.

About daylight we got to the town of Woodstock and got our rations served out then took the Road again to the Town of Edenburg whare we staid that night, and on the morning of the 24th fell in with the Rebs at Mount Jackson. It [was] hear thay had promised to make a stand but we got them agoin and that day I Witnessed the Grandest sight. The Valley hear is Whider and the land better. Hear was massed all Sheridans Cavlery and has the 3 Corps couled be all seeing at one time with the long lines of the Cavlery, it was a most Beautifull sight with the different Corps Flags waving.

Sheridan rode through the lines with is Body Gard. Sheridan is a young looking man, Light Complexion & Sandy Beard and a good looking man and the Hansomest Cavlery Officer that I have seeing. He Rides a Beautifull light Grey Horse, some times a Jet Black one, none of your old Plugs, but a Horse that is a horse and he is a Beautifull rider, and taken all to gather his turn out can not be beat in this Show.[394] He is as full of Pluck and fier as the horse he rides. I shall all ways rember him when I hear Winchester mentioned. He was Buley that day.

He came and complimented the 12th has we was waiting a few mineutes for Ammunition after making that Charge that Brock the Rebl line and drive them out of the Woods. He rode up to us, the Shells was coming thick and fast from the Rebl line on a hill in our front. A great Shell burst right over his head, the Peices flying right and left. He turned on his horse and Seluting it with his hand, turnd to the Regiment and said, all right Boys, all right, we can whip them. In a few mineutes we was served with the Cartridges and moving again, and on the 24th he was with foremost Batterys. Has fast has thay fell back, our Batterys followed up and the 19th Corps Moved by Colloum and not beaing wanted, I or all of us, had fair vew of all that was goin on in our front and the sight was truley imposing.

---

[394] *Rienzi,* the black horse, was favored by Sheridan, and after the Battle of Cedar Creek, he changed the horse's name to Winchester. He was a tall horse, sixteen hands high [some sources say seventeen], and Sheridan described him as "an animal of great intelligence and immense strength and endurance." The horse has been mounted and is on display at the Smithsonian Institute. "Rienzi or Winchester," Civil War @ Smithsonian, accessed April 19, 2012, http://www.civilwar.si.edu/cavalry_winchester.html.

The Johneys tryed hard to keep up a Bold front, but we was to many for them. Thay had thair best men in line that day and Braver men can not be found, I will say that for them, that it was no disgrace to fall back has thay did. Thay kept a good line. We Captuerd 2000 of them that day. This was in New Market. We staid thair that night and the next morning Marched to this Place Harrisonburg.

This makes the 3rd day we have been hear. The Train came in last night and at midnight we got up and was served with 3 days hard Bread, 3 days Sugar and 4 days Coffee, and with orders to March at 5 this morning and did strike tents, but after waiting a spell, had orders to Put them up again. The reson we did not move, I hear we are waiting for reinforcements has thair will be some opersition made to stop our further advance.

What ever it may Please Providence that I shouled go through, I hope to be Able to do my Duty. Thair must be some heavey Fighting hear befor we shall get to our destination, which is Lynchburge. So many of us suspect Soldiers are expected not to know whare thay are goin and I sopose that is about has well, so that we are suckcessfull is the main point. I am anxiouley looking toward the End. I want Richmond and the Reble Armey and must have them before winter sets in.

Give my respects to Mr. Brooks. Tell him that his Paper comes safe to me and has my Chum, Sargent Larkum of Hartford is with me, it is as much of a Plesuer to him as to me to read it.[395] His time will be out soon as he whouled not renlist and I shall Lose a kind frend and the Regiment a true Soldier.

Give my love to the Chirldren and keep up your hearts. I shall come out safe and Victory will crown our eforts to Brake this many headed Reblion.

My love to you all your Affactnat Husband & Son,
CW Sherman on his way to Richmond so Cleer the Track and get out of the way Johney Reb.

The Maile did not get up last night as we expected it wouled. I have writen to Henry to see to Virtue till I can get my Pay

---

[395] See Sergeant Larkum's letter of October 29 to Charles's family at the end of this chapter.

Mount Crawford, Shenandoah Valley, September 29, 1864

Dear Wife & Chirldren Parents,

I am in good health this morning and have been through this fataguin march. We reached this place yesterday noon. Our Cavelery are coming Back from Staunton having accomplished all that thair orders allowed them to do. Thay went about seven mile above Staunton. Thair Orders whare to distroy everything except Dwelling Houses and thay have raided to some purpose. The Rebs had a new suply of Clothing, Sadles, Bridles and most every thing that a Armey needs, and thay never knew of Earley defeat till our Cavelery Charged through the Streets. Thay thought that the day of Judgment was upon them and that thay whare about to meet thair Punishment for thair many fold Crimes.

In going up, the Cavelery whouled ride up to a trembling Sesash and tell him to hand over in Silver & Gold or thay whouled Burn his House, and I hear that some of the Cavelery have made a good thing of it, but how thay must Swear when our Cavelery, in coming back, whouled ride up to theas very men that had Paid to have thair Houses saved from the Flames and set thair Barns on Fier, Wheat Stacks & Hay Stacks and corn, every thing that couled give Aid and comfort. Yesterday you whouled have thought that t[h]ings was suffering by the Huge Clouds of Smoke in the Distance and last night any one whouled sopose that the Southron Confederacy was burning up from the number of Barns & Stacks on fier.

5 Brigades of Cavlery came in from the front last night and we are goin to fall back after distroying every thing. Grants orders are to make this Valley a desert so that the Rebs can not Subsist an Armey hear this winter. Thay are driving all the Cattle & Sheep Back with them. Our Boys are living high on fresh Pork & Mutton, Chickings making up for Short Rations. What a Sight of Wheat & Flour thair is in this Valley. In Harrisonburg was found 20,000 Barrles of Flour, but thair has been non Isued to us and I sopose that it will be all distroyed. We are in a ticklish Position at this time, beaing 100 mile from our Base of suplies and so many Pases through the mountains for a enterprising Cavelery force to Push thair way through and cut off our Waggon trains.

October 2nd

We have fallen back to our Old Camp at Harrisonburg and have been waiting for our Train to come up. We have been out of rations 2 days and are Hungray.

I recved a letter from Henry this morning. He told me that you was all well at that time. I have been waiting to hear from home. The Train is up but no Mail for us. The Wether is wet and Cold and disagreeable and some wish thay was back to Louisisana again and the Chances are that we shall go back. I shouled like to come home befor we go, but that can not be. When we shall get Paid I can not see but hope soon. I have written to Henry to let virtue have some Money till I can send some. Give my love to the Chirldren and keep up your hearts all will be well yet.

Your Affactnat Husband & Son,

CW Sherman

having no more time to write has the train is going Back

Harrisonburg, Shenandoah Valley, VA, October 4, 1864

Dear Mother & Father,[396]

We are Camped hear at this Town. Thair are two Hospitals hear full of Reble Wounded & Sick and thay have to be suplied with Medical Stores by our Sergons. I have conversed with some of them. Some want to get well so has to Fight us again, so thay tell us, and others want to have this War Close, thay having had anuff of War. Now, thay talk like sensable men and Echo my sentiments to a Charme, for I have had about all the War I want, but then I want a Peace that will be lasting, non of your compromses that are brocken has soon has made, and Jeff Davis is geting into a bad fix and his condition will be much worse before it is better. That last dich is not far off. I hope it may be deep anuff that when Lee finds it, we can buery this Wicked Reblion in it, and all that have upheld them both to home and hear. I do wish that we couled have all of that large Class that have given the south Aid and comfort couled be made to come and Join thair Fortuns with the Rebs so that we couled Cleen it all up at once and the same time.

Sunday night we moved our line so as to Join the 8th Corps and make one great line of Battle across the Valley. Our Position is on the right, on a range of Hills and the left of the 8th Corps rest on a range of Hills to the left. The 6th

---

[396] This letter is transcribed from copies.

Corps is in the Rear and has far has you can see is Camps and at night the sight of the small fiers in the Distance is very Beautifull. You cannot get up such a Alumination North. The sight of the long Circul of Camp fiers must be very Pleasant to the View of the Rebls as thay Climbe some tall tree and look down the Valley upon the Sleeping hosts of Northern Freemen that have left thair homes to uphold the right of free Speech, free Press and Civle and religious Liberty.

In our front is our Cavelery, back of them is a Brigade of Infantry on Picket and how Johney Reb will get down on us with out our knowing of thair movement is an impossibility. This Valley has escaped the Ravedges of War till this time, all though Hunter went through it this last Spring[397] and Freemont had one Campaing here and Banks and Genral Milroy.[398] We went to the Old Battle Ground of Cross Keys where Fremont Whiped Stone Wall Jackson and, faith, those Old Hills must have Shook some with the Thunder of so many Peices of Artllery.[399] The Echo of Canon in theas Mountains is Sublime has I can testifie to.

Our Cavlery Skirmish with the Rebls every day. What we are kept hear for now, I can not see, unless it is to invite A. P. Hill or Longstreet to come down on us.[400] Has for Earley, we shall hear from him no more. He is played out, gone up the spout whare all Rebles will go is thay do not mind thair Eye. Thair has been a great distruction of Grain & Hay in this Valley latley, and the People are frightend out of thair Witts for fear of the Rebs, as thay say thay will Murder them when thay come down again. All Grist Mills we Burn and Barns that hold Hay & Wheat, so the Rebs can not Winter hear.

Today I have been out to whare our Pickets are. Thair are about a Dozen Houses scatterd hear and thair, with good Farms Atached to them and Barns

---

[397] Gen. David Hunter

[398] Robert Huston Milroy of Indiana

[399] This apparently was a rumor, but in error. After the Union defeat at the First Battle of Winchester, Lincoln ordered two additional armies to the Valley. One commanded by Gen. John Fremont, the other by Gen. James Shields. Confederate Gen. Trimble, General Richard S. Ewell's right flank, repulsed Fremont's pursuit of General "Stonewall" Jackson during the Battle of Cross Keys in June 1862. Robert K. Krick, "Momentous Results at Cross Keys: The Battle of Cross Keys," Civil War Trust, accessed February 20, 2014, http://www.civilwar.org/battlefields/crosskeys /momentous-results-at-cross.html.

[400] Confederate Lt. Gen. Ambrose Powell Hill, Jr.; Confederate Gen. James Longstreet

full of Hay & Grain. The Owners have left thair homes and gon to Ohio, taking thair Clothes but having to leave thair Furneture, Stoves and every thing els for fear of the Rebs. Theas People, has I learn, belonged to a Socity called Dunkers and do not beleave in War.[401] Thay have been Taxed by the Confederates till thay couled stand it no longer and thair Lives have been Threatend this time and thay have left for thair frends in Ohio.

I was remined of my home has I wanderd over the House. Thair was the high Chair for the little one to sit up to the Table and the little Cot Bed for him. Thair was one small Pillow left, every thing els beaing gon. I took that and have made a small Bag of it to put my hard Bread in has we have to Carrey 4 days Rations hear. The House was full of our Fellows and had been used by the Picket for quarters and was getting Preaty dirty. Every thing was thrown about in confusion. Good Milk House and a Spring of Watter in it, with good Churn, set [of] Kettles and Washroom, and everything that belongs to a good Farm House, and it forceabley remined me of one of the Worst featuers of this Crule War; Famleys Fleeing from thair homes and fiersides.

In one of our late Battles our Batterys had to throw thair Shell over some dwelling houses and the thought came to me what whouled my Poor Old Mother & Father do if thay had to be situated in such a Cuntry. I did Heartley wish that cirtain Houses & Famleys that I wrote of couled have been Placed in the same condition with straglin Soldiers coming into the House and find no one thair, take whatever thair Fancy Promted them, and Strew the rest over the Floor.[402] I do think that it whouled be a good Lesson to and for them and to have thair Orchards strip[p]ed, thair Poultry taken, Fences torn down and every thing distroyed, Cattle & Sheep shot and what was once Rich and Thriving Famley, Reduced in a few hours to Poverty, and have to leave thair Comfortable Homes and go among Straingers or Cold Frends. It is this of the War that the Inhabitans of this Valley are goin through and many of them may deserve all and more than has been inflicted on them for not doing all that thay might to

---

[401] Dunker is a name for a people of faith, so-called because they fully immersed or "dunked" their baptismal candidates. They were a peace people and were opposed to war and did not participate in the Civil War. They are known more formally as the German Baptist Brethren. Carl F. Bowman, *Brethren Society: The Cultural Transformation of a "Peculiar People"* (Baltimore, MD: Johns Hopkins University Press, 1995), 212, 227, 350, http://books.google.com/books?id=8ew2f4nPlM8C&q=dunkers#v=snippet&q=dunkers&f=false.

[402] Referring again to the Copperheads

have prevented this War, but many Inocent men must suffer the same as the most Rabid Reble. It can not be otherwise. This is not a Plesing Pictuer, but it is what I have had to look on every day, ever since I left home 3 years ago. It is this Pictuer of the War that maney to home are down on, but it can not be helped. We do not make it any worse that the Rebs do for us when thay have the Chance, and we are compeld to do as we do by the exigences of this War. Let them come into our lines and help us all thay can and the Goverment will make up to them what thay Lose or what is taken for the use of the Armey.

I do not see when I shall get any Pay and what Virtue will do if Henry failes to send her any Money, I cannot see. I have written to him and I expect to hear from him soon to know what he can do to help her through this Fall & Winter if I have any difficulty in getting my Just dues on the next Pay day, let that be when it may. I shall go to my Corps Comand, who ever it may be at that time, and Claime my discharge on the Grounds that the United States have failed in thair agreement with me. I may not meet with any truble. My Bountys & Pay are all down on this Pay Roll that we expect to be Paid on and it may be all right and I am anxious to know.

I must Close having but five Mineutes to write. Pleas let me know whare I shall Direct my Pay to if I get it. I have thought that Stafford whouled be the most direct way. Give my love to Virtue and the Chirldren and tell them that I do not forget them if I do not send them any Money. My love to you, Father and Mother, and may God bless and Preserve you to me many years yet.

Your affactnat son,

C W Sherman, Shendandoah Valley, Va.

October the 5—1864

All well at this time.

Strausburg, Shenandoah Valley, Va., October 11, 1864

Dear Wife, Chirldren and Parents,

I am well at this time and most Froze on top of this Mountain. We have fell back to the Reble Position held by them Called Fishers Hill. The Papers Call the place Flint Hill but that is not the Name.[403]

It is a Strong Place and we shouled have lost heavley if we had had to Carry the Mountain Directley in front, has the onley way we couled have reached the Position was by a narrow Road and that was strongley Fortified. And Sheridan, to spair the lives of his men, sent the 8th Corps to the right and across the Mountain. At the same time the 6th & 19th Corps forced the Front, and when we heard the Canon of Crooks men, we knew he was coming on thair Flank & Rear and then we moved and the way the Rebs got up and took [to] thair heels was fun for us, but Death to them. We lost but few men in the 19th Corps and for one, I was satisfied with the 2 days work. I looked on to many of our dead at Winchester to fancey the Sight. A Battle Ground is a sad sight to look on and I hope that we shall never have to Wittness but few more, if any.

You have heard of our suckcess in this Valley and it still continues. The Cavelery have don imense Damadge hear and yesterday thay captuerd 8 more Guns and nine Hundred more Prisnors.[404] We are worn out by hard Marching and want rest and Warme Clothing. Maney of the men are Bare foot and with out Clothing. The Water Froze in our Canteens last night. I had to get up and Warme my self severale times in the night. I do hope we shall get whare it is warmer or have some Clothing come up.

I recved your kind letter of the 18th of September and one from Mr. Lillibridge and shall Answer it to day if we stay long anuff. I cannot write any time as we have to be moving all the time and when we halt, we know nothing, how long we shall stay, & so you must excuse me if you do not get letters reguler. I write when I can and have to carry the letters about with me till thair is a Chance of sending them. The Last one I did not have time to get it Franked. Has I have not heard frome the 3 last letters, you will Please say what Letters you do recve and then I shall know if you get them.

---

[403] There was a Flint Hill captured by Union Gen. James B. Ricketts about the same time. Wert, *From Winchester to Cedar Creek*, 117.

[404] This would be after the clash of cavalries at Tom's Bridge.

I have Jot[t]ed down a few things and my impresions of Matters, and shall send it, of our Journey back to this Place so that you can see us and what we have to do.

I whouled say that the Letter I recved from Burnham Lillibridge was a good and Cheering one[405] and tell him from me that I thank him and that it will help me to still March and Fight, if need be, till the end shall come and has the good Cause is Prospering with us the last Dich will be reached soon, that Jeff has told us of so many times, and Grant will see that the Reblion and its backers are buerd in it, and then shall the good time come that we have beleved in, trusted to see. I recvd two Papers from Henry in the Mail that brought your lest letters and one frome Mr. Brooks. I sopose it came from him, it was the Curent . . .[406]

Ceedeer Creek, Shenandoah Valley, Va., October 12, 1864

I am well at this time and the Corps has fell Back to this Place. Has I have told you Preaty much of our travles up this Valley, I thought I whouled keep you Posted in regards to our falling back. I have written to Burnham Lillibridge by this Mail and shall try to send this by the same. We have small Chances of writing, have to write as we can.

October the 6th

We broke up our camp this morning, fell in at 5 A.M. [I was] loathe to leave my Nest of Cleen Straw as that is a Luxury that seldom falls to our lot to enjoy. Had to go. Straglers all mounted on Poor Old Horses that thay had captuerd. Laughed to see some fall down with thair Burdens of Camp Kettles & Drums; thought that all the drumers in the service was mounted by the Number of them. Thought that if all the Old Horses that we Brought away was North and Boiled down, what a fortune it whouled be to some Sope Manufactuer.

---

[405] A friend or neighbor from Willington, about Charles's parents' age. Also mentioned in the letter dated October 28, 1863.

[406] The rest of the pages of this letter are missing, but the next pages, dated October 12, are the jottings and "impressions of matters" mentioned above.

It was a Grand sight to see the long lines of men file a cross the Hills. The Differant Corps taking thair Position that thay Maintain during the march. We are falling Back Burning every Barn and Wheat Stack. All the Hay & Wheat in the Valley has been Cut & Planted by the Reble Armey and for themselves and Sheridan is bound not onley to Whip them in Battle, but to starve them at the same time.

The men go out Foragin and some are taken by the Rebs and thay get no Mercy shown them. On the 2nd of this Month, Genral Sheridans Cheef of Staff was out with two Ordleys and was taken by the Rebs and Murderd by them. Sheridan gave Orders that every thing within 5 Mile of the Place shoulel be burnt.[407]

We had a hard days March this day. At night Camped at New Market Gape. Went to the Shenandoah River, had a Wash, found some Straw and thought what a lucky Chiled I was when I arived in Camp. Was told that I was wanted on Picket for the night. If that was not Cold Water thrown on my hopes of rest, I know not what is. Had to go some two mile tierd as we was and keep Watch.

Pased some 40,000 Dollers worth of Contrabands through the lines. This is a kind of Property that dose take to its self feet and Walkes away. One Womon had 3 little Chirldren Barefoot and bare headed who had been after us two days. Thay was more then half White, how tickled that Mother was when I told the Gard to let them Pass. Thay wanted to get to our Wagon train before Morning. Thay all told me that thair was nothing for them to Eat and thay had been waching for a opertunity of geting away, but couled not till we came. I Pased another Mother and two small Chirldren the next day which I had Pased through to the train, but thay couled not get a Ride. I sopose how Weary thay must have been. I was beat out myself and it was coming on night and I wonderd whare

---

[407] Charles's reference concerns Sheridan's Chief Engineer, Brevet Capt. and Maj. John Rodgers Meigs and two of his men. On October 3, while returning to camp after conducting a military survey, they met three Confederate cavalrymen who demanded that Meigs and his men surrender. Gunfire was exchanged, Meigs was killed and one of his men captured. The other escaped and told Gen. Sheridan that Meigs had no chance to defend himself, in essence having been murdered. This infuriated Sheridan, who ordered the whole town of Dayton, Virginia, and a five mile area surrounding, to be burned. He later rescinded the order after hearing that the first report may have been exaggerated, but many homes and barns surrounding the town had already been destroyed. Wert, *From Winchester to Cedar Creek*, 145; Faust, *Historical Times Illustrated*, 485.

the Poor things whouled put for the night. War is a tirrable visitation for any People, but the Inocent have to suffer has well has the Guilty. I have looked on many hard sights, but helpless Chirldren and Wemon all ways make me feel sad, for it is out of my Power to help them.

I was kept up all night Passing dispach Cares, Ordleys, staff Officers and straglers through the lines, answering all maner of questions. Had orders to fall back on the reserve Picket and go to Camp about 5 A.M. The first Division was rear Gard today, October the 7th, to suport the Cavelery in thair work of Burning. The sight was Grand to day, the Burning of so many Barns & Pased by one large House seround by Barns & out Building all on fier; the Wind blowing the Flames directley onto the House; Wemon Whring thair hands, the Old man & son running hear and thair. Fortunateley the Wind shifted and the House was saved.

All day the Work continued and in this way the South is reaping a Wirlwind of distruction and it must have an important baring on the Work goin on round Richmond. The Loss of so much Grain & Hay can not be replaced this year. This has been a big Raid and Lee must feel it the most. His pet Genral Earley and his Armey that has been kept to Theraten [threaten] Washington, Distroyed and all his Canon Captuerd, his Trains taken and burnt.[408] We have been waiting for the other pet of the Southron Armey, the Tirrable Longstreet, to come down on us, but so far we have seeing nothing of him. The Rebs followed us down and thay have been learnt that it is not healthy to be in the Valley. Thay lost all thair Guns, trains and to day thair is nothing in it but Yankees and hard Bread and not much of that. The Meat is most Played out and in fact, the Rebs will long remember the Day when thay met Genral Sheridan in Battle Aray.

I wish that we was goin to stay hear has we want rest, but the indacations are that we have a Winter Campaing in Louisisana. Well, if it must be, so the Rebs will wish the 19th Army Corps back in this Department for the men will distroy what is left thair and, for one I shall try and set the Missispipi on fier, for if thay wont give in in one way, thay must in a nother.

I hope that Henry will Atend to what I have him to do till the Corps is Paid off. Give my love to the Chirldren and Virtue, bare up a spell longer. We must be Paid sometime and that soon. Give my love to Father & Mother and tell them

---

[408] This is a little premature, as Early had one more strike to make in the Valley at Cedar Creek, much to the misfortune of the Twelfth Connecticut and Charles.

to be of good Cheer. All things will work for our good, if we onley have Faith. Give my respects to Mr. Brooks & Famley and to all enquiring frends.

Your Affectionate Husband & Son,

CW Sherman Va.

Cedar Creek, Shenandoah Valley, VA, October 13, 1864

Dear Wife and Chirldren, Parents,[409]

I am well at this time and was Pleased to recve a Letter from home last night of October 2nd and was Glad to hear that you was all well. I am thankful to that good Beaing who has Preserved me through so many daingers. The Bulets of the Enemy has rained round me like hailstones in a thunder storme, and how so many of us Escaped beaing killed or Wounded is a mystery that I cannot explain except that we was Protected by our good Gardin Aingles [Guardian Angels].

I have Written five letters since the 19th of September and this is the first one of those Letters you speak of recving. It must have been Dated the 18 of September, written on Picket Sunday.

Sunday night at 2 O'clock we moved for Winchester. At daylight we got to Winchester. I see by the papers that the 19th Corps is reported two hours Late and that we disarranged Sheridan's Plan of Battle. Now I Pronounce the man that wrote that for the Papers a most unmitigated Lier and Skoundrel. The fact is we had 4 hours to spaire before the Battle comenced in Earnest and was kept in reserve right under the Guns of Earley's Battery. The statement was writen by a Corespondent in the Pay of the 6th Corps, thay beaing out Fought that day by the 19th Corps and have all ways held the front rank has a Fighting Corps, but thay have had the Conceit taken out of them by Old Ben Buttler's Louisiana men. The Rebs themselves owned to our men that the 6th & 8th corps was good men but it was the 19th Armey Corps that Whipped them. Thay gave the First Division of the 19th Corps the Compliment of Br[e]aking thair Line and that thay never was fairly whipped before in this Valley.

Genral Sherican rode to our Regiment and Complimented us has I have told you in one of my Letters. A Major Genral has not much time for Compliments in a

---

[409] This letter is transcribed from photocopies.

Great Battle with the Enemys' Battery Playing on him and the Brave Fellows that is around him. You ought to have seeing our Genral, Officers and Staff Colls, and in fact every man was a host in themselves. Do not tell me that the Rebs can not be whipped; thay can. Stonewall Jackson's Best Troops are no whare in comparison to good Yankee Vollenteers. The Veterans can Fight and Earley had the Best men in the Southron Armey; men that had never been whipped, and thay couled not realize thay was beaten, but such was the Fact and Glory Hallelujah we can do it again, and now Sheridan has had that Corespondent Arrested has he states in Genral Orders that it was not the first time that he had given False information, and Sheridan states that if we was late, he knew nothing about it and that Ends the matter, and if he knew nothing about the Fight I shouled like to know who did.

I hear the Mail that left hear yesterday has been Captuerd and in that Mail was the Letter that I had sent to Burnham Lillibridge, and if he dose not recve it Please let me know. Our Train that left yesterday was fierd into by Gurrillas and we Lost 25 men, killed and Wounded, and it may be that my Letter may be gone up and I wish I knew.

I was sorry to hear that Faney had Scalded her feet, but Acidents will happen in the best regulated Famleys. I hope nothing serious will Grow out of it. I am glad that Virtue has got better. She must keep up a good heart. I can not send her any Money yet, but the Pay Masters are with us. I understand that our Corps is to report in Washington by the 19th of this month and that we will be paid off thair. I do not want to recve Money hear with the Chance of beaing Shot, or if I send it by Mail, of its being Captuerd by the Enemy. I want my Money to reach my Family, and has soon has I can get any Money, it will be sent, and if Henry dose has I have requested, Virtue need not want, for the Money will be sent has soon has recved. I am sorry that it shouled have hapened this year in regard to my Pay has it as, but I couled not help it. It was through having a Drunken Captain and my Beaing in the condition I was when to home. If I was sick, it was not through any Fault of mine and if not Paid up in full this time, I shall Carrey it to my Corps Comander, let it Injuer who it may. I shall demand Justice and I am not afraid but it will be accorded to me. Do the best you can. It will all come right soon.

This has been a beusey Campaing and not much time to look after Money. My accounts are on the Pay Roll that was sent in last, and it may come all right. I see Captain Clark, who is in Command of the Regiment at this time, yeseterday in regard to my Pay and he told me that any thing he couled do to help me, he whouled do, and that he whouled see Captain Roch in regard to what couled be don, and when the Regiment is next Paid, and it may be all right next time. I know that it has been a hard year for you all and it has been a source of truble to me that I couled not have had it all straightend out befor I left home.[410]

I wish I knew wether Sarah Hobbs, has we must call her for the Futuer, had moved to Washington or not, has I wouled try and see them when we go back if it was in my Power, and it may be barley Posabley that we stay a few days thair befor leaving. Please let me know, and, if Posable, the Number and Name of street Block and what other information. I thought of writing to Derrick, but he has not Answerd my Letter that I sent to him from New Orleans, and if you whouled send to him, and he might send right to me, send the Directions to him. I shouled feel sorry to go through Washington and not see them if thay whare thair.

The Wether is very Cold hear and we suffer nights and I do not care if we go back to Louisiana to Winter if it shouled Cost us a Winter Campaign, but events are thicking and we may hear of the taking of Richmond in a few days and then the War is narrowed down so that we can see the end.

Give my love to the Chirldren and may Heaven Bless you all. Keep up a good curadge. All things are working for our good. Tell the weak hearted and those that have nearly despaird of our success not to give in. We shall win and bring this War to a close this Winter. Give the Coppers fits and we will give the Rebs the Lead and the Bayonet and that will give us the Victory.

Your Affactnate Husband and Son,
CW Sherman

Ceedeer Creek, Shenandoah Valley, Va, October 14, 1864
Dear Wife & Chirldren, Parents,

We are still Camped hear but how much longer we shall be allowed to Desacrat this secrad Soil by our presence, I know not.

The Rebs came down in great Wharth yesterday and by the noise thay made, one would have thought that our time was short, but Sheridan made a

---

[410] Sarah was Charles's cousin and the daughter of James and Elizabeth Derrick.

few moves that took the conceit out of them. We got ready for a warm time. I cannot say the wether is warm, it is very cold up hear in the Mountains. All the Troops was moved and Massed in the Woods when it came night but our Solitary Brigade and one Battery of six Guns. We was lef to the Tender Merceys of the Wharthfull Rebs all night, but wether thay would have fanc[i]ed our reception of them is a question not decided yet, but it was not to be. Thay thought having better of thair Blood Thirsty intentions concerning us for we was let alone and at Noon to day the Troops all returnd to thair Old Camps and things gose on has usal.

Col Lewis has returnd to the Regiment. You rember that he was Wounded at Port Hudson and has he was Major when Coll Peck was made full Coll, he steped into the Leautenant Colls Place and in the Death of Coll Peck he will be Promoted in his Place. We neve thought of seeing him with us again. The men never liked him and thay would much rather some one else comanded them then Coll Lewis but he may treat them better has thair Coll then has thair Major. For my self I have nothing to say eath for or against him.

A nother Featuer in our Soldiers life is that we all Voted to day. It was all fair and above board. Every man had two Tickets, a Lincoln Ticket and a McClleand Ticket, and a Envelop he could Put wich Ticket he Pleased into the Envelop and seal it up.[411] Thair is two Commisners apointed who wrote each mans Name & Town on the Envelop and Each Voat will be sent to the differant Towns and thair counted.

I wish you or Burnham Lillibridge to see that my Name is on the Voting List all right so that I shall not lose it and let me know. Thair will be a great many Votes lost on account of the men not beaing made freemen of in the Differant Town whare thair homes are at this time.

Tell our frends that the Soldiers are all right. Thair will be a Larger Majority for Uncl Abraham among the Soldiers then could have been Polled if the Rebs had not a went in for McClleand, has McClleand had many frends among the Soldiers, but his Reble frends have spoilt his Broth, and he is gon up and the fourth of November will show Uncl Abraham spliting Railes for us to fence this Cuntry in has we mean to have it well fencd in. Please tell our frends to go in and win for we are bound to win and thay must not be behind us. This Regiment can speak both hear and at the Ballot Box and it has spoken

---

[411] George B. McClellan, the presidential candidate for the Democratic Party

well today and can speak to Longstreet to morrow in a way that he can understand.[412] We have Shoved the Constitution through the Shenandoah Valley in a way that Thomas Jefferson did not anticapate it ever would be.

October the 15th

We have Just returned from a Look after the Rebs. Orders came round in the night to be ready to move at 5 in the morning. The first Division of the 19th Corps was sent on that service. We Crossed Ceeder Creek and sent out our Skirmsh line, formed line of Battle and moved on Strasburg, but after travling some 6 Mile, found that the Rebs had left and then returnd to Camp.

Thair is some thing that comes over a man in looking at the Praperations for Battle. It is not fear, but a Sad feeling when you see the Skirmshers deploy into line and the Regiments unfold themselves into a Line of Battle, the Artllery coming on in the rear, and those detailed to carrey off the Wounded with thair Streachers, and you waiting as you March along to hear the first shot from the Skirmsh line that is in your front. When thay come upon the Enemy, the Skirmsh line all ways goes in advance to feel of the Enemy and far anuff to allow any Chaing to be made in the formation of the Line that is coming on in thair rear. When the thunder of the Artllery comes upon you, you forget every thing els and look out for the Shells that come Screming toward you, not that you can Dodge any thing, but you want to see whare thay come from. When the Enemys line begin to fier, you have anuff to do in returning it, and have your Ears open for Orders for on obeying Orders Prompley depends your life, and the lives of others.

Has we found no Enemy, we returned to Camp and a man feels better in goin away from Dainger then goin into it. I do wish this Cruell War would come

---

[412] On October 16, it was reported to Sheridan that a message to General Early from Longstreet was intercepted. The message stated that Longstreet's forces would be joining Early's in the Valley. Sheridan correctly believed the message "a ruse"; however, he decided it best to play it safe and to keep Merritt's cavalry in the Valley. Had he not done so, there may have been a different outcome. Early's ruse backfired. During the actual Battle of Cedar Creek on the nineteenth, Sheridan again received an erroneous report of Longstreet moving toward Winchester and delayed his counterattack until 3:30 p.m. when it was reported not to be true, thus clearing the way for Sheridan to attack. Wert, *From Winchester to Cedar Creek*, 172, 212, 229–30.

to an end, for this goin about to Kill one another has a unchristian look to me, when you come to look at it in that light, but it has to be don, I sopose.

I want to hear from you to see if my Letters get to you safe and to know if Henry has done any thing to help Virtue till I can get my Pay and to know how Faneys Burn gets along. A Mail lef hear last night and by it I sent a letter. I have to have them wrote, ready so that I can send when a Mail leaves and that will account for the differance in time. That I write often, you must know if you get all my letters. Please [do] not get discuradged by the delay of that money. I do wish I could get it for you. Kiss those Babys and take Curadge, for it dose no good to fret and worry your selves. Some thing will be don soon round Petersburg & Richmond that will give us all hope and encuradgement. Give my love to the Girls and Lewis. Tell them that I should like to see them.

your Affactnat Husband & Son,
CW Sherman

Please send me a hank of Black thread in a Letter or Paper & I am in want of some very much for I am Rag[g]edI turnd this Sheet wrong has you see.[413]

Ceeder Creek, Oct. the 23, 1864

Mr. Sherman

Dear Sir,

It devolvs on me as a tent mate of your son to line the sad news of his death, which accured in terible battle of the 19th of the present month. As a soldier he was much respected. He was courteous alike to ever one and there was not a man in his regiment that did not respect him. He was killed in the formost rank, bravley fighting for his country whic he thought so much of, and what he had fought so much for. His lasting resting place is on a high spot very near where he fell. His grave[414] is marked with head board. His name and

---

[413] These last two sentences were written upside down at the top of two different pages of this letter. He occasionally did that with when running out of room for a postscript.

[414] Initially, C. W. Sherman was buried, as Sergeant Larkum states, at Cooley's Farm, Virginia. The family apparently did not choose to send his body home, and the graves of soldiers killed at the Battle of Cedar Creek were moved to Winchester National Cemetery: "Sherman, C W, d. 10/19/1864, CPL K 12 CONN INF, Orig Burial

compay and regiment are upon it and it will be a very easy matter if you so choose to remove his body to his home. Any information that I can give will be gladly attended to and, if be of any benefit to you in any other way, willingly will my services be offerd and gladly will I pay the last tribute to him who was so brave and so kind. I remain your obedient servant,

Serg. E. S. Larkam[415] Com K 12 Reg. Co Voll

Cooley's Farm Va, Winchester National Cemetery Section 87 Site: 4053." United States Department of Veterans Affairs, Nationwide Gravesite Locator, s.v. "C W Sherman, Winchester National Cemetery, October, 1864," accessed April 24, 2012, http://gravelocator.cem.va.gov/index.html.

[415] His signature spells his name as E. S. Larkam; however, *Record of Service of Connecticut Men* lists his name as Edward S. Larkum. Other records, such as *1860 Census* and *Massachusetts Deaths*, 1841–1915, concur. He died of "pneumonia and alcohol" at age fifty-five on January 2, 1899, in Boston, Massachusetts, occupation is listed as salesman. Sergeant Larkum was mentioned in Charles's letters as his tent mate, or "chum." Larkum was born in Hartford, Connecticut, in 1844 and was discharged from the army on November 28, 1864. *Record of Service of Connecticut Men*, 496; Massachusetts Vital Records, 1911–1915, s.v. "Edward Larkum," New England Historic Genealogical Society, Boston, Massachusetts.

Afterword

The Battle of
Cedar Creek

There has been a lot written about the Battle of Cedar Creek, which was fought on October 19, 1864. It was a decisive turning point in Maj. Gen. Philip H. Sheridan's Shenandoah Valley Campaign, which included the Battles of Third Winchester, Fisher's Hill, and Tom's Brook, and essentially ended the Confederate Army's pursuit of control of the valley. Confederate Lt. Gen. Jubal A. Early, commander of the Army of the Valley, marched his troops stealthily through the woods, under cover of darkness, to spring a surprise attack on Sheridan's troops in a dense fog at dawn. Union Bvt. Maj. Gen. William H. Emory's Nineteenth Corps was situated to the west of the Valley Pike forming the left flank. Southeast of that position were situated two divisions of Bvt. Maj. Gen. George Crook's Eighth Army Corps (Army of West Virginia): Col Joseph Thoburn's First Division and Col. Rutherford B. Hayes's Second Division. They were the first attacked by Early's troops, were quickly routed, and the survivors pushed back towards the Pike by Confederate Maj. Gen. Kershaw's and Confederate Maj. Gen. Gordon's troops. Thoburn's and Hayes's surviving troops retreated towards Emory's Nineteenth Corps, which had in its command Brig. Gen. Cuvier Grover and Brig. Gen. James W. McMillan. The left flank was exposed and in danger of immediate attack. Emory knew that he needed to buy time for the Union supply wagons to withdraw north, and allow the Sixth Corps time to organize a defense line. He therefore directed McMillan to bring one of his brigades from the breastworks and move it across the Pike. The brigade chosen was the Second under Col. Stephen Thomas of the Eighth Vermont, and included the four regiments of the Eighth Vermont Infantry, the Twelfth Connecticut Infantry, the Forty-Seventh Pennsylvania Infantry, and the 160th New York Infantry. They proceeded east across a ravine, crossed the Pike into direct line of fire, and fashioned a battle line in the woods on a piece of high ground. The ensuing fight with the enemy was bloody with hand-to-hand combat, muskets used as clubs, and bayonets wielded. Loss of life was great in all four regiments. The Twelfth Connecticut alone suffered casualties of twenty-two killed, fifty-seven wounded, and ninety-three missing.

Although forced to retreat, Thomas's brigade held the enemy's attention for a good thirty minutes and bought valuable time for Emory to reposition his troops to protect his left and front. The gallant and courageous fighting displayed by the brigade earned the respect of both Union and Confederate troops alike. For his leadership and actions, Thomas was awarded the Medal of Honor in 1892.

The attack by Confederate troops continued so quickly that the Union troops had little time to organize and prepare, and were forced to retreat. However, the Eighth and Nineteenth Corps held off the enemy long enough to allow units and wagons to load up and withdraw buying time for Brig. Gen. James B. Rickett's Sixth Corps to organize its resistance, but all were eventually forced back. Later, Early's troops, surprisingly, became pre-occupied with looting and pillaging the abandoned Union camps and did not keep pursuing the retreating Union troops, assuming they were leaving the area. Meanwhile, Sheridan, who had spent the night in Winchester, arrived and began rallying his discouraged troops. The survivors joined in the charge led by Sheridan later that afternoon. That charge, strengthened by Brig. Gen. George A. Custer's cavalry, decided the victory for the Union after what started out to be a sure loss for them in the morning hours.

The above is merely a brief description of the battle with the intent to highlight the Twelfth Connecticut's involvement. Jeffry Wert has written a very detailed accounting of all troop movement during the day's action in *From Winchester to Cedar Creek*. This editor highly recommends it to anyone who is interested in learning more about the battle. In addition, Jonathan A. Noyalas has published an excellent, thorough description in *The Battle of Cedar Creek (VA): Victory from the Jaws of Defeat.*

It is not known at which point in time during the Battle of Cedar Creek that Charles W. Sherman gave his life for his adopted country. It most likely occurred in that first, bloody hand-to-hand combat with Confederate forces when the most casualties were suffered, but it could have been during the second charge in the afternoon. Three days later, the regiment returned to the battleground to collect the bodies and bury the dead. Sergeant Larkum states that Charles was buried "on a high spot very near where he fell." Chaplain J. H. Bradford wrote: "the bodies of all the men of the Twelfth who had fallen on the field were collected, and decently buried within a neat little inclosure [sic],—a substantial head-board at each grave . . ."

The Twelfth suffered great losses at Cedar Creek, and those losses, coupled with death by disease and the mustering out of those that did not reenlist, ended the regiment's fighting days. The regiment was disbanded with surviving members being consolidated into the Twelfth Battalion with other companies. The campaign in the Shenandoah Valley was essentially over, with the Union victories playing a major part in turning the war towards the ultimate victory the following spring.[416]

Charles W. Sherman fought bravely for his adopted country and for his belief in freedom and a person's individual rights. His great faith in God and his deep love for his family carried him through nearly three years of brutal hardship and fighting. As he wrote, just days before his death, "I do wish this Cruell War would come to an end, for this goin about to Kill one another has a unchristian look to me, when you come to look at it in that light . . ." Six months later, it did come to an end. The rights and freedoms enjoyed by Americans today owe him, and thousands of others who lost their lives in that war and others since, a huge debt of gratitude.

---

[416] Wert, *From Winchester to Cedar Creek*, 177–219; *Record of Service of Connecticut Men*, 478; Croffut and Morris, *The Military and Civil History of Connecticut*, 725, 727–8; *The Connecticut War Record*, "From the Twelfth Regiment," James H. Bradford, Chaplain, Vol. II, No. V, (New Haven, CT: Morris & Benham), 322–323, PDF e-book.

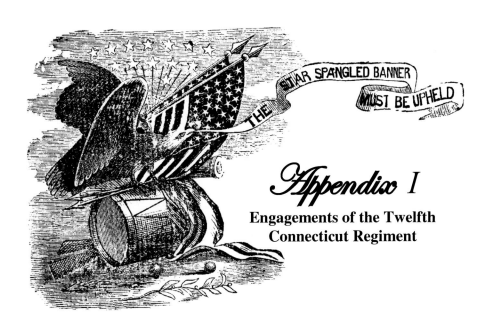

Appendix I
Engagements of the Twelfth Connecticut Regiment

Georgia Landing, Louisiana, October 27, 1862.
Capture of Gunboat *Cotton*, Louisiana, January 14, 1868.
Pattersonville, Louisiana, March 27, 1863.
Bisland, Louisiana, April 13, 1863.
Siege of Port Hudson, Louisiana, May 25 to July 9, 1863.
Brashear City, Louisiana, June 23, 1863.
Winchester & Opequan, Virginia, September 19, 1864.
Fisher's Hill, Virginia, September 22, 1864.
Cedar Creek, Virginia, October 19, 1864.
(From *Record of Service of Connecticut Men*, 473)

Winchester National Cemetery
(The following photographs are credited to Dick and Marge Sharp.)

Charles W. Sherman's Headstone

Twelfth Connecticut Monument

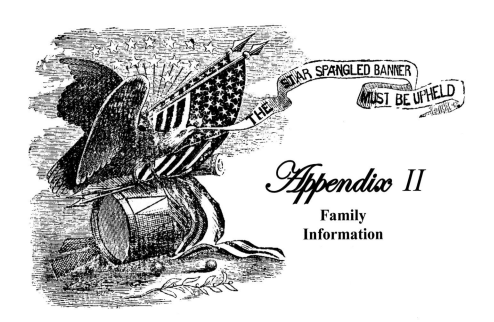

Appendix II

Family Information

Charles William Sherman was born in Gloucester, England, on October 25, 1828. He came to the United States in 1838 with his mother, Sarah, and brother, Thomas Henry. (I have not yet established when his father, Thomas, arrived; however, it is certain that it was at an earlier date.) He married Virtue M. James in 1848, and they had five children: Fanny Louisa, Angeline Maria, Lewis William, Henry Arthur, and Charles Butler. In the 1850 Census, he was listed as a harness maker in Connecticut. In 1860, he and Virtue lived in Webster, Massachusetts, and his occupation was listed as a carpenter. His brother, Henry, also lived there at that time. It is evident that Charles moved the family back to Connecticut sometime before the end of 1861. He enlisted in the Twelfth Connecticut Volunteer Infantry and was mustered into Company K on January 31, 1862. He was killed at the Battle of Cedar Creek on October 19, 1864.

Relatives of Charles:

Parents: Thomas and Sarah

Charles's father, Thomas H. Sherman, was born in 1808 in Gloucester, England, to William and Prudence (Turner) Shearman. On April 6, 1828, he married Sarah Ann Collier, born in Gloucester in 1805. They had two children, Charles William and Thomas Henry. As previously mentioned, they immigrated to America in 1838, settling in Connecticut. These letters and various census documents list Thomas as working in the woolen mills. Some letters are addressed to Rockville, Connecticut, where the mills were located. One letter mentions Thomas's promotion to supervisor. After the war, the 1870 Census shows Thomas and Sarah living with Virtue and the children in Putnam, Connecticut. Thomas died in 1882 and Sarah in 1885 in Putnam. She and Thomas are buried at the Grove Street Cemetery in Putnam in a family plot with their son Henry, grandson Lewis, and his wife Mary A. Grant Sherman.

Brother: Henry

Thomas Henry Sherman, ("Henry" in these letters) was born on February 22, 1830 [H. T. Sherman, T. H. Sherman, and Henry T. Sherman]. He lived in San Francisco from 1852–1854 during the gold rush, working as a carpenter, which was his trade. He married Elvira B. Paul, and they had three children: Elias Dwight, 1864 (mentioned in the letters); Ella P., 1866; and Etta B., 1869. The 1870 Census shows them living in Putnam. Public records show that Elvira died in 1872 of insanity. It appears as though Henry remarried on July 5, 1873, to Emma Jane Derrick. The 1880 Census shows Henry and Dwight in Wallace, Kansas, working as house carpenters and living in a boarding house or hotel. Ella married a George B. Stacy in February 1887 and died on December 3, 1887, from burns. Etta died July 22, 1870, at the age of ten months and twelve days. It is not known what happened to Dwight. Henry lived with his new wife and their three children—Emma N., William R., and Alice E.—in Putnam, in 1900. Henry died March 5, 1903, and is buried at the Grove Street Cemetery in Putnam with his parents, Thomas and Sarah, and his nephew Lewis and his wife Mary. Henry and Emma's daughter, Emma, married Fred M. Cole on April 13, 1892, and, according to the 1910 US Census, was living in Putnam with her husband, a son Howard, her mother Emma Jane, and her sister Alice.

Wife: Virtue

Charles's wife, Virtue M. James, was born on July 15, 1825, in England. Her father's name was Joseph. Her mother's name is unknown, but may have been Mary. Virtue arrived in the US in 1844. She married Charles on April 1, 1848. After Charles was killed in battle, she continued to live for several years with his parents and/or the children and received $8 per month in pension, plus $2 month for each child until he/she reached the age of sixteen. Pension records were signed with her "mark," an indication that Virtue could not read or write. (The same is true for Charles's mother, Sarah. Both Virtue and Sarah were raised in England; it was quite common for women who were not in the "upper class" to be uneducated in England in the 1800s.) The 1870 Census lists Virtue as "keeping house" and living with all five children, as well as her in-laws, Thomas and Sarah, and Albert Sherman, a relative. In 1880, she was living with Charles B. and Arthur Henry in Webster, Massachusetts. Sometime between then and 1900, she went to live with Fanny and her family; Virtue died on August 27, 1911, in Baldwinville, Massachusetts, of dysentery. Her son, H. A. Sherman (Arthur in these letters), signed her death certificate. It is interesting to note that Virtue outlived not only her husband, but four of her five children as noted below. Birth information on the five children comes from family records passed down as well as from the family bible as stated in official US Pension Records.

Children of Charles and Virtue:

Fanny Louisa Sherman was born on July 28, 1850, in Willington, Connecticut. She worked in the woolen mill (most likely in Pomfret, Connecticut) until she married Ezra Ayers, listed as an undertaker, in 1873. They had two children: Charles Sherman Ayers and Edith V. Ayers. Fannie died on October 22, 1910, in Baldwinville, Massachusetts, of heart complications due to diabetes.

Angeline Maria Sherman was born on May 27, 1852, in Broad Brook, East Windsor, Connecticut. In 1870, she was living at home with Virtue in Putnam and working in the woolen mill. According to Connecticut death records, she died of "consumption" (tuberculosis) on May 13, 1872, in Putnam, Connecticut, at age nineteen, just fourteen days short of her twentieth birthday.

Lewis William Sherman was born on October 29, 1854, in Willington, Connecticut. The 1870 Census from Putnam shows his living at home and working as a carpenter's apprentice. After his father died, Lewis started his apprenticeship at age thirteen, according to family records, and became a master carpenter and stayed in Putnam from 1868 on. His obituary states that he had gone into partnership with a Victor Chase in a building and repairing business; prior to that, he worked for Charles H. Kelly, a prominent building contractor in Putnam. He was a member of the Second Congregational church in Putnam and the United Brotherhood of Carpenters and Joiners. He married Mary A. Grant of Woodstock, Connecticut, in 1877. They lived in Putnam in a house that he built, the same house in which the letters were found. Lewis and Mary had a stillborn child on March 16, 1880, and then three children: Marsha Ernestine Sherman (Gilbert), February 12, 1882; Florence Etheline Sherman (Munroe), May 19, 1884; and Byron Grant Sherman, March 8, 1887 [my grandfather, Ed.], who became a doctor. Lewis died on June 17, 1909, at the age of fifty-five. Cause of death is listed as cerebral spinal sclerosis (multiple sclerosis). Mary passed away on February 26, 1924, of ovarian cancer. They are both buried at the Grove Street Cemetery in Putnam with his grandparents, Thomas and Sarah, and his uncle, Henry.

[What started as genealogy research on this family for the book has turned into a fascinating hobby for me. One of the more intriguing discoveries was that a family myth about being related to Ulysses S. Grant is true after all. He and Mary A. Grant Sherman were seventh cousins. Considering that Charles essentially fought under Grant's orders to General Sheridan in the Shenandoah Valley, I find it oddly coincidental that his son married a distant relative of Gen. Grant.]

Henry Arthur Sherman ("Arthur" in these letters) was born on February 21, 1860, in Putnam. He became a doctor in New London and Groton, Connecticut. Henry sometimes went by Henry A., H. A., or Arthur H. Sherman. He married a woman named Marie from Virginia sometime between 1880 and 1900. [I am not sure what year and can't find any children.] He signed Virtue's death certificate H. A. Sherman in 1911. He died in 1915.

Charles Butler Sherman (the "baby," "Butler," and "the little general" in the letters) was born on January 6, 1862, in Willington, Connecticut, a few weeks before Charles enlisted at the end of January. He was living with Virtue in 1880 in Webster, Massachusetts, occupation was listed as bookkeeper. He married Harriet Spalding on June 23, 1886; they had no children. He was a guardian of Althea Hazard, a survivor of the Hassanamisco tribe of Indians, and on March 1, 1898, an annual annuity of $250 was awarded her, which was to be paid to him as guardian or to his successors. She died in October 1903. Charles was cashier of the Oxford National Bank, Massachusetts, and was apparently a prominent citizen and very well liked and respected. He was chairman of the board of Selectmen, a member of the Oxford Lodge of A. F. and A. M., I.O.R.M. and S. of V., vice president Oxford Board of Trade, president Oxford Agricultural Society, member of I.O.O.F. of Webster, and Tyrian chapter R.A.M. of Millbury. He died of apoplexy on January 4, 1903, just two days short of his forty-first birthday. His obituary states that the whole town closed down for his funeral.

Uncles & Aunts of Charles:

Charles's mother, Sarah, had a sister named Elizabeth who married James Derrick. They had three children: Anne, Sarah, and George, Charles's cousins. Anne married Henry Wolcott Phelps and lived in East Windsor, Connecticut, until her death in 1896 at age fifty-eight. Sarah married Amos Hobbs in 1864 and also lived in East Windsor, Connecticut, until her death in 1926 at age eighty-six. George married Mary, and settled in Cambridge, Massachusetts. He died in 1901 at fifty-eight years of age.

Charles's father had a brother, John, who was the father of Edwin. While John remained in England, Edwin settled in Massachusetts with his wife Harriet and four children: George, Frank, Frederick, and Minnie. He died in 1897.

Appendix III

A Connecticut
Soldier's Pay

Charles often mentioned back pay that was due him, and it is well known that the federal government was frequently well in arrears in its payment to the soldiers who should have been paid every two months. At the time of his death in October, Charles had not been paid *any* of his monthly salary for 1864, nor certain bounty payments owed. This editor has attempted to discover what payments would have been due to him and his family, as well as what was actually paid; the latter, with one exception, has proven to be difficult to discover in official records.

Charles Sherman would have earned the following pay and bounties from the US Government during his term of service:[417]

- A monthly pay of $13 from January 31, 1862–April 30, 1864, $16 in May and June 1964, and $18 per month starting July 2, 1864, when

---

[417] Sources for some of the information in this Appendix: William C. Moffat Jr., *Soldiers Pay*, January 1965, Cincinnati Civil War Round Table, http://www.cincinnaticwrt .org/data/ccwrt_history/talks_text/moffat_soldiers_pay.html; Croffut and Morris, *The Military and Civil History of Connecticut*, 141; *Encyclopedia Britannica*, s.v. "Bounty System," accessed May 30, 2012, http://www.britannica.com/EBchecked/topic /75684/Bounty-System; *General Orders of the War Department*, Embracing the Years 1861, 1862 & 1863, Vol. I & II (New York: Derby and Miller, 1864), Orders #191, p. 218–219, 305, 412, PDF e-book.

he was promoted to Full Corporal. Monthly pay up to October of 1863 has been confirmed through his mention in various letters.

- A Federal Bounty of $100 for enlisting in 1862, which was payable to him as of February 16, 1964, when he was mustered out (discharged) and reenlisted.

- A Federal Bounty for Veteran Volunteers reenlisting was $402 including a $2 premium. $75 was payable when mustered in, which consisted of $13 as an advance of one month's salary, $60 as part of the bounty, plus the $2 premium; the remaining bounty ($340) was paid in six $50 installments plus one final payment of $40. The total paid was $415, however since $13 was a salary advance, the total bounty equaled $402.

- There was an additional payment awarded of $100 to a widow (or rightful heir) of a soldier that died in battle. Additionally, all unpaid bounties and back pay would be due upon the death of a soldier in battle. The widow also received pension payments.

In addition, the State of Connecticut would have paid the following:

- A bounty to the enlisting soldier in 1862 of $30 per year; $10 paid initially with the next $10 paid four months later, and the final $10 four months after that. Through his letters, it has been confirmed that he received these payments in 1862 and 1863. It is assumed that the reenlistment bounty listed below replaced this $30 in 1864.

- Those reenlisting for three more years in the beginning of 1864 were paid an additional $300 ($100/year) with a thirty-day furlough and a special chevron for their uniform.

- He received one payment of $10 in 1862 by the town of Stonington. The nature of the payment is unknown and could have been pay for carpentry work done before he enlisted.

- In addition, his wife was paid $6 per month plus $2 for each child, limit of two, for a total of $10 per month paid quarterly, to continue for the length of his term of service, even if killed in battle. These payments, by the town of Willington to the family, were confirmed in the *Comptroller Records of Payments to Civil War Soldiers and*

Families, Vol. I and II. A total of $424 was paid to Virtue from May of 1862 to November of 1865.[418]

In January 1864, Charles mentions that the bounty of $800 to reenlist "was some temptation." It appears that two components are: 1) the federal bounty of $400 (plus a $2 premium) and 2) the state bounty of $300. The remaining $100 was most likely the old 1862 bounty that would have been due immediately upon discharge. Those who reenlisted were "mustered out" or "discharged," which meant they would collect their original enlistment bounty, provided that they had served two years. They then were "mustered in" or "enlisted," thereby collecting enlistment bounties.

From his letters, it has been possible to determine most of the pay he either received or should have received. There were no letters while he was on furlough, but by deduction from subsequent mentions of money, it appears that he received his back pay of $26 from November and December 1863, his $75 advance on Federal reenlistment bounty, and his $300 reenlistment bounty from the State of Connecticut while he was on furlough. He mentions in June 1864 that he had given Henry $250 while he was at home, presumably to repay him for money he lent Virtue while Charles wasn't receiving his pay. He would not have had the means to do so without his receiving those payments. In his letter of July 30, 1864, he states "for the record" that he was owed at that time "340 Dollers United States Bounty, one 100 Dollers Old Bounty, and 20 Dollers Back Pay, and Pay from the 16th of Febuary to the 30th of July. . . ." The "20 Dollers Back Pay" would have been January and half of February 1864, before his reenlistment date. On October 4, he states that the payroll that was drawn up on August 31 included his pay and the bounty due. By the time he was killed in October, the regiment had received no pay, so his arrears would include pay from July 31–October 19, plus bounty payments. Research has shown that the Twelfth was paid four months' pay immediately after the Battle of Cedar Creek. One can only hope that his pay would have been forwarded to his widow.

---

[418] The payments listed in this paragraph are the only official payment records the editor has been able to access to date. The rest of the amounts listed in this Appendix are what he *should have been paid*. Some of the bounty information has been difficult to determine in terms of what he would have been promised at the actual time of reenlistment, particularly by the state; however, the 1862 Federal and State bounties are known. It is known that he was due several months' pay and bounties when he was killed.

The total of all payments (theoretically) would have been $1,735.00 for nearly three years in the Army. The contrast between an enlisted man's pay and an officer's pay, especially that of a general, was vast. Even if one did not include the "allowances" officers received, a general's monthly pay was close to nine times that of an enlisted man.

The monthly pension that Virtue received was $8 plus $2 per child (until age sixteen) to March 1886, at which point new legislation increased her monthly pension to $12. As closely as this editor can calculate, the total pension payments, including the $100 death benefit, equaled $6,678.00 over a span of forty-six years.[419]

---

[419] Actual copies of pension application, claim for widow's pension, testimonies, and other pertinent records for Virtue. National Archives, *Case Files.*

Acknowledgments

One never knows from where one might get that final push or from whom that final word of encouragement will come to undertake a huge project. Initially, mine came in 2009 from my mother's gentle persistence in her quest to be able to read the letters that had been in her possession for forty-nine years. Life's duties and activities had gotten in the way over the years, and her failing eyesight was threatening her ability to read them at all. At first, the transcription of the letters was a solution to Mom's vision impairment; however, it began to evolve into a much bigger undertaking as feedback from friends who read "the first translation" suggested that the letters should be shared with a larger audience. Yet doubt and procrastination set in; how in the world would I ever compile a book? Was I just biased, or were they really that interesting?

As fate would have it, the Civil War Round Table meeting at which James I. Robertson Jr. spoke was scheduled during one of my family visits to New Jersey. He was kind enough to read a few copies of the letters and later sent a message stating that he thought they had "the makings of a good book." He offered several solid suggestions on how to tackle it—not the least of which was to leave the original spelling intact, although it meant "re-doing" the letters since, in the first transcription, I had corrected all of the spelling, capitalization, and grammar while adding punctuation and paragraphs. Without that final word of encouragement, and a bit of guidance along the way, I never would have had the nerve to get off square one! So, Dr. Robertson, you have my deep appreciation for your time and helpful advice; my best wishes to you and your lovely wife for a happy, peaceful retirement. Sincere appreciation also goes out to my brother-in-law, Kenneth, for his invitation to attend that serendipitous meeting with him.

Nancy Disher Baird (Editor, *Josie Underwood's Civil War Diary*) very graciously spent many hours with me in June of 2012 discussing the project and offering valuable suggestions on portions of the manuscript. Nancy, I am ever so grateful and look forward to visiting with you on my next trip to Kentucky.

A great BIG thank-you goes out to my friends, Dick and Marge Sharp, who generously spent time on a recent trip to Virginia visiting Winchester National Cemetery and photographing Charles's gravestone and the Twelfth Connecticut Monument. A professional photographer couldn't have done better!

I would like to express a very special thank-you to my second cousin, Nancy Hinkle, for sending the photo of Charles with permission to use it in this book.

Without a doubt, the team at BookLogix deserves to be acknowledged for their superb job in bringing this work to press. Special kudos to my copyeditor, Kelly Nightingale, for her invaluable suggestions and for getting me up-to-date on style—a lot has changed since I went to school! The layout and appearance of the book and its back cover are products of the wonderful work by Laura Kajpust and Ellina Dent. Thank you so much! And many thanks to Jessica Parker for her guidance along the way and to Ahmad Meradji for sticking with me.

Unfortunately, Mother passed away a few weeks before the publication of this book, and although she never got to see it in print, I know she was pleased and proud that Charles's "story" was finally going to be shared and his place in our country's history recognized.

It would be a serious omission if I didn't also thank my children, relatives, and friends who cheered me on with their endless encouragement. And, finally, I extend my eternal gratitude to my husband whose love and support is a true blessing in my life.

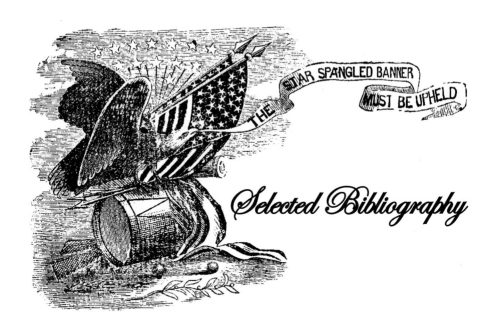

Selected Bibliography

Allen, Dan Sumner, IV. *The Mason Coffins: Metallic Burial Cases In The Central South*. Paper presented at South Central Historical Archaeology Conference, Middle Tennessee State University, Jackson, MS, September 20–22, 2002. PDF e-document.

Benedict, G. G. *Vermont in the Civil War, A History of the part taken by the Vermont Soldiers and Sailors in the War for the Union, 1861–5*. Vol. 1. Burlington, VT: The Free Press Association, 1888. PDF e-book.

——*Vermont in the Civil War, A History of the part taken by the Vermont Soldiers and Sailors in the War for the Union, 1861–5*. Vol. 2. Burlington, VT: The Free Press Association, 1888. PDF e-book.

Bowman, Carl F. *Brethren Society: The Cultural Transformation of a "Peculiar People."* Baltimore, MD: Johns Hopkins University Press, 1995. http://books.google.com/books?id=8ew2f4nPlM8C&q=dunkers#v=snippet&q=dunkers&f=false.

Brewer, E. Cobham. *Dictionary of Phrase and Fable 1898*. Philadelphia, PA: J. B. Lippincott Company, 1905. PDF e-book.

Carpenter, George N. *History of the Eighth Regiment Vermont Volunteers. 1861–1865*. Boston, MA: Press of Deland & Barta, 1886. PDF e-book.

Catton, Bruce. *The Civil War*. New York: American Heritage Press, 1971.

Commager, Henry Steele, ed. *Living History: The Civil War, the History of the War Between the States in Documents, Essays, Letters, Songs and Poems*. With revisions and expansions by Erik Bruun. New York: Tess Press, 2000.

Croffut, W. A. and John M. Morris. *The Military and Civil History of Connecticut During The War of 1861–65.* New York: Ledyard Bill, 1869. PDF e-book.

Cunningham, Edward. *The Port Hudson Campaign, 1862–1863.* Baton Rouge: Louisiana State University Press, 1963. http://books.google.com/books ?id=It-y_Y65X-kC&printsec=frontcover&dq=cunningham+port+hudson +campaign&hl=en&sa=X&ei=GKD_UqypA8XY0gHzmIHwCg&ved=0CC sQ6AEwAA#v=onepage&q=cunningham%20port%20hudson%20campaign &f=false.

De Forest, John William. *A Volunteer's Adventures, A Union Captain's Record of the Civil War,* Edited by James H. Croushore. New Haven, CT: Yale University Press, 1946.

Dyer, Frederick H. *A Compendium of the War of the Rebellion.* Des Moines, IA: The Dyer Publishing Company, 1908. PDF e-book.

Faust, Patricia L., ed. *Historical Times Illustrated Encyclopedia of the Civil War.* New York: Harper Perennial, 1991.

Flood, Charles Bracelen. *1864 Lincoln at the Gates of History.* New York: Simon and Schuster Paperbacks, 2009.

Gluckman, Arcadi. *United States Muskets, Rifles and Carbines.* Harrisburg, PA: The Stackpole Company 1959. PDF e-book.

Hines, Blaikie. *Civil War, Volunteer Sons of Connecticut.* Thomaston, ME: American Patriot Press, 2002.

Irwin, Richard B. *History of the Nineteenth Army Corps.* New York: G. P. Putnam's Sons, 1892. PDF e-book.

Keegan, John. *The American Civil War, A Military History.* New York: Alfred A. Knopf, 2009.

Maitland, James. *The American Slang Dictionary.* Chicago: R. J. Kittredge & Co., 1891. PDF e-book.

Maryniak, Benedict R. and John Wesley Brinsfield, Jr., eds. *The Spirit Divided, Memoirs of Civil War Chaplains.* Macon, GA: Mercer University Press, 2007.

McPherson, James. *Encyclopedia of the American Civil War: A Political, Social, and Military History.* Edited by David Stephen Heidler, Jeanne T. Heidler, and David J. Coles. New York: W. W. Norton & Company, 2000. http://books.google.com/books/about/Encyclopedia_of_the_American_ Civil_War.html?id=SdrYv7S60fgC.

Moat, Louis Shepheard, editor. *Illustrated History of the Civil War.* New York: Mrs. Frank Leslie, 1895. PDF e-book.

Noyalas, Jonathan A. *The Battle of Cedar Creek (VA): Victory from the Jaws of Defeat (Civil War Sesquicentennial).* Charleston, SC: The History Press, 2009.

——*The Battle of Fisher's Hill, Breaking the Shenandoah Valley's Gibraltar.* Charleston, SC: The History Press, 2013.

Patchan, Scott. *The Last Battle of Winchester: Phil Sheridan, Jubal Early, and the Shenandoah Valley Campaign, August 7–September 19, 1864.* El Dorado Hills, CA: Savas Beatie LLC, 2013.

Sandler, Stanley. *Battleships: An Illustrated History of Their Impact.* Santa Barbara, CA: ABC-CLIO, Inc., 2004. http://books.google.com/books?id=i9-0ZuKsMvIC&printsec=frontcover&dq=stanley+sandler+battleships&hl=en&sa=X&ei=upECU7SROMidyQGylYCoDA&ved=0CCkQ6AEwAA#v=onepage&q=manassas&f=false.

Shorey, Henry. *The Story of the Maine Fifteenth: Being a Brief Narrative of the More Important Events in the History of the Fifteenth Maine Regiment.* Bridgton, ME: Press of the Bridgton News, 1890, PDF e-book.

Sprague, Homer B. *History of the 13th Infantry Regiment of Connecticut Volunteers During the Great Rebellion.* Hartford, CT: Case, Lockwood & Co., 1867. PDF e-book.

Stillwell, Leander. *The Story of a Common Soldier of Army Life in the Civil War, 1861–1865.* 2nd ed. Kansas City, MI: Franklin Hudson Publishing Co., 1920. PDF e-book.

Taylor, Richard. *Destruction and Reconstruction, Personal Experiences of the Late War in the United States.* London: William Blackwood and Sons, 1879. PDF e-book.

Wert, Jeffry D. *From Winchester to Cedar Creek, The Shenandoah Campaign of 1864.* Mechanicsville, PA: Stackpole Books, 1997.

The Wesley Study Bible, New Revised Standard Version. Nashville, TN: Abingdon Press, 2009.

Whitehorne, Joseph W. A. *Self-Guided Tour, The Battle of Cedar Creek.* Washington, DC: Center of Military History, United States Army, 1992.

Winters, John D., *The Civil War in Louisiana.* Baton Rouge, LA: Louisiana State University Press, 1991. http://books.google.com/books?id=PjicJWUQhPYC&printsec=frontcover&dq=the+civil+war+in+louisiana&hl=en&sa=X&ei=nekCU9eSJuXw0QGZyoHgBQ&ved=0CCsQ6AEwAA#v=onepage&q=order%20no.%2041&f=false.

Regimental Histories, Official Records, Catalogues

Annual Report of the Adjutant-General of the State of Connecticut for the year ending March 31, 1865. New Haven: Carrington, Hotchkiss & Co., State Printers, 1865.

Catalogue of Connecticut Volunteer Organizations with additional enlistments and casualties to July 1, 1864. Compiled from Records in the Adjutant-General's Office. Hartford, CT: Press of Case, Lockwood and Company, 1864. PDF e-book.

Catalogue of the Twelfth and Thirteenth Regiments Connecticut Volunteers. Compiled from Records in the Adjutant-General's Office. Hartford, CT: Press of Case, Lockwood & Company, 1862. PDF e-book.

Civil War Papers. Vol. 1. Read before the Commandery of the State of Massachusetts. Boston: F. H. Gilson Company, 1900. PDF e-book.

Civil War Papers. Vol. 2. Read before the Commandery of the State of Massachusetts. Boston: F. H. Gilson Company, 1900. PDF e-book.

Connecticut, State Comptroller of Accounts. *Record of returns from towns and payments to soldiers and families during the Civil War, v. 1–2, 1861–1866,* Salt Lake City, UT: Filmed by the Genealogical Society of Utah, 1988. Microfilm.

The Connecticut War Record, "From the Twelfth Regiment," James H. Bradford, Chaplain, Vol. II, No. V., 322–323. New Haven, CT: Morris & Benham, December 1864. PDF e-book.

The Connecticut War Record. Issues August 1863–July 7, 1864, New Haven, CT: Peck, White & Peck. PDF e-book.

The Connecticut War Record. Issues August 1864–December 12, 1864. New Haven, CT: Morris & Benham, PDF e-book.

General Orders of the War Department, Embracing the Years 1861, 1862 & 1863, Vol. I & II. New York: Derby and Miller, 1864. PDF e-book.

The National Archives, *Case Files of Approved Pension Applications of Widows and Other Dependents of Civil War Veterans,* ca. 1861–ca. 1910, Catalog ID 300020, Record Group 15. www.fold3.com.

Official Records of the Union and Confederate Navies in the War of the Rebellion, Series I, Volume 17. Published under the direction of the Hon. William H. Moody, Secretary of the Navy, by Mr. Charles W. Stewart. Washington, DC: Government Printing Office, 1903. PDF e-book.

Record of Service of Connecticut Men in the Army and Navy of the United States During the War of the Rebellion. Compiled by Authority of the General Assembly under the direction of the Adjutants-General. Hartford, CT: The Case, Lockwood & Brainard Company, 1889. PDF e-book.

The Union Army. Vol. 1. Madison, WI: Federal Publishing Co., 1908. PDF e-book.

The War of the Rebellion, A Compilation of Official Records of the Union and Confederate Armies. Series I, Vol. 34, Part IV. Washington, DC: US Government Printing Office 1880–1901. PDF e-book.

The War of the Rebellion, A Compilation of Official Records of the Union and Confederate Armies, Additions and Corrections to Series III, Vol. I. Washington, DC: Government Printing Office, 1902. PDF e-book.

About the Editor

Ann K. Gunnin is the great-great-granddaughter of Charles W. Sherman. Her mother was a Sherman, descended from Charles's son, Lewis, and his grandson Byron Grant Sherman.

Ann was raised in New Jersey and graduated from Skidmore College with a BS in Marketing/Quantitative Analysis. She worked in the corporate world as a VP and Director of Administrative and Financial Services for many years before starting her own business, Nice Touches. Ann is now retired and resides in the North Georgia Mountains with her husband.

She is a quilter and recently completed a quilt as a tribute to Charles W. Sherman. Civil War reproduction fabrics were used, incorporating into the quilt some of the letters that were transferred onto fabric. The quilt features the photo of Charles as the center block. As a result of researching her family roots, Ann has discovered a passion for genealogy which, in turn, has led to her becoming a member of the Daughters of Union Veterans of the Civil War (DUVCW) as well as the Daughters of the American Revolution (DAR).